T4-AHF-581

Aggression American Style

AGGRESSION AMERICAN STYLE

William H. Blanchard

Goodyear Publishing Company, Inc.
Santa Monica, California

0885221

41847

Library of Congress Cataloging in Publication Data

Blanchard, William H.
    Aggression American style.

    Includes index.
    1.   United States—Foreign relations—1945–
2.   Aggressiveness (Social psychology).   3.   United
States—Politics and government—1969–1974.
4.   United States—Politics and government—1974–1977.
I.   Title.
E744.B583   327.73   77-28051
ISBN 0-87620-040-4

Copyright © 1978 by Goodyear Publishing Company, Inc.
Santa Monica, California 90401

All rights reserved. No part of this book may be
reproduced in any form or by any means without
permission in writing from the publisher.

Y-0404-7
ISBN: 0-87620-040-4

Current Printing (last digit):
10   9   8   7   6   5   4   3   2   1

Printed in the United States of America

Text design: Jim Van Maanen
Copyeditor: Suzanne Knott
Production editor: Pam Tully

to my
Pamplemousse

Contents

0885221   41847

4181/7   U85023

Preface

This book is a study of the American approach to aggression by a humanistic psychologist. However, it is a psychological study only in the largest sense of the word. It is a study of the relationship between a person's style of thinking and the decisions he makes. It could have been written by a sociologist, a political scientist, or an anthropologist. In my initial interest in this type of study I was influenced by Karl Mannheim's *Man and Society in an Age of Reconstruction*, by Jean-Paul Sartre's *Being and Nothingness*, and by the works of Abraham Maslow and Harold Lasswell. The early approach of Maslow has been carried a step further by Floyd Matson and Charles Hampden-Turner, to make a more direct link between the way people think and their capacity for personal and political freedom. In his book, *Power and Innocence*, Rollo May has made an attempt to associate a specific style of thinking with the American culture. His work is closely related to my own in his effort to deal with the American ambivalence about power. He has shown that it is possible to deny our power while, at the same time, enjoying the pleasure of acting on it.

This denial cannot take place on a massive scale without a gradual movement from innocence to hypocrisy and finally to cynicism. According to May, one of the central features in the aggravation of aggressive acts is the sense of personal innocence, a lack of awareness of one's own aggressive intent. This, I believe, is central to an understanding of American foreign policy. Within recent years this striving for innocence has been allied with a growing cynicism, a striving for the "appearance" of innocence. We see the most extreme form of this cynicism in the Watergate case and the denial of responsibility by the president. But Watergate did not appear suddenly without any warning signs. It is not a fluke or an anomaly in American political life. It is the culmination of a growing tendency that began with the justification of inadvertence and ended with the cynical pretense of inadvertence. It will be one of the goals of this book to show the historical precursors of Watergate in our culture and in our way of thinking about the world. Watergate was an act of aggression by one political party against another. As such, it does not fit into the framework of national policy. But "national security" was so often used in the initial attempts to justify Watergate that it has come to represent an integral part of the American style of aggression—an aggression carried out through inadvertence, for which no one is willing to accept responsibility.

The ideas for this book have been germinating for several years but they were first expressed during a course on the Psychology of Revolution that I gave at San Fernando Valley State College. It was a course in which I learned a great deal from my students, both in classroom discussions and in the informal sessions and parties that accompanied and followed the class. Much of the last part of this book is the product of that interaction. I am grateful to Richard Doctor, Chairman of the Psychology Department, for his willingness to experiment with an untried course on a controversial subject. I have since used some of this material for lectures in a course on Humanistic Psychology at the University of California at Los Angeles and in the Urban Semester at the University of Southern California. On both occasions, I have found that the comments of students and faculty have helped me to take the concept of the systematization of thought from the realm of abstraction and demonstrate its direct application to policy.

While the present work was in the process of development, I presented some of the chapters to professional and scientific societies and journals. The lively discussion they stimulated has served to reinforce some of my basic ideas and to correct some of my overstatements. I prepared some material from the "Changing Nature of Aggression" for the American Orthopsychiatric Association Convention in San Francisco and read an earlier version of "The Systematization of Thought" at the International Political Science Association in Munich, Germany. In 1971, I was a member of a panel on the Violence of Normal Man at the American Association for the Advancement of Science in Philadelphia where I gave most of the material from "Inadvertent Aggression." The Los Angeles Times, December 15, 1968, carried a small excerpt from this chapter under the title "Aggression—American Style."

An earlier version of the U-2 chapter appeared in the Revue de Psychologie des Peuples at the Centre de Recherches et d'Études de Psychologie des Peuples et de Sociologie Economique at the Université de Caen in 1961 and in *The Journal of Conflict Resolution* in 1962.

I am particularly indebted to Marjorie Jensen of the Center for the Study of Armament and Disarmament for her painstaking review and comment on an early draft of this study. Her suggestions have proved to be of great value to me, but it has taken a long time to assimilate them. I am grateful to Arthur Schlesinger, Jr., for his review and comments on the chapter on the "Invasion of Cuba." Through a fortunate meeting on a plane, I have had the help of Carl Kisslinger, whose expert knowledge of seismology has been helpful in my study of the Rainier shot (in the chapter on "The Scientific Test"). I have included some of his comments in the notes to this chapter. Some of the ideas for the chapter on "Inadvertent Aggression" evolved from an earlier study of mine on American bargaining and negotiating behavior financed by the Advance Research Project Agency under the direction of Gerald Shure, who provided valuable criticism of my ideas at that time. My thinking has altered so markedly since that work was completed that the study would scarcely be recognizable in its present form.

Irving Janis, as one of the readers for the book, has provided valuable criticism of the general rationale as well as specific commentary on a number of issues. I am most grateful for the time and care he has given to the manuscript.

My good friend, Rafe Dubrovner, whose views on almost all the issues in this book are different from my own, has challenged me with the kind of moral criticism that has forced me to rethink and rewrite a number of times. Much of the material in the final chapter is a product of this challenge.

Joe Fink has been, in many respects, the guardian of this project in its initial stages. In creating time, space, and some of the resources, he has helped to bring this work to a conclusion at an earlier date than might otherwise have been possible.

Space does not permit a description of the help and advice I have received from many friends and colleagues who have looked over and commented on the manuscript of this study in its various stages of development. They are Richard Barnett, John Cogswell, Steve Crain, Barbara Cohen, Charles Hampden-Turner, Floyd Matson, Murray Korngold, Bon Lessing, Harold Lasswell, Lou Pattison, Arnold Rogow, J. David Singer, David Scott, Gene Dvorin, Ursula Caspary-Ruoss, Richard Sennett, Norman Palmer and Tom Milburn. My wife, Hitchie, who helped with the research, was a constant source of hope and encouragement.

The comfortable working relationship established with the Good-year staff has been an invaluable and significant influence on the direction, development, and final implementation of this book. Among those who have been particularly helpful are my editor, Jim Boyd and the people in production and advertising who worked on my book, Pam Tully, Stacey Maxwell, Chris Wain, and Jim Van Maanen.

Introduction

I

This study began as an investigation of American foreign policy, but I soon realized that the phenomenon of inadvertence influenced much domestic policy as well. Furthermore, there are many antecedents to policy in the form of studies and tests by government scientists. Here, too, the phenomenon of inadvertence or self-deception operates to produce an experiment or a study in line with the general consensus of policy makers. These studies, then, become the basis for policy formulation. In order to examine this phenomenon of inadvertence in some detail, I have confined myself to the study of certain incidents in foreign and domestic relations rather than attempting to examine the broad area of policy formulation. As it stands it would be easy for a student of American foreign policy to point to sins of omission and commission in the incidents I have described. Nevertheless, I believe they provide an important insight into the style of American leadership and our failure to deal directly with aggression in American policy.

1

The way we define aggression will depend, in large measure, on the purpose of a definition. For legal purposes I would be willing to accept the definition arrived at by the United Nations on April 12, 1974. It is complex and consists of several articles, but its essence is the use of armed force by one nation against another, either directly or through an intermediary such as mercenaries or irregulars. However, Tedeschi, Smith, and Brown[1] have suggested that the term *aggression* may not be adequate to classify human behavior and the concept of coercive action may be more useful. They have pointed out that lack of clarity about *intent* is a major difficulty in defining aggression. As all individuals and nations rationalize their coercive actions, to some extent, to avoid giving the impression they are aggressive, it is difficult to determine which side began the process of provocation that led to armed conflict.

This is the era of the preemptive strike, the time in which we justify our acts of aggression on the grounds that, "I had to do this to him or he would be in a position to do that to me." Not that he would *necessarily* have done it, but he would be in a position to do it. It is the era in which the building of a weapon can be an act of provocation in itself since, once the weapon is built, there is no defense against it.

It is also the era of "inadvertent" aggression—a form of aggression that takes place, not from a desire for conquest, but from an effort to increase the security of one's people. I have placed the word *inadvertent* in quotes because it often happens that the behavior in these acts of "inadvertent" aggression is indistinguishable from an act of conquest. There is the usual lie about one's motives and the rationalization as to why the act was necessary. Nevertheless, the acts are inadvertent in one sense. Unlike the deliberate lie for reasons of state, the lie in inadvertent aggression represents a form of self-deception, a lie to oneself. In the case of a nation committing these acts they are a form of national self-deception. It is a process of thinking in bad faith by admitting the reality of the acts, but denying their significance. It is what I have called, in this book, "aggression American style."

In selecting American aggression for study (and not Soviet or Chinese aggression), I do not intend to imply that the United States is more aggressive or more dangerous to the peace of the world than other nations. However, I do believe that the American style of aggression is more influential and that there is evidence to indicate a general trend toward American methods of coercion and persuasion not only in Europe but in the Soviet Union as well. Nevertheless, the purpose of this study is not to demonstrate the Americanization of other nations but to discover the roots of American aggression and examine some of its manifestations in our national policy.

The American style of aggression is similar in some respects to that of the British, from whom we derive the notion that a world empire is (and should be) a burden and not a source of pleasure. However, the major part of the British Empire was created during the period of a genuine monarchy, and its development was deliberate. It was achieved through the conquest of territory in a conscious motive of acquisition and growth. In the growth of the American Empire, a different process is apparent. Even the early conquest and settlement of the American continent was conceived, not so much in terms of a quest for power, but as part of a "Manifest Destiny," a sense of mission through which we would set an example of our goodness for the rest of the world.[2] American annexation of territory would proceed not by wars, but simply by consenting to the request of other republics for annexation. At one time William H. Seward believed that the United States would embrace the entire continent through such a peaceful process. However, with the growing power of the United States, the urge to thrust "democracy" upon the other nations of the world has grown accordingly. We began with a desire to protect South America from the European powers. Later we determined to "open up" Japan to the influence of the Western world. Today we have a policy, not yet disavowed, of coming to the aid of "free people" everywhere in the world. In most of these moves outside the continental limits of the United States, it has been apparent that we were after influence, business connections, and raw materials—never territory. In the more recent expansion of American power, there is an effort to continue the early myth of Manifest Destiny. The chief characteristic of this myth was that things happened to us because of our essential goodness. Others wanted to be like us, to join us, to submit to our gentle domination. We did not seek power. If we became powerful, it happened to us without any conscious intent on our part.

It has been difficult to continue such a myth during the American military efforts in Cuba, Korea, Santo Domingo, and Vietnam. Nevertheless, for the great majority of the American people, this myth has persisted up to the later stages of our conflict in Vietnam. How is it possible to maintain this belief that we do not actively seek power in the face of our active intervention in the affairs of other nations? Can the people really be deceived about such things in a so-called "open" society? It is in the effort to examine this question that the present study was undertaken.

Clearly, the United States is not the only nation in the world in which the government deceives the people about its policies. However, in a nation that preaches openness as a national virtue, that provides more information to its citizens about government operations than any other nation, and that cannot prevent investigation and exposure of government secrets on the scale of the *Pentagon Papers* and the Watergate affair, a different means of concealment is required than that used by the more "closed" societies. If the people are to remain unaware of what the government leaders are really doing, but the leaders themselves cannot successfully keep factual information from the public, there is only one way to keep the intentions of government leaders from the American people: the leaders themselves must remain unaware of what they are really doing. On the face of it, this sounds absurd. We have one of the most extensive information-collection networks in the world. The government is filled with committees that sift and process information, that develop contingency plans, and that attempt to make the president aware, in great detail, of the consequences of each policy option available. But if a national leader does not know his own intentions, knowledge of the consequences of certain options will not help him very much. It is this concealment of intent from one's self, this process of self-deception, that is particularly characteristic of American leaders.

However, we cannot play such games with our own consciousness indefinitely. When the game is played again and again, it becomes more visible, more obvious, and more mechanical. There are more deliberate attempts to *make sure* that one does not know. As the incidents in this book develop, you will notice a shift from genuine inadvertence toward a deliberate preparation of the *appearance of innocence.* This is nowhere more obvious than in the Watergate affair, but there are signs of its development much earlier. In this later stage real innocence is no longer preserved, but only "deniability," as John Dean has described it.[3] The national leader is now very conscious of his intent, but he makes sure that his intent cannot be traced by any direct order to his subordinates. His subordinates anticipate his needs without telling him the messy details. In his policy of "openness," then, he can truthfully say that he did not know what was happening. But in reality, in the larger sense, he did know. Here we have moved from inadvertence to deceit.

On the surface these two forms of behavior appear the same until the actions are exposed. Then the person who is genuinely unaware of his own intentions will reveal everything. He believes himself to be innocent. He has nothing to hide, and he is forgiven and loved by the American people. When the national leader is conscious of his own intent, he is less inclined to reveal all the facts. He knows he is guilty, even though he has a built-in system of deniability. But there is seldom such a clear-cut distinction. Intent is seldom completely known or completely unknown. Even Richard Nixon believed that he was a "good" person throughout the Watergate affair. He tried to present an appearance of openness, but he was blocked by strong feelings of distrust of the American press, and he did not really believe that he had nothing to hide.

So powerful is the pressure of public opinion in regard to the characteristic of frankness and candor that a stigma attaches to public officials who consistently give a "no-comment" response to inquiries from the press. The elaborate apparatus of secrecy that has been established in the United States government is expected to apply more directly to the lower ranking, appointed official. A leading public figure, particularly an elected official, who shows an attitude of caution, qualification, and guardedness in his speech appears unsavory to most Americans. He is not loved and therefore is generally not reelected. It was not because of the *actions* of Watergate that President Nixon was threatened with impeachment and finally resigned; it was because he covered them up. Had he confessed early, he would probably have been forgiven.

II

American openness has been noted by a number of observers. It may derive, in part, from our Puritan traditions in which an Elder had a right to inspect the homes of the faithful at any time to see if they were keeping a good Christian household. But it clearly has its modern counterpart. Grund[4] has remarked on the openness we demand of our politicians; Dickens,[5] Mackay,[6] and Dicey[7] have all commented on our frankness. Birmingham seems to imply a relationship between our openness and a belief in our virtue; "The American has no objection to this publicity. He is not doing anything of which he is the least ashamed."[8] But Parkes suggests a more menacing element; "While the American was less eager to protect his own privacy than was his English ancestor, he was also more prone to interfere with that of others."[9]

Although openness is an American virtue, it functions within the context of the high value placed on success. Since a certain amount of concealment and self-protection is necessary in a highly competitive society, a conflict arises between the desire to be open and sincere with others and the desire to climb above others in the hierarchy. One can fulfill both desires only by deceiving one's self. Since the individual does not want to "knowingly" conceal anything, he is inclined toward a rather superficial honesty, in which the only plans and actions available for recall are those that are well intentioned and relatively harmless to others. In this book I will refer to this attitude as one of "unreflective sincerity." Public officials avoid many embarrassing confrontations with the press simply by keeping a clean mind and placing the most optimistic and innocent interpretation upon their own behavior and national policy moves. The result is that Americans often appear to be candid and spontaneous with others, but also rather flip and lacking in depth. To some degree, of course, this is simply deliberate concealment. But deliberate concealment produces an abrasive effect on the concept of one's self as an open person. There is a persistent urge to break through the secrecy and tell all. This combination of the guilt about being secretive and the high probability that secrets will be leaked to the public produces an unstable situation for most Americans in business and public affairs. The revelation of a partial truth serves as a catalyst to the press. Reporters can exert an intense pressure on public officials by the implied threat to publish their own version of a story (based on the facts already revealed) if more information is not forthcoming. As a result, a national leader may become so concerned about his image among his own people that he will himself reveal secret information or take public responsibility for a decision that was actually made by a minor functionary, all in the interest of being more "open."

But in the process of telling everything a peculiar transformation takes place. The very revelation of the facts serves as a basis for concealment of the motive. Truth telling in this context becomes a form of emotional release. If a leading public figure accepts responsibility for an act, the act must be justified somehow or we will condemn ourselves in condemning one of our heroes. Thus, the American style of revelation is one in which great emphasis is placed on the facts, as though this factual revelation in itself were a proof of virtue. In the process it becomes possible to turn the klieg lights on the factual honesty of our hero in order to leave his motives in greater darkness.

It is in this way that the gathering of information (particularly the more quantified, categorized, factual information) can be used to conceal one's intent—from oneself as well as from others. By concentrating attention on the external facts, the decision maker takes the position that he is being "objective." This helps to justify his neglect of the internal and subjective aspects of the decision process. Calling upon social scientists for aid in the decision system does not improve the situation if these scientists study the system with the same methodological bias. Charles Hampden-Turner has pointed out that in the social sciences the attitude of scientific detachment leads to a concern with physical variables instead of an attempt to understand human motives. The tools used by the social scientist and the manner of their application tend to produce a conservative political bias. "Moreover their conservatism is unaware, non-ideological, unowned, and is latent in the tools they employ."[10]

It is my contention that in the United States these two factors—(1) the desire for a sense of innocence and personal goodness and (2) the development of a mechanical system for gathering information and reaching a decision—tend to work together to suppress awareness of our intentions. If the decision process is mechanical and the self is not involved, it is possible to remain innocent of the consequences. Injustice in both foreign and domestic policy results from technological errors in the system and not from human malice. Therefore, it is only a question of gathering more "hard data" to correct the error. Self-reflection is not necessary; there is no guilt, only a lack of knowledge.

In the initial chapters of this book, I have tried to show the fallacy of this type of thinking by highlighting the human element in the decision process. I have also attempted to show some of the ways in which we try to remain unaware of our aggressive intent. Obviously, the problem of unawareness in the United States is not confined to aggression. I have concentrated on this area because I believe that with the recent massive increase in American military power, this form of unawareness represents a major threat to world peace. It is for this reason that I have selected for study those incidents that illustrate the particular relationship between human volition and action in our *recent* (post-World War II) foreign policy. I have confined each study to a period of limited duration in order to focus on the details of the behavior of national leaders in each crisis situation. I have tried to determine the motives, desires, and fears as well as the national myths and traditions that have influenced their actions. These are the influences that have been masked by an emphasis on objective factors and the need for logical explanation. Because of the need to look closely at the person making a decision, this is a very personal book. It could not have been otherwise. One cannot attempt a psychological study of the behavior of a public official in the detail I have employed without making use of his name and the personal factors in his decision.

However, I want to emphasize that, although I make no apology for the conclusions of each chapter, they are strictly relative to the situation. When an individual is described as lacking in awareness, this is not intended as a description of his habitual response to all life situations. No one can be fully aware of everything at all times. My purpose is to characterize the psychological functioning of American policy makers, not the particular deficiency of any one individual. For this reason, I have tried to sweep over the entire range of American public life to include Republicans, Democrats, presidents, secretaries of state, State Department intellectuals, scientists who work for the government, CIA leaders, and military officers. I have had to say some difficult and painful things about some men whom I admire very much. In other cases I must confess that I have enjoyed the process of taking apart the decision of a public official for whom I have less regard. My own bias will be evident in each case. I have not tried to conceal it, but I have observed a policy of careful documentation in order to provide you with the information you may need to examine my errors. A work of this kind must be very selective. The requirement for an extensive examination of each case places a severe limitation on the number of incidents examined. Those of you who are disappointed by certain omissions may share my hope that this study will stimulate others of its kind.

The chapters are arranged in a general historical sequence, although there is some overlap for incidents that have occurred close to each other. Following the incidents, I have made some general statements about the role of the systematization of thought in the development of American policy. This chapter covers some of the ways in which this apotheosis of method tends to shield the decision maker from an awareness of his intent. I have tried to show how the need for innocence, the desire to avoid the painful confrontation with the self, has fostered the use of "objective" or nonself-related procedures in the decision system.

The need for a heightened self-awareness in the modern world is accentuated by the changing nature of aggression. In former times, aggression was clearly marked by the crossing of physical boundaries and the conquest of territory. Today, we may well despair of finding any satisfactory definition of the term. It is possible to exercise influence and control over other nations through control of air space, through satellite television stations and radio stations that flood the communications space, and through economic pressures and trade barriers. Our sophistication in the use of indirect means of aggression has increased enormously in the last half-century. There is also a movement toward a more psychological type of aggression.

Persuasion, or a combination of persuasion and coercion, is now more common than the almost exclusive reliance on physical force or the threat of force that characterized earlier periods. This does not mean that aggression is *confined* to the realm of psychology or that we have less physical aggression than before. If anything, it appears that the psychological element in aggression has increased the threat of physical violence. One can lose psychological influence more rapidly than one can lose territory. If this influence is threatened, there may be a sudden resort to physical force to preserve the national image.

There is also a trend within nations toward an increase in the psychological aspects of repression. There is a movement, most pronounced within democratic nations, to change the meaning of repression through the rise of such terms as *pacification* and *control*. B. F. Skinner has suggested that a "technology of behavior" might make the more obvious forms of repression unnecessary and a government could learn to control the lives of its people largely by psychological means.[11] In this psychological approach to political and social problems, Skinner has extended the possible influence and range of technological thinking in our society.

At the present time, there is a growing recognition that our culture has become dangerously limited and stifled in its emphasis on the technological approach to social and political problems. The experience of awareness is often seen as a joyful escape from this restricted way of thinking and being. However, in the development of retreats and "growth centers," where people can get away into the country to experience awareness, we have fostered an unfortunate dichotomy between thinking and feeling. Thinking is regarded as methodical and dull. The experience of awareness (which is often limited to feeling) is regarded as beautiful and exciting. In an earlier work[12] I have emphasized that this confrontation with the self can be a moment of ecstasy or terror and that the element of ecstasy has perhaps been oversold by those who make a business of providing experiences of awareness—just as the merits of systematized thinking have been oversold by the professional systems analyst and the "scientific" psychologist. We are presently experiencing a dehumanization of man through a glorification of his analytical faculties and a separation of his emotions from his intellect. It is this process that makes possible the blind and unreflective use of the intellect in the development of instruments of repression and control, destruction and "pacification." Under such circumstances, the new emphasis on physical sensation and emotion, provided by the counterculture, is a healthy antidote to the methodical style of American aggression. But as a new way of life, it suffers from the same lack of balance that is characteristic of the present culture. To describe the rediscovery of the emotions as a return to humanism is to miss the important element of balance that is central to the notion of a unified person. Ralph Barton Perry has outlined the guiding principle of the humanist philosophy as follows: "Emotion and intellect are designed to correct one another. Man is meant to profit both by heat and light. Nature provides him with power and with a steering gear. When either is lacking he falls into evil ways. . . . So to serve one another they must not be divided into different social clubs, as the intelligensia and the mob."[13]

Global aggression and the concomitant dehumanization of man are obviously problems that extend far beyond the boundaries of the United States. Global aggression is a phenomenon of the modern world. However, the democratic state has long been credited with having a peaceful and humanizing influence on its citizens. If the present study can throw some light on the failure of democracy in this regard, I will consider it well worthwhile.

Critics tell me that my theory of inadvertence serves as a perfect escape for those who rule America. They maintain that American policy is deliberately manipulated by a "power elite," a group of people who know what they are doing, and that I am naïve in ascribing the acts of this group to inadvertence. I do not deny the existence of a power elite, but it is a different kind of power elite than the one described by C. Wright Mills. If there is a conspiracy to control America, it is an implicit, not an explicit, conspiracy. It is based on a tacit, and not an overt, understanding. Most importantly, it is a conspiracy in which no one admits that he is conspiring, *not even to himself.* Furthermore, it is a conspiracy that has the full cooperation of the members of the American middle class, who find that it serves their ends very well. It absolves them of responsibility for injustice.

I do not intend that the inadvertence of the officials, described in this book, should serve as an excuse for their behavior (in the sense that they should be forgiven because they know not what they do). They have a responsibility to know. The determination to remain innocent of one's own intentions must be a conscious act at some point in the development of the individual. But the innocence of American officials cannot be perpetuated without the cooperation of the electorate. It is as though the citizen is saying to his elected leader, "I have placed you in office so you can help me rationalize what I am doing. You must lie to me in order to help me lie to myself—and I will cooperate by believing you."

I would not contend that the American approach to policy, which

I am describing in this book, is unique to the United States. The very fact that we are a leading world power has led other nations to imitate us to some extent. Although the emphasis on the systematic method of thinking and the development of "technique" has been more pronounced in the United States, it is gaining favor in Europe as well. Furthermore, many world leaders disavow aggression, and some of them fool themselves. The aspect that is distinctive about the American experience is the pressure for openness combined with the extent of American power. The result is that we run a greater risk of an inadvertent and fatal miscalculation. Like most of the nations of modern Europe, we began the twentieth century as a success-oriented, capitalist democracy. But the United States is different from other democracies in its status as a major world power. I have described some of these differences in more detail in Chapter 14, "The Changing Nature of Aggression."

What I have provided in this study is a working hypothesis that the phenomenon of inadvertent aggression, if not unique to the United States, is at least American in origin. The converse of this hypothesis would be that there is not, nor has there ever been, any real (significant) difference in the extent or the way in which major nations of the world deny responsibility for their aggressive acts. I have not disproved this null hypothesis. I have tried to account for contrary evidence, but I am aware of my own bias, and I may have overlooked sources that would refute my views. Only a complete comparative historical study of cultural styles could do justice to the evidence from all sources, and that is beyond the scope of this study. It is my hope that the case I have presented will be sufficiently provocative to stimulate further studies of this kind.

NOTES

1. J. T. Tedeschi, R. B. Smith, III, and R. C. Brown, Jr., "A Reinterpretation of Research on Aggression," *Psychological Bulletin*, vol. 81, no. 9, (1974), pp. 540–562.

2. F. Merk, *Manifest Destiny and Mission in American History* (New York: Vintage, 1963).

3. J. Dean, *Blind Ambition* (New York: Simon & Schuster, 1976).

4. F. J. Grund, "Religion and Morality Preside over Their Councils," *America in Perspective*, ed. H. S. Commager (New York: New American Library, 1948), pp. 72–73.

5. C. Dickens, "It Would Be Well if They Loved the Real Less and the Ideal More," *America in Perspective*, pp. 78–79.

6. A. Mackay, "Every American Is an Apostle of the Democratic Creed," *America in Perspective*, p. 86.

7. E. Dicey, "God Made America for the Poor," *America in Perspective*, p. 126.

8. G. Birmingham, "The American at Home and in his Club," *America in Perspective*, p. 174.

9. H. B. Parkes, *The American Experience* (New York: Vintage, 1959), p. 50.

10. C. Hampden-Turner, *Radical Man* (Cambridge: Schenkman, 1970), p. 13.

11. B. F. Skinner, *Beyond Freedom and Dignity* (New York: Knopf, 1971).

12. W. H. Blanchard, "Psychodynamic Aspects of the Peak Experience," *Psychoanalytic Review*, vol. 56, no. 1 (1969): 87–112.

13. R. B. Perry, *The Humanity of Man* (New York: Braziller, 1956), pp. 85–86.

Inadvertent Aggression

I

Many political theorists have subscribed to the notion that democratic governments are more peaceful because war is not in the best interest of the common people and the people are, presumably, free to advance their own interest. The United States has often been used as an example of the peaceful consequences of a democratic form of government. Joseph Schumpeter, who felt the United States was less imperialistic than the other nations of the world, associated this tendency with capitalism rather than democracy per se. It was not, he said, in the interest of the average citizen to support a warlike policy, and the policy of the United States confirmed this view.[1] Alexis de Tocqueville had more reservations about the relationship between democracy and peace. Although he believed that "democratic nations are naturally prone to peace from their interests and their propensities," he felt they were drawn into war by their armies.[2] Schumpeter, too, believed that the existence of a military class provided a danger to world peace, but he regarded this condition as

13

atavistic, a hangover from earlier autocratic societies. He recognized that nationalism and militarism could reach an alliance with capitalism, but he believed this was more likely in those European nations where the heritage of the autocratic state was strong and where the people were economically and psychologically influenced by this prior condition. The United States, he felt, was least burdened by these precapitalistic influences. He supported this view by pointing out that the United States was the first advocate of disarmament and arbitration, the first to conclude treaties concerning arms limitation, and the one to initiate plans for the surrender of her own possessions and territories.[3]

Earlier public opinion research supported the notion of the peaceful inclination of the American people. In a study of the way nations perceive each other, Buchanan and Cantril found, in part, that Americans were generally rated as more peace-loving than Russians.[4] But the Buchanan and Cantril study was published in 1953, using data obtained in 1948, long before the United States was drawn into the conflict in Southeast Asia. In 1948 the United States was already beginning to suffer the negative effects of a too-hasty postwar demobilization. Our European allies, fearful of the Russian presence in Europe, had begun to feel we were a bit too peace-loving. It is unlikely that the ratings, if taken again, would still show such a universal opinion of Americans as lovers of peace. Images tend to change, depending on the times and the needs of the observer. The fraternity boy and football hero of yesterday has become the jock of today. The men of the heroic U.S. Air Force, the wild-blue-yonder boys of World War II who came to the rescue of an embattled civilization with crushed caps and an engaging American smile, have become part of a major nuclear strike force that dominates half the world. The image of Dr. Oppenheimer has been replaced by that of Dr. Strangelove and Jimmy Stewart, the boy next door, has become a general.

It would be convenient, at this point, to hark back to the warning of Tocqueville and contend that we have been betrayed by the ambitions of our military leaders, the thesis being that the people want peace, but the generals have conspired against them. However, some of our most successful military leaders have been opposed to our growing militarism. General (and later President) Dwight D. Eisenhower warned of the ominous alliance between the military and industrial organizations.[5] General Smedley Butler of the U.S. Marines, who was twice awarded the Congressional Medal of Honor, said, with obvious disgust, that he had spent his life advancing the interest of large American corporations.

> I spent 33 years . . . most of my time being a high-class muscle man for
> Big Business, for Wall Street and the bankers. In short, I was a rack-
> eteer for capitalism . . . I helped purify Nicaragua for the interna-
> tional banking house of Brown Brothers in 1909–12. I helped make
> Mexico and especially Tampico safe for American oil interests in
> 1914. I helped in the rape of half a dozen Central American republics
> for the benefit of Wall Street . . . In China in 1927 I helped to see to it
> that Standard Oil went its way unmolested . . . I had . . . a swell racket.
> I was rewarded with honors, medals, promotions . . . I might have
> given Al Capone a few hints. The best he could do was to operate a
> racket in three city districts. The Marines operated on three conti-
> nents.[6]

Although General Butler's remark suggests that there is a dangerous alliance between American capitalism and militarism, it is not at
all clear that this mutual encouragement is the result of a conscious
conspiracy. Conspirators generally do not warn the public that their
colleagues are dangerous. There are other inconsistencies. Seymour
Melman has pointed out that it was Eisenhower in 1946 who put
together the military–industrial complex. Yet before he retired,
Eisenhower felt constrained to warn the American people that this
concentration of power was a threat to American liberty and the
democratic process.[7] The warnings of Eisenhower and Smedley Butler seem to result from a belated awareness that they have been a
part of something that is not altogether in the best interest of the
nation, that they are a bit uncomfortable about it (in Butler's case
more than a bit uncomfortable), and that they would like to make
some kind of restitution—if only a verbal restitution—to the people.
In the generals' remarks, as in the earlier statement by Tocqueville,
there is an implication that the best interest of a democratic people
will not be served by a large military organization. If the people can
be made to see their interest clearly, they will reduce the size of their
armed forces.

But why should this be such a problem? If it is simply a matter of
explaining something that makes sense from a logical point of view,
we should have ended the problem of military domination long ago.
We should be able to provide a reasonable defense against aggression without proposing to build a military force large enough to save
the world. The people are more numerous than the generals. If they
are free to oppose the power of a growing military establishment and
fail to do so, we are justified in suspecting that they derive some
satisfaction from being represented by such an impressive show of
force. It may not be in their best "interest" to escalate the arms race,
but perhaps it satisfies some need that they are not willing to admit
openly.

At the time of the Boer War, Schumpeter remarked that there was not a beggar in London who did not speak of "our" rebellious subjects.[8] Of course, it is not acceptable for the leadership in a democracy to give voice to the satisfactions expressed by Schumpeter's beggar. The thirst for power in a democracy must be experienced as a painful necessity. It must be cleansed of any obvious libidinal satisfaction. Thus, in the United States we hear that we did not seek our position of world leadership. It was thrust upon us. During the ceremony of lighting the White House Christmas tree in 1969, President Richard M. Nixon reiterated this point several times. He spoke of "the role of leadership which is ours, one that we accept, one that we did not ask for. . . . America did not seek this role of world leadership. . . . This, as I said, is a role America did not seek. We are the first power to be the major power in the world that did not ask for it."[9] Why this need to deny the intention to become powerful? Clearly, the reality of power is not denied, nor is there any suggestion that we are about to give it up. But to seek power is to be openly aggressive. It is therefore aggression, and particularly the pleasure in aggression, that is denied by Mr. Nixon.

It is my contention, which I hope to demonstrate in the chapters that follow, that this speech is not merely a reflection of Richard M. Nixon, but of the American style in general. It is characterized by the belief that our power came to us through some kind of innate goodness and that we have never been intentionally aggressive. The word *intentionally* is critical in this statement. Americans have always been proud of being strong. Children in our country are taught to be tough, to defend themselves. But the notion of a deliberate, conscious struggle to dominate others is foreign to our national ethos. Of course, we do it in both our domestic and foreign policy. But it is characteristic of the American style that it must happen without conscious intent. The ancient warrior king pounded his chest and challenged his enemies. He measured his worth by his power and the extent to which he had expanded his territory. He took an open delight in warfare as a form of sport, and when he was victorious, he would drag the conquered chieftain through the streets in chains behind his chariot. Democratic imperialism must take a different form. If a democratic leader takes open delight in the exercise of power, he cannot remain in office. To secure the pleasures of command, he must put on a long face. The aggressive intent of an action must be concealed not only from the other nations of the world but from the people who help to perpetrate the aggression.

How is this possible? First, the whole culture must come to regard pleasure in aggression as something nasty, very much the way our forefathers regarded sex. One never takes an aggressive action against another person for the fun of pushing him around, the sheer delight in one's power. In fact, fighting is bad unless one is justified by some clear provocation. Margaret Mead describes it this way.

> So the American boy learns a series of lessons: aggression and fighting are wrong and are to be avoided as low, liable to arouse his mother's and often his father's disapproval; but aggression and fighting are also necessary. . . . Out of a series of conflicting traditions, out of the confusion which can be built in the male mind when females are those who urge his maleness insistently upon him, there has emerged a special American form of aggressiveness: aggressiveness which can never be shown unless the other fellow starts it; aggressiveness which is so unsure of itself that it has to be proved.[10]

A number of writers have supported this contention that there is a uniquely *American* attitude toward aggression (in the sense of a struggle for power and influence). Martin and Sims comment,

> It is true, as many others have pointed out in different connections, that we in this country have an instinctive revulsion against the term "power." It carries immoral connotations for us. . . . Furthermore, though we glorify ambition in the abstract, we frown on its practice and are distressed by the steps which must be taken if ambition is to be transformed into actual advancement. Thus when power is coupled with ambition, we shy away and try to pretend that neither really exists.[11]

If it is true that we act in an aggressive manner without being willing to admit to our aggressive desires and that we deny to ourselves the aggressive nature of our acts, we are in a dangerous position in regard to our domestic and our foreign policy, particularly the latter. We are likely to take actions that invite retaliation without recognizing that we have been provocative, and we are likely to regard the retaliation as an unprovoked act of aggression. In this book I will examine some cases in which I believe this has happened.

II

If Americans can take the sensual enjoyment out of fighting, it should also be possible to remove the pleasurable element from other more indirect forms of aggression, such as economic domination. When Max Weber first identified what he called the Protestant ethic and pointed out its relationship to the spirit of capitalism, it was in the work of an American, Benjamin Franklin, that he found one of the more striking examples of this belief.[12] Weber regarded the United States as a place where the pursuit of wealth, stripped of its religious and ethical meaning, had reached its highest development. However, although he remarked that Franklin treated honesty, frugality, industry, and so on, as strictly utilitarian virtues in the sense that they served the purpose of increasing a man's income, he did not fail to observe that moneymaking had become a religion. He recognized that the pursuit of money, as it was practiced in the United States, seemed to be an end in itself, devoid of any admixture of hedonism. In short, it functioned in much the same way as any other virtue, the money-making activity being a duty rather than a delight.[13]

It is this ability to remove conscious pleasure from an act that makes it possible for the American to avoid becoming aware of what he is really doing. Thus, it is possible for President Nixon to be proud that the United States consumes more than its share of the world's goods without becoming aware that there is anything aggressive about economic domination. In the Christmas-tree speech, Mr. Nixon remarked, ". . . there are 85 million television sets, there are 80 million automobiles, there are 300 million radios in America, and 150,000 airplanes . . . today America is the richest nation in the world, we are the strongest nation in the world. . . ." and he asserted the continued intention of the United States to have more than other nations. "So I say to you that as we enter the decade of the seventies, American will continue to be rich, America will continue to have more of the world's goods, there will be more television sets and more radios and more automobiles. . . ."[14] Yet the ceremony was titled "The Pageant of Peace," and in his speech Mr. Nixon called for increased efforts toward world peace and improvement of the environment. It would seem that there was no *connection* in the president's mind between the enormous disparity in the wealth of the world and the chronic problem of international wars and domestic strife.

The delicate balance by which this innocence is maintained is, I believe, characteristically American. It is dependent on two important drives that both conflict and complement one another.

1. The desire for success that has pushed us into the position of one of the major nations of the world.[15]

2. The desire for virtue that makes it necessary for us to deny the aggressive aspects of this success motivation.[16]

An important aspect of the American quest for virtue has been the denial of the inevitability of evil in human relationships. This is consistent with the eighteenth-century notion of the infinite perfectability of man, an idea that was very popular during the formative stages of the United States. One can also find the roots of this attitude in the American experience. In American colonial life nature was the enemy, and there was little to be gained by one man appropriating the possessions of another. Life was hard and many of the colonists died during the attempt to gain a foothold in the new world. Every man who lived and prospered was an additional source of protection for others. It was to the mutual advantage of the colonists to help one another. This view was in striking contrast to the stark inequality and the hardships resulting from differences in wealth and status that prevailed in Europe. For the European, evil was a natural consequence of human relationships. For the American, there were problems to be solved and natural obstacles to overcome. From the beginning, American attitudes were characterized by an elemental faith in the natural goodness of man. Henry Bamford Parkes has characterized this "weakening of the sense of sin" as follows:

> What appeared as evil was not a fundamental and permanent element in the nature of things, but should be regarded merely as a problem to which the correct solution would one day be discovered. The American was therefore a voluntarist and an optimist. . . . The American came to believe that . . . any obstacle could be mastered by means of the appropriate methods and technology. A failure was the result either of weakness or an incorrect technique.[17]

From this basic assumption it became a central feature of the American philosophy that patience, good will, and well-intentioned reasonableness would overcome disagreements among men. If this is not entirely corroborated by the reality of the American experience, it certainly remains today as one of our most popular myths. Thus, the observation of Margaret Mead on the style of American aggression is deeply rooted in our historical experience.

If it is not necessary to take from others in order to survive, then unprovoked aggression is unnecessary. What is more, it does not make good sense. Evil in the sense of malice is seldom considered. Instead, wrongs tend to arise from a lack of knowledge or a failure to be reasonable. Jean-Paul Sartre has contrasted this American belief with the European attitude. Speaking of a trip to America, he remarked that Americans regard their thought as universal

> . . . above all there is that concrete, daily presence of a flesh and blood Reason, a visible Reason. Thus most of the people I spoke with seemed to have a naive and passionate faith in the virtues of Reason. An American said to me one evening, "After all, if international politics were in the hands of well-balanced and reasonable men, wouldn't war be abolished forever?" . . . I, for my part, said nothing; discussion between us was impossible. I believe in the existence of evil and he does not.[18]

If evil is not an inevitable aspect of human relationships, it no longer becomes necessary to balance competing interests in international relations but only to find the correct or reasonable solution to the problem. Thus, as far as public discussion is concerned, there is no American interest, only world interest. In order to maintain this belief, it is necessary to ignore the various attempts to define our national interest by a long line of theoreticians from Mahan to Kissinger. Presidents from Monroe to Truman have used the national interest as a justification for the expansion of American influence. The concept of a national interest is implicit in our complaints that our foreign aid has not shown a satisfactory "payoff." Nevertheless, there is a persistent myth that, even in our most self-serving acts, we are really working, not for ourselves, but for the good of mankind and that we can be trusted to interpret this good to others. The potency of this myth can be seen in its influence on our foreign policy as well as in its acceptance by the average citizen.

Kissinger has summarized the problem as follows:

> It is part of American folklore that, while other nations have interests, we have responsibilities; while other nations are concerned with equilibrium, we are concerned with the legal requirements of peace. We have a tendency to offer our altruism as a guarantee of our reliability. . . . We find it hard to articulate a truly vital interest which we would defend however "legal" the challenge. This leads to an undifferentiated globalism and confusion about our purposes. The abstract concept of aggression causes us to multiply our commitments. But the denial that our interests are involved diminishes our staying power when we try to carry out these commitments.[19]

When we speak of the myth that there is no American interest, it is important to remember that we are not talking about propaganda—although there are times when a national leader has made clever use of this myth for propaganda purposes. In the myth of American altruism we are dealing with a vast, pervasive, tacit assumption that is held with an almost religious conviction by the American electorate.

Because most people do not deal with this assumption explicitly, it is not the sort of thing one could discover by direct questions to a cross section of the American people. It is not really part of our rational, conscious process of decision making. Gabriel Almond has described such beliefs as part of the "largely unconscious patterns of reaction and behavior" that influence our perception of political reality.[20] These reactions are not unconscious because we have repressed them—in the psychoanalytic sense. Instead we are unaware of them in the sense that we no longer notice them. In the Gestalt expression one might say that they are part of the ground, not the figure.

But there are breaks in this total mythical environment. Kissinger could perceive the myth of American altruism because he was both an American and an outsider. Foreign visitors have noted it as well. S. N. Eisenstadt has remarked that this attitude appears on several levels in the American psyche. "The moralistic attitude, the self-assurance that American policy is guided only by considerations of justice and right, seem to be very widespread, perhaps because it provides some sort of anchor in a very uncertain field."[21] Bryce has remarked on the feeling that, for Americans, national honor is rooted in national fair dealing,[22] and Brogan points to a strong emphasis on altruism that cannot really be maintained in practice.[23]

This belief in a "good" that reaches beyond self-interest is related to the strong religious conviction in the United States. It must be a good in the larger sense of being good for mankind and not just good for us. It must be a godly kind of virtue. This association between religious and political beliefs in the American has been noted by a number of observers. P. von Zahn speaks of our desire to eradicate evil in the world.[24] Sarc emphasizes that this idealism is not a mere cover for other motives but that the American believes it himself.[25] Tocqueville tells us that there is no country in which the Christian religion has a greater influence on the souls of men, that this control is reflected in our manners and in our political life, and that it is a religion that "clings to the interests of the world" rather than the narrow interest of a party.[26] Grund contrasts the superficial acceptance of the forms of religion in France with American seriousness about religion. He believes there is a direct connection in the United States between religion and morality. Private virtue is an indispensable requirement for political office. If he is not a saint, the public man must at least be regarded as one by passing a test of public scrutiny.[27] In his review of a number of these observations, Commager was struck by their consistency and the extent to which this element in our character seemed to persist from the early observations of Tocqueville to the twentieth century.[28]

But is there not a certain hypocrisy in all this? Can we really be so naïve as to believe that we can free ourselves from all self-interest—that is, national interest—and work only for the good of the world? Skeptics have sometimes claimed that American morality is a mere cover, a facade behind which the old national interest continues to operate. "Israelis," says Eisenstadt, "tend to think that Americans and American policy are naïve or to suspect that they are Machiavellian, because nobody could be that naïve."[29] America is the land of a highly sophisticated technology in which information is gathered and processed from all over the world. Can we really be

0885221

that ignorant about our own motives? Many observers contend that it is this very concentration on the *external* aspects of information and the knowledge of *facts* and *things* that enables us to avoid the subtle nuances of human motivation. Muller-Freienfels points out that in America technique is a "despot of life." Although it is associated with the superficial in Europe, it has achieved a high positive value in the United States where the bookstores are filled with how-to-do-it books. This emphasis on technique produces a "rationalization of the soul"—that is, "the prevalence of practical thinking . . . useful and efficient, and the obverse of this attitude is the repression and suppression of all that is merely agreeable, emotional and irrational in the personality."[30]

W. L. George tells us that the American is more easily impressed and less likely to doubt. "He is altogether more literal; he uses the words, 'right' and 'wrong', as to the meaning of which many Europeans have become rather shakey."[31] Gurowski says the American mind tends toward the objective. "In its intellectual, positive turn, it yields more easily to the pressure of outward events and combinations. Intellect finds more food, more stimulus in externalities, and therefore it overpowers the spirit . . . [The American mind is] of great mobility, expansive, but not deep . . ."[32] But it is Raymond Aron who tries to relate this thinking directly to policy. American leaders, he says, are convinced that their point of view is "less unilateral" and more complex because they are gathering information from the whole earth. But instead, they oversimplify. One explanation is that Americans apply technical thinking "that expresses itself in terms of problems to be solved and a search for means to reach an end. . . . This tendency to confuse political thinking with technical thinking sometimes leads Americans to assume implicitly that they can change the world at will."[33] D. W. Brogan also describes this concentration on externals, on the effort to change behavior rather than examine motivation. He points out that in the effort to control human actions by external means we may breed violence because we have ignored man's inner nature.[34]

III

The American leadership is placed in a difficult role by the myth of American altruism and objectivity. Poll data seem to indicate that the American people do not want to become involved in the details of foreign policy. They prefer global prescriptions for peace and order in the world.[35] However, our public officials know that we do not really want to surrender American power. In fact, we want to expand it, but we must not do it deliberately or "aggressively." There is also, as Almond has shown, "an extreme dependence of public interest in foreign affairs on dramatic and overtly threatening events."[36] This situation tends to tip the scales in the direction of using some event, either real or manufactured, as a pretext for action—rather than a long-range policy that has the support of the electorate. If American leaders were truly Machiavellian, as some have supposed, they would simply manufacture a series of these events to justify the expansion of American power. Instead, the character of the American leader usually reflects that of the people. He is highly moralistic. He wants both world peace and American power, and he believes that his own motives and those of his people are "good." This means that, for the most part, he cannot consciously manufacture a pretext for aggression, but he can "misunderstand" an event or arrange to get false information regarding it. However, knowing his own people as he does, knowing that they will forgive an "inadvertent" error, he is sometimes tempted to push dangerously close to the borders of his own innocence. In some of the cases studied in this book, we will see that the line between self-deception and the outright lie has been crossed. But in the initial stages it is apparent that the American president and many other leading public officials have a strong belief in their own good intentions and in their capacity for altruism.

The power of this myth of American altruism is evident in the pronouncements of President Woodrow Wilson at the close of World War I. Wilson had the conviction that the United States, as a nation, was not influenced by the narrow concerns of national interest but by the broad principles of world justice. He concluded, therefore, that we had no need to recognize the claims and counterclaims of the various European states but that the Europeans, once they understood that we had nothing to gain, would be "converted to America."[37] His message had a demonstrably religious quality.

> You can see that the representatives of the United States . . . have laid down for them the unalterable lines of principle. . . . They [Americans] came as crusaders, not merely to win a war but to win a cause; and I am responsible to them, for it fell to me to formulate the purposes for which I asked them to fight, and I, like them, must be a crusader for these things, whatever it costs and whatever it may be necessary to do, in honor, to accomplish the object for which they fought.[38]
> . . . I do not mean any disrespect to any other great people when I say that America is the hope of the world. And if she does not justify

that hope results are unthinkable. Men will be thrown back upon bitterness of disappointment not only but bitterness of despair. . . .[39]

The notion of a "crusade" for the right, rather than a war to protect or
advance American national interest, was invoked, once again, by
Eisenhower in World War II. In postwar negotiations the role of the
United States as an impartial referee, a nation that made no claims
for itself and had no national interest to promote, was put forth by
President Franklin D. Roosevelt. In Roosevelt's conversations with
his son Elliott it is clear that this was not mere American propaganda
but that the president attempted to act on his model of personal and
national disinterest.

> "The biggest thing," Father commented, "was in making clear to Sta-
> lin that the United States and Great Britain were not allied in one
> common block against the Soviet Union. I think we've got rid of that
> idea, once and for all. I hope so. . . . That's our big job now, and it will
> be our big job tomorrow too: making sure that we continue to act as
> referee, as intermediary between Russia and England."[40]

Roosevelt's belief that every problem had a single solution which
was reasonable, regardless of one's nationality or bargaining position, was echoed by Bernard Baruch in his attempt to negotiate a
disarmament agreement after World War II. Baruch felt that, if the
Russian people really understood what was going on, they would
support the American position—even against their own negotiator.
He said to Gromyko, "Can't you see it's in your interest as well as
ours to agree to this plan? Someday the Russian people are going to
hold your government responsible if we fail to control the atom."[41]
Baruch offered to supply the newsprint if Gromyko would publish
the American plan in full in the Soviet press, apparently in the conviction that the Russian people would see the superior merit of the
American position. Baruch assumed that the American position was
not part of a game of proposals and counterproposals, but an aspect
of moral truth to which the "people of the world" would subscribe if
given all the facts.

Although this American approach may be confusing to other nations, it is not inherently aggressive. In fact, it would be possible for
a clever bargainer to make use of the American need for virtue in
such a way as to come out ahead in the bargain. Our allies have often
accused us of giving away territory and power (their power as well
as ours) in order to prove our sincerity and support our contention
that we have no special interest to protect. It is part of the American
quest for virtue that the good intentions of the nation should be evident from the manner of the negotiator. In an effort to achieve this

atmosphere of generosity and warm heartedness, there is sometimes an excessive stress on the *appearance* of sincerity, which may not come across very well to a person who does not share the American attitude. A. H. Birse, the interpreter for Winston Churchill, described Roosevelt's behavior at the Yalta Conference:

> He beamed on all around the table and looked very much like the kind, rich uncle paying a visit to his poor relations. . . . It was not enough, as he evidently thought, to clap Russians on the back and say they were good fellows, in order to reach a mutually advantageous agreement with them. . . .[42]

In this connection, David Riesman has remarked "it appears that American delegations, regardless of the issues at stake, entered each (international conference) placing much glad-handed emphasis on the emotional value of conference moods. . . . Americans place a great stress on international mood engineering in order to persuade other countries to like them and vice versa."[43] If mood engineering were viewed for what it is—a kind of international application of American salesmanship—the diplomatic consequences of its failure would not be so momentous. But in the *confusion of intent,* which is often a part of the denial of American interest, the American position is accompanied by a sense of *moral rightness,* a feeling that we are extending ourselves toward another people in the person of our representative. Under such circumstances, the cold rejection of the American position may mean much more than the opposition to a point of view. It opens the door to sudden and unexpected reversals in American policy based, not on a change in the realities of the bargaining situation, but on a change in the bargaining atmosphere or emotional climate. In this connection, Riesman has remarked, "when the glad hand is rebuffed, the mood of tolerance may change abruptly to a mood of hurt. The result may be a desire not to reach an agreement—again, irrespective of trading advantages."[44] In a similar vein Kissinger recalls, "When the Paris summit meetings collapsed, a sudden reversal took place in the West. . . . Personal diplomacy, which had been thought capable of ending the Cold War, was now held responsible for perpetuating it. As Mr. Krushchev's mood changed, the West seemed as much in danger of being mesmerized by his frown as it had earlier been beguiled by his smile."[45] Embodied in this belief is the notion of psychological representation— that is, that another man cannot only present our proposal but that he can "be sincere" for us. It is for this reason that protestations of personal sincerity are so characteristic of American bargaining behavior. In his first speech before the Geneva Conference Arthur Dean, the American disarmament negotiator, said:

> When I was asked to accept the honor of leading the U.S. Delegation
> . . . I first investigated. . . . I wanted to know the purpose of my gov-
> ernment. . . . The fact that I undertook this job is clear evidence not
> merely of my own personal desire to conclude a just and reliable treaty
> . . . but also of the very real and sincere determination of President
> Kennedy . . . to support every reasonable effort to achieve this noble
> and humane end.[46]

Mr. Dean proposes that, since he is personally sincere, he could not
possibly support an unfair policy—that is, one that held some special and as yet unspecified advantage for the United States. If his
government were to propose such a policy, he would not take it to
the bargaining table. This assumes, of course, that Mr. Dean would
be sufficiently unbiased to recognize such unfairness if it existed in
the American proposal.

In proposing his open-skies plan at Geneva, Eisenhower injected a
similar personal note. Departing from his prepared text, he turned to
Bulganin and Khrushchev to remark:

> Gentlemen, since I have been working on this memorandum to present
> to this conference, I have been searching my heart and my mind for
> something that I could say here that could convince everyone of the
> great sincerity of the United States in approaching this problem of
> disarmament.[47]

The chief problem here is the fact that the aggressive and self-
serving aspects of American policy have not been adequately recognized. Thus, although the protestations of our desire to serve mankind may be quite genuine, they are also superficial in the sense that
the role of our own interest in policy formation has never been
examined. Such a situation not only places us at a disadvantage in
dealing with our opponents, it also unsettles our allies who expect
some consistency in our policy.

One does not find such personal expressions of sincerity coming
from Russian negotiators. Although they make frequent references to
the value of an "honest attempt to reach agreement," these statements are a formal part of the Soviet argument and are not tied to the
personality of the negotiator. They are not really aimed at the other
person as an individual. This difference in negotiating behavior is
quite consistent with other differences between the United States
and Russia in general moral standards. In America it is acceptable to
be proud of one's personal virtue and to place a high value on one's
personal reputation for honesty, particularly if it helps to advertise
one's country. In the Soviet Union, egotism of any kind, whether it be
a desire to accumulate personal capital or a virtuous reputation, has
long been regarded as one of the great sins in the morality of Bolshevism.[48] The worst egotist is the one who refuses to dirty his

hands for the party. Moral purity in the communist system is not the refusal to act immorally, but the willingness to sacrifice even one's moral principles for the good of the party.

IV

It is easy for an American to discover how this cynicism, inherent in the communist approach, provides a serious barrier to the development of mutual trust. It is more difficult for us to understand how our emphasis on personal goodness can give rise to a kind of righteousness that interferes with our awareness of our own aggressive intent. Clearly, our urge for goodness can serve to mitigate our aggressive impulses, but it often happens that the need for virtue is fused with ambition in such a way that the total thrust is intensified into a kind of messianic zeal—the ambition to be more virtuous than anyone else. It is under these circumstances that one hears such themes as "making the world safe for democracy," "coming to the aid of free people everywhere," and other glorious phrases that imply America can be a savior of the world.

At other times the need for virtue does serve as a check on ambition, but only in a restraining sense. Ambition is dammed up behind a wall of virtue until it reaches a point at which further restraint is no longer possible. It is then that the former restraint becomes, ironically, a justification for a release of aggression: "We have held ourselves back too long. We have been fools, suckers, patsies!" Although we are restrained in our desire for achievement by the thought that we must not take from others, must not be bullies, we can strike all the more forcefully if we are provoked, that is, if we can believe that the other fellow started it. Evil may not be a necessary aspect of life for the American, but there are certain circumstances under which it can be fully acknowledged. Clearly, the starting of a fight is one of these situations. The very fact that the other person strikes first releases us from all restraint. He becomes a "bad" person (or nation), and it becomes acceptable for us to punish him. This is why our foreign policy appears to be reactive.[49]

In both world wars, it was the American style to strive for peace, to refuse to fight until provoked. When the provocation came, it was "a day that will live in infamy," and there was a great flood of righteous anger when the nation moved as one body to break the bonds of restraint. When the war was over, we began to disarm, but we soon discovered that there were those who would take advantage of our peaceful intentions. The idea of "massive retaliation," which fol-

41847

lowed this experience, did not originate with John Foster Dulles or the atomic bomb. It is related to the American style of holding back and letting go: a welling up of righteous anger behind the wall of restraint and a release of this energy, accompanied by a thrill of national indignation. The very experience of playing the fool or the patsy serves as a basis for the sense of righteous anger that follows. It is a basic aspect of the American ideal of the triumph of virtue and the final and overwhelming retribution for evil.

However, a nation that grows to a major world power finds it increasingly difficult to find other nations, particularly smaller ones, who will oblige it with a significant provocation. Power has its burdens. While the world is open to conquest, innocence recedes even farther from one's grasp. If the desire for virtue were not as intense and personal as it is in the United States, such provocations would be easy to arrange. The justification of offensive acts as "defensive" is as old as Caesar. Hitler's cry of pity for the persecuted Sudeten Germans represents a rather flagrant example of this type of thing, as was his elaborate fake of a Polish attack on Germany by dressing Germans in Polish uniforms.[50] But such an approach is not congruent with the American character. A pretext for aggression is not satisfactory in the United States. The sincerity of the leader in such acts must not be open to question, at least not by the majority of the people. When Hitler made his accusations against Czechoslovakia, the Germans smirked. They were proud of their bully boy. Americans, on the contrary, must believe in the virtue of their leader. His essential goodness is even more important than the virtue of their cause, since his position as president is the result of the decision of the American people.

This has led to an interesting feature of the American style, namely, the phenomenon of innocent provocation. If an American leader manages to engage in aggressive acts without being aware of the provocative aspect of his behavior, he will be forgiven and supported by his people, even if his policy proves to be wrong. In this respect, innocence is more important than responsibility. This is a critical aspect of American morality. The fact that an act was "inadvertent" or an "honest mistake" constitutes an important basis for justification in the American mind. For a person to act without thinking, without reflecting on what he is doing, is not only congruent with the American style, but it constitutes a basis for removal of the guilt of an action. An act that is thoughtless becomes innocent thereby.

However, it is important to distinguish between the so-called "crime of passion," which absolves the criminal from guilt because

TABIA

of his intense emotion (more characteristic of the morality of the Latin countries), and the style of justification, which has become associated with the cooler and more deliberate American temperament. In America it is not the passion associated with an act that makes it guiltless but the individual's lack of awareness of his motives. When we were a small nation, our size served as a natural check on our aggressive impulses. Since the United States has emerged as a major world power, it is easier to be aggressive without "intending" it that way. The mere abundance of force makes inadvertent aggression more likely and, if the provocation be countered, the same force tempts us to retaliate.

Thus, the twin ideas of innocent provocation and massive retaliation are both essential aspects of the American style of aggression. Of course, it is not possible to know just when an administration official really does not know what he is doing and when he is making cunning use of the American tendency to forgive an act committed in innocence. One often has the feeling that innocence and guile are working so closely together that it is impossible to determine where the one leaves off and the other begins. Despite the fact that congressional investigations usually clear those involved and indicate that the errors were "inadvertent," there is a strong feeling that careful planning and deliberate concealment have often been involved. Yet in another sense, it would seem that, despite their acts, U.S. officials have shown a remarkable capacity to remain unaware of the aggressive *implications* of their behavior. This attitude of innocence is a characteristic response. It fits with the American ethos and is supported, in general, by the attitude of the American people.

In many instances, the clumsy nature of the concealment and the guilty confession of public officials, once the facts are exposed, suggests that the aggressive implications of the act have never really been examined. This is particularly true at the highest levels of government. One often has the impression that members of the lower echelons are much more conscious and deliberate in their plans, but there is apparently a certain conspiracy of silence between the higher and lower levels. Administration officials seem to feel that if they can avoid coming to grips with the hard realities of a situation (avoid conscious, aggressive intent), they are somehow free from complicity, or at least they will be excused for their complicity by the people. In this, their judgement is probably correct.

Dissonance theory would suggest that if a person holds two inconsistent beliefs (or if his public behavior is inconsistent with his avowed beliefs), he experiences a certain discomfort and that he strives to reduce this dissonance by modifying his actions or his be-

liefs.[51] But the early experiments on cognitive dissonance were conducted in laboratory situations and dissonance phenomena have
been difficult to demonstrate in actual life situations. Tedeschi,
Schlenker, and Bonma have pointed out that the subject in these
experiments is sometimes more concerned with appearing to be consistently fulfilling others' expectations than he is with actually privately structuring his beliefs to be consistent.[52] In accordance with a
larger and more inclusive theory of "impression management," they
have suggested that our society teaches us to justify all our behavior.
Virtuous behavior requires no justification, but if we do harm to
others, an effective strategy might be to attribute this activity to un-
controllable emotions or accidents. The need for consistency, then,
is seen as being rooted in the *socialization process*. It would follow
from this that the particular culture in which one is socialized might
have an influence on the manner in which one strives for credibility.
A culture in which a high value is placed on one's personal virtue
might require more concealment of one's intent and more accidental
behavior. However, if personal virtue is also indicated by openness,
the concealment of one's intent must not be a conscious lie. It must
be a concealment from oneself as well as from others.

V

If American international policy is characterized by "inadvertent"
aggression, perhaps there is a domestic counterpart that sustains it.
If the American people support the actions of their president on the
grounds that he did not really intend to be aggressive, we may find
that a similar attitude prevails in their own behavior. In this context,
of course, it should be apparent that the term *American people* really
refers to a particular class of people: those who share the ambition of
their leader, as well as his values and his desire for innocence,
namely the American middle class and upper-middle class. We are
dealing with the people who do the voting—those who have the
power but who avoid becoming personally aware of their power.
However, few people would relinquish the pleasure associated with
a personal consciousness of power unless there were some reward
associated with this sacrifice. Some bargain must be struck with the
people if they are to give up what is rightfully theirs. They must
share some of the pleasures of their leader without admitting to each
other that they have enjoyed themselves. Freud has suggested that
there is a dynamic relationship between the desire to dominate

others and the willingness to be dominated ourselves.[53] Rousseau made a similar point in regard to politics, pointing out that people can only be induced to sacrifice their freedom and independence if they can be instructed in the pleasures of command. "Individuals only allow themselves to be oppressed so far as they are hurried on by blind ambition, and, looking rather below than above them, come to love authority more than independence, and submit to slavery, that they may in turn enslave others."[54] If this is true, then the relationship between democracy and peace, implied by both Tocqueville and Schumpeter, does not necessarily hold. However, unlike autocratic regimes, democratic governments cannot forcefully oppress the majority of the people. If the people are to be conquered, they must submit willingly—that is to say, they must be seduced. Tocqueville was aware of this process in his early observation of the United States when he remarked that monarchs institute material repression but that democratic republics have rendered repression entirely an affair of the mind. "Under the absolute sway of one man the body was attacked in order to subdue the soul; but the soul escaped the blows that were directed against it and rose proudly superior. Such is not the course adopted by tyranny in democratic republics; there the body is left free, and the soul is enslaved."[55]

However, *slavery* is a rather dramatic term to describe what has happened to middle class whites in the United States. In this nation there is a pervasive belief in the "rightness" of the majority. Americans identify so completely with what they believe to be the opinion of the majority that they do not feel a sense of obeying anything but themselves. David McClelland has pointed out that Americans will resist any form of pressure, even group pressure, if it is overt. Americans do not like being told what to do. Instead, the American code of behavior is *implicit*. One absorbs it from the culture. "Americans want to freely choose to do what others want them to do. . . . The American should find out for himself what the group norm is and then, of his own free will, conform to it. Many experimental studies of opinion formation in small groups show that this in effect is what most Americans do. . . . Years of experience in many group activities have taught them *how to be sensitive to others without being told.*" [Italics mine][56]

Since he is not told what to do, the American is not conscious of obeying anyone, even the mythical "majority." Thus, the words of Tocqueville about the overwhelming, soul-crushing power of the majority seem strange to him. Tocqueville spoke of "the American republics where the power of the majority is so absolute and irresistible that one must give up one's rights as a citizen and almost abjure one's qualities as a man if one intends to stray from the track which it prescribes."[57] The image presented is that of a great commanding autocratic power that demands obedience. The average American, however, is not conscious of himself as something separate from that great majority. He searches eagerly to find the opinion of the majority, and when he discovers it, he believes he has made up his own mind. In the same manner, he also gains a sense of participation in the power of the majority since he identifies his own opinion so completely with that of the majority. If others do not conform to this opinion, he is willing to make them outcasts. He cannot understand why people with deviant opinions, peculiar dress, or manner of behavior should not be excluded from his neighborhood or his place of employment. After all, they could get a job if they would only dress and act in a respectable manner.

In the United States, where the psychological pressures for conformity are greater, there is a correspondingly greater political freedom. The American middle class adult can be "trusted" with this freedom precisely because he has been thoroughly indoctrinated— by his education, by the advertising culture, and by his neighbors in the same middle class neighborhood. His notion of individualism is contained within the social limits and the type of aspirations accepted by his society. He is interested in discovering his own unique way of becoming successful, but he does not question the merits of the success ethic itself. He has learned to equate freedom of choice with the freedom to choose among those things his society offers him. He does not recognize that he has the power to create his own alternatives. He is unaware that he is free and there is, therefore, less danger that he will make use of his freedom. Repression is more effective if people can be sold on the idea of their own foolishness and peculiarity. If the police can be kept in the background, the people can be taught to restrain themselves because they will look ridiculous or because their behavior might be bad for business. If a man feels himself tremble at his own fear of a beating, he knows that his manhood is being attacked. If he is afraid of being socially inappropriate, he is unaware of his own surrender. This is why the revolution of awareness in young people has been directed toward bringing the repressive aspects of our society into the foreground— that is, in refusing to cancel a protest march because it blocks traffic in front of the business establishments, flouting their own fears of looking ridiculous by wearing the most outlandish and unconventional garb, and defying what Norman Mailer has called the "middle class terror of excess."[58]

VI

In domestic as in foreign policy, then, the innocence of intent is preserved by a denial of the desire for power. If people can be made to conform by psychological pressure, there is no need to use force. If they fail to conform, their disturbance represents, not a challenge to power, but a problem to be solved. Under such circumstances the use of force is not aggression but an attempt to "stabilize" or "pacify" the situation. As Richard Barnet has pointed out, our metaphors suggest the field of physics and internal medicine. We seek a healthy balance of power in the world that will be good for mankind. We describe our role in Vietnam as that of the good doctor. If there is internal dissent within a nation, a "power vacuum" has been created. If we don't do something, power will flow into the vacuum from some other part of the world.[59] On this basis our vast intelligence network represents, not aggressive pressure against other nations, but an attempt to know and understand the world in order to improve world conditions.

Intelligence gathering within the United States is justified on similar grounds. The emphasis on communication and information contains an implicit assumption that the formulation of policy is a problem with a scientific solution. In this concentration on externals the internal and more human influences on policy are ignored. These are the subtle attitudinal variables that make it possible to have a different form of law enforcement for the wealthy and for the poor, although the policy is ostensibly the same. The information approach assumes that if we can only find out, in great detail, what is going on in the ghetto, we can correct the situation. It takes for granted the good intentions of policy makers and the malleability of the police. In a similar manner American foreign policy is based on the assumption that international disagreement is caused by some misunderstanding. If only all the facts were known, both sides would see the mutuality of their interests, and cooperation would be assured.

The understanding of international disagreement must take into consideration the urge for national aggrandizement and the will to dominate. This does not mean that a few clever conspirators have made the United States into an imperialist power against the will of the people. It means that the spokesmen for American imperialism have learned to make use of the urge for power that exists in all of us to forward their own ambitions. But even this statement is sugges-tive of too much deliberation. Those who have been the most active in advancing American imperialism have been "decent respectable citizens" with all that this phrase implies for the American middle class. They are not conscious of their greed. They feel that they have earned the right to what is called "success." They regard competition, in both the individual and the international sense, as a healthy form of sportsmanship. They have managed to avoid looking at its deadly and destructive aspect. They have a genuine desire for peace, a peace that will leave them in full possession of all they own with the opportunity to accumulate more. This attitude is common, not only to the "power elite," but to the majority of the American middle class.

How, then, can we understand American generosity as exemplified by the Marshall Plan and our vast foreign aid programs? Is this a cynical effort to keep others in check, to make them dependent on us? Is this merely the carrot that accompanies the stick?[60] To describe American behavior in this manner is to make the mistake of assuming that there is a calculating demon directing American policy, who is conscious of his power and who delights in its use. Americans oppress others in the same way they are oppressed themselves. They would not think of demanding that a foreign leader obey them if he is to receive American aid. David McClelland has described the implicit bargain.

> Americans, in giving aid to underdeveloped countries, frequently state publicly that "no strings are attached," that the recipient government is free to do what it chooses politically, that we are bringing no pressure to bear on it, etc. If it should do something we don't approve, however, we may immediately proclaim our disapproval and threaten to cut off our support. Other countries are apt therefore to consider Americans hypocritical: they talk one way and act another. But the fact is that behaving in this way is quite consistent with the American value formula: we do not believe in bringing pressure to bear on people (we resent it and resist it when applied to ourselves). We do want people and governments to feel free to choose what to do, but we also expect that they will choose to do what others (including especially ourselves as an influential friend) expect them to do.[61]

George Allen, a former Director of the United States Information Agency, has protrayed this development eloquently in his report of an exchange between the U.S. Senator, William Knowland, and Prime Minister Nehru of India. Knowland had just left Korea for India and was full of enthusiasm for the American military effort in South Korea. He reported to Nehru: "Mr. Prime Minister, the United States has created, in South Korea, a little nation of only 18 million people, the fifth largest army in the world, with tanks and jet planes and all the modern instruments of war."[62] This speech did not increase Nehru's confidence in the United States. Speaking to Allen a few days later, he pointed out that the United States had created vast dependent territories by their support of the regimes in South Korea, Nationalist China, and South Vietnam. India, like other former colonial territories, had hoped for many years that she might gain her independence, but now she began to see other excolonials losing their independence and coming under the control of the United States. Speaking of the fate of the former colonial powers, Nehru said:

> They couldn't buy gasoline for their tanks and airplanes, nor bullets for their guns nor even shoes for their soldiers, if the United States didn't supply the wherewithal. So you see, without your being diabolical or scheming, you have unwittingly let it happen and they have let it happen, that they have become dependent on your continued support. . . . That's why many people consider the United States to be the new imperialist power. You Americans aren't wicked people. We know perfectly well that you're not going to send governors to Korea the way imperialist powers did in the past. But, in a sort of new, streamlined, twentieth-century manner, more or less the same thing is happening.[63]

Thus, although the American desire to save the world from chaos and misery seems, on the surface, to be a very positive quality, there is a darker side to this image that manifests itself from time to time. Most behavior is really overdetermined; that is, people act, not for one reason alone, but for a variety of motives. Therefore, it is not surprising to discover that an American action that begins as a generous and unselfish response to a call for help can become mixed with motives of national aggrandizement, without anyone intending that it should happen that way.

In his observation that American imperialism is inadvertent, Nehru has put his finger on the primary defect in American foreign policy. Unlike the conquerers of the past, we do not have an acknowledged policy of American expansion. We have condemned aggression, and we have managed to remain unaware of our own aggressive intent. We do not use anger as a means of frightening an opponent, as did Hitler. If we become angry, it must be a righteous anger. It must be a "backlash" against someone else's aggression rather than a deliberate and calculated attempt to get our own way. Yet in the very intensity of our search for goodness, in our attempt to eliminate evil from the American psyche, we seem to have developed a particular blindness to our own greed, lust, and aggressiveness.

This does not mean that we should return to the early Puritan attempt to root out the sin within ourselves. We cannot seek to discover the evil in ourselves if we are determined to eliminate it before we start. Such an attitude will leave us completely unready for the darkness inside ourselves. We must be prepared to accept our own impulses to dominate and destroy. For we cannot find ourselves unless we are first ready to love ourselves. If we are to build the universal and international morality to which we have aspired, we must learn to take a look at our own diabolical potentiality. We must face the possibility that we may not be destined to be the moral leaders of the human race. If we can question our own righteousness, if we can learn to admit, at least to ourselves, what rascals we are, we may be less insistent upon forcing our way of life on others. We may become more tolerant of their moral defects and more willing to accept them into an international community. In short, we may take an important step toward world peace.

The purposes of this examination of specific cases is not to suggest that Americans are less honest than other people. It is to suggest that we are less aware when we are being dishonest. It does not mean that American aggression is more dangerous or more reprehensible than a deliberate aggression. However, it does mean that our growing power has added a new and frightening dimension to our inadvertent aggression. If we can become fully aware of the hostile implications of a particular act, we may be more inclined to discontinue it during peace negotiations and be less likely to be surprised and outraged if the offended nation forcefully interferes with our operations. If we can learn to admit that we have an interest and define it within the limits of our existing power, we may be less grandiose about advancing the interest of mankind and therefore have less need to expand our power.

NOTES

1. J. Schumpeter, *Social Classes and Imperialism* (New York: World Publishing, Meridian 1966), pp. 72–73.

2. A. de Tocqueville, *Democracy in America*, vol. II, (New York: Vintage, 1959), pp. 279–281.

3. Schumpeter, *Social Classes and Imperialism*, pp. 72–73.

4. W. Buchanan and H. Cantril, *How Nations See Each Other* (Urbana: University of Illinois Press, 1953), pp. 46–47.

5. D. D. Eisenhower, "President Eisenhower's Farewell to the Nation." *Department of State Bulletin*, February 6, 1961, pp. 179–182.

6. S. Butler, *The World Tomorrow* (October 1931), *Great Quotations*, ed. G. Seldes (New York: Lyle Stuart, 1960), p. 134.

7. S. Melman, *Pentagon Capitalism: The Political Economy of War* (New York: McGraw-Hill, 1970), pp. 88, 231–234.

8. Schumpeter, *Social Classes and Imperialism*, p. 12.

9. R. M. Nixon, "The Pageant of Peace Ceremony," *Weekly Compilation of Presidential Documents*, 1969, vol. 5, no. 51, pp. 1757–1758.

10. M. Mead, *And Keep Your Powder Dry* (New York: William Morrow, 1965), pp. 150–151.

11. N. H. Martin and J. H. Sims, "Power Tactics," *Readings in Managerial Psychology*, ed. H. J. Leavitt and L. R. Pondy (Chicago: University of Chicago Press, 1964), pp. 217–218.

12. M. Weber, *The Protestant Ethic and the Spirit of Capitalism* (New York: Scribner, 1958), pp. 48–56, 75–76.

13. Ibid., pp. 52–53, 182.

14. R. M. Nixon, "The Pageant of Peace Ceremony," 1969.

15. D. C. McClelland, *The Achieving Society* (Toronto: Collier Macmillan, 1967).

16. See particularly Mead, *And Keep Your Powder Dry*, pp. 38, 115, 120, 134, 136, 142–152, 162–163 and G. Gorer, *The American People* (New York: Norton, 1948), pp. 40–60, 93. Both Mead and Gorer emphasize the feminine source of American morality.

17. H. B. Parkes, *The American Experience*, (New York: Vintage, 1959), p. 9.

18. J. -P. Sartre, *Literary and Philosophical Essays* (New York: Collier Books, 1965), pp. 108–109.

19. H. A. Kissinger, "Central Issues of American Foreign Policy," *Agenda for the Nation* (Washington, D.C.: Brookings Institution, 1968), pp. 610–611.

20. G. Almond, *The American People and Foreign Policy* (New York: Praeger, 1962), p. 29.

21. S. N. Eisenstadt, "From Israel," *As Others See Us*, ed. F. M. Joseph (Princeton: Princeton University Press, 1959), p. 168.

22. J. Bryce "The Faults and Strength of American Democracy," *America in Perspective*, ed. H. S. Commager (New York: New American Library, 1948), p. 158.

23. D. W. Brogan, *The American Character* (New York: Vintage, 1956), p. 76.

24. P. von Zahn, "From Germany," *As Others See Us*, p. 98.

25. O. C. Sarc, "From Turkey," *As Others See Us*, p. 140.

26. A. de Tocqueville, *Democracy in America*, vol. I, (New York: Vintage, 1955), pp. 314–323.

27. F. Grund, "Religion and Morality Preside Over their Councils," *America in Perspective*, pp. 70–72.

28. Commager, *America in Perspective*, p. xiii.

29. Eisenstadt, "From Israel," *As Others See Us*, p. 161.

30. R. Muller-Freienfels, "The Mechanization and Standardization of American Life," *America in Perspective*, p. 190.

31. W. L. George, "The Sentimentality, Kindness and Innocence of the American," *America in Perspective*, p. 179.

32. A. G. de Gurowski, "The Practical Genius of the American," *America in Perspective*, p. 116.

33. R. Aron, "From France," *As Others See Us*, p. 62.

34. D. W. Brogan, "From England," *As Others See Us*, p. 8.

35. G. Almond, *The American People and Foreign Policy,* pp. 69–70.

36. Ibid., p. 72.

37. W. Wilson, *Messages and Papers of Woodrow Wilson,* vol. II (New York: George H. Doran, 1924), p. 642.

38. Ibid., p. 622.

39. Ibid., p. 644.

40. E. Roosevelt, *As He Saw It* (New York: Duell, Sloan and Pearce, 1946), pp. 206–207, 240.

41. B. Baruch, *The Public Years* (New York: Holt, Rinehart and Winston, 1960), p. 378.

42. A. H. Birse, *Memoirs of an Interpreter* (New York: Coward-McCann, 1967).

43. D. Riesman, *The Lonely Crowd* (New Haven, Conn.: Yale University Press, 1950), pp. 260–261.

44. Ibid., p. 261.

45. H. A. Kissinger, *The Necessity of Choice* (Garden City, N.Y.: Doubleday Anchor, 1962), p. 187.

46. A. Dean, Statement of the U.S. Representative at the Geneva Conference on the Discontinuance of Nuclear Weapons Tests, April 28, 1961. *Documents on Disarmament 1961* (Washington, D.C.: U.S. Government Printing Office, 1962), pp. 127–134.

47. Proposal by the President at the Geneva Conference of Heads of Government, July 21, 1955, *American Foreign Policy 1950–1955, Basic Documents II,* U.S. State Department, p. 2842.

48. N. Leites, *A Study of Bolshevism* (Glencoe, Ill.: The Free Press, 1953), p. 114.

49. Mead, *And Keep Your Powder Dry,* p. 139, "Aggression in the American character is seen as response rather than as primary behavior."

50. W. L. Shirer, *The Rise and Fall of the Third Reich* (Greenwich, Conn.: Fawcett, 1962), pp. 784–790.

51. L. Festinger, *Conflict, Decision and Dissonance* (Stanford, Calif.: Stanford University Press, 1964).

52. J. T. Tedeschi, B. R. Schlenker, and T. V. Bonma, "Cognitive Dissonance: Private Ratiocination or Public Spectacle?" *American Psychologist* 26 (1971): 685–695.

53. S. Freud, *The Basic Writings of Sigmund Freud,* trans. A. A. Brill (New York: Modern Library, 1938), pp. 569–570.

54. J. J. Rousseau, *The Social Contract and Discourses* (New York: E. P. Dutton, Everyman, 1950), p. 264 (from "A Discourse on the Origin of Inequality").

55. Tocqueville, *Democracy in America,* vol. I, pp. 274–275.

56. D. C. McClelland, *The Roots of Consciousness* (New York: Van Nostrand, 1964), p. 74.

57. Tocqueville, *Democracy in America,* vol. I, p. 277.

58. N. Mailer, *The Armies of the Night* (New York: New American Library, Signet, 1968), p. 310.

59. R. Barnet, *Intervention and Revolution* (New York: World, 1970). See particularly the chapter on the national security manager.

60. In this regard note the cancellation of all foreign aid by the U.S. Congress after the vote in the United Nations went against the Two-Chinas policy of the United States.

61. McClelland, *The Roots of Consciousness,* pp. 76–77.

62. G. V. Allen, "The Overseas Image of American Democracy," *Annals of the American Academy of Political and Social Science,* vol. 366 (1966):62.

63. Ibid., pp. 62–63.

3

The Truman Doctrine

I

In this chapter I will focus on the role of George F. Kennan and James Forrestal in the development of the Truman Doctrine. Kennan provided a large measure of the intellectual muscle, and Forrestal accentuated the anticommunist aspect of the final position paper, but neither man would have exercised his particular influence on policy without the personal interaction that occurred between them. In fact, Kennan was shocked by the global nature of the doctrine as it finally emerged and was profoundly disturbed to find that he was credited with its development. Yet it would seem that he played a major role, albeit inadvertently, in this new departure in American foreign policy. I would not contend, however, that Kennan and Forrestal were alone responsible for the development of the Truman Doctrine. Clearly, Vandenberg played a vital role in his insistence on a public explanation, in global terms, for the American decision to aid Greece and Turkey. Truman himself made the final decisions on how the policy was to be explained to the American people. it is necessary, therefore, to examine the historical background of the times before developing Kennan's and Forrestal's roles.

II

It is appropriate to begin this series of events with the creation of the Truman Doctrine. It set the tone for much that was to follow. Coming at the end of World War II, it began a new phase in Soviet–American relations that has influenced American policy toward communist nations to the present day. Although the step was a sudden one, it was the product of forces, both political and intellectual, that had been at work in the previous administration long before the close of the war. Immediately after World War II, President Truman continued the strenuous effort that had been made by President Roosevelt to get along with "Uncle Joe" Stalin. During the three power conferences prior to the close of the war, it had been Roosevelt's conviction that he should act as a mediator between British and Russian demands for the postwar era. He had leaned over backwards to create an atmosphere of harmony and good fellowship among the "allies." In the initial stages of the new administration, Truman attempted to follow a similar policy. The new president, conscious of the reputation of his illustrious predecessor, did not want to "rock the boat" and spoil the atmosphere of camaraderie that was alleged to exist between the Americans and the Russians. Thus, the Truman Doctrine, when it was finally proclaimed, came as one of those "sudden reversals" that have been described as characteristic of American behavior in international relations.

The reason for this is apparent when one examines the situation in the United States at the time. Although there had been a number of curt diplomatic exchanges between the Americans and the Russians, the American people, as a whole, were demanding a policy of disarmament. The boys must come home, taxes must be reduced, and business must begin to play the dominant role in American life once again. The memory of the Roosevelt–Stalin relationship dominated the American scene, and Truman was regarded as a pale shadow of his former chief. If he had difficulty with the Russians, no one was surprised. After all, he lacked the Roosevelt charm. Conflict between Washington and Moscow had been evident since the end of the war, but it was on March 2, 1946, that the first major confrontation occurred. On this date Russia failed to comply with the terms of an agreement that had been made the previous September between

Bevin and Molotov at the London conference of foreign ministers. The Russians had agreed that all foreign troops would be withdrawn from Iran by March 2. When it became evident that the Russians did not intend to live up to their agreement, President Truman sent a blunt message from the United States, and on March 24 the Russians announced that all troops would be withdrawn from Iran at once.[1] However, by July the Russians were again on the move. They sent a note to Turkey proposing a new regime for the Dardenelles (which would exclude the United States and Great Britain) and suggesting the straits be put under joint Turkish–Russian defense. To Truman the move was unmistakable. "This was indeed an open bid to obtain control of Turkey."[2] Truman offered the Turks support and suggested they give a firm reply to Moscow.

By the following February the situation had deteriorated further. It was now evident that Great Britain was no longer a major world power. After British withdrawal from India, Egypt, Palestine, and Burma, the British ambassador arrived in Washington on February 24, 1947, to announce that Greece was on the verge of economic collapse and that the British government was no longer able to sustain either the economic or military support of Greece or Turkey. Britain hoped the United States would be able to take over this responsibility.

On March 12, 1947, the policy that later became known as the Truman Doctrine was presented to a joint session of Congress. The president asked Congress to appropriate $400 million for aid to Greece and Turkey, but in this same speech he put forward a new role for the United States in world affairs. Announcing that the United Nations would not be able to help in this crisis, he accepted American responsibility for the support of "a democratic Greek government." Then, in a few sentences he announced an American policy of support for the other "free peoples" of the world. As a unilateral action, outside the purview of the United Nations, it was a clear challenge to the Soviet Union.

Although most Americans favored the aid to Greece and Turkey, many were profoundly disturbed by the sweeping implications of the Truman Doctrine that accompanied the announcement. It was nothing less than an extension of the Monroe Doctrine to the entire world. Walter Lippmann did not see how such a fantastic program could be carried out. He was certain that, in attempting to intervene everywhere in the world, we would jeopardize our position in Europe. George F. Kennan, an experienced Russia observer and one of the chief policy planners in the State Department, was shocked when he read the draft of the president's speech around March 6 and found, along with the proposed aid to Greece and Turkey, an ideological position that pitted the United States against the Soviet Union (even though the latter was not specifically named) and committed the United States to aid free peoples without reservation as to where they might be in trouble. "It implied that what we had decided to do in the case of Greece was something we would be prepared to do in the case of any other country, provided only that it was faced with the threat of a 'subjugation by armed minorities or by outside pressures'."[3]

Kennan objected to the language of the speech.[4] He evidently felt it was sufficiently inflammatory to start a war.[5] He tried to have the language changed, but it was already too late. In retrospect he wondered about the origin of some of the more grandiose sentences, such as:

> I believe it must be the policy of the United States to support free peoples who are resisting subjugation by armed minorities or by outside pressures.

> I believe that we must assist free peoples to work out their own destinies in their own way.[6]

What was there about the American character that seemed to give rise to such grand generalizations?

> On many occasions, both before and after this Greek–Turkish episode, I have been struck by the congenital aversion of Americans to taking specific decisions on specific problems, and by their persistent urge to seek universal formulae or doctrines in which to clothe and justify particular actions.... To this day I am uncertain as to the origins of this persistent American urge to the universalization or generalization of decision.[7]

Kennan learned that the language describing the open-ended commitments had been produced "at the initiative of the [State Department's] public relations office ... which evidently felt itself under the necessity of clothing the announced rationale for the President's decision in terms more grandiose and more sweeping than anything I, at least, had ever envisaged."[8] Kennan's finding is certainly consistent with what has often been said about the influence of the advertising man in American society, but it leaves certain important questions unanswered. Can we assume that the Truman Doctrine originated in the mind of a public relations man? If so, the president clearly had an opportunity to object to it. He went over the speech carefully before he delivered it, crossing out certain phrases and adding others.[9] If he had objected to any aspects of the content, he would certainly have changed them. In his own account Truman clearly indicates that, whatever the origin of some of the more sweeping statements in the Truman Doctrine, they reflected the intent of the president at the time.[10] It would seem that Kennan's original thoughts about the role of American character in the evolution of the president's position merits a more detailed examination. How did we manage to go so much farther in words than we intended to go in deeds? How did we manage to extend ourselves into a position that was so far beyond our military or economic capability at the time or in the years to come?

III

To capture a feeling for the political climate that served as a background for the Truman Doctrine, it is necessary to return to February 1947, a time when the American people were preoccupied with the idea of adopting the old prewar economy. President Truman had been concerned, for some time, by the wholesale manner in which ships were being placed in "mothballs," men were being sent home, and airplanes were being scrapped. His suggestion for an extension of the draft was vigorously opposed by Congress, as was his request for universal military training. Finally, on February 20, after the House had voted a full $6 billion slash in his budget, including a $1.5 billion cut in the Army's appropriation, Truman made a partial capitulation. He said he would probably renew his request for universal military training at a later date, but he indicated he would not ask Congress to extend selective service, which expired at the end of March. Secretary of War Patterson warned that the budget cuts would leave the army too weak to carry out the duties assigned to it and made the continued occupation in Europe and Japan impossible.

At that time, it was the custom to speak of a "bipartisan foreign policy," but, in the face of the Republican enthusiasm to cut taxes, the party leadership found it difficult to muster the necessary votes to support the president. On February 26 the Republican leadership, under the direction of Taft, Vandenberg, White, and Millikin pushed an amendment through the Senate that would hold the budget cuts to $4.5 billion, but the amendment received more Democratic votes than the Republicans could muster among their own party.[11] So unpopular was the president's program among the majority party that even the Republican leadership could not control the vote.

Truman was acutely aware of the effort that Taft, Vandenberg, and others had put forth in order to defeat a most severe cut in his budget. He realized that he was indeed fortunate to get by with a $4.5 billion cut instead of a loss of $6 billion from his program. The British request for aid to Greece and Turkey could hardly have come at a more difficult time as far as Truman's status was concerned. His power over Congress was at one of its lowest points in the history of his administration. Wary as he was of the Republican fiscal axe, he had to go to Congress and ask for an additional appropriation to support Greece and Turkey.

The president decided to convene a meeting of Congressional leaders at the White House on February 27 in which Secretary Marshall and Undersecretary Dean Acheson would brief those present on the British position and the need for American aid to Greece and Turkey. The events of that meeting are covered in Joseph Marion Jones' book, *The Fifteen Weeks*. According to Jones, Secretary Marshall's effort to convey the need for aid to Greece, on grounds of loyalty and humanitarianism, did not sit well with the congressional leaders who were interested in reducing taxes and making a favorable impression on their constituents. The statement that aid to Turkey would strengthen Great Britain's role in the Middle East brought forth the general reaction that it was not America's task to "pull British chestnuts out of the fire." This was followed by further complaints about the costs of such aid. Things were going very badly until Acheson requested an opportunity to speak. Avoiding the humanitarian approach, he directed the attention of the members of Congress to the growing power of the Soviet Union and the pressure the Soviets were exerting on Turkey, Greece, Germany, and some of the other nations of Europe. He dismissed the remark about "pulling British chestnuts out of the fire" by pointing out that Britain was through as a world power. She no longer had any chestnuts in the fire. If the United States did not take action, the advantage would go to the Soviets. American security and the cause of freedom itself was in danger, said Acheson.

Senator Vandenberg was the first to break the silence following Acheson's presentation. He had been deeply impressed by the undersecretary's remarks. The president asked for comments, but he no longer received any opposition. Mr. Jones summed up his impression of the meeting with the remark that, although no commitments had been made,

> the very definite impression was gained, and was conveyed to the State Department staff the next day as a working hypothesis, that the Congressional leaders would support whatever measures were neces-

> sary to save Greece and Turkey, *on the condition*, made by Senator
> Vandenberg and supported by others present, that the President
> should, in a message to Congress and in a radio address to the Ameri-
> can people, explain the issue in the same frank terms and broad con-
> text in which it had been laid before them.[12]

Thus, the congressional support was contingent on the president's ability to explain the problem to the American people in a
broad context. The justification that Greece was a friend of the
United States, her dire financial situation, and the precarious position of the British and the Turks might all represent satisfactory
arguments in such a speech, but obviously they were not going to be
sufficient. Something more was needed. In a nation with a history of
isolationism, in which there was already widespread resentment at
the cost of postwar involvement in Europe and Japan, some very
heroic arguments would be necessary. As Jones remarked,

> at the meeting with the Congressional leaders, Acheson discovered
> that he had to pull out all the stops and speak in the frankest, boldest,
> widest terms to attract their support for a matter which, in parliamen-
> tary democracies without a tradition of isolationism, would have been
> undertaken quietly and without fanfare. . . . They were deeply im-
> pressed and felt that on that basis they could go before their constit-
> uents. It was Vandenberg's "condition" that made it possible, even
> necessary, to launch the global policies that broke through the re-
> maining barriers of isolationism.[13]

We have here the basis for the grand generalizations in the president's speech of March 12. Mr. Truman reports that he had already
become concerned about supporting "the cause of freedom wherever
it was threatened" before talking with congressional leaders.[14] However, it is one thing to have such ideas and something else to pro-
claim them before the world. It is clear that he was given a strong
push in the direction of gradiosity by the congressional leadership.

The details of these meetings with Congress are important because of what we so often hear about U.S. foreign policy. We hear
that the public statements of U.S. policy are mere window dressing,
that the real reasons for policy are more hardheaded and practical,
devoid of the sentimentality that politicians sometimes provide for
the press. Indeed, this is the way the Truman Doctrine seems to have
begun. In his talk with congressional leaders, Acheson is said to
have dismissed humanitarian motives, but he also spoke in the
"frankest, boldest, widest terms" about the Soviet threat. However,
in the final preparation of the Truman Doctrine, humanitarian considerations were not only introduced once again, but we were placed
in the position of saving the entire free world—not just Greece and

Turkey. Was this a hard-headed and practical policy? On the contrary, it seems to have been an earlier version of the domino theory. Was it mere window dressing? In fact, it would seem to have set the stage for our involvement in a series of interventionist wars from Korea to Vietnam.

According to Joseph Marion Jones, Francis Russell, Director of the State Department's Office of Public Affairs, was told to start work on a program of public information, which would explain to the American people the background of the decision to give aid to Greece and Turkey. The controversial portions of the president's speech containing the statements about the "choice between two ways of life" and the support for "free peoples who are resisting attempted subjugation by armed minorities or by outside pressures," was taken directly from a report by Russell's Subcommittee on Public Information. It survived subsequent revisions intact.[15] This is, no doubt, the source of Kennan's opinion that the president's more sweeping statements were the product of the "public relations office." However, it is clear that Russell's report merely reflected the instructions of Dean Acheson, who had made the successful presentation to the small group of Republican and Democratic leaders gathered in the president's office and who was under no illusions in regard to the kind of justification Congress demanded of the president when he spoke to the American people.

IV

Whatever the pressures on President Truman at the time of his decision, he took an active role in forming the doctrine that bears his name. The president makes it clear that he was in full agreement with the idea of generalizing the response to the Greek–Turkish situation into a statement about the cause of freedom and the containment of communism. He remarked on this subject in his *Memoirs:*

> The ideals and the traditions of our nation demanded that we come to the aid of Greece and Turkey and that we put the world on notice that it would be our policy to support the cause of freedom wherever it was threatened.
>
> . . . the studies which Marshall and Acheson brought to me and which we examined together made it plain that serious risks would be involved. But the alternative would be disastrous to our security and the security of free nations everywhere.

What course the free world should take in the face of the threat of Russian totalitarianism *was a subject I had discussed with my foreign policy advisors on many occasions in the year just past.* To foster our thinking in long-range terms, I had approved the establishment in the State Department of a Policy Planning Staff. George F. Kennan, one of our foremost experts on Russia, was to head this group. [Italics mine][16]

Truman's account would seem to indicate that his new doctrine was not a spur-of-the-moment decision. He indicates that it was a product of a position that we know Forrestal had been urging upon him for some time.[17] The mention of Mr. Kennan's name in connection with the decision suggests that he found Kennan's opinions very important in formulating his final position. The fact that he mistakenly dates the formation of the State Department Policy Planning Staff (of which Kennan was the head) prior to his March 12 speech is a further indication that he regarded the ideas of Kennan as a part of the general intellectual background on which his decision was based. In the light of the fact that Walter Lippmann was later to accuse Kennan of being the architect of the Truman Doctrine, it would seem worthwhile to examine, in more detail, Kennan's role in the years prior to Truman's decision.

In his *Memoirs*, Kennan describes himself as a rather shy, retiring person, who was accustomed to remaining in the background in political situations. His role was that of an advisor and, during his period at the American embassy in Moscow, he had accustomed himself to the idea that his telegrams to Washington would not receive much attention. However, Kennan was a man with a powerful intellect, who was not afraid to speak his mind. He was quite willing to make controversial statements and to give his opinions freely when asked. He did not have the traditional reticence of the foreign service officer. Brooks Atkinson describes him as a man with "a roving, speculative mind and considerable intellectual independence, he does not fit comfortably into an organization that is weighed down with inertia in which the ambitious foreign service officer is inclined to play safe . . ."[18]

On February 22, 1946, Kennan had sent a long telegram of over 8000 words to the State Department in response to a routine request for information about the Russian attitude toward the World Bank and the International Monetary Fund. The telegram described the basic features of the Soviet outlook and its effect on their diplomatic behavior. The telegram arrived at a critical time in American–Soviet relations, a time when the "soft line" was already under question and the slow, persistent Russian testing of the Western position was gradually being recognized. The telegram made a profound impression on Forrestal, then Secretary of the Navy. In January of the following year, in response to a request by Forrestal for criticism of a policy paper, Kennan sent him a long and detailed paper on the sources of Soviet conduct. On February 17, Forrestal acknowledged the paper, indicated that he thought it was very well done and said that he would suggest that it be read by the "Secretary," presumably the Secretary of State.[19] For years, Forrestal had been a leading advocate of the containment of communism. He was one of the most aggressive spokesmen on this subject, but it was Kennan's paper that gave him some of the intellectual force that his arguments required. It is not clear at what point Kennan began to realize the profound impression his telegram and his paper had made on Forrestal. His observations and deductions were the product of his own diplomatic experience. Although he was aware of the need for extreme "discrimination of judgement and prudence of language" in dealing with a foreign power, he was accustomed to letting himself go and giving his opinions quite frankly when dealing with his fellow Americans.

Forrestal, already intensely involved with his idea of a Russian conspiracy, was eventually to push himself to the point of a complete breakdown which resulted in "involutional melancholia" with decided paranoid ideation and, finally, his suicide.[20] It is difficult to determine to what extent Forrestal's attitude toward communism was a product of his delusion. However, as Rogow has remarked, it is also difficult to avoid the conclusion that "Forrestal's personality needs and policy recommendations were closely related."[21] In any event, there is little doubt that he found Kennan's paper useful in promoting his own point of view. The paper reached Forrestal just 24 days before President Truman and Secretary Marshall called him in to confer on the Greek–Turkish situation. It may have already been in Secretary Marshall's hands at that time. Kennan's previous long telegram was already well known by the administration. It is, of course, impossible to determine the extent of the influence of Kennan's paper on the Truman Doctrine. When the paper was later published as an article in *Foreign Affairs* under the title "The Sources of Soviet Conduct," it was signed only with the name X.[22] However, Arthur Krock soon ferreted out the name of the author and revealed it in his column in the *New York Times*. It was at this point that Walter Lippmann began to put together the "estimates, the calculations, and the conclusions" of Kennan's article and to find in them the very sources of the Truman Doctrine. Lippmann, like Kennan, was in general agreement with the United States policy toward Greece and Turkey. He also agreed that the Soviet pressure could not be "charmed or talked out of existence." However, he quoted and challenged Kennan's assumption that the Soviet power was inherently weak and impermanent and that the United States should enter with "reasonable confidence upon a policy of firm containment, designed to confront the Russians with unalterable counterforce at every point where they show signs of encroaching upon the interests of a peaceful and a stable world."[23]

With this quotation as his primary wedge, Lippmann proceeded to take apart what he regarded as the intellectual foundation of the Truman Doctrine. He questioned the capability of the State Department, under the Constitution, to provide the money and military power for the appropriate "counterforce." He referred to the policy as a "strategic monstrosity" and pointed out that its open-ended nature left no limits to American commitment. He emphasized the importance of diplomatic techniques for driving the Soviet army out of Europe and urged that we limit our immediate concern to the European community. Contrasting the Truman Doctrine with the Marshall Plan. Lippmann remarked:

> the difference is fundamental. The Truman Doctrine treats those who are supposed to benefit by it as dependencies of the United States, as instruments of the American policy for "containing" Russia. The Marshall speech at Harvard treats the European governments as independent powers, whom we must help but cannot presume to govern, or to use as instruments of an American policy.[24]

Thus, Kennan, who was proud of his association with the Marshall Plan and embarrassed by the generalities of the Truman Doctrine, was divorced from the former and associated with the latter.

The experience was a painful one for Mr. Kennan, particularly when his "oversights" were exhibited with such deadly accuracy in Lippmann's column. In his *Memoirs*, he describes his reaction:

> It was doubly painful by reason of the great respect I bore him [Lippmann]. I can still recall the feeling of bewilderment and frustration with which—helpless now to reply publicly because of my official position—I read these columns as they appeared and found held against me so many views with which I profoundly agreed. A few months later [April 1948], lying under treatment for ulcers on the 16th floor of the naval hospital in Bethesda, very bleak in spirit from the attendant fasting and made bleaker still by the whistling of the cold Spring wind in the windows of that lofty pinnacle, I wrote a long letter to Mr. Lippmann, protesting the misinterpretation of my thoughts which his articles, as it seemed to me, implied. I never sent it to him. It was probably best that I didn't.[25]

Kennan reacted to the Lippmann columns with what he describes as a "peal of anguish over the confusion about the Truman Doctrine and the Marshall Plan. To be held as the author of the former, and to have the latter held up to me as the mature correction of my youthful folly, hurt me more than anything else."[26]

In his later reflection on Lippmann's comments, Kennan deplored his own lack of careful editing, his failure to mention that his idea for the containment of Soviet power was not containment by military means or a military threat, and his failure to mention the satellite area of Eastern Europe in terms of the involvement of Soviet power. He admitted that his use of such expressions as "a long-term, patient but firm and vigilant containment of Russian expansive tendencies" and "the adroit and vigilant application of counterforce at a series of constantly shifting geographical and political points"—"was at best ambiguous, and lent itself to misinterpretation . . ."[27] For the most part, Kennan, in his *Memoirs*, seems mystified by the errors and oversights that he acknowledges in his article. At one point, however, he mentions that he suspects his failure had something to do "with what I felt to be Mr. Forrestal's needs at the time . . ."[28]

V

This is the extent of the evidence. There is little else to confirm my own hunch that the status of Forrestal (and the knowledge that he was impressed by and interested in Mr. Kennan) had a powerful influence on the direction of Kennan's paper. It is at least a possible explanation for the manner in which Kennan admittedly found himself misrepresenting his own views. What we have here is not a deliberate cooperation. Kennan was a man of high intellectual integrity. It is my contention, however, that there was a subtle influence of Forrestal's power on Kennan's ideas, in such a way that the intellect of Kennan was, to some extent, swept into the vortex of Forrestal's general goals.

Forrestal was not the kind of administrator who thought he could hire an intellectual to justify his opinions. Such a person would have made no progress with Kennan. On the contrary, Forrestal had a genuine respect for ideas. Although his position on communism was similar to that of the political right, he often considered himself a liberal, particularly in his early years. He and his aides took detailed notes for a book he was planning. He had a habit of sending books and magazine subscriptions, or photostats of articles, to his friends and associates in an attempt to "educate" them. For many years he was a financial contributor to *The Nation*. But he also admired Ayn Rand and the ultraconservative magazine, *Plain Talk*.[29]

He was one of the few government officials with an interest in the
ideas behind policy, but he lacked the intellectual depth to provide
the kind of thinking required to substantiate some of his own opinions. For this reason, he was particularly eager to photostat and send
"attention" copies of those articles and position papers that he
admired—and to give encouragement to the author. He had been
impressed by Kennan's analysis in the long telegram of the previous
year, having entered the entire contents in his diary.[30] On February
24, 1947, the day that Secretary Marshall handed him the memorandum from the British ambassador, the Kennan telegram was still on
his mind. That day he entered in his diary, without further explanation, the words, "Ideology is the figleaf for Soviet respectability," a
quotation from Kennan's telegram of the year before.[31] His inquiry as
to whether Kennan would criticize the policy paper from his department was both a high compliment and a request for help. Kennan, being aware of Forrestal's views, was inclined to try to meet the
secretary's needs without knowingly compromising his own beliefs.

We do not really know what use Forrestal made of the Kennan
paper before the drafting of the Truman speech. He probably gave a
copy to his own information officer, who attended the Subcommittee
on Foreign Policy Information, the group that was so influential in
drafting the critical sentences in the Truman Doctrine. Certainly, it
must have had wide distribution in other quarters as well. Kennan
did not participate in the actual drafting of the Truman speech.
When he read the draft around March 6, he says he was "extremely
unhappy."[32] Joseph Marion Jones puts the matter even more
strongly: "To say that he found objections to it, is to put it mildly."[33]
Yet a careful reading of the X paper in Foreign Affairs reveals a
number of parallels between Kennan's ideas, which were for private
circulation, and the public speech by President Truman on March
12. According to Jones, Kennan was the only one who offered
strenuous objections to the speech prior to March 12. Perhaps the
intensity of Kennan's feeling was based, in part, on his belated
awareness that he had contributed "inadvertently," in large measure, to the intellectual foundation for the very policy he found so
reprehensible.

Kennan was an intellectual, a man who believed in a rational
approach to world problems. Viewing himself as a person who provided technical advice in dealing with foreign powers, he was not
inclined to consider his subjective feelings in the preparation of his
reports. He warned against the growing power of the Soviet Union,
but he did not intend that others would translate his words into such
aggressive and global policy initiatives. Said A. J. P. Taylor, in

commenting on Kennan's statement that "Americans stand as a lonely, threatened power on the field of world history,"

> When Americans were addressed by the rational Mr. Kennan in these frightening terms, they naturally responded violently. They flung themselves into the Korean War, and Mr. Kennan protested in vain that they had learnt the wrong lesson. He had meant to preach "containment." Instead he had helped to launch a crusade. . . . He never appreciated the deeply emotional basis of his own outlook and was therefore surprised when he evoked emotion in others.[34]

VI

Regardless of the attitude of Kennan toward his role in providing a justification for the Truman Doctrine, it is clear that President Truman's policy statement was inadvertent in one important aspect. The president, like many other Americans of the time, regarded it as a declaration of virtuous intent, not as a declaration of hostility. With the possible exception of such people as Walter Lippmann and George Kennan, the belligerent character of the Truman Doctrine seems to have escaped both the president and his contemporaries. At the time of its inception, it seemed to most Americans not only reasonable but heroic—and well within our capabilities. It was not until the stalemate in Korea, or perhaps until the hopeless involvement of American men and matériel in the jungles of Vietnam, that the full implications of the Truman Doctrine became apparent to the American people.

NOTES

1. H. S. Truman, Memoirs, vol. II; Years of Trial and Hope (New York: Doubleday, 1956), pp. 93–95.
2. Ibid., p. 97.
3. G. F. Kennan, Memoirs: 1925–1950 (Boston: Little Brown, 1967), p. 320.
4. J. M. Jones, The Fifteen Weeks (New York: Harcourt Brace and World, 1955), p. 155.
5. Ibid.
6. Kennan, Memoirs, p. 320.
7. Ibid., pp. 322–323.
8. Ibid., p. 315.
9. Truman, Memoirs, vol. II, p. 105.
10. Ibid., pp. 97–107.

11. J. D. Morris, "Senate Coalition Votes 51–33 to cut Budget 4½ Billion," *New York Times*, February 27, 1947, p. 1.

12. Jones, *The Fifteen Weeks*, p. 142.

13. Ibid., p. 143.

14. Truman, *Memoirs, vol. II*, p. 101.

15. Jones, *The Fifteen Weeks*, pp. 151–153.

16. Truman, *Memoirs, vol. II*, p. 101.

17. J. Forrestal, *The Forrestal Diaries*, ed. W. Millis (New York: Viking, 1951) and A. Rogow, *James Forrestal* (New York: Macmillan, 1963).

18. B. Atkinson, "America's Global Planner," *New York Times*, July 13, 1947, section VI, p. 9.

19. Kennan, *Memoirs*, p. 355.

20. Rogow, *James Forrestal*, p. 9.

21. Ibid., p. 399.

22. G. F. Kennan, "(X) The Sources of Soviet Conduct," *Foreign Affairs*, July, 1947.

23. W. Lippmann, *The Cold War* (New York: Harper, 1947), p. 11.

24. Ibid., p. 54.

25. Kennan, *Memoirs*, pp. 360–361.

26. Ibid., p. 361.

27. Ibid., pp. 358–359.

28. Ibid., p. 358.

29. Rogow, *James Forrestal*, pp. 250–260, 269.

30. Forrestal, *The Forrestal Diaries*, p. 135.

31. Ibid., p. 246.

32. Kennan, *Memoirs*, p. 315.

33. Jones, *The Fifteen Weeks*, p. 155.

34. A. J. P. Taylor, "American Metternich," *Observer* (London), January 28, 1968, p. 30.

The Clean Bomb and the Scientific Test

4

I

When a nation has adopted a doctrine that calls for a wider range of international influence, it must have the power to back up this new policy. A critical aspect of this power is the development of more ingenious, more effective weapons. Weapons development, then, is a generalized form of international aggression. It is also a more subtle form of aggression, since it can be undertaken in the name of defense. It is significant in this regard that 1947, the year of the Truman Doctrine, was also the year in which the War Department had its name changed to the Department of Defense.

But the creation of new weapons requires research and hence the cooperation of scientists. Just how this cooperation was achieved in the United States is a long story. It did not come about overnight. From the very beginning, there was strong resistance on the part of leading scientists, such as J. Robert Oppenheimer, to the extensive involvement of scientists in the defense establishment. However, once the scientific community began to develop a vested interest in the arms race, a new element had entered the picture—the expert adviser. Research corporations and "think tanks" began to develop under the not-for-profit category. It was assumed that, since these corporations were not making a profit from defense business, their advice would be "objective." Such an assumption was only possible if one ignored the salaries of the staff, the "management fee" paid in lieu of profit, and the tremendous sense of power that the individual scientist derived from his new role. The scientist discovered that he could exert a potent influence on policy by virtue of his specialized knowledge. What is more, he managed to convince himself that he was not exerting his influence to enhance his own personal power. It was his "duty" to urge the administration to appropriate funds for weapons. He was protecting the nation from a potential aggressor. Thus, the American scientist became involved in the sorcery of self-deception.

Whole new industries were created, based on scientific developments for the defense establishment. The increased need for weapons had created a need for more scientists in all categories: communications technology, solid state physics, space research, psychological warfare, the chemistry of defoliation, and the development of biological weapons. However, the scientist soon discovered that his new-found position was dependent on the continuation of the arms race. He could always return to the university, but he had become accustomed to the life of power and prestige. There was no longer a sufficient number of university or nondefense positions to employ the vast number of scientists created by defense business. If more scientists were to be produced by the university every year, the arms race must continue. Furthermore, many valuable scientific discoveries had occurred as by-products of weapons research. The arms race had become not only good for science, but essential to its continuation at its newer, more expanded level of activity. However, during the period of 1956 to 1959, the United States had begun to lose a different kind of battle—the struggle for the support of the neutral nations of the world. We found ourselves holding out for further experimentation in weapons development while India, Japan, and most of the major uncommitted nations of the world had joined the Soviet Union in a massive international movement to ban further testing of nuclear weapons. This move was a threat, not only to the further growth of American power, but to the weapons scientists as well. The need for defense was no longer an adequate justification for the continuation of weapons development. The Soviet Union had agreed to cease further testing of nuclear weapons and to open its territories to inspection if we would do the same. The time had come for a combined effort by scientists and public relations men to demonstrate the humanitarian value of further weapons development.

In the American mind the idea of virtue is closely allied to that of wholesomeness, freshness, and cleanliness. American tourists are frequently heard to express their disgust about the dirtiness of the French and Italian cities and their strong preference for clean restaurants, antiseptic toilet facilities, a room with a bath, and freshly washed people. Thus, when the United States found itself backed into a corner by the offer of a nuclear test ban agreement, it is not surprising to find the American government attempting to counteract this position by the development of a "clean" bomb. The belated awareness of this requirement for a smaller tactical nuclear bomb is an indication of the degree to which the administration and its scientific advisors had been caught up in the fascination of developing larger and more impressive weapons and the extent to which weapons development had become separated from the total requirements of national policy, including the peace and disarmament efforts of the Eisenhower Administration. To understand how this situation came about, it will be necessary to return to the first comprehensive U.S. policy on disarmament—the Baruch Plan—following World War II.

II

The Baruch Plan for disarmament was proposed by the United States in 1946. It was thoroughly coordinated with the State Department (Byrnes) and President Truman. It was a rather amazing example of American generosity. In this plan the only nation with a monopoly on the atomic bomb put forward a proposal to control all nuclear material and destroy existing nuclear weapons, while asking for no controls on conventional weapons, a field in which it suffered a serious disadvantage relative to the Soviet Union.

However, the Baruch Plan was proposed at a time when Stalin was still in power in Russia. His attitude of suspicion infused all Soviet policy. The reluctance of the Soviets to accept the Baruch Plan was due, in part, to the fact that they felt there must be some catch in it. Their own suspicion blinded them to its obvious advantages for Soviet power. It is true that the Baruch Plan was imperfect in many respects. It called for international ownership of uranium and thorium mining, but in December 1946 it was conceded that this was not really necessary. Nevertheless, the Soviets were suspicious of the American offer. The American demand for inspection posts was perceived as a disguised attempt to spy on the Soviet Union. Surely, they thought, the Americans could not be offering something for nothing—even for the cause of peace.

Stalin died in 1953, shortly after Eisenhower assumed office. Eisenhower seized the initiative to deliver a major policy speech on April 16, 1953, entitled "The Chance for Peace." He gave considerable encouragement to Emmet John Hughes, who urged him to push a policy of disarmament in the early years of his administration. However, the State Department was out of step with the Eisenhower plan for peace from the beginning. In March 1954 John Foster Dulles announced the policy of "massive retaliation" by nuclear weapons against any aggressive communist activity. This was a policy based on the acknowledged Russian superiority in tactical weapons. Knowing that we could not meet a Soviet thrust with their land army and that we did not have the manpower to counter the massive communist armies building in Asia, Dulles proposed to make use of U.S. nuclear capability, which was our strong point. However, he failed to consider two important factors: (1) the tremendous moral disadvantage that would result from American retaliation with nuclear weapons to a relatively slight communist provocation and (2) the fact that the Baruch Plan, which had never been disavowed, proposed the elimination of nuclear weapons and the control of fissionable material. At this point the policy in the State Department was completely out of phase with our disarmament policy.

By 1955 it was already clear that the policy of "massive retaliation" had presented a very poor image of the United States to the rest of the world. However, the United States was at a serious disadvantage in terms of its tactical military capability. If we should disavow the use of "massive retaliation," it was clear that the lead times required to develop a conventional capability equal to the Russians was prohibitive. Consequently, a plan evolved to develop smaller, tactical nuclear weapons. This was conceived as a rapid means of developing a tactical capability. Nevertheless, in June 1954 the United States had subscribed to a British–French plan calling for a total prohibition of nuclear weapons as a first step. Conventional weapons were to come later. The situation was clearly loaded for a major Soviet move.

By May 1955 the new Russian regime, under Bulganin and Khrushchev, had recognized that it would be to their advantage to accept the Western proposal. On May 10 they put forth a plan in which they accepted the conventional force levels proposed by the West and agreed to the establishment of inspection posts.

It was apparently only when the United States was faced with a possibility of real action on their plans that they seriously considered its relationship to State Department policy. If they allowed the Russians to accept the Western proposal, it could mean the end of the development of tactical nuclear weapons. There was already strong pressure for a test ban agreement. Thus, the United States had no way out of the situation except a reversal of their previous policy. Eight days after the Russian proposal was tabled, the United States insisted on a recess. The U.S. negotiators said that the approaching summit conference necessitated a review of the whole problem. This was surprising since the Western proposals had been on the table for almost a year.[1]

The open-skies plan, which was then offered by Eisenhower, was apparently a counter to Soviet propaganda. This was followed by the American negotiator, Stassen, putting "a reservation on all its [the United States'] previous substantive positions." Stassen was placed in an extremely difficult position. He did not want to admit that the United States was withdrawing from its own disarmament plan, now that the Soviets had accepted it. His statement to the Disarmament Subcommittee on September 6, 1955, makes his embarrassment quite clear: "In placing this reservation upon our pre-Geneva positions, may I make it perfectly clear that we are not withdrawing any of these positions, we are not disavowing any of them. But we are indicating clearly that we do not now re-affirm them . . ."[2]

However, the matter was not allowed to rest at that point. Pressure for a test ban agreement began to mount. The American newspapers published statistics on the contamination of the atmosphere caused by the explosion of atomic weapons. On December 6 the government of India drafted a resolution calling for the suspension of nuclear weapon tests. On July 12, 1956, a similar proposal was again introduced in the Disarmament Commission by the government of India. By October the situation had reached the point at which President Eisenhower found it necessary to make a full policy statement on the question of nuclear tests. It was in this statement that he first announced the goal of developing tactical nuclear weapons with a lower yield.[3] This statement came at the height of a presidential campaign, in which Eisenhower's opponent, Stevenson, was stressing the merits of a test ban agreement.

It is Schlesinger's opinion that Eisenhower was actually moving toward such an agreement, but when Stevenson made it a political issue, test ban discussions were halted within the government.[4] Another factor that might well have caused Eisenhower to change his position at this point, was an aggressive campaign of letters by

Bulganin on the subject of the test ban. Bulganin referred to the presidential campaign and the statements on disarmament that had acquired the form of a polemic. In a pointed reference to Stevenson, he remarked, "We fully share the opinion recently expressed by certain prominent public figures in the United States concerning the necessity and the possibility of concluding an agreement on the matter of prohibiting atomic weapons tests . . ."[5] Eisenhower replied sharply to Bulganin's letter, and his public statement on the need for further nuclear tests followed.

However, by June 1957 the clamor for a test ban agreement was mounting to another pitch both inside and outside the United States. According to Marcus Childs, popular opinion was strongly opposed to John Foster Dulles and his public speeches opposing such an agreement. In June the president seemed about to come around to the view of his advisor on disarmament, Harold Stassen, that it was possible to separate a test ban agreement from the other elements of the complex American disarmament proposal.[6] It was clear that the president was strongly drawn toward the idea of a test ban agreement, both from the standpoint of the world demand for the cessation of atomic tests and his own feelings that it would be a step toward world peace. In the London disarmament conference toward the end of June, the president said he would be, "Perfectly delighted to make some satisfactory arrangement for temporary suspension of tests."[7]

On the following day, Lewis Strauss, Chairman of the Atomic Energy Commission, took a major step to dissuade Eisenhower from what appeared to be a move toward a test ban agreement. He arrived at the White House for a talk with the president with three internationally known physicists, Edward Teller, Ernest O. Lawrence, and Willard Libby. These men were firmly opposed to any cessation of testing. It was apparently his interview with the scientists that caused the president to reverse himself on the policy of a test ban. From this point on, the status of his disarmament advisor, Harold Stassen, seemed to have deteriorated. After their conference with the president, Doctors Teller and Lawrence used the steps of the White House to make their announcement regarding the clean bomb. They opposed the cessation of atomic tests and called upon the president to continue testing of the new weapon: ". . . to neglect it, would be a 'crime against humanity' . . ."[8] The clean bomb had become an humanitarian gesture.

Backed by the powerful Atomic Energy Commission (AEC), which was developing the bomb, Teller and Lawrence played down the effects of fallout and urged further experimentation for the development of nuclear weapons. Thus, the agency that held the responsibility for developing the bomb was also the primary government spokesman in evaluating the risks of continuing this development. A number of scientists questioned the objectivity of the AEC in private and were particularly critical of the ability of the AEC to speak in the name of both testing and public interest. A few of them spoke out, but most maintained a discreet silence. As one reporter put it, "In spite of their training in logic and professional dedication to the ideal of truth, they [physical scientists] have been no more courageous than anyone else in risking the displeasure of a powerful government agency with a practical monopoly on easy money for atomic research."[9]

The press, however, proved to be more skeptical. In its editorial, "A Clean Death," the *New Republic* openly wondered whether it was "cleaner" to be vaporized by a hydrogen bomb than to be poisoned by fallout.[10] In London the *New Statesman* found the whole thing rather ridiculous:

> On Monday Admiral Lewis Strauss, Chairman of the Atomic Energy Commission, arrived at the White House with three top physicists, who disclosed to the President their progress in the development of "clean bombs." They had achieved 96 percent purity already, just 3 percent under Ivory Soap. . . . In the face of such an advance toward civilized bombing, it was clear that the question, as the President said was "not black and white." . . . After all, why should we use clean bombs on an enemy and have them, by default, drop dirty bombs on us? "I would hope," the President told the Press, "that they would learn how to use clean bombs" . . .[11]

The American failure to advertise its way out of a difficult situation was due to the mistaken assumption that American middle class values were universal values. The first assumption was that a cleaning of almost anything could make it better and more worthy of praise. The second assumption was that it was possible to set an example and make one's own things "clean," thereby embarrassing others and making them want to be clean, too. This is the way it works in the United States among middle class families, but these values do not hold up in the arena of world politics. It was Norman Cousins in the *Saturday Review* who prepared the most vitriolic attack on the line coming from the White House. Surely, he felt, we could not realize what we were doing or what we were saying. We were pretending—pretending to ourselves as well as to the rest of the world—that we were doing something nice instead of something evil. It was the extent to which Americans were fooling themselves that seemed to concern Cousins.

> Almost without realizing it, we are adopting the language of madmen.
> We talk of "clean" hydrogen bombs as though we are dealing with the
> ultimate in moral refinement. . . . What kind of monstrous imagination
> is it that can connect the word "clean" to a device that will put the
> match to man's cities? . . . to call a hydrogen bomb or any bomb
> "clean" is to make an obscene farce out of words.

> Or we will use the term "sunshine units" to measure the amounts of
> radiation suffered by people as the result of nuclear explosions. Seri-
> ous research reveals that any added radiation shortens life. . . . Yet all
> this now goes by the name of "sunshine units." It is made to sound as
> though something beautiful and gleamingly wholesome were coming
> into man's life . . . To use the pretty words of the nursery in connection
> with such an effect is to engage in a fiendish act of moral shrinkage.[12]

Cousins was trying to tell us that we were not willing to face some
moral implications of what we were doing, that we were attempting
to deny our own responsibility for evil by covering it with advertising slogans.

By September 23, 1957, Dulles began to use the new tactical nuclear bomb as a basis for retreating from his embarrassing policy of
"massive retaliation."[13] But shortly thereafter, Nehru of India renewed his request for a cessation of atomic testing, and Prime Minister Kishi of Japan sent a letter to President Eisenhower making a
similar request. On October 5, 1957, Mr. Nehru visited Japan to lay a
wreath on the memorial to victims of the first atomic bomb at
Hiroshima, and on the same day the Russians announced they had
successfully launched a man-made earth satellite into space. This
was held up as an example of Russian interest in discovery versus
American interest in bombs. The United States was again on the defensive. When Henry Cabot Lodge offered a U.S. peace plan for outer
space to the United Nations on October 10, the Soviets were openly
contemptuous. Pointing out the Russian Sputnik was merely a scientific experiment, Andrei Gromyko called again for agreement on a
test ban. Late the same month France announced her intention to
develop her own atomic bomb in the absence of any testing agreement. The American stock market, which had been falling for
months, took a sharp drop directly after the launching of Sputnik,
and on October 22 the president had to warn of the danger of "mor-
bid pessimism" about the economic picture.

By the following year, the Eisenhower Administration finally
conceded that the Soviet Union was ahead in the propaganda battle
on disarmament. With the offer of a plan for outer space and the call
for a summit conference, they were rapidly gaining the sympathy of
many of the neutral nations of the world. The Soviets were calling
for a summit meeting of the heads of state, and Vice-President Nixon

was asked by a British correspondent during a speech in Chicago, "Why is the United States dragging its feet to the path of the summit?"[14] Soon the United States was bracing itself for the next Soviet move. It was not long in coming. On March 30 the Soviet Union announced a unilateral cessation of atomic testing. Both India and Japan praised the Russian move.

On April 2 John Foster Dulles held a press conference in which he made a final attempt to justify the clean bomb. He told the reporters:

> as a country which is governed by humane considerations . . . we want to get away, if we can, from having these weapons inevitably involve a vast destruction of humanity and turn them into smaller, tactical, cleaner weapons which can be used effectively for defensive purposes without this great possible danger to humanity . . . We operate, as is visible right here, in terms of a free and independent and a highly intelligent press. If I came before you with something that was a phony you would recognize it in a minute and tear it apart publicly.[15]

III

The problem of the clean bomb was not merely one of international credibility. An advertising culture is characterized by a certain tolerance for exaggeration. If the opening of a frosty bottle of pop causes snow to fall in the living room, this is all part of the wonderworld of advertising. It is not to be taken seriously. Testimonials and the claims that "scientific tests" have shown the superiority of one's product are discounted in the light of a natural enthusiasm for success. It becomes a struggle to see who is going to be more clever in the use of words. Instead of being used for communication, words are manipulated for effect, meanings become blurred, speech is divorced from reality, and the individual suffers a loss in general awareness. An advertising culture does not really produce a more critical and analytical attitude toward advertising. Instead the advertising man comes to believe his own pitch.

The "clean bomb" was not merely poor advertising in that it failed to "sell" the American position to the neutral nations of the world. The chief difficulty was the extent to which it presented an unrealistic picture of the world situation to administration leaders and to the American people. Secretary Dulles' challenge to the reporters—to call him a phony if they dared—is, I believe, indicative of the extent to which the secretary believed in his own rationalizations. He was not speaking with tongue in cheek. He was morally committed to a point of view that involved his own rightness and the essential evil of his opponent. The story of the "clean bomb" was a disservice precisely because it *was* accepted by the administration and by a large segment of the American people. It was a false picture of the world. This is not to say that the tactical nuclear weapon had no importance in promoting American interest. It is simply that American interest was not the issue, at least it was not an issue that the administration was willing to acknowledge.

There was, of course, considerable conflict concerning the clean bomb within the Eisenhower Administration at the time. There were those who pushed actively for a test ban agreement and who often had the ear of the president: Emmet John Hughes and Harold Stassen among others. There was the president's general belief in peace and disarmament and his own vacillation on the issue of a test ban. There was the firm opposition to any test ban agreement on the part of Dulles, Strauss, and their supporters. The president himself was strongly moved by moral arguments. In such a situation it is difficult to determine where the "real reasons" came to an end and the "public reasons" began. However, in retrospect, it is clear that we were embroiled in a dangerous situation. The United States was developing a policy of reliance primarily on nuclear weapons for tactical warfare. This policy had two important implications. First, there was a strong probability that in entering a tactical conflict at a nuclear level, we would produce an almost immediate escalation, thus increasing the threat of a general war. Second, if our policy in limited wars was to be based on tactical nuclear capability, we could not cease research, development, and testing in this area. The American requirement for tactical nuclear weapons tended to postpone indefinitely any agreement on the discontinuance of nuclear testing. To make such an agreement would be to permit a lapse in our tactical capability vis-à-vis the Soviets, who placed their primary emphasis in tactical warfare on conventional weapons.

Once having taken the position that the "clean bomb" was not merely a temporary military expedient but a moral necessity for the good of mankind, it was more difficult to retreat. In attempting to win over the American public, the administration leaped from the practical and situational to the idealistic and ethical. In the process the degree of commitment and the rigidity of the position were greatly intensified. This is the great dilemma in American foreign policy. Explanations of policy must be prepared, first of all, for domestic consumption. The American people want to believe that their policy is virtuous and humanitarian. On the other hand, the people want their own interests to be paramount. American interest is therefore unmentionable or, if it is mentioned at all, it must appear in the guise of humanitarian considerations. If one is engaged in a bargaining situation, seeking private advantage, it is easy to yield a point when it seems expedient. But if one is acting on a matter of universal moral principle, it becomes immoral and "weak" to change one's mind. In the case of the test ban treaty it required a change of administration to reverse the American position.

The Dulles speech was the last attempt to promote the humanitarian aspects of the clean bomb. Within the Eisenhower Administration pressure was already beginning to mount for a separation of the issue of nuclear testing from other aspects of a disarmament agreement. If we could forego the requirement to detect all forms of nuclear fission and fission products and limit ourselves to the detection of nuclear explosions it might be possible to set up inspection stations for this purpose, stations that would be acceptable to the Soviet Union. Harold Stassen had already obtained the support of Dr. Harrison Brown of the California Institute of Technology for this point of view.

However, the Stassen–Brown position was directly opposed by scientists who contended it would require a great mass of detection stations to be sure the Soviets were not testing. The men who opposed their own scientific evidence to that of Professor Brown represented some of the most outstanding names in the field of physics: Ernest O. Lawrence and Willard Libby, both nobel prize winners, and Edward Teller, winner of numerous international awards and the man often described as the father of the hydrogen bomb. Dr. Teller was quite outspoken and emphatic in his opposition, remarking for the benefit of reporters that "disarmament is a lost cause" because there were "very serious, very effective possibilities of hiding nuclear tests."[16] He dismissed the Soviet offer to permit inspection stations on their territory as meaningless since it would take a vast number of detectors to be sure the Soviets were not testing.

Nevertheless, Stassen continued to push his arguments, bringing forth his own experts and calling for hearings and testimony. To counter Stassen's argument, his opponents within the administration proposed a test of the range at which underground nuclear explosions could be detected. The test was also designed to provide other basic data on the phenomenology of underground nuclear explosions. However, this particular test was conducted by scientists in the pay of institutions under contract with the government. It demonstrated that inadvertent errors can occur, even among scientists working in their own field of study, when their awareness is clouded by political considerations.

IV

The Rainier shot was conducted in Nevada on September 19, 1957, in the early days of the controversy about the feasibility of a treaty to ban nuclear tests. It was a small bomb, about a tenth the size of the one that was dropped on Hiroshima, and the AEC picked a nice soft spot for the explosion. It consisted of a partially congealed tulfa volcanic ash, which was quite porous. As Dr. Willard Libby later told a Senate committee, "we picked the softest, spongiest mountain we could find."[17] The analysis of the results of the blast took several months. In the following February the data from the shot still had not been released to the general public, but Harold Stassen felt sufficiently confident of his information to report to a Senate Disarmament Subcommittee hearing that the shot had been detected by every seismic instrument within 1000 miles. It appeared there were solid grounds for Stassen's original contention that the detection problem would not prove to be an insurmountable barrier in a test ban agreement. However, on March 6 the AEC issued a detailed report of its findings, which directly contradicted Stassen's testimony. The AEC report claimed that the maximum distance at which the shock had been recorded was about 250 miles.

The report touched off a controversy that continued for weeks. I. F. Stone who published a small independent weekly newspaper, called the AEC to check the report. He uncovered stories in *The New York Times* at the time of the test shot that indicated the shock had been detected as far away as Toronto and Rome. He called the U.S. Coast and Geodetic Survey, which provided him with information that the test had been detected in College, Alaska, 2320 miles from the test point. Then he asked the AEC for an explanation.[18]

On March 10 the AEC issued a correction of its previous report, and on the following day Senator Hubert Humphrey, Chairman of the Senate Disarmament Subcommittee, said he felt the AEC statements gave the impression that scientific facts were "being used by someone to prove a political point."[19] The error in the AEC report was so gross and it so strongly supported the known bias of its leaders that it was difficult to believe that it could have been a mistake. The odor of politics was so strong that a special hearing of the Joint Committee on Atomic Energy was called for March 15 to determine how such an error could have occurred in the report of a respected scientific body.[20]

Dr. Willard Libby, Acting Chairman of the AEC, admitted the error in the tradition of unreflective candor that is appropriate for such occasions. "We regret it, we assume full responsibility, but there was absolutely no intent to deceive anyone."[21] There it was again. That matter of intent. How, then, did the error occur? It appeared that the mistake became possible through a series of oversights. The San Francisco information officer had detected the error in a draft of the report. He phoned Albuquerque, New Mexico, recommending that the sentence containing the incorrect maximum distance be deleted. But the publicity representative at Albuquerque became ill after receiving the message and did not return to work until the report was ready for publication. The statement was reviewed in Washington and approved on March 2, circulated to the commissioners on March 4, and issued in Washington and Nevada on March 6 without anyone catching the error. After listening to the testimony, the congressional Joint Committee on Atomic Energy cleared the AEC of any intention to deceive. Said the chairman, Carl Durham of North Carolina, the AEC made an "honest mistake." Dr. Libby concluded the matter by assuring Senator Humphrey, of the Disarmament Subcommittee, that the AEC error was "entirely inadvertent."[22]

Actually, this tale of inadvertence is not difficult to believe. In view of the numerous agencies making measurements of seismic data from the test, which were independent of the AEC, it would have been foolish for the AEC to believe it could really get away with deliberate falsification of the results. How, then, did such a foolish thing happen? The explanation offered to the Joint Committee on Atomic Energy, while it supports the contention that there was no conspiracy to deceive the American people, does not really help us understand the mistake.

V

Freud first began to examine the process by which people make mistakes in a book called *The Psychopathology of Everyday Life*. He investigated common errors, such as slips of the tongue and acts of absent-mindedness, and he concluded that an unconscious wish was often responsible for the mistake.[23] Other psychologists have emphasized the importance of what they call "set" or expectation and its influence on behavior.[24] It has been demonstrated in a number of experiments that the expectations of an individual will have a marked influence in determining what he will see or hear in a particular situation. The set causes a person to notice certain things and fail to notice others. There are a number of factors that help to determine a person's set: anxiety, physical needs, desire for achievement, and predetermined attitudes or beliefs. However, many of these experiments with set have been conducted using animals or college students as subjects. Could we not expect a reputable scientist to be less influenced by such subjective factors? Unfortunately in order to deal with one's own personal expectation, it is first necessary to acknowledge that it exists. There is no evidence to indicate that scientists are more adept at this form of self-understanding. Jerome Wiesner, a physicist with extensive experience in government work in the fields of disarmament and weapons technology, is one of the few who have been able to take account of his own bias. He described the problem this way:

> I've been billed as an expert on arms control, and I think I'm an example of what's wrong with the American posture in this field. . . . I come to the arms control field with all the biases, prejudices and skepticism to be expected of someone who has been working very hard on military weapons. Unfortunately, most of the people who work on arms control problems have the same background.[25]

The scientists in the AEC who directed the Rainier shot were the very ones who advocated further testing in order to develop a clean bomb. The reasons for their opposition to a test ban are not clear. It may have been due to a genuine concern about the security of the United States, a need to support the more powerful faction in the administration, a desire to continue their work on weapons without any interference, or a mixture of these motives. *In any event, their opposition to a test ban agreement was clearly related to their belief in the difficulty of detecting nuclear explosions.*

But how can we make a connection between belief and expectation? Would it not be possible for a scientist to believe in the difficulty of detecting nuclear bursts and still keep an open mind toward a particular shot? Unless we can return to the day of the shot and examine the expectations of the scientists, it will be difficult to establish that there was any "set" or expectation that may have biased the results. Fortunately, the shot was of sufficient importance that reporters roamed the Nevada test site in an effort to pick up some scraps of information. Gladwin Hill of *The New York Times* reported that:

> Scientists—particularly those involved in the earth research of the International Geophysical Year program—had been hoping that the extraordinary explosion might provide some seismological information.
>
> But the top ranking AEC test scientists said today that, according to their seismological consultants, the size and location of the blast would preclude any far-reaching repercussions . . . the detonation will have only a very small fraction of the power of a very small earthquake, and most of the force will be absorbed in the immediate area.[26]

Immediately after the blast the scientists involved apparently made a quick check of their predictions. This information also was given to the press. Hill again reported

> There were reports in California about 300 miles away that some seismographs recorded a small tremor at the moment of the blast. . . . But in general, the experiment seemed to have conformed with predictions of AEC scientists that the explosion would not be detectable more than a few hundred miles away . . .[27]

In the same paper there were reports of readings from Tokyo and Rome, but no one bothered to question the scientists on these discrepancies. Obviously, they would need time to examine all the data. The AEC took plenty of time to prepare the report, but there is a question as to whether they made a serious attempt to examine the data. For the final conclusions did not differ significantly from the first brief observation made directly after the test. Their own expectations and their immediate observations had produced a powerful bias against any further discoveries.

The hearing suggests that information from Alaska was available to contradict these initial observations as early as January 21, 1958, almost a month and a half before the official report was released, but although members of the investigating committee were aware of this information, Dr. Libby, the chairman of the AEC at the time, appears to have overlooked it until a much later date. His explanation to the congressional committee supports this conclusion.

> Chairman Durham [of the Joint Committee]: I believe we were told in January by Dr. York that it [the shock wave] was picked up in Alaska. That was January 21 of this year. So I do not see why these people in making the official report did not have the same information. Dr. Libby have you anything to say on that point?

> Dr. Libby: I personally know myself it was picked up in Denver. I had not heard about Alaska until the last couple of weeks. I think the situation is, Mr. Durham, that the seismological records are coming in and have been coming in quite recently . . . These records are coming in. For example, we knew Berkeley had heard it the first day, and Berkeley is three hundred and fifty miles from the Rainier site. So certainly this two hundred and fifty mile statement was a complete inadvertence [sic], there never was a basis for it.[28]

Dr. Libby seems to have been aware of the evidence of smaller discrepancies from the official reported results, in the range of 100–200 miles, while ignoring the 1750 mile discrepancy in the information from Alaska. It is as though he cannot bring himself to admit that a finding of such significance could have been overlooked by the AEC scientists. The joint committee returned to this point to question him further.

> Chairman Durham: After the test shot when the AEC and the test of-
> ficials [were] advised that the Alaska station over two thousand miles
> away had detected the shot—when was that received by the Commis-
> sion?
>
> Dr. Libby: I believe our first information was on March 4, but I must
> check with the General Manager.[29]

The memory of the general manager, Mr. Fields, supported that of
his chief, Dr. Libby, but at least one member of the commission had a
better memory for dates.

> General Starbird: The first time I heard it, sir, was in testimony be-
> fore the Joint Committee given in executive session. The date as I re-
> member was about January 21.[30]

But the general was examining the problem of shock hazard close to
the site. His area of concern did not include the problem of distance
of detection. ". . . personally, at the time I heard the remark before
your committee, I did not take this to be of any great significance to
what I was trying to achieve. Perhaps I should have; however, my
objective was to find out what was the nature of that shock and the
possible hazard close in."[31]

It is apparent that the division of responsibility was a factor in the
failure to catch the significance of the Alaska report. It is one of the
problems of science by committee that the man who was aware of the
Alaska report did not consider it significant and the man responsible
for approving the report (Mr. Fields) managed to avoid the data until
two days after he had signed it. The AEC commissioners themselves,
including the chairman, Dr. Libby, apparently were not responsible
for approving the report but were circulated copies for their "information."[32] The report was filtered through a kind of sieve of responsibility in which the people who were officially accountable for the
work of the AEC did not approve it, but merely reviewed it. Mr.
Fields, the man who approved the report, was an administrator. On
the basis of the hearing, it would appear that no working scientist
held responsibility for examination of the data, verification of the
conclusions, and final approval of the report. However, in examining
the nature of the error in reporting the Rainier shot results, it is important to remember that it was a group error. No one among the AEC
scientists reviewing the report raised any objection. It almost seems
as though there was something about this group of scientists, operating together, that prevented them from speaking out as individuals.

The work by Irving Janis, on the decision-making process in
groups, is particularly valuable here.[33] Janis studied a number of
American policy decisions and noted the tendency of groups to in-

crease their solidarity in the face of an external stress. There is a general tendency of group members to try to win over the nonconformists and to reject them if this proves impossible. Although the results of the Rainier shot did not constitute a policy decision, it was understood that these results could have an important influence on policy. In this sense, there was stress on the group as a whole. Men of the stature of Teller, Lawrence, and Libby, all of whom opposed a test ban, undoubtedly had a profound influence on their colleagues. In this connection it is probably significant that the one man who did suggest that the report be changed was not a member of the scientific team. He was an information officer. As such, he was outside the immediate influence of the group of scientists conducting the test.

VI

In the previous discussion, we have touched on only some of the factors involved in the erroneous report of the Rainier shot. There are many questions that remain unanswered. Perhaps we could go further into the problem with more information—information that is not likely to be made available.

We have heard from those who accepted official responsibility for the error, but it would be interesting to know who actually made the mistake. It would be fascinating to trace his sources of information, look at his sheets of data, and compare this information with the official report. Perhaps here, too, we would find a similar sieve of responsibility with several people sharing the task in such a way that no one really felt a sense of personal involvement in the experience of knowing—for there is a vast difference between assembling data and understanding its significance.

NOTES

1. R. J. Barnet, *Who Wants Disarmament?* (Boston: Beacon Press, 1960), p. 35.

2. Statement by the deputy United States representative to the Disarmament Subcommittee, September 6, 1955, *Documents on Disarmament: 1945–1959* (Washington D.C.: U.S. Government Printing Office, 1960), p. 513.

3. Statement by President Eisenhower regarding nuclear tests, October 23, 1956, *Documents on Disarmament: 1945–1959*, p. 698.

4. A. M. Schlesinger, Jr. *A Thousand Days* (New York: Fawcett, 1966), p. 417.

5. Ibid., p. 694.

6. M. Childs, *Eisenhower: Captive Hero* (New York: Harcourt, Brace & World, 1958), p. 279.

7. "Cleaning The Monster," *Newsweek*, July 1, 1957, p. 48.

8. Ibid.

9. J. Lear, "On Serving Two Masters," *The Saturday Review*, August 3, 1957, p. 38.

10. "A Clean Death," *The New Republic*, July 15, 1957, p. e.

11. R. Bendiner, "Clean and Dirty," *The New Statesman*, July 13, 1959, p. 39.

12. N. Cousins, "Clean Bombs and Dirty Wars," *The Saturday Review*, July 20, 1957, p. 1.

13. J. Raymond, "U.S. Dilemma on Defense Views," *New York Times*, September 23, 1957, p. 1.

14. T. J. Hamilton, "Soviet Is Exploiting Its Propaganda Lead," *New York Times*, March 23, 1958, p. E3.

15. *New York Times*, April 2, 1958, p. 6.

16. J. Reston, "Mine Atom Blast Felt 2000 Miles. AEC Admits First Report on Detection of Explosion in Nevada Was Wrong," *New York Times*, March 12, 1958, p. 1.

17. U.S., Congress, Senate, Committee on Foreign Relations, *Control and Reduction of Armaments: Hearing Before a Subcommittee*, 85th Cong., 2d sess., 6 March 1958, p. 1366. Actually tulfa was picked for several reasons besides the desire to minimize the shock wave. It was necessary to find material on the Nevada test site into which a tunnel and instrument emplacement hold could be excavated at reasonable cost. There are other materials that will hide an explosion more effectively than tulfa. One reason for selecting a small nuclear device was also lack of experience in containment.

18. "Underground Test Error," *Science*, April 18, 1958, p. 866.

19. Ibid. There is a possible explanation for the discrepancy between the AEC report and the newspaper account of the detection range. It lies in the difference between the scientific meaning of "detection" and the public understanding of the word. Professor Carl Kisslinger has pointed out to me that, although the signal was certainly "detected" in College, Alaska and in Rome, the observer would have to be waiting for it. "I think it can be guaranteed that if no previous announcement of the event (which was well publicized in advance to the seismological community) had been made, the seismologists in Alaska, Japan, Rome, and other places would have overlooked or ignored the signal. We cannot expect the violator of a treaty to tell us ahead of time when to look for a signal from his test. It would be foolish for me to deny that AEC omitted the fact of the observations— even though it was known to them. I have no data about this, and you present a convincing account. But might it not have been because the public would almost certainly misunderstand the significance of the observations, and any attempt at explanation would look like special pleading?" (Personal communication.)

20. The report of this hearing is not listed in the *Daily Digest* of congressional hearings nor in the index of publications for the Joint Committee on Atomic Energy. Edward J. Brunenkant, the AEC Director, Division of Technical Information has indicated (in a letter to me) that the hearing was held, but never published. The information in this study is based on a transcript contained in a bound volume in the offices of the congressional Joint Committee on Atomic Energy. I am grateful for the cooperation of John T. Conway, Executive Director of the Joint Committee and his staff for locating and releasing the transcript to me. It is titled *Transcript of the Hearing of the Joint Committee on Atomic Energy*, vol. 101, 85th Cong., 2d sess., 15 March 1958.

21. Ibid., p. 4.

22. "Political Shock Wave," *Time*, March 24, 1958, p. 23.

23. S. Freud, *The Psychopathology of Everyday Life*, trans. A. A. Brill (New York, Norton, 1966).

24. For a discussion of this phenomenon and some of the experimental studies concerning it, see A. J. Bachrach, *Experimental Foundations of Clinical Psychology* (New York: Basic Books, 1962), pp. 116–124; R. Brown, Social Psychology (New York: The Free Press, 1965), pp. 510–514, 642, 643; R. S. Woodworth and H. Schlosberg, *Experimental Psychology* (New York: Holt, Rinehart and Winston, 1962), pp. 830–838; and B. G. Andreas, *Experimental Psychology* (New York: Wiley, 1960), pp. 528–530.

25. J. Wiesner, *Where Science and Politics Meet* (New York: McGraw-Hill, 1961), p. 173.

26. G. Hill, "First Underground Nuclear Explosion Set for Today," *New York Times*, September 19, 1957, p. 4.

27. G. Hill, "First Atomic Blast Set Off in a Tunnel," *New York Times*, September 20, 1957, p. 1.

28. *Joint Committee Hearing*, 85 Cong., 2d sess., 15 March 1958, p. 16.

29. Ibid., pp. 29–31.

30. Ibid.

31. Ibid., p. 31.

32. Ibid., p. 16.

33. I. L. Janis, *Victims of Groupthink* (Boston: Houghton Mifflin, 1972).

The U-2 Incident

I

In the previous chapter I pointed out the cultural pressure for an American leader to formulate and explain international policy in such a way that it can be accepted by the American middle class, regardless of what foreign governments might think of this explanation. George F. Kennan has commented on this same tendency of American statesmen

> to make statements and take actions with regard not to their effect on the international scene to which they are ostensibly addressed but rather to their effect on those echelons of American opinion ... to which the respective statesmen are anxious to appeal.... Until the American press and public learn to detect and repudiate such behavior, the country will not have a mature and effective foreign policy.[1]

In his acceptance of personal responsibility for the U-2 incident, President Eisenhower clearly exhibited the kind of manly and forthright behavior that Americans admire. But the consequence of this acceptance was to put an end to further deliberations with the Soviet

Union. Further investigation of the U-2 incident suggests that the president was himself relatively unaware of the significance of the U-2 flights in relation to peace negotiations at the impending summit conference and that the possibility of their temporary suspension during the conference was never brought to his attention.

Again we are brought face to face with the separation between the aggressive acts and the peace deliberations in an administration. This is due in large part to the fact that espionage and weapons development are kept secret, whereas maximum publicity is generally given to peace negotiations. Although there are practical reasons for this, the psychological effect is the creation of a kind of national unconscious, in which are included all peacetime espionage activities and other illegal acts performed by the government.

Under such circumstances there is a strong tendency to repress, if not the secret activity itself, the implications of this activity. Although a national leader must consider it in the planning session, he is inclined to forget it when he leaves the meeting. Although the knowledge of peacetime espionage is never repressed in the sense that it is unavailable for conscious recall, it may remain at a lower level of awareness in which it is never coordinated or integrated with other plans for peaceful negotiation or cooperation with other world powers. In this sense, an American national leader may be unaware of the negative consequences that may occur when his secret plan reaches fruition. For this reason, the revelation of his secret acts to the American public may come as a shock and produce a feeling of guilt in the leader. He is inclined toward a full confession for the same reason that a public figure caught in a scandal of self-interest may seek to redeem himself by a return to the ethic of openness. The basic idea behind this ethic is that actions will become innocent once they are voluntarily exposed to public view.

II

This reluctance to look at the negative side of ourselves was dramatically illustrated by the U-2 incident of May 1, 1960, in which an American intelligence agent, Francis Gary Powers, under the aegis of the National Aeronautics and Space Agency (NASA) violated Russian air space by flying over Soviet territory for at least 1200 miles. The plane was shot down by the Russians, and Mr. Khrushchev accused us of spying. Without knowing if the pilot, Mr. Powers, was dead or alive, NASA gave a rather detailed description of his mission, which was summarized as "weather reconnaissance."

Khrushchev then released the information that Powers was, in fact, his prisoner and that he had confessed to spy charges, naming names of his supervisors and his subunit within NASA. Finally, the U.S. State Department, with the president's approval, admitted that Powers had been spying—or, as they put it, "seeking information now concealed behind the Iron Curtain." (We are not really spying; it is you who are concealing.)

The European press was shocked by this sudden and unprecedented revelation. The French particularly were taken aback. It violated the well-known rule number 2 in every spy's handbook, namely, "If you are caught, never admit guilt" (rule number 1 is "Never get caught"). The incident, and admission of U.S. involvement, occurred within weeks of a summit meeting of the leaders of the major world powers. Many observers of the international scene wondered if, by taking personal responsibility for the U-2 incident, the president had destroyed all hope for amicable discussions regarding world peace.

In America the Powers incident received a different reaction. The "Letters to the Editor" column in newspapers all over the country were filled with criticism of our government for having permitted the overflight to take place. Perplexed and disillusioned, many Americans were wondering how their government could be guilty of such an immoral act. It was almost as though no one had been willing to admit that the United States would, could, or ever had engaged in peacetime espionage or sabotage; that red-blooded American spies might commit murder, suicide, or steal in order to accomplish their mission. As values crumbled on the New York Stock Exchange, Burton Crane of the New York Times, attributed the falling market to the plane incident and the Russian response.[2]

Other readers began to defend our intelligence activities. They pointed out that these activities are part of the facts of life we must all face and that we couldn't let the Russians bluff us into dropping our guard and cancelling all overflights every time they called for a peace conference. Many remembered the old Pearl Harbor strategy in which the Japanese struck against our unalerted defenses while they were talking peace in Washington.

Yet it seemed clear that the Powers flight was not intended to provide warning to the United States against imminent attack but was for purposes of gathering information on Soviet capability. This type of intelligence can tolerate long lead times—up to several months. Again the question was raised, "Why a flight of such a provocative nature so close to the summit conference?" It was the incisive Walter Lippmann in his column of May 10 who struck home on this point with all its implications.

Why, then, knowing that such flights were being made, did the President fail to realize the risks of continuing them right up to the meeting at the Summit?

Is it because he was not paying sufficient attention?

It looks like that.

It seems as if the country has been humiliated by absent-mindedness in the highest quarters of the government.[3]

Various government officials, concerned by the impression that was developing in the press regarding administrative control, attempted to imply that the question of continuing the flights had been carefully considered and that a decision had been reached to go ahead with them. Secretary Herter said, "The decision not to suspend this program of flights, as the Summit meeting approached, was a sound decision." However, when pinned down by questions from Senator Fulbright and Senator Gore, he admitted that the flights had never really been examined in connection with the approaching summit conferences.

THE CHAIRMAN [FULBRIGHT]: Thank you very much. One other statement, Mr. Secretary, on page 5, point 2: "The decision not to suspend this program of flights, as the Summit meeting approached, was a sound decision." Can you tell us who made that decision, and when, and of the circumstances?

SECRETARY HERTER: That is a decision that I think has been carried over the whole four-year period. Here, sir, we get into certain technical aspects of when these flights would properly be conducted and could not be conducted, but I think the technical reasons had better be kept in executive session. . .

THE CHAIRMAN: I don't think I make myself clear. I understood from your previous statement and others that the program was agreed upon, and it was running along without being suspended. But this statement seems to leave the implication that a specific decision was taken not to suspend them in view of the conference approaching. Was such a decision taken?

SECRETARY HERTER: That I can't tell you. I was not a party to that.

THE CHAIRMAN: Well, this says: "The decision not to suspend this program of flights, as the Summit meeting approached, was a sound decision." Was there any decision taken not to suspend it?

SECRETARY HERTER: I know that when the matter came before me, which was some time previous from the point of view of the continuation of the program, when conditions were appropriate, I did not interpose any objection to it because of any diplomatic event that was coming up.

THE CHAIRMAN: Is it fair to say then that no specific decision not to suspend them was taken? It was allowed to go along without any decision being taken to suspend them.

SECRETARY HERTER: I think that is correct.

THE CHAIRMAN: Therefore, the other way around is that no positive decision was taken not to suspend them; is that correct?

SECRETARY HERTER: That is right.

THE CHAIRMAN: That statement, I think, needs clarification. I think, to me, it means that at some point prior to May 1 a specific decision was taken not to suspend them in view of the Summit. Isn't that a legitimate interpretation of that sentence?

SECRETARY HERTER: I think that is correct. May I read what the President said on that subject? He said: "As to the timing, the question was really whether to halt the program and thus forego the gathering of important information that was essential and that was likely to be unavailable at a later date." The program went forward.

THE CHAIRMAN: Then the decision was made by the President.

SECRETARY HERTER: Oh, he was certainly consulted with regard to the continuation of the program . . .

SENATOR GORE   [Some time later]: Well, my specific question is this: Did you participate in a conference or were you aware of a decision; did you make a decision? What is the full extent of your knowledge of a decision that the flight would not be discontinued?

SECRETARY HERTER: I know of no conference at which the matter was discussed . . .

SENATOR GORE: To return to the question, insofar as either of you know, or any official of the Department, no actual decision to proceed with the flight or not to proceed with the flight was made. If such a decision was made, it was beyond your knowledge. Is that a correct statement?

SECRETARY HERTER: Yes; I think that I ought to say this. When the matter came before me, I had an opportunity of disapproving it and did not do so. Not it, but the program . . .

SENATOR GORE [later]:   Well, what would be the proper agency to consider whether these flights should or should not be discontinued?

SENATOR HERTER: If the question of discontinuance had come up, if there was a decision to be made, we would have been asked advice on it. We were not asked for advice on it.[4]

That a certain degree of absent-mindedness was responsible for the blundering over the spy-plane incident is clear. The situation was further compounded by our giving out an embarrassingly detailed first version of the incident (NASA's "weather reconnaissance" story) and finally by our belated confession of the true situation.

Perhaps the root of the problem is revealed in Mr. Herter's admission that the possible suspension of the U-2 flights was never considered worthy of discussion. If the pros and cons of continuing the flights had been considered, we might have been prepared for what followed. However, U-2 flights, which violate international law, are exactly the type of immoral act that no good American wants to think about. To deal in such matters is to remind one's self of an unpleasant side of American foreign policy. To ignore them is to maintain the fiction of American innocence. It is this desire to forget about our negative side and think only of the good that is our greatest source of vulnerability.

III

However, there remains another curious event in the story of the U-2 incident. If it was the serious intent of the president and the top government officials to conceal the details of overflights, why did they blurt out the whole truth when caught in the act? Such statements are extremely unorthodox and certainly not necessary. Many government scandals have been hushed up by promising that "the matter will be fully investigated and the details revealed after further study." Such an approach would be even more acceptable in the case of intelligence information, which requires the highest security restrictions. As Lippmann pointed out in his column of May 12,

> all great powers are engaged in the spy business, and as long as the world is as warlike as it has been in all recorded history there is no way of doing without spying.
>
> All the powers know this and all have accepted the situation as one of the hard facts of life.
>
> Around this situation there has developed a code of behavior. The spying is never avowed and, therefore, the government never acknowledges responsibility for its own clandestine activities. If its agent is caught, the agent is expected to kill himself. In any event he is abandoned to the mercies of the government that he has spied upon . . .
>
> The cardinal rule which makes spying tolerable in international relations, is that it is never avowed. For that reason it is never defended, and, therefore, the aggrieved country makes only as much of a fuss about a particular incident as it can make or as it chooses to make.
>
> We should have abided by that rule. When Mr. K. made his first announcement about the plane, no lies should have been told. The administration should have said that it was investigating the charge and would then take suitable action. We should then have maintained a cool silence . . .[5]

Why, then, did our officials feel compelled to admit that Mr. Powers was a spy? To examine the basis for this strange disclosure one
must know more about the American concept of truthfulness and its
supposed relation to virtue. Such a concept is vividly illustrated by
the folk tales of George Washington, which were created during the
lifetime of our first president by the notorious Parson Weems. When
we dismiss these innocent stories of the cherry tree and the dead colt
as fictitious, we tend to overlook the fact that such widely read and
repeated myths correspond to a profound psychological truth about
a people. The folk myths of a people represent a basic, generally
unverbalized aspect of their character.

When we read the story in its many variations, it is never really
clear why George wanted to cut down that cherry tree. His intent is
masked by the sincerity of his confession. We are also inclined to
forget the fact that it was rather obvious who had done the cutting.
It is the spontaneous openness of the young Washington that we remember. George was forgiven because he told the truth in a manly
fashion and accepted full responsibility for his act. If his father suspected that George was expressing anger toward him by an attack on
his tree, it is nowhere indicated. Since George had just received a
new axe, it is assumed that he was curious to discover its power and
the object of his attack, his father's tree, was incidental. George's aggression was inadvertent in the sense that he was not thinking about
the owner of the tree, but only the power of his axe. In the original
tale by Parson Weems, George's confession brings forth not merely
an emotional release followed by forgiveness, but an outpouring of
love from his father.

> . . . looking at his father, with the sweet face of youth brightened with
> the inexpressible charm of all-conquering truth, he bravely cried out,
> "I can't tell a lie, Pa; you know I can't tell a lie. I did cut it with my
> hatchet." "Run to my arms, you dearest boy," cried his father in trans-
> ports, "run to my arms; glad am I, George, that you killed my tree; for
> you have paid me for it a thousand fold. Such an act of heroism in my
> son is worth more than a thousand trees, though blossomed with sil-
> ver, and their fruits of purest gold."[6]

Although perhaps fashionable in its day, there is something excessive about this outburst of fatherly love. The father seems to be protesting too much. It is as though this concentration upon the external, physical fact of George's cutting the tree enabled the father and
son to ignore the internal sources of friction between them.

I believe that the story of the cherry tree can serve as a paradigm
for the style of confession in American public life. The public figure
plays a role similar to that of George Washington, and his confession

is delivered to some representative of the general public: the press, a congressional hearing, etc. When a nationally known educator or the president of a large corporation is exposed in a scandal involving private greed, it represents a form of aggression against the public interest. But when the figure is also a popular hero, there is a strong tendency to deny the significance of his act. There is a general willingness to believe that the public hero was basically good, like the rest of us, but that he simply did not realize what he was doing. In fact, this belief is probably at least half valid, for in a society that encourages people to avoid facing the reality of their more destructive, acquisitive, and antisocial impulses it is not surprising to discover that most people repress such feelings. This does not mean that we do not act on these desires; it only means we are not willing to acknowledge them.

The development and spread of this myth of George Washington, the man of truth, has been beautifully illustrated by Henry Cabot Lodge, grandfather of the former ambassador to the United Nations. Weems concocted the cherry tree tale and many others of the same character from his own imagination.

> The biography did not go, and was not intended to go, into the hands of the polite society of the great Eastern towns. It was meant for the farmers, the pioneers, and the backwoodsmen of the country. It went into their homes and passed with them beyond the Alleghenies and out to the plains and valleys of the West. The very defects of the book helped it to success among the simple, hardworking, hard-fighting race engaged in the conquest of the American continent. To them its heavy and tawdry style, its staring morals, and its real patriotism all seemed eminently befitting the national hero, and thus Weems created the Washington of the popular fancy. The idea grew up with the country and became so ingrained in the popular thought that finally everybody was affected by it, and even the most stately and solemn of the Washington biographers adopted the unsupported tales of the itinerant parson and book-peddler . . .[7]

> Weems was not a cold-blooded liar, a mere forger of anecdotes. He was simply a man destitute of historical sense, training, or morals, ready to take the slenderest fact and work it up for the purposes of the market . . . In a word, Weems was an approved mythmaker.[8]

The cherry tree morality developed by Weems has become a basic ingredient of the American conscience. However, it is important to emphasize that this belief in the virtue of confession is not a clearly enunciated tenet of American policy (either foreign or domestic), but rather a popular belief that exists at various levels of awareness in various people within our national community. For many Americans it is a part of that intuitive feeling of right and justice in which the source is never clearly identified and that is not based on rational considerations.

On the other hand, the morality described by Lippmann and the procedure he recommends of maintaining a "cool silence" is part of our approved diplomatic morality. It is a veneer that we adopt in diplomatic circles because it has been found to be effective in international relations. It is logical, carefully thought out, but above all, it is conscious. When there is plenty of time for sober consideration, it is generally diplomatic morality that prevails. But when we act under the pressures of the moment, we are more likely to respond to a highly localized and parochial view of what constitutes right action.

This was the situation that prevailed when the president and his advisers were faced with the U-2 incident. It was a period of hurried conferences and little time to think. The international situation was serious. The "weather reconnaissance" story had been exposed and there was pressure from the American press for an explanation. It was in this atmosphere that the decision was made to cast aside diplomatic morality and tell the truth. Why? Was it not an acute sense of guilt about being caught in a lie, an unconscious conviction that a full confession was the only brave and manly way out, the only *American* way? There was, of course, no question about the facts. The U-2 was intact. Powers was alive. Both were in Russian hands, and Powers had confessed. In fact, as the previous discussion has already indicated, the president was technically responsible, but he had not ordered the particular flight in question. It was clearly unnecessary to pretend that he was more involved in the decision than was actually the case. Why, then, did the president feel he had to make a public confession? Was this, too, a product of his sudden feeling of guilt over what had happened?

No doubt there were many "rational" reasons for the decision. Cater suggests that, in addition to the humiliation of being caught in a lie, there was a desire to reveal our penetration of the boasted Soviet air defenses during the past four years.[9] Some felt it offered an opportunity to propagandize about "open" societies versus "closed" societies. However, we must remember that unconscious forces often operate behind the facade of "rational" motives. The sudden and impulsive nature of the spy-plane admission suggests the behavior of a man who has not given much attention to these espionage activities until they are discussed in a hurried conference after the U-2 incident is made public. When he realizes the moral impact of what he is doing, he is so guilty and horrified by the details that he must make a "clean breast" of the affair at once and accept personal responsibility for it. According to David Wise and Thomas Ross, who have investigated the U-2 incident in considerable detail, Eisenhower favored full disclosure and an acceptance of presidential responsibility from the moment it was evident that the U-2 and Powers were both in Russian hands. He did not like Herter's rather guarded statement admitting espionage, but not implicating the president. He felt it was his "duty" to accept full blame for what happened. He did not feel it would be honorable to pass off the responsibility onto a subordinate.[10]

At first, however, Herter had been able to convince Eisenhower that he should not accept responsibility for the overflights. After the telephone conversation with the president, Herter, Cumming, and Bohlen prepared a statement admitting that the overflight had taken place but indicating that "as a result of an inquiry ordered by the President, it has been established that insofar as the authorities in Washington are concerned, there was no authorization for any such flight as described by Mr. Khrushchev."[11] The statement was released on Saturday, May 7. Nevertheless, by Sunday the president had changed his mind, and it was necessary to draft still another statement. The next statement admitted presidential responsibility, but blamed the overflights on Moscow's rejection of the president's open-skies proposal, indicating that it was necessary for the United States to have the U-2 flights in order to protect itself against surprise attack. The statement came out under Herter's name.

There were, of course, many political factors behind the president's decision to accept full responsibility. Wise and Ross have described the criticism, both foreign and domestic, that was being directed at Eisenhower during this period. The president, it was said, was not really in control of his own administration. The democrats had claimed he was out of touch with events and that most of his decisions were made by his planning staff and his advisors. Khrushchev had claimed the military was making the president's decisions for him. Eisenhower's determination to accept full responsibility was a product of his desire to "stand up and take the blame like a man" and to counter the charge that he was weak and ineffectual in his leadership.[12] It was the first time in history that an American president had accepted personal responsibility for espionage.

However, we have already seen, from the previously quoted interrogation of Herter, that the president did not really authorize the particular overflight in question. His attempt to be *honest* in the classical American sense of that term, was more a dramatic gesture than a true description of events. Furthermore, he did not really admit responsibility in the sense of a breach of international law. He blamed the Russians for his need to spy, since they had rejected his open-skies program. The Russians had been provocative. Therefore, we had to violate their air space.

The general popularity of President Eisenhower was an important source of support and acceptance for his explanation of the U-2 incident, but there were many Americans who did not believe him. They felt the situation was deliberately set up to sabotage the scheduled summit meeting of world leaders on the subject of peace and disarmament. The charge was a public one, and it came from sources as diverse as the Republican party in the United States and the Communist party in Russia. On May 7, 1960, Harold Stassen called the Associated Press in Washington to charge that the U-2 had been deliberately scheduled to fly over the Soviet Union by "some of our military officers" in order to torpedo the summit meeting scheduled for May 16.[13] Mr. Stassen was the chief disarmament negotiator for the United States. He was very serious about his mission, and the U-2 incident angered him considerably. On May 9 Premier Khrushchev remarked at a reception in the Czechoslovakian embassy in Moscow, "I have already said, Comrades, and now I repeat, that this was done deliberately and deliberately timed for the summit meeting in Paris."[14]

As late as June 1967, certain elements of the American left were still providing evidence of deliberate sabotage. In an article in Ramparts, Paul Jacobs, who was in Moscow at the time of the incident, described how he stared in disbelief at the collection of items that the Russians displayed from the cockpit of the U-2. There were bundles of 50 ruble notes, each one the equivalent of an American hundred dollar bill. Jacobs asks us to imagine a comparable situation of a Russian spy walking into a gas station in Iowa and attempting, by sign language, to get the attendant to break a hundred dollar bill so he could call the Soviet embassy in Washington. "My God, I thought as I moved around the hall, is the CIA really that stupid?"[15] Jacobs' answer was, of course, in the negative. He proceeded to speculate on the real cause of the incident.

> Had Powers' plane been deliberately brought down by the CIA, because the agency wanted the Russians not only to capture him but to have his connection with the CIA revealed to the world? That was a plausible explanation of how the plane was brought down; if the Russians hadn't succeeded in shooting one down in more than four years, why should they have been able to knock off Powers' U-2? And if Powers' capture was what the CIA wanted, this would also explain his survival and the weird collection of paraphernalia he carried with him. It would explain, too, why his connection with the CIA was admitted instead of being denied and disowned, the normal procedure in such cases.[16]

To follow this line of reasoning to its ultimate conclusion, one would have to assume that President Eisenhower was a party to the sabotage, since it was he who assumed responsibility for the incident and since it was his assumption of this responsibility that formed the basis for Khrushchev's disruption of the summit meeting. I have already indicated that my own view of the American character is not congruent with such a theory of conspiracy. Eisenhower's belief in the virtue of peace is evident from his memoirs and from the entire history of his efforts in this direction.[17] Although there was obviously considerable ambivalence about disarmament and peace talks throughout the Eisenhower Administration, the barriers placed in the way of peace were inadvertent rather than deliberate. As such, they were a product of bad faith rather than conspiracy.

IV

The president's belated honesty became the basis for a number of congratulations from the press. Ernest Lindley gave him "cheers for candor."[18] When Secretary Herter came before the congressional committee he was thanked, in the usual manner, for his candor. On May 15, George V. Allen, Director of the United States Information Agency even attempted to make a virtue out of Gary Powers' "truthfulness" when his plane was shot down in Russia. When questioned by Miss Dodd on the "ABC College News Conference" program regarding how far the United States should go in backing Powers, Allen replied

> . . . I do think I ought to point out and that more people ought to recall it: When he went down he told exactly what his mission was and exactly what he was expected to do, and he was under instruction to do that. He wasn't wearing a false mustache and a cloak and dagger and that sort of business that you usually think of as a spy pretending that he is somebody that he isn't. He gave an honest report of what his mission is and I think that ought to be recalled by everybody concerned.[19]

He remarked that President Eisenhower had already offered an open-skies program to the Soviet Union and "urged the Soviet Union to get rid of this closed society." He felt that U.S. admission of the overflight "was one of the most important things that has been done in this whole field of trying to build an open society. The frank admission on the part of the United States that we did it."[20]

The false statements in Mr. Allen's above remarks were probably inadvertent in the same sense that many of the statements that our

government put forth in connection with the U-2 incident were inadvertent. They were blurted out in a more or less unthinking and
uncritical manner, supported by a general belief in the value of spontaneous sincerity. There is something about Allen's response and the
general tenor of his remarks throughout the interview that suggests
that, at the moment he was speaking, he *really believed* our spy was
a good sincere spy because he was American, that Powers told the
truth when he was captured because he wanted to do the right thing
and not because he was frightened, and that his government would
not have wanted it any other way. How else can we explain his remark that Mr. Powers was instructed to tell the truth when it is so
patently obvious that he was not so instructed?

It is easy to laugh at Mr. Allen's discomforture and remove ourselves from his predicament. Yet, if we will turn to look at the cam-
era, we will see that we are all on television with him. His remark
reflects our culture and our style of thinking. It is a product of the
American belief that we conceal our behavior only because of the
secrecy practiced by "closed" societies and that we would really like
to tell everything to the whole world because we are really fully justified (in a worldwide sense) in what we are doing.

But if a man cannot be honest with himself, it may be risky for him
to be open with others on issues of great international significance.
Furthermore, if he attempts to be open in the traditional American
style, he may find that his spontaneous honesty does not have the
same significance in the court of world opinion that it had in his own
country. On the international scene honesty may not represent an act
of repentance, a throwing of oneself on the mercy of the court. Instead, it may signify a heedless defiance of international law, a denial of guilt, an assertion of one's own righteousness—particularly if
the honesty is accompanied by justifications in the name of a morality that is assumed to be international in scope and above the law. In
short, it may be, not an apology, but a notice that the provocation will
continue. Clearly, this is what happened. One can follow the sudden
escalation of international tension from the moment Mr. Herter made
the announcement that the president was personally responsible for
the U-2 flights.

On May 7 it appeared that, despite the capture of Powers and the
Soviet protest, the incident would be allowed to subside. There was
a move toward an official announcement that the flights would be
discontinued (they had already been compromised and were clearly
vulnerable to attack) and a suggestion that those responsible for the
latest incident would be punished. The official U.S. statement on the
plane was that "there was no authorization for any such flights as

described by Mr. Khrushchev. Nevertheless it appears that in endeavoring to obtain information now concealed behind the Iron Curtain a flight over Soviet territory was probably undertaken by an unarmed civilian U-2 plane."[21] After a meeting by Secretary Herter and President Eisenhower the following day, information was quietly leaked to the press that the CIA was about to be investigated. The *New York Times* reported that "no announcement was made of this [Herter–Eisenhower] meeting, but elsewhere it was stated on responsible authority that the President had ordered a halt to all flights over or near Communist frontiers pending an executive investigation of the intelligence apparatus of the government."[22]

But with the official acceptance of presidential responsibility, all of these conciliatory statements had to be denied. The following day, in the course of his announcement that the president had personally authorized the U-2 flights, Secretary Herter denied that there was any planned investigation of the CIA. He followed this with a statement seeking to justify the U-2 flights as a legitimate means of gathering information. As in the past, U.S. policy was justified not on the narrow grounds of its right to compete with the Soviets, but on the larger scale that we had a duty to protect mankind.

> I will say frankly that it is unacceptable that the Soviet political system should be given an opportunity to make secret preparations to face the free world with the choice of abject surrender or nuclear destruction. The government of the United States would be derelict in its responsibility not only to the American people but to free peoples everywhere if it did not, in the absence of Soviet cooperation, take such measures as are possible unilaterally to lessen and to overcome this danger of surprise attack.[23]

The newsmen surrounded Press Secretary Hagerty for further clarification. Not only did Hagerty deny the earlier story of a CIA investigation, but he denied that any order had been given to halt the U-2 flights. In the *New York Times* column headings of this story ("Secretary is Firm," page 1, and "Herter Indicates Further Flights," page 18),[24] it was an obvious conclusion that the U-2 flights would continue.

Khrushchev was outraged. The Americans were not really doing anything he would not do secretly if he had a U-2 and the bases to support it. But such behavior was a clear violation of Soviet territory, a breach of international law. The least an offending nation could do was to indicate indirectly that it would not continue the violations, that it would withdraw now that secrecy of the operation was no longer possible. To do otherwise was to assert that the United States had a right to fly over Soviet territory and that they would continue to do so. Without any conscious intent to provoke hostilities, an American president was telling the Soviets that, since they did not have an open society like ours, and since they tried to keep secrets from us, we would no longer respect their frontiers. Khrushchev was about to depart for the Czechoslovakian embassy when he received news of the Herter announcement. During the reception he warned that if the Americans would not stop the U-2, the Soviets would bomb the bases (in countries like Norway and Turkey)[25] from which the U-2 was launched. This was followed by an official note to the American government in which the same statement was made but in more veiled terms. He warned of "retaliatory measures, the responsibility for the consequences of which will rest on the government of the state committing aggression against other countries."[26] At a press conference in Moscow the following day Khrushchev repeated his threat to attack the U-2 support bases to foreign journalists including the Americans present. He said

> The danger is aggravated by the fact that the United States Secretary of State, Mr. Herter, in his statement on May 9, not only sought to justify the aggression committed, but even said that the United States government intended to continue such flights. This is a direct threat to peace. We shall bring down such planes and shall strike at the bases from which they are sent to our country. You are well aware that if such aggressive acts continue, they may lead to war.[27]

This was followed by an American pledge to defend those bases that might be attacked by Soviet missiles or planes.[28] The only defense against Soviet missiles would have been to strike at their bases within Soviet territory. The two nations had moved up one more step on the ladder of escalation. Fortunately the United States did discontinue the U-2 flights over Soviet territory, and the summit conference gave Chairman Khrushchev an opportunity to demonstrate his anger toward President Eisenhower in words instead of deeds. The president kept his head in the face of considerable humiliation, and the tension between the two nations gradually subsided.

V

In the United States it would seem that the justification for the U-2 flights was based, not on the legal aspects of the act of overflight, but on the American intent. The American reply to the Soviet protest over the U-2 incident reads, in part, "The United States government does not deny that it has pursued such a [espionage] policy for purely defensive purposes. What it emphatically does deny is that this policy has *any aggressive intent.*"[29] [Italics mine] Is it really possible to separate the intent of the observer from the total act of looking and its consequences? American support for "open" reconnaissance activities has consistently emphasized this belief that looking itself is innocent, if the observer does not seek to do any harm at the moment of observation. In the American system of beliefs, information is neutral. It can be used for good or evil. The proof of innocence is to be found in the immediate intent of the observer. Thus, our justification for reconnaissance always stresses the fact that these ships are "unarmed" and therefore harmless. The U-2 in particular was alleged to be used to defend us from a surprise attack by the Soviets. In fact, the time required to fly the mission, interpret the data, and communicate the information to Washington precluded the collection of any valuable data on immediate Soviet preparations for attack. The chief mission of the U-2 was to gather data on potential Soviet targets—airfields, missile sites, factories, arsenals, etc.—in the event that we should want to attack them, either in retaliation for a Soviet strike or, as one possible measure to prevent a Soviet attack. Allen Dulles, the chief of CIA at the time of the incident, makes it quite clear that the U-2 was to gather information on Soviet targets.[30] This does not mean that the U-2 was devoid of any defensive purpose, but it does demonstrate that one cannot separate the offensive from the defensive aspects of the U-2 and justify our right to look on the grounds that looking is an innocent act.

What, then, can we say of the statements of American leaders in regard to the U-2 incident? Was the statement that we had "no aggressive intent," like the "weather reconnaissance" story, just another lie directed not at the Soviets but at American public opinion? To say that these men were lying, assumes, first of all, that they were conscious of their desire to deceive their fellow Americans and, secondly, that they understood in all clarity exactly what they were doing. Sartre makes a distinction between the lie and what he calls "bad faith." The lie is a conscious project to deceive the other, made in entire clarity. It assumes the existence of the other as a separate consciousness from the self. Bad faith has the structure of falsehood, but it is a lie to one's self. Thus, the duality of the deceiver and the deceived is no longer evident.[31] There are certain situations that encourage bad faith as opposed to a deliberate lie. A king may lie to his people because he is conscious that his interest is different from theirs. He knows it would be to his disadvantage if they learned the truth. In the United States the bad faith of the national leader is something that is invited by the people. The American people want to be a major world power. They seek a power advantage over other nations, but they also expect that their national leader will tell them that they are a virtuous people, that they are acting in the interest of mankind, and that they have "no aggressive intent" against another nation. The bad faith that results from this total situation is a cooperative venture. It is initiated by the American leaders, but it requires the cooperation and acquiescence of the people.

Does this mean that the U-2 should not have been built and used? On the contrary, the U-2 was a product of the fear of nuclear attack and the total competitive situation that existed between the United States and the Soviet Union at the time. Its construction was inevitable, but its use in the overflight of another nation's territory could not be justified *on moral grounds*. This was the major American policy failure in connection with the incident. We found it impossible to withdraw from the argument and allow the Soviets a moral victory. It was this need for moral righteousness that constituted the act of bad faith. It is this same need for moral righteousness that has made it so difficult for us to face the reality of our policy in Cuba and South America.

NOTES

1. G. F. Kennan, Memoirs 1925–1950 (Boston: Little Brown, 1967), pp. 53–54.
2. B. Crane, "Values Crumble in Edgy Market," New York Times, May 11, 1960, p. 56.
3. W. Lippmann, "Plane Blame Falls on Ike, Advisers," Boston Globe, May 10, 1960, p. 12.
4. U.S., Congress, Senate, Committee on Foreign Relations, Events Incident to the Summit Conference: Hearings, 86th Cong., 2d sess., pp. 57–58, 93, 98.
5. W. Lippmann, "U.S. Invites Trouble by New Spy Policy," Boston Globe, May 12, 1960. p. 5.
6. M. L. Weems, The Life of George Washington with Curious Anecdotes Equally Honorable to Himself and Exemplary to His Young Countrymen (Philadelphia: Lippincott, 1877), p. 16.
7. H. C. Lodge, George Washington (New York: Houghton Mifflin, 1889), p. 78–79.
8. Ibid., p. 85.
9. D. Cater, "A Chronicle of Confusion," The Reporter 22 (1960): 15–17.
10. D. Wise and T. Ross, The U-2 Affair (New York, Random House, 1962), pp. 105–106.
11. Ibid., p. 106.
12. Ibid., pp. 110–112.
13. Ibid., p. 103.

14. *Events Incident to the Summit Conference,* 86th Cong., 2d sess., p. 189.

15. P. Jacobs, "Did the Real Gary Powers Really Fall Down?" *Ramparts,* June, 1967, pp. 6–10.

16. Ibid.

17. D. D. Eisenhower, *Mandate for a Change* (Garden City, N.Y.: Doubleday, 1963) and D. D. Eisenhower, *Waging Peace* (Garden City, N.Y.: Doubleday, 1965).

18. E. K. Lindley, "Cheers for Candor," *Newsweek,* May 23, 1960.

19. *Events Incident to the Summit Conference,* 86th Cong., 2d sess., p. 215.

20. Ibid., p. 216.

21. *New York Times,* May 8, 1960, p. 29.

22. J. Reston, "Flights Stopped," *New York Times,* May 9, 1960, p. 1.

23. *New York Times,* May 10, 1960, p. 18.

24. W. Jorden, "Secretary Is Firm," "Herter Indicates Flights Will Continue," *New York Times,* May 10, 1960, p. 1., p. 18.

25. *New York Times,* May 10, 1960, p. 14.

26. "Russ and U.S. Notes on Downing of American Pilot in the Soviet Union," *New York Times,* May 11, 1960, p. 4.

27. *N. S. Krushchev's Statement and Replies to Questions, Gorky Park, Moscow, May 11, 1960* (New York: Crosscurrents Press, 1960), p. 3.

28. W. J. Jorden, "Washington Firm," *New York Times,* May 11, 1960, p. 1.

29. "U.S. Disclaims 'Aggressive Intent' in Sending Aircraft Over Soviet; Krushchev Sees Peril of War," *New York Times,* May 13, 1960, p. 1. Text of U.S. Note on U-2, *New York Times,* May 13, 1960, p. 6.

30. A. Dulles, *The Craft of Intelligence* (New York: New American Library, 1965), p. 67.

31. J. P. Sartre, *Existential Psychoanalysis,* trans. Hazel E. Barnes (Chicago: Henry Regnery, 1966), pp. 157–159.

The Invasion of Cuba

6

I

The Truman Doctrine had proclaimed American determination to go to the aid of "free people" everywhere and to contain communist influence throughout the world. The Korean War represented an early expression of this determination. The CIA sponsored invasion of Cuba was another manifestation of our belief that the "people of Cuba" sought rescue from Castro and that it was our duty to come to their aid. However, specific acts such as the Cuban invasion do not evolve directly from doctrine. The implementation of policy is a matter of individual interpretation and the ambition of those close to the source of power within the administration.

The invasion of Cuba by forces directed by the CIA represents a striking example of the power that a planning staff can exert on an American administration. The influence exercised by the CIA in this case was due, in large measure, to the fact that it was allowed to operate for a long time unchecked by presidential supervision and control. Another reason for this influence is that the plan for the invasion was

92

initiated in one administration and carried out in another. The CIA served as the only source of detailed knowledge of *intent* from one administration to the next. It functioned, in this instance, as a planning staff for the president. The president and other elected officials are designated as initiators of policy. The CIA is expected to exercise merely a coordinating function. However, the nominal function of coordination, in the absence of specific instructions from the executive authority, can evolve into the complete development and definition of policy. Leaders in the CIA are sensitive to the charge that they have such a profound influence on American policy. Allen Dulles handles the issue by a general statement that "the CIA has never carried out any action of a political nature, given any support of any nature to any persons, potentates or movements, political or otherwise, without appropriate approval at a high political level in our government *outside the CIA*."[1] This was certainly true of the CIA role in the Cuban invasion, but it does not come to grips with the issue of the influence of the CIA on policy decisions.

Toward the end of the Eisenhower Administration, there was a growing dissatisfaction with the Castro government and its obvious communist orientation. A plan was developed to give support to Cuban refugees in the United States who sought to recapture their homeland. Although there was no question regarding the intent of the Eisenhower Administration to encourage these refugees, it seems clear in retrospect that the involvement of American forces and the degree of our participation and direction of these plans was inadvertent, in the unreflective sense in which this term has been used in the previous chapters. This means essentially that our official policy was out of step with the unexpressed desire and intent of those who were influential within the Eisenhower Administration. It was this unexpressed intent that was conveyed to those responsible for action.

The Eisenhower plan for the support of Cuban refugees, in their opposition to Castro, was restricted to the organization and training of guerrilla forces in Guatemala. There was no plan for an invasion in the initial stages.[2] It was the president's order that no United States military personnel were to take part in the activity. However, in the process of planning the operation, CIA people began to doubt whether a guerrilla force would succeed. They had some information that there was a Cuban resistance movement, but their agents had difficulty making contact with it. Gradually they began to evolve the idea of a full-scale landing force equipped with U.S. ships and air cover. The decision to go all the way in Cuba was, in part, a result of the growing influence of the "black operations" branch of the CIA, which had successfully engineered the overthrow of Guatemala's president, Jacobo Arbenz Guzman, in July 1954. It was also a product of the free hand given to the CIA during the final stages of the Eisenhower Administration. Knowing that the next president would have to give the final authority for the execution of the mission, President Eisenhower gave it little attention.

The massive growth of the scope and size of the CIA plan is a long and involved story, which has been told at length by a number of writers. The best account is to be found in Schlesinger's book, *A Thousand Days*. In the description of these events, one is reminded of the peculiar distortions that can take place in any specialized in-group that is isolated from the world of reality. The people involved in the planning of the Cuban invasion were members of a group strictly limited to "operations." They were concerned with the technology of military action, with know-how. The freedom from questioning by policy experts and politicians enabled them to ignore such factors as political considerations and international treaties.

Richard Bissell, the CIA official who had assumed responsibility for the day-to-day operation of the Cuban plan, was deeply submerged in the details of the operation. A colleague reported later that Bissell had been overworking himself for weeks, being in his office 12 to 14 hours a day. Then he added, "I'm sure he thought he was serving his country, but he might have served it better by leading a more normal schedule, reading the newspapers, and keeping in contact with common-sense reality. As it was, he was isolated in a kind of weird world of secret reports day and night."[3]

The plan, being a "secret," continued to evolve and expand in the private reality of the CIA. By the time of the presidential election of 1960, there was no longer any trace of the modest goal of supporting a small group of revolutionaries in the Escambray Mountains. Guerrilla exercises were discontinued and a conventional landing force was assembled for training.[4]

In December 1960 the new CIA plan was reviewed by the Special Group, an interdepartmental committee that supervised such special operations. However, as Schlesinger has remarked, the Special Group itself was infected with "interregnum uncertainties." Not knowing how the new president would view this new plan, it did not look too closely at the details. It merely encouraged the CIA to continue.[5] The Special Group does not appear to have recognized the significance of this change in plan—that is, the change from an operation in which the United States played primarily a supporting role to one in which American artillery, landing craft, and air cover would be used. This meant a change from the training of guerrillas to the active intervention in the affairs of another nation. Schlesinger has discussed the complications of such a decision. It required a considerable increase in the size of the expeditionary force. Since the United States could no longer disown the operation, it could not afford to let the expedition fail. Thus, the plan advanced into a full-scale invasion.

> As the expeditionary force enlarged its hold, the CIA men argued, now introducing a new idea, a provisional government could be flown in; and, if the invaders could sustain themselves for ten days or two weeks, this government could receive recognition as the government of Cuba. Once this was done, the new government could request United States aid, though this aid was carefully defined as "logistic" and, therefore, presumably excluded military intervention ... The scheme envisaged victory by attrition rather than by rebellion and no longer assigned a significant, immediate role to the internal resistance. As the invaders strengthened their position, this, along with the command of the skies and the acceptance of the new government by our American republics, would produce a steady withdrawal of civil support from Castro and his eventual collapse . . .[6]

II

There can be little doubt that the United States and Cuba were moving in opposite directions by the time John F. Kennedy took his oath as president of the United States. There was a good deal of clandestine operation on both sides. While the United States was engaged in active attempts to subvert the government of Cuba, Castro agents had infiltrated many of the South American nations with the goal of exporting the Cuban revolution. However, unlike the communist system, American public morality does not support the idea of political subversion as a "fair" means of combat. The CIA intervention in Guatemala was and still is denied by official government sources. When it was discovered that the CIA was secretly supporting various American student organizations, the revelation caused a scandal and the tactic had to be abandoned.

For this reason there is often a temptation for an American president to avoid inquiring into the details of a CIA operation. There is a subtle but unexpressed feeling that there are certain questions that should not be asked. CIA officials recognize this in dealing with the president. They are careful not to dwell on certain points or to make statements that would obligate him to further inquiry. It is a matter of personal tact, a tacit understanding based on "you know what I mean," without spelling out all the details. Such was the case with the Cuban invasion plan. Neither President Eisenhower nor Presi-

dent Kennedy wanted to examine the degree of American involvement in the operation and the implications of this involvement for
America's position of moral leadership in the West. When Arthur
Schlesinger, Jr. asked President Kennedy what he thought about the
proposed invasion, Kennedy replied, "I think about it as little as
possible,"[7] a witticism that proved to be painfully accurate. One of
the factors that predisposed the new president toward this attitude
was the air of inevitability that had already surrounded the operation
by the time Kennedy was briefed by the CIA. He was led to believe
that the former president, a military leader and war hero, had already
approved the plan. Kennedy tried to keep his alternatives open, refusing to give a final approval of the plan, but on March 11 Allen
Dulles, Director of the Central Intelligence Agency faced him with a
crisis.

The morale of the Cuban forces was at a peak, their training had
been completed. The presence of the training base for Cubans was
becoming an increasing embarrassment to President Ydígoras of
Guatemala, and he had insisted that they depart by the end of April.
"Don't forget," said Dulles, "that we have a disposal problem." Presumably the existence of the invasion plan was still a secret from the
rest of the world, but if the Cubans in training in Guatemala were
transfered to the United States, they could wander around the country and the secret would soon be out. They would tell everyone how
the United States had prepared an expedition against Cuba and then
lost its nerve.[8] Thus, the plan that was initiated as a contingency,
one of many possible approaches, had generated its own momentum. It seemed there was no stopping it. In the final days before the
invasion began, Kennedy was to offer this same disposal problem as
one of the primary reasons for going ahead with the CIA plan.[9]

Of course, the existence of a band of Cuban revolutionaries opposed to Castro was not a secret. The secret part of the operation was
the involvement of the CIA and the extent of U.S. support and direction. This aspect of the operation was so carefully concealed that
even the president did not understand the full extent of U.S. participation until it was too late. In a number of speeches prior to the
invasion, President Kennedy referred to the possibility of participation by United States armed forces. In every case he denied it, both
as a general policy and in the specific case of Cuba. On April 12 he
gave this assurance to the American people in a press conference.

> Well, first I want to say that there will not be under any circumstances,
> an intervention in Cuba by United States armed forces. This Govern-
> ment will do everything it possibly can, and I think it can meet its
> responsibilities, to make sure there are no Americans involved in any
> action inside Cuba . . .[10]

Despite the President's assurances, the first frogmen on the Cuban mainland, who came ashore to mark the invasion points, were American.[11] But these details were only some of the factual violations of the president's assurances. In spirit, the President's promises were violated to a more extreme degree. Although Kennedy had remarked that the opposition to Castro was a Cuban affair, the direction and control of the Cuban forces had been completely taken over by the CIA. It is probable that the president did not know of the plans for the frogmen. It is clear that he did not know the extent of CIA control. When Kennedy later discovered that the Cuban Revolutionary Council had been held virtual prisoner during the invasion while a public relations man for the CIA issued dispatches in their name, he was shocked.[12]

III

Many writers, both within and outside the newspaper fraternity have criticized the American press for its role in the Bay of Pigs affair. In the United States the press is not only a vehicle for letting the people know, it also serves as a means for administration officials to retain a certain contact with the real world of events and their impact on the American people. President Kennedy was an avid newspaper reader. He would often pursue a story in detail and question reporters about it later. In the minds of many critics there was a feeling that the press had failed the president. While Kennedy was critical of the New York Times for revealing too much about the Cuban invasion, he said later in an aside to the managing editor, "If you had printed more about the operation, you would have saved us from a colossal mistake," and he was later to remark to the publisher, "I wish you had run everything on Cuba . . . I am just sorry you didn't tell it at the time."[13]

It is true that to some extent the press could have improved the president's view of the situation. If the president is forced into an awareness of the full significance of an illegal CIA operation and if he knows that the public is also aware of the details, he must take action to prevent a complete loss of respect for his administration. The earlier this information is brought to his attention, the more effectively he can act. The longer he is allowed to believe that he is engaged in a "secret" operation, the longer it is possible for him to avoid awareness of what he is really doing.

However, James Reston has raised the question as to whether the press is behaving in a more responsible manner when it withholds information that might damage the security of the United States or when it reports such information as news. He says that he knew of the U-2 flights for over a year before the incident, but that the New York Times did not publish the information. He reminds us that premature publication of the movement of American ships during the Cuban missile crisis, which followed the invasion fiasco, could have interfered with a critical move in American policy.[14] But it is also clear that the press is not responsible for American security. The function of the press is to inform. If there is a security leak, can we not assume that the press of other nations will discover the information? Will enemy intelligence agents remain ignorant of our plans because the press fails to report them, or is it only the American people who must be kept unaware of the position their government is taking in their name? Meyer and Szulc have pointed out that the CIA agents in Miami and elsewhere used no discretion whatsoever.[15] They organized a revolution to overthrow another government, recruiting on American soil and financing the operation with the money of the American taxpayer. Yet the American people were among the last to discover what was taking place. Of course, the news was not completely suppressed. Although some Florida editors became active accomplices of the CIA—even concealing information from their newspaper colleagues—other papers printed some of the facts as early as January 1961, including the location of the training bases and U.S. financial aid for the exiles. However, it would have been necessary to piece together several reports to understand the significance of what was happening.[16]

In bringing the news to the attention of the American people, the press is not a single entity but a multilayered institution. It is difficult to measure individual awareness of events, but general public awareness can be indicated objectively by a statement of where the news is printed. Excluding television coverage, if an event appears on the front page of the New York Times, together with a signed article outlining its significance, the American people have the greatest opportunity to become aware of it. Moving an issue to the back pages is a way of minimizing its importance. When a story appears only in a few small papers or specialized political magazines, its impact is already considerably reduced. Furthermore, as far as the American public is concerned, its credibility is suspect. As President Kennedy remarked, in regard to some of the information on the Cuban crisis, "But it was not news until it appeared in the Times."[17]

Thus, as in most situations that require action, it becomes a question not only of awareness but of the level of awareness of the president and the American people regarding the impending crisis in Cuba. Although the CIA was engaged in open recruiting throughout Florida and although the training base in Guatemala was known to everyone in the vicinity, the American press continued to report "both sides" of the situation as though the whole operation was still just a matter of opinion. Finally, in the 11th hour, James Reston of the *New York Times* became sufficiently concerned to editorialize on the coming invasion. Mr. Reston was distressed by the absence of public debate on our intervention in Cuba. On April 12, 1961, pointing out that intervention had been considered at previous times in American history, he remarked that at such times

> the issues of right and wrong were debated in Congress and in the country.
>
> No such debate is going on now. President Kennedy and his advisers are discussing the question on an urgent basis, but the Congress is not talking about it, the press is ignoring the moral aspects of the question, nobody knows where the funds are coming from or where they are going, though Article 15 of the OAS Treaty which we have signed (prohibits armed intervention by the United States) . . . the defense of the West rests not only on its physical power, but on the moral and intellectual allegiance of peoples in the hemisphere and elsewhere.[18]

Mr. Reston's concern for the moral question and the lack of public information and debate on Cuba is commendable, but even at this late hour he was covering for the administration. It was not really true, as he said in his column, that no one knew where the funds were coming from to recruit and train the invasion army. Mr. Reston knew, but he wasn't telling. On April 6, Tad Szulc had filed a long dispatch with the *Times* clearly linking the CIA to the proposed invasion of Cuba and indicating that the crisis was "imminent." When the publisher, Orvil Dryfoos, and the managing editor, Turner Catledge, called Reston in Virginia, he advised them to withhold some of the critical features of Szulc's story including the CIA connection and the references to the imminent nature of the invasion.[19]

The role of the CIA had already been documented in some of the stories in other newspapers, but Reston clearly recognized the enormous increase in national attention to the crisis that could be provided by the *Times*. At this same time, the story was changed from a four-column head to a one-column head.[20]

On April 6 the invasion was less than two weeks away. In failing to report some of the facts while calling for debate on the moral issue, Mr. Reston was exercising a conscious choice. He was aware of the facts but decided to suppress them. He may have felt, as did Mr. Dreyfoos, the publisher, that the invasion would go ahead anyway and that further disclosure of the preparations might merely result in the *New York Times* being blamed for the failure of the administration's plans.[21] The decision to suppress portions of the Szulc story and decrease its impact by reducing the size of the heading given to it, was not implemented without objections on the part of the *Times* staff. The news editor Lou Jordan and Theodore Bernstein, the assistant managing editor protested vigorously to Turner Catledge. "Mr. Jordon's face was dead white, and he was quivering with emotion. He and Mr. Bernstein told the managing editor that never before had the front-page play in the *New York Times* been changed for reasons of policy."[22] However, Reston's advice prevailed.

To some extent one can understand the reluctance of the *Times* to print all the facts at this late date. This reticence may have been due, in part, to a sense of complicity with the administration, for the *Times* had the facts on the Cuban story long before Szulc filed his dispatch. As early as Friday, November 11, 1960, editors had received a report on the invasion plans, but somehow the report did not receive attention.[23] If the *Times* withheld the news in the final stages of the invasion preparations because it was too late to stop the operation, why did awareness of the administration plans develop so slowly? How did it happen that the major independent news agencies, the Associated Press and the United Press International, who normally compete with each other at a furious pace, were so slow to pick up information on the actions of the CIA?

On November 11, 1960, over five months before the invasion, *The Nation* discussed a report by Dr. Ronald Hilton, Director of the Institute of Hispanic American and Luso-Brazilian Studies at Stanford University. Dr. Hilton had reported the training of Cuban exiles at the secret base in Guatemala for the invasion of Cuba, under the direction and funding of the CIA. The editorial in *The Nation* called for a check on the reports by all U.S. news media and insisted that, if the report proved to be true, pressure should be brought on the administration to abandon the plan.[24] Proofs of the *Nation* editorial, together with copies of a news release on which the editorial was based, were distributed by Jesse Gordon of *The Nation* to all the major news media. However, only the York (Pa.) *Gazette and Daily* published the release. The reaction of some of the major wire services was a peculiar inability to hang onto the information, once it was placed in their hands. After Gordon followed his news release to the Associated Press with a telephone call, he received the following response.

> The phone calls elicited some puzzling reactions. The Associated Press was called three times; each time a different desk man answered,

professed interest in the story, but said he hadn't seen either the release or a proof of the editorial. Could duplicates be sent immediately? Three duplicates were sent in as many hours, apparently to end up on the desk of someone in the AP hierarchy who didn't want them to go any farther. In the end neither the AP nor the United Press International used the story . . .[25]

The Times also professed an interest in the story, but sent its reporter to check it by a visit to President Miguel Ydígoras Fuentes of Guatemala who branded the reports as lies. It was probably this questioning of Ydígoras, at first by the Times and later by the AP, that caused him to indicate his "embarrassment" to the CIA and demand that they get the exiles out of Guatemala. Although the Guatemalan newspaper, La Hora had previously published the story on October 30, neither the Times nor the AP reporter bothered to check it with the newspaper's publisher. On November 20, nine days after the story appeared in The Nation, it was finally published briefly in the Times, along with the denials of President Ydígoras.[26]

Meanwhile, the Times continued to print without comment U.S. denials of Castro's accusation that an invasion was in preparation. Such ravings from Castro were a mere "smoke screen,"[27] said the Times. When the United States broke diplomatic relations with Cuba in response to Castro's demand for a reduction in the size of the staff of the U.S. embassy, the Times editorialized in the Sunday summary of weekly news, describing how Castro had pushed U.S. patience too far with his unfounded allegations and his provocations. The impression was created that Castro's preparation for the invasion was merely a side-show put on for the benefit of Cubans—to distract them from their low standard of living. The base in Guatemala and the CIA recruiting in Florida were not mentioned.

> The [UN] Council, in effect, rejected the Cuban charges by adjourning without taking any action.
>
> However, the Castro Government went right on preparing defenses. In Havana artillery pieces sprang up along shore roadways . . . in all cases, places where the Cubans could see them easily . . .
>
> The break in the U.S.–Cuban relations raised two main questions about Castro's course. They are: Why has he deliberately sought to portray the U.S. as Cuba's enemy? And why push to the breaking point now?
>
> As to Castro's generally anti-American course, the principal reason advanced is the unrest within Cuba. Taxes are high, shortages have been increasing, the future remains bleak. As things have worsened, the Castro Government has become increasingly shrill with its anti-American propaganda to busy minds that otherwise would be preoccupied with dissatisfactions at home . . . as to why the breaking point should be reached now, observers point to the number of Cubans seek-

ing visas to flee to the U.S. . . . . Another reason advanced is that Dr.
Castro wanted to cut down on the number of diplomatic reports to
Washington—especially those on Communist arms shipments. The
Castro Government has taken elaborate security measures to cloak
their arrival, but leaks will occur.[28]

One does not have to assume that the one-sided picture that
emerges from the above article resulted from a deliberate policy of
concealment on the part of the *Times*. In all likelihood the writer was
"unaware" of actual invasion preparations that had provoked Castro
into his action. He may never have read the editorial in *The Nation*,
or he had forgotten it. After the first perfunctory investigation of Dr.
Ronald Hilton's charges and the denial of President Ydigoras, the
Times was apparently content to drop the matter and report the news
as it appeared from Washington. But one of its readers was not so
easily mollified. He had read the story in *The Nation*, and he sent a
letter to the *Times* editor asking if the story were true. The allegations were serious. With its greater news gathering capability why
had not the *Times* investigated them?[29] Clifton Daniel, who read the
letter, had not seen the *Nation* editorial. Now he read it, and apparently so did others on the staff. Finally, Paul Kennedy, an experienced reporter, was sent to Guatemala to look into the matter. His
investigation was already underway while the *Times* was explaining
away Castro's charges and his "anti-Americanism."

It was the Paul Kennedy story, appearing on January 10, 1961, that
was later cited by President Kennedy as an example of premature
disclosure of information vital to the security of the United States.
However, the story, although more detailed than previous accounts,
was reported in the form of "allegations." The base (Retalhuleu) in
Guatemala was described, but it was represented as a base for the
training of Guatemalans for an expected invasion by Cuba. The presence of Cubans on the base was admitted, along with other foreigners from various countries, including the United States. As
Bernstein and Gordon have indicated, the report was so circumspect
as to be misleading ". . . each time he [Paul Kennedy] offered a sin-
ister interpretation, he balanced it with an innocent one."[30] The
story concluded with a rather convincing denial that the base was
planned to be used or even could be used to launch an invasion.

> One authority who has negotiated with the United States for assistance
> in the Retalhuleu land and air operations said that application for cer-
> tain amounts of war materials over the amount already received had
> been turned down by the United States.

The reason, he said, was that Washington considered that the amount
and type of materials applied for went beyond the needs of defensive
operations.

> ... the field is not a military installation in the true sense. It could not possibly serve in its present state as a large-scale offensive base. It has no dispersal areas, hardstands for plane parking or lateral exiting and entering runways.[31]

With a few exceptions the attitude displayed in the Paul Kennedy report was adopted by most of the major newspapers and wire services. Although some newspapers remained guarded or silent, others accepted the administration's denials and repeated them with emphasis. Castro's charges were "hysterical" and "preposterous." In summing up the account of press gullibility during this period, *Newsweek* quoted one newsman as saying, "Many of us may have gone off the deep end, but I can't help thinking that at some point we were pushed."[32]

There was one man in the Kennedy Administration whose reputation for veracity and whose pointed denials of American involvement in the invasion plans may have had a strong influence on the press. Adlai Stevenson was widely regarded as a man of integrity. It was felt that he must surely know the details of any invasion plan. But Stevenson confounded reporters from the beginning with his categorical statements on February 14, to the effect that the United States was not training the exiles and his ridicule of the charge that the "innocent winter resorts" of Florida were involved in the invasion preparations.[33] Schlesinger has admitted that Stevenson was given false information at a later point.[34] It is not clear to what extent he was deceived by administration aides at this earlier date. Kennedy is reported as having only the best of intentions in regard to Stevenson: "The integrity and credibility of Adlai Stevenson constitute one of our great national assets. I don't want anything to be done which might jeopardize that."[35] However, somehow there was a "mistake" in communication, and the intentions went awry. Stevenson may never have received full information on the invasion.

But on April 6 it was no longer possible for the *New York Times* to deny the significance of what was happening. With the arrival of the dispatch from Tad Szulc, the *Times* was faced with the reality of the impending crisis in Cuba. In the very act of cutting the story (not because of space limitations but for reasons of national interest), the staff was forced to admit, at least to themselves, that it was significant.[36] The act of cutting the report of a highly regarded correspondent like Szulc is hard on the conscience of a newspaperman. It may have been a certain malaise in the role of censor, coupled with the realization that he should have been more zealous in his earlier inquiries, that provoked Reston's series of editorials and his belated concern with the moral issues. Reston apparently consoled himself, to some extent, by the fact that the president had insisted he would not allow American forces to be used in any Cuban adventure. As though to remind himself once again of the president's words, Reston repeated the assurances in his editorial of April 11. "One decision has already been made here. The President has made it clear that in any military moves against the Castro regime United States forces are not to be used."[37] There is little question that President Kennedy planned to live up to this statement at the time he made it.

IV

But the world of President Kennedy and that of the Cuban brigade were far apart. The Cuban exiles were not familiar with American character, and they had not talked with Kennedy. Their major contacts with American policy had been mediated by CIA agents. There is no doubt that the Cuban leaders had heard the president's public statements about "no American involvement." There is also no question about the fact that they did not believe these statements. They all understood that some kind of "cover" story would be necessary. When Kennedy began to discover that there was a serious misunderstanding between himself and the Cuban leaders, he attempted to rectify the situation. Under instructions from the president, Schlesinger, Adolf Berle, and John Plank met with Miró Cardona, Castro's former Prime Minister and now the provisional president of the Cuban Revolutionary Council. Miró seemed unable to accept their statement that there would be no U.S. military support. Said Schlesinger, "He waived the President's news conference disclaimer aside as an understandable piece of psychological warfare and kept pressing us to say how far the administration really meant to go."[38] Schlesinger returned to Washington depressed by Miró's refusal to believe the United States would not provide military support. He reported the situation to the president who called Bissell of the CIA, insisting that Miró be made to understand the American position. Bissell sent Tracy Barnes to New York to talk to Miró once again, but Barnes was also under the impression that Miró, although he gave formal approval of the position, did not really believe him.[39]

Schlesinger remarks that Miró was a driven man and did not really want to believe he would get no support. There was surely an element of wishful thinking in Miró's misunderstanding. Schlesinger, who kept careful notes on their discussion, reports that Miró claimed 10,000 Cubans would align themselves wtih the invading forces, and Berle then promised arms for the 10,000 men. Miró apparently later remembered this conversation as a promise of

10,000 U.S. troops.[40]   But perhaps there was something beyond Miró's own needs that contributed to his misunderstanding. There is a strong suggestion that somewhere in the CIA hierarchy the idea developed that American aid would be forthcoming if things looked bad for the invaders. It is not clear where this idea took root and how it was communicated. However, on the lower levels the charge is very explicit. If the leaders of the Cuban brigade are to be believed, they had been given a very distorted version of the intended role of the United States in the coming invasion. The CIA agent in the field, a man known as "Frank," reportedly told the Cuban leaders that their unit was not the only one involved. He further added that, although the U.S. Marines were not a part of the invasion force they would be close at hand if needed.[41] Furthermore, if the Kennedy Administration tried to call off the invasion Frank had plans to counteract this move. Pepe San Roman describes Frank's instructions:

> If this happens (cancellation of the invasion order) you come here and make some kind of show, as if you were putting us, the advisors, in prison, and you go ahead with the program as we have talked about it, and we will give you the whole plan, even if we are your prisoners.
>   . . . Frank never said who opposed the invasion—it was just "forces in the administration," or "politicians," or "chiefs above." He did say that if he received the order to stop the invasion, "I have also orders from my bosses, my commanders to continue anyway."[42]

Countless other Cubans, talking to reporters after the event, insisted that they were given assurances of air cover and naval support and that these promises were never withdrawn. In a letter to Stewart Alsop, Dr. Manuel Antonio Verona, one of the leaders of the Cuban Revolutionary Council, said, "I find myself forced to declare that at no time were we advised that the Cuban patriots would lack the promised air and naval protection . . ."[43] Describing an interview with one of the ransomed Cuban prisoners, Howard Handleman reports, "Officially, Mr. Cuervo never was told that Americans or other non-Cubans would join the attack—but, unofficially, he was given to understand that they would."[44] A similar tale of American assurances is told by Manuel Penabaz, a young Cuban lawyer who was on the beach with the invasion forces at the Bay of Pigs.[45]

In the light of these stories from numerous different sources it seems difficult to believe that the idea of American support was conceived solely by the Cubans and elaborated by no other means than the heat of an active Cuban imagination. It appears very likely that, at some level in the CIA, there developed a belief that President Kennedy did not really "mean it" when he said there would be no in-

volvement of American forces. Or perhaps—and this is a more ominous suggestion—there was a feeling that the president would
panic and call in the Marines, once he saw the plan beginning to fail
and his own prestige on the line. If this is true, there was a major
blunder in the attempt to take the measure of President Kennedy and
predict how he would act in a crisis.

To make such a suggestion, as I have done here, is not to imply
that there was a deliberate conspiracy on the part of Dulles, Bissell,
and the entire CIA organization to push an American president into a
policy to which he was opposed. The theory of deliberate conspiracy
is too simplistic in its view of the American character. Dulles and
Bissell are members of "good families," a part of the American upper
class. Such people are as deeply moved by the need for virtue as
the need for success. If there was an intention to push the president
into full military involvement, it would have to take place without
the conscious awareness of either Dulles or Bissell. One of the ways
in which this inadvertent involvement of the president might be arranged is by providing him with an invasion plan that could not
succeed without American support—again, without intending that
it should happen that way.

The preparation of the invasion plan was a complicated process.
As originally conceived it was merely an infiltration by guerrilla
forces. Such a plan could have been executed without overt American involvement. The change in plans occurred while Eisenhower
was still president—although he appears to have been unaware of
what was taking place.[46] The Special Group, assigned to review
these plans, also gave little attention to the change.[47] The invasion
plan was simply not adequate to do the job. However, the inadequate
plan was not due to a failure in intelligence gathering, as has often
been claimed by reporters reviewing the incident. Dulles himself has
denied this assertion.[48] However, he failed to convey his doubts to
the White House staff. In addition, the CIA had full knowledge of the
strength of the Cuban forces. As early as mid-November, the State
Department revealed the fact that Castro's army was ten times the
size of Batista's and fully supplied with modern Soviet equipment.[49]
The last possibility that might have been counted on for success,
namely surprise, was effectively excluded by the CIA itself. CIA
agents in Miami, say Meyer and Szulc, used "as much discretion as
carnival shills before a sideshow tent."[50] Recruiting offices were
everywhere. Castro had been announcing to the world, through the
United Nations, that invasion was imminent. Another factor that
made success difficult was the fact that the invasion plans were
never discussed with the only people who could have evaluated

them and who were expected to execute them—the Cuban exiles. The Cuban leaders were kept in complete ignorance of the launch date, the place of the invasion, and even the strength of their forces until the brigade was actually at sea.[51] It was even decided it would be a good idea to lock up the Cuban Revolutionary Council until after the invasion was over. The rationale for these acts was the need for secrecy. But an additional reason may have been the fear that the CIA would have no invasion force if the Cubans knew all the facts.[52]

When the Cubans finally discovered what was about to happen they were incredulous. Penabaz says that when an American crew member explained to the Cubans that they would be carried in and left on the beach

> we took this as added assurance that we would be covered by air and naval support, for it was unthinkable to us that any civilized government would send men to battle without ample means either for complete victory or honorable retreat. . . . No one expected our 1,500 volunteers alone to conquer Castro's forces of 300,000 militia and regulars.[53]

One can accept all the facts of Penabaz's story without accepting his conclusion that he and his fellow exiles were "betrayed." This is not an instance of using a nice word when a dirty word might be more truthful. It is a matter of the American style of thought and the acceptance of inadvertence as a part of American morality. The CIA had the information that would have told them their mission could not succeed, but failure was not acceptable. Despite President Kennedy's statements to the contrary, there must have been those who believed he could not hold out against failure. Surely, at the last moment, he would throw aside his scruples and plunge in with all the armed forces of the United States behind him. How else can we explain the CIA's continued recommendation to push ahead with the invasion plans?[54]

Janis has pointed out the strong pressure for group conformity on a policy staff may induce a group to become soft-headed but to make hard-headed decisions when dealing with out-groups and enemies. Members consider loyalty to the group the highest form of morality. Certainly, the fact that Dulles and Bissell were part of Kennedy's team was an influence that led the members of the advisory staff to suppress any criticism of a plan that already had the acceptance of the group. They were members of the team.[55] If they suspected that something had gone wrong and there would be pressure on the president to call out the marines, it would not be sporting of them to throw cold water on a plan to which the group was already committed. It would be presumptuous and a sign of a "lack of faith" in their fellow members to imply that the group had supported a plan that would fail. Instead, the tendency was to "talk it up," as they say in baseball, in the hope that the confidence generated at the top would work its way down through all the echelons of command and "make" it all come off properly. Most Americans are so familiar with this style of "talking it up" that they are inclined to expect it and discount it at the same time. This is not always true of foreigners. In his account of the final briefing for the Cuban Brigade, Schlesinger described the American predictions that Castro's air force would be neutralized and the brigade would move on to Havana without serious opposition. Then he added, "The Cubans, still regarding the Americans with veneration and not used to locker-room pep talks, left the briefing in a state of exaltation."[56]

Although Americans are inclined to discount each other's sales talk, there is always an element of uncertainty in this process. One American never really understands another until he is able to get behind the façade of words that seems to separate them from one another. Kennedy did not understand the salesmanship of the CIA until it was too late, but they did not understand him very well either. The president had given his word to the American people that he would not make use of U.S. armed forces in the Cuban affair. He intended to stand by his word.

V

The decision to hold the members of the Cuban Revolutionary Council incommunicado was the result of an agreement between Miró and the CIA. However, it was not part of the plan that the CIA would be giving out press releases in the name of the CRC. Apparently as a part of the urge to "talk it up," a New York public relations man named Lem Jones began releasing his canned announcements of the progress of the "liberators." Shortly after the landings of April 17, when the forces of Fidel Castro began to close in on the small brigade of exiles, Lem Jones was pouring out his propaganda.[57] The newspapers were filled with reports issued in the name of the CRC, the organization that was supposedly directing the invasion. The Cuban Navy was in revolt! Now the Isle of Pines had fallen! The invaders were moving in! Peasants, workers, and militia were joining the "freedom front."

But things were different in the Bay of Pigs. On Monday, April 17, the invasion floundered on the coral reefs that had not been considered in the landing plans. Some of the landing craft were sunk.

When the path was charted through the reefs, the B-26s and Sea Fury fighters from Castro's air force began strafing and bombing the landing party. The equipment had to be unloaded under fire. One ship was disabled by rocket fire. Another, carrying supplies for the first ten days of fighting—including the communications trailer, ammunition, food, and hospital equipment—was completely destroyed. The men jumped overboard and were strafed by Castro's planes in the water. Pepe San Román, the brigade commander, led a successful assault on the airport at Girón, but when some of his Cuban prisoners wanted to join him and asked for weapons to fight, he had none to give them. Soon the American ships were forced to withdraw under fire and Castro's militia moved in. By Tuesday, Pepe was on the radio in constant communication with the American task force commander demanding the help he had been promised. The wounded were around them. They had no medical supplies. They were out of ammunition. They were badly outnumbered and were being bombed and strafed. Where was the American air support? The invaders could not even receive supplies without air cover to permit the ships to come in.[58] The news of the impending failure of the invasion was transmitted to Washington, to the only man who could lift the restriction on aid from the U.S. armed forces: John F. Kennedy.

Kennedy had known for some time that the invasion was failing. On Tuesday evening, April 18, the night of the congressional reception, after waiting until the last moment for news from the front, the president arrived at the ball with Mrs. Kennedy and mingled for an hour and a half with his guests. After the reception he went to his office where Rusk, McNamara, Bissell, Lemnitzer, and Burk were waiting. Schlesinger was aroused from bed and arrived later. It is not clear what pressures were brought to bear on the president that evening, but the plight of the men on the beach was unmistakably clear. Without American support they were lost. Admiral Burke strongly supported the request for air power that was presented by Bissell. Rusk was opposed. Although Pepe San Román had already refused evacuation for himself and his men, there is a suggestion in Schlesinger's account that Kennedy finally relaxed his ban on air power in the hope that the brigade might be evacuated and the lives of some of the men saved.[59] The president authorized the use of jet fighters from the carrier, Essex, to defend the B-26s flown by Cuban exiles. The B-26s could then knock out Castro's tanks. As it turned out, the B-26s arrived over target an hour ahead of time and were largely ineffective. Attempts to press Kennedy into sending more air support ended in failure. He stood firm against any further commitment of American forces. From that point it was simply a matter of time. Refusing evacuation, the brigade fought on. In his last messages from the beach, Pepe San Román was still calling for the expected air cover: "In water. Out of ammo. Enemy closing in. Help must arrive in next hour." "Fighting on beach. Send all available aircraft now."[60]

VI

There is no question that the United States was deeply involved in the Cuban invasion from the very beginning. It was financed and supplied by the CIA. American ships transported the invaders. American officers trained them. An American planning staff conceived of and directed the entire operation up through the actual landing of the invading forces. However, President Kennedy believed that somehow U.S. armed forces could be kept clear of the actual fighting and, if this were accomplished, we would not become involved in "aggression." One must admire the courage with which he held to this conviction against the enormous pressures that were placed on him and his willingness to face the world after the event without self-pity or excuses. But the courage of Kennedy must stand beside that of Pepe San Román, who was captured by Castro, and his comrades who died on the beach at the Bay of Pigs. The tragedy of the Cuban invasion was primarily a refusal on the part of those involved in the planning and execution of the mission to face their real intentions.

Senator William Fulbright, who was opposed to the plan from the beginning, suggested the risks for the American conscience in a memorandum to the president prior to the launch date. "To give this activity even covert support is of a piece with the hypocrisy and cynicism for which the United States is constantly denouncing the Soviet Union. ... This point will not be lost on the rest of the world—nor on our own consciences."[61] It may well have been a sense of guilt about the invasion that paralyzed the entire mission. The president's unwillingness to think about it and his reluctance to smell out all the details may have affected the attitude of his staff. As Margaret Mead has pointed out in reference to another war, "There is one further absolute necessity if Americans are not only to start fighting but to keep on fighting. ... We must feel we are on the side of the Right."[62]

However, although the story of the Bay of Pigs reveals a flaw in the character of President Kennedy, it also reveals one of his great strengths. He was unable to extricate himself from the plans of the previous administration, but he understood the meaning of limits in the use of power. He was able to face the agony of failure and hold back the force that was available to him. This ability to look tragedy in the face is a rare quality among American leaders. It was our failure to recognize the limits of our power and our inability to face the tragedy of an American defeat that led to our full-scale military involvement in Vietnam.

NOTES

1. A. Dulles, *The Craft of Intelligence* (New York: New American Library, 1965), pp. 174–175.

2. A. M. Schlesinger, Jr., *A Thousand Days* (Greenwich, Conn.: Fawcett, 1965), p. 213.

3. K. E. Meyer and T. Szulc, *The Cuban Invasion* (New York: Praeger, 1962), p. 104.

4. Schlesinger, *A Thousand Days*, p. 218.

5. Ibid., p. 220.

6. Ibid., p. 223.

7. Ibid., p. 231.

8. Ibid., p. 227.

9. Ibid., p. 241.

10. *New York Times*, April 13, 1961, p.18.

11. H. Johnson, *The Bay of Pigs* (New York: Norton, 1964), pp. 103–104.

12. Schlesinger, *A Thousand Days*, p. 265.

13. C. Daniel, "Excerpts from a Speech on Coverage of Bay of Pigs Buildup," *The New York Times*, June 2, 1966, p. 14.

14. J. Reston, *The Artillery of the Press* (New York: Harper & Row, 1966), pp. 20–21.

15. Meyer and Szulc, *The Cuban Invasion*, p. 116.

16. Ibid., pp. 114–115.

17. Daniel, "Bay of Pigs Buildup" (speech).

18. J. Reston, "United States and Cuba: The Moral Question, I," *New York Times*, April 12, 1961, p. 40.

19. Daniel, "Bay of Pigs Buildup" (Speech).

20. Ibid.

21. Ibid.

22. Ibid.

23. V. Bernstein and J. Gordon, "The Press and the Bay of Pigs," *The Columbia University Forum*, Fall 1967.

24. Ibid.

25. Ibid.

26. Ibid.

27. L. Parrott, "UN Sets Hearing on Cuba's Charge of U.S. Aggression," *New York Times*, January 2, 1961, p. 1.

28. "Castro's Motives," *New York Times*, January 8, 1961, section 4, p. E1. The complete editorial can be found in the appendix.

29. Daniel, Op. Cit.

30. Bernstein and Gordon, "The Press and the Bay of Pigs."

31. P. Kennedy, "U.S. Helps Train an Anti-Castro Force at Secret Guatemalan Air-Ground Base," *New York Times*, January 10, 1961, p. 1.

32. "Pushed Off the Deep End?" *Newsweek*, May 1, 1961, p. 25.

33. Statement by Ambassador Stevenson, *Department of State Bulletin*, April 2, 1962, p. 556. [Statement made on February 14, 1961.]

34. Schlesinger, *A Thousand Days*, pp. 253–54.

35. Ibid. Schlesinger points out that CIA actually deceived the State Department in regard to the origin of the air attack on Cuba. "Why CIA should have misled State has never been clear. Possibly the agency, having worked out its deception plan, felt obliged to deceive even the rest of its own government; or possibly the CIA source, if in the Intelligence Branch, was himself 'unwitting'."

36. The *New York Times* was not the only paper to withhold important news just prior to the invasion. Schlesinger reports that Gilbrert Harrison of the *New Republic* suppressed Karl Meyer's "careful, accurate, and devastating account of the CIA activities among the [Cuban] refugees" at the request of the president, Schlesinger, *A Thousand Days*, p. 244.

37. J. Reston, "Top U.S. Advisers in Dispute on Aid to Castro's Foes," *New York Times*, April 11, 1961, p. 1.

38. Schlesinger, *A Thousand Days*, p. 247.

39. Ibid., pp. 248–249.

40. Ibid., p. 248.

41. H. Johnson, *The Bay of Pigs* (New York: Norton, 1964), p. 74.

42. Ibid., p. 75. In fairness to "Frank" it should be said that he has denied this story. See A. Dulles, *The Craft of Intelligence* (New York: New American Library, 1965), p. 176.

43. J. T. O'Rourke, "Who Bungled the Cuban Invasion? Another Version," *U.S. News and World Report*, July 31, 1961, p. 57.

44. H. Handleman, "The Real Story of the Bay of Pigs," *U.S. News and World Report*, January 7, 1963, p. 39.

45. M. Penabaz, "We Were Betrayed. A Veteran of the Cuban Invasion Speaks Out," *U.S. News and World Report*, January 14, 1963, pp. 46–49.

46. Johnson, *The Bay of Pigs*, pp. 54–55; Schlesinger, *A Thousand Days*, pp. 219–220.

47. Ibid.

48. Dulles, *The Craft of Intelligence*, pp. 157–158.

49. Johnson, *The Bay of Pigs*, p. 54.

50. Meyer and Szulc, *The Cuban Invasion*, p. 116.

51. Penabaz, "We Were Betrayed"; O'Rourke, "Who Bungled the Cuban Invasion?" Op. Cit.

52. Of course, the CIA had other good reasons for secrecy. Having recruited everyone from former members of Batista's army to some of the more outspoken advocates of social revolution there was much dissension in the Cuban Revolutionary Council and in the brigade itself. Someone was always threatening to resign because a political opponent had too much power. With the constant threat of defection, CIA agents could trust no one. So they trusted no one.

53. Penabaz, "We Were Betrayed," p. 47.

54. Schlesinger has suggested this possibility as an alternative, but on analysis, his statement appears very much like my own.

> There was plainly a logical gap between the statement that the plan would work if one or another condition were fulfilled and the statement that the plan would work anyway. One cannot know whether this gap resulted from sloppiness in analysis or from a conviction, conscious or unconscious, that once the invasion were launched, either internal uprising or external support would follow, and, if not the first, then the second—that, in short, once the United States government embarked on this enterprise, it could not risk the disaster of failure. [Schlesinger, A Thousand Days, p. 224.]

Dulles has himself dismissed the idea of an internal uprising. As to the explanation of "sloppiness in analysis," one must raise the question as to why the analysis was sloppy in this particular situation when it is not always sloppy. If one believes that mistakes or "sloppiness" do not simply happen in a random fashion, it becomes necessary to look for a reason in terms of the motivation of the participants. Of the explanations suggested by Schlesinger, only one remains plausible.

55. I. L. Janis, Victims of Groupthink (Boston: Houghton Mifflin, 1972), pp. 12, 19–49.

56. Schlesinger, A Thousand Days, p. 252.

57. Ibid., p. 257.

58. Johnson, The Bay of Pigs, pp. 140–151.

59. Schlesinger, A Thousand Days, p. 260; see also Johnson, The Bay of Pigs, pp. 152–153.

60. Johnson, The Bay of Pigs, p. 161.

61. Schlesinger, A Thousand Days, p. 236.

62. Margaret Mead, And Keep Your Powder Dry (New York: William Morrow, 1965), p. 115.

The Incident in the Gulf of Tonkin

7

"So you thought then, you scoundrel, that together with Dmitri I meant to kill my father?"

"I didn't know what thoughts were in your mind then," said Smerdyakov resentfully; "and so I stopped you then at the gate to sound you on that very point."

"To sound what, what?"

"Why, that very circumstance, whether you wanted your father to be murdered or not? . . ."

"What next! Come answer, answer, I insist: what was it—what could I have done to put such a degrading suspicion into your mean soul?"

"As for the murder, you couldn't have done that and didn't want to, but as for wanting someone else to do it, that was just what you did want."

FROM: Fyodor Dostoyevsky,
The Brothers Karamazov,
trans., Constance Garnett,
(New York: Random House, 1950)

I

If innocent desires are transformed into questionable deeds, there must be a communication of intent from the higher to the lower echelons of power. The man at the higher level knows what must be done, but he does not admit it to himself. He manages to avoid thinking about the details. The man at the lower level must work out these details for himself. If he is guilty of criminal violence, it is his own responsibility, but he has reason to hope that his chief will look upon his acts with indulgence.

In the early days of American foreign policy it was easier to dissociate a president from direct involvement in military provocation. It was possible to speak in generalities without being responsible for the particulars, since any correction of a misunderstanding had to travel over a great distance and arrive in a changed situation. We find this convenient misunderstanding in Commodore Perry's report to Washington on the progress of his mission to establish commercial relations with Japan. Since the Japanese did not want any contact with foreigners, Perry decided he must be firm. He reported: "It is very certain that the Japanese can be brought to reason only through the influence of their fears, and when they find that their seacoast is entirely at the mercy of a strong naval force they will be induced, I confidently hope, to concede all that will be asked of them."[1] Of course, this was not the avowed "intention" of the president or Congress. The secretary of the navy hastened to reply:

> [The president] desires to impress you with his conviction that the great end should be attained, not only with credit to the United States, but without wrong to Japan. I need not remind you that your mission is one of peaceful negotiation, and that, although in consideration of the peculiar character of the Japanese much importance may well be attached to the exhibition of impressive evidences of the greatness and power of our country, no violence should be resorted to except for defense.[2]

But what was really the intention of the United States toward Japan? Had Perry failed to grasp the point, or was it merely that the president and the secretary of state became somewhat uneasy when they saw their rather vague philosophical notions about "commerce" transformed into action? Let us return to the original instructions to Perry. After being ordered to proceed with his "whole force" to the coast of Japan, Perry received, through the secretary of the navy, these rather ambiguous instructions from the secretary of state:

> In his intercourse with this people, who are said to be proud and vindictive in their character, he should be courteous and conciliatory, but

at the same time, firm and decided. He will, therefore, submit with patience and forebearance to acts of discourtesy . . . but, at the same time, will be careful to do nothing that may compromit, [sic] in their eyes, his own dignity, or that of the country. He will, on the contrary, do everything to impress them with a just sense of the power and greatness of this country. . . . It is impossible by any instructions, however minute, to provide for every contingency. . . . For this reason, as well as on account of the remoteness of the scene of this operation, it is proper that the Commodore should be invested with large discretionary powers, and should feel assured that any departure from usage, or any error of judgment he may commit will be viewed with indulgence . . .[3]

Thus, the administration conveniently disposed of responsibility for direct military action. In effect, Perry was told that it was perfectly acceptable to frighten the Japanese with a display of force, but it would be preferable if his adversary fired the first shot. In any event, if he was a bit too zealous in the prosecution of his mission, his "errors of judgment" would be looked upon with indulgence. One is reminded of the strange conspiracy that obtained between Ivan and Smerdyakov in *The Brothers Karamazov*, in which the communication of intent was so subtle that the man who talked in generalities was hardly aware of what he was saying, but to the man of action the message was unmistakable.[4]

Today, with the increased effectiveness of modern communication, the time span is no longer a satisfactory means of establishing the inadvertent character of an aggressive act. The president, whether he likes it or not, is responsible for the actions of the armed forces on a daily, if not an hourly, basis. The higher echelons must be split off from the lower by more subtle means—through compartmentalization and fractionation of plans and a division of responsibility. In short, it is necessary to forget that certain things are taking place by leaving the details to someone else. Delegation of responsibility, a method of improving the strictly mechanical efficiency of an operation, becomes, then, a method of removing an unpleasant thought from consciousness. A man who is planning the details of an operation must think about what he is about to do, but he is not necessarily responsible for the diplomatic consequences. The man who delegates the details to others is technically responsible, but it is possible for him to avoid thinking about what he is doing. It is by a substitution of other values, such as efficiency and professionalism, that it becomes possible to direct one's attention away from the intent of one's actions. If one can succeed in avoiding the question, "What are we really trying to do?" a great step has taken place in the emancipation of action from responsibility. Although this step has become increasingly difficult for an American president, the matter of urgency makes it possible for Congress and the people to avoid direct responsibility for the actions of the administration.

II

In contrast to the sudden crisis in Cuba, American involvement in Vietnam was a slow process. Although there were many grand speeches about protecting a "free people," it was not necessary to keep these general motives separate from our commercial interest in Vietnam. The need to sell our surplus goods and bring back tin and tungsten were clearly outlined by President Eisenhower in a speech to the Governor's Conference of 1953 as a justification for our aid to the French forces in Vietnam. If we lost Southeast Asia, he said,

> the tin and tungsten that we so greatly value from that area would cease coming. . . . So when the United States votes $400,000,000 to help that war [the French in Vietnam], we are not voting a giveaway program. We are voting for the cheapest way that can prevent the occurrence of something that would be of a most terrible significance to the United States of America, our security, our power and ability to get certain things we need from the riches of the Indonesian territory and from Southeast Asia . . .[5]

One is reminded of Richard Nixon's remark that the United States will continue to have more of the riches of this world than other nations. At this point we had not yet reached the level of desperation at which more urgent "reasons" would be needed for our continued involvement in Vietnam. We were far removed from the immediacy of the violence. If our simple desire for commerce supported the questionable deeds of the French, we were not telling them what to do and were, therefore, not responsible for the consequences. Altogether we spent $2.6 billion to support the French from 1950 to 1954. But with the fall of the French forces at Dien Bien Phu in 1954, it was no longer possible to act through others. First, American advisors were sent, and steps were taken to create a new government under the direction of Ngo Dinh Diem. With the American encouragement given to the overthrow of Diem in 1963 the situation in South Vietnam became more clearly an American problem. Our commercial interests, although crucial to our initial involvement, were no longer a satisfactory justification for a continuation of the war. By 1964 the cost of the war was already excessive compared to any possible commercial advantage to be gained from it. It was now

clearly American pride that was at stake—our position and our reputation as a world power.[6] However, as representatives of a nation that
"did not ask for power," American leaders could not tell this directly
to the American people. We were still ostensibly in South Vietnam
as advisers to the government. We were helping them fight communist invaders.

As the situation in Vietnam became more difficult and more
costly, the tacit understanding between the U.S. government and the
people began to break down. The war protest movement was gaining
momentum. As the people and the administration began to move
further apart, greater cynicism was required to function within the
government organization. Bad faith cannot be maintained indefinitely since it is dependent on the suspension of reflection. As
one's nose is rubbed in the truth, one must either abandon the lie or
cynically invent a bolder one—a more dramatic justification for
one's behavior. Gradually the Johnson administration came to recognize that some dramatic event would be required to show the
people that their security was threatened. The United States must be
provoked by some incident that would justify our outrage and a
deeper involvement in the war.

This does not mean that the administration deliberately conspired
to trick Congress and the American people into supporting a full-
scale war policy. The basic American urge for personal virtue would
not permit the deliberate creation of a fake provocation. However,
members of the inner circle of government had already begun to tell
each other that such an incident would be necessary. It was therefore
only a matter of time before one was discovered. The draft of a congressional resolution, which the administration regarded as the
equivalent of a declaration of war, was drawn up in May 1964.
Targets were selected and clandestine military operations against
North Vietnam were begun. Chief among these operations was 34A,
a program of military attacks and sabotage, planned jointly with the
South Vietnamese, using mercenaries for actual operations, but
under the direct command of an American general. Like earlier activities, however, 34A was funded under the guise of advice and
information collection. General Paul D. Harkins ran 34A under a
branch of his command called the Studies and Observation Group.[7]

III

The incident in the Gulf of Tonkin was the beginning of the deep
American involvement in Vietnam. It was following this incident

that the massive deployment of American troops was initiated and the American casualties began to mount. Although President Johnson had been contemplating an increased American commitment in Vietnam for some time, it is likely that the decision to make use of North Vietnamese PT boat attacks as a basis for gaining congressional support occured shortly after August 2, 1964, when two Vietnamese PT boats attacked the destroyer *Maddox*. At this time, the incident was minimized. Secretary of State Rusk assured the reporters that there was no major crisis and that the United States had sufficient strength in the area. The impression was left that in destroying or damaging the attacking craft the *Maddox* had already administered the degree of retaliation that was necessary. "The other side got a sting out of this," Secretary Rusk told the reporters. "If they do it again, they'll get another sting."[8] There is a suggestion, from Secretary Rusk's remarks, that the sense of American outrage did not occur until after the second attack.

On the morning of August 5, the American public was greeted with the news that the communist PT boats had renewed their raids and that U.S. planes had engaged in a "limited" retaliation (64 sorties of American bombers attacking PT boat bases and support facilities in North Vietnam). In his address to the American people, President Johnson termed the attacks "open aggression on the high seas."[9] It was just a month before a major political election and Mr. Johnson's Republican opponent, Barry Goldwater, was an avowed exponent of escalation of the war. President Johnson had espoused the cause of moderation. In his announcement of the American raids into North Vietnam, the president was still taking the role of a moderate, while letting his actions speak to the "hawks" in his own party. In his address he called for wider authority, while promising not to widen the war.

> We Americans know—although others appear to forget—the risk of spreading conflict. We will seek no wider war. I have instructed the Secretary of State to make this position totally clear to friends and to adversaries and, indeed, to all. . . . finally I have today met with the leaders of both parties and the Congress of the United States and I have informed them that I shall immediately request the Congress to pass a resolution making clear that our government is united in its determination to take all necessary measures in support of freedom and in defense of peace in Southeast Asia. . . . It is a solemn responsibility to have to order even limited military action by forces whose overall strength is as vast and as awesome as those of the United States of America. But it is my considered conviction, shared throughout your government, that firmness in the right is indispensable today for peace. That firmness will always be measured. Its mission is peace.[10]

The resolution that would permit the president to "take all necessary measures in support of freedom and in defense of peace" was
the famous Tonkin Gulf Resolution. It enlisted congressional support and "all necessary measures to repel any armed attack against
the forces of the United States and to prevent further aggression." It
further emphasized that "the United States is, therefore, prepared as
the President determines, to take all necessary steps, including the
use of armed forces, to assist any member of protocol state of the
SOUTHEAST ASIA COLLECTIVE DEFENSE TREATY requesting
assistance in defense of its freedom."[11] The resolution passed 88 to 2
in the Senate and was unanimous (416 to 0) in the House, a striking
show of unanimity of congressional opinion, in the face of what was
perceived to be "open aggression on the high seas."

The attack on the American destroyers *Maddox* and *Turner Joy* on
August 4 was represented to the American people as an entirely unprovoked attack. The *Maddox* and *Turner Joy* were allegedly on
routine patrol in international waters. In short, they were innocent. It
was the enemy who was guilty of aggression. Although the South
Vietnamese were engaged in armed attacks on the mainland of North
Vietnam in the same general area at the same time and although we
had supplied the boats for their mission, our own ships, the *Maddox*
and *Turner Joy,* were represented as being "unaware" of the hostilities of the South Vietnamese against the North. In his testimony
before the Committee of Foreign Relations on August 6, 1964, Secretary McNamara said, "First, our Navy played absolutely no part in,
was not associated with, was not aware of any South Vietnamese
actions, if there are any. I want to make that very clear."[12] Subsequent investigation has revealed several interesting details. (1) Despite the fact that most communist nations claim a 12-mile limit for
their territorial waters, the *Maddox* had been given orders that
would permit it to penetrate beyond those limits, on the assumption
that the territorial waters extended only to three miles.[13] (2) The
Maddox and *Turner Joy* were part of an intelligence mission to
gather information on North Vietnamese coastal defenses for future
use by the South Vietnamese. As part of the mission, the *Maddox*
stimulated the electronic networks on the coastal defenses of North
Vietnam, ostensibly to obtain intelligence information.[14] (3) But the
U.S. commander in South Vietnam clearly saw that one of the effects
of his mission would be to "possibly" draw North Vietnamese patrol
boats northward away from the area of the 34A operations (the South
Vietnamese attack boats).[15] As Senator Morse later remarked, "'possibly,' in that context, could be interpreted as 'hopefully.'" (4) The
operational commander of the mission, who was aboard the *Maddox*

at the time, felt that the North Vietnamese forces considered his patrol directly involved with the South Vietnamese operation; they considered him a part of the attacking forces.[16] (5) But perhaps more significant than any of the above details is the general fact that the United States had shown by its presence, by its commitment of land, sea, and air forces to the area, and by the official statements of the administration that it was an ally of South Vietnam, that it was allied to a power engaged in activities against North Vietnam.

In view of this provocation and the fact that there was no damage to the American ships, the sense of outrage and the degree of retaliation (64 sorties) is rather surprising. It is clear that the retaliation and the resolution that followed it was based, not so much on the attack by the North Vietnamese PT boats, as on the general war aims of the administration. It was also based on a sense of unlimited American resources and power, the conviction that the North Vietnamese could not strike back with equal force. This is demonstrated by the fact that, when another American intelligence ship, the Pueblo, was later attacked, captured, and some of the crew killed and wounded off the coast of North Korea, the United States took the case to the United Nations rather than attempt military action. In an interview on "Meet the Press," Secretary McNamara indicated that air cover had not been provided for the Pueblo because it might have been "provocative" to the North Koreans. Yet, under questioning by the Senate Committee on Foreign Relations, he denied that the air cover provided to the Maddox and Turner Joy was provocative to North Vietnam.[17]

IV

It would appear that the chief justification for American innocence in the affair of the Gulf of Tonkin rests on the allegation that we really did not know what we were doing; i.e., it rests on our refusal to admit that we knew what we were doing. This seems to be the position taken by Secretary McNamara in his testimony before the Senate Committee on Foreign Relations on February 20, 1968. Since the extent of our retaliation could only be justified on the basis that we were attacked without provocation, McNamara's testimony was designed to show that we were not provocative, or if we were, we did not know that we were being provocative. The question of "knowing" plays a primary part in these hearings. During his questioning before the committee, Secretary McNamara did recall that he had said, "Our Navy played absolutely no part in, was not associated with, was not aware of, any South Vietnamese actions if there were any." However, he explained to the committee that he was really talking about the *Maddox* and not the entire U.S. Navy when he made that statement. He admitted that the statement was rather "ambiguous," but claimed that the committee must have known what he meant since he had already informed them that the navy had supplied boats for the "South Vietnamese" 34A operation.[18] Although this explains to us what the committee "should have known," it does not explain the source of that peculiar ambiguity that crept into the secretary's speech, unless it was based on a desire to deny knowledge of provocation while, at the same time, being provocative.

After it was pointed out to Secretary McNamara that cables directed to the *Maddox* made reference to Operation 34A (the South Vietnamese attacking force), he was willing to admit that the *Maddox*, too, "knew" of 34A, but insisted that they were "not aware of the details" of the operation (targets, times, etc.).[19] If a man wishes to avoid "knowing" or understanding what is going on, there is always a level of specificity to which he can retreat and claim a "lack of awareness." The man who pulls the trigger of a gun is not aware of the chemistry of gunpowder, yet he still knows the consequences of his acts.

However, the committee carried the issue even further. Senator Fulbright presented a cable from the operational commander of the *Maddox*, which indicated that, even aboard the *Maddox*, there was awareness that the D.R.V. (Democratic Republic of Vietnam—North Vietnam) had confused the American operation with 34A. The cable by the commander stated, in part, "evaluation of information from various sources indicates that the D.R.V. considers patrol directly involved with 34A operations. D.R.V. considers U.S. ships present as enemies because of these operations and have already indicated readiness to treat us in that category."[20] At this point, Secretary McNamara's retreat from awareness appears almost unbelievable. He told the committee that even if the commander claimed to be aware that the D.R.V. regarded his patrol as an enemy, he could not *really* have been aware, since he had no knowledge on which to base his awareness. In short, the commander could not really have been aware unless he knew why he was aware.

> SECRETARY McNAMARA: Mr. Chairman, may I comment on this specific cable?
>
> THE CHAIRMAN: Yes.
>
> SECRETARY McNAMARA: Two points: First we can find no basis for the commander making this statement, that the D.R.V. considered

the DeSoto patrol directly involved in 34A operations. Second, Harrick [the Operational Commander] himself states he can recall no basis for coming to that conclusion. Third, the PT boat officer that we captured and interrogated in July, 1966 told his interrogators that it was clear in his mind that the DeSoto patrol was separate from 34A operations.

THE CHAIRMAN: Well, you are not saying this cable was not sent.

SECRETARY McNAMARA: I simply stand on what I said, Mr. Chairman. Of course, the cable was sent.[21]

Nevertheless, after this detailed discussion of the commander's cable and the fact that the term, *34A*, had appeared in previous cables directed to him, it was still possible for Secretary McNamara to contend that the commander did not know the nature of Operation 34A.

SECRETARY McNAMARA: . . . he did know that he was to stay out of certain restricted areas. He knew the term "34A" because it was included in a message that was sent to him.

SENATOR GORE: But did not know what it stood for?

SECRETARY McNAMARA: I do not believe he knew what it stood for, and he certainly did not know anything about these particular targets or dates, or the nature of operations. One good evidence of that is that he misidentified 34A vessels as Russian vessels.

THE CHAIRMAN: Didn't he later say in one of his cables that the North Vietnamese were very agitated about their presence there and regarded them as part of the 34A operations, in one of the later cables? I think he said that was why he was apprehensive and suggested that they call off the further operation. "The above patrol will"—this is to the *Maddox*—"clearly demonstrate our determination to continue these operations. Possibly draw North Vietnamese Navy patrol boats to northward away from the area of 34A operations and eliminate DeSoto patrol interference with 34A operations." Then, on the 4th of August, some 15 hours before the second incident, the Operational Commander . . . sent the following to the Commander of the Seventh Fleet: "Evaluation of information from various sources indicates that D.R.V. considers patrol directly involved with 34A ops. The D.R.V. considers the United States presence as enemies because of these ops and have already indicated readiness to treat us in that category . . ." I cannot imagine a Commander who sent that saying that they considered him part of the 34 operations without knowing anything about what 34 operations was.

SECRETARY McNAMARA: Well, I can only tell you what he tells us, which is that he did not know the nature of 34A operations, the targets, the times, the boats, the courses, or anything at that time.[22]

Of course, it is unnecessary to know the specific targets of an operation in order to understand that the operation is hostile and to understand the risks involved in a confusion between DeSoto and

34A. Yet, although Secretary McNamara contended that the right hand of DeSoto did not know what the left hand of 34A was doing, he asserted that the North Vietnamese understood both operations and could not possibly have confused them. It is only the enemy who is allowed to know what he is doing and, consequently, he must bear the full responsibility for this knowledge. Again, I quote Secretary McNamara:

> May I go back to the point you made that it is your belief that the DeSoto patrols on the 2nd of July, 2nd of August, and the 4th of August were carried out in such a way that North Vietnam could reasonably assume there was coordination between them and operations 34A, I do not believe so. . . . The North Vietnamese radar tracked both of them; we can be confident of that. They knew they were separated in place and time, but importantly, and most important of all, the North Vietnamese knew they had nothing to fear from our DeSoto patrol. This was the fourth one carried out. They were all carried out essentially in the same fashion and operating procedures. At no time did any of these patrols carry out hostile action. At no time did they contribute in any way to the success of 34A operations and, therefore, there was no basis whatsoever for the North Vietnamese to consider them a part of or associated with 34A operations.[23]

The North Vietnamese are expected to assume that since we have not engaged in hostile actions against them in the past, we will not change our tactics, despite the fact that we are an ally of the South Vietnamese. Furthermore, if they have no concrete evidence, no precisely measureable and quantifiable facts indicating that we might engage in hostile action, they have no justification for regarding us as hostile. We are inside what they regard as their territorial waters, stimulating their electronic network, in the general area where our ally is conducting an attack against them, but they are expected to regard us as friendly until we fire the first shot. They really know what we are doing better than we do ourselves.

V

But the innocence of the U.S. Navy was not the real issue in the hearing. Everyone understood *that*, even though there were moments when the discussion was swamped with the details of what a commander knew or did not know. The issue was the intent of the Johnson Administration. It was Senator Wayne Morse who brought the committee back to that point in his summary statement.

> You see, what I think we never come to grips with is what we were doing long before the second and the fourth, long before the incidents

of Tonkin Bay. The fact we had this kind of presence there, that we were stimulating the electronic devices of the North Vietnamese, that we were carrying on intelligence operations was wrong. The *Maddox* was, on this occasion, a spyship and quite a different body of international law applies to spy activities than applies to other activities. So I only want to say for the record that I don't think we should have been there and especially under the circumstances when the navy and the administration knew that South Vietnamese naval vessels that we had furnished and the personnel whom we had trained were on their way in that period of time to bombard North Vietnam and its two islands. The *Maddox* and the *Turner Joy* were in the area, despite all our talk about the distances. The fact is that the North Vietnamese had no reason to believe that we were trying to keep separate from the South Vietnamese boat operations in our patrol. They had no reason to know or believe that. We don't know what conclusions they reached. I think it would be a very reasonable conclusion if they thought there was a connection.

I happen to think there was a very clear connection.

The very fact that you were electronically invading, so to speak, North Vietnam, while at the same time, in that series of time, the South Vietnamese boats were going to make their attack, put us, I think, in the position where the North Vietnamese and the rest of the world, for that matter, would see some interrelation.

But I still go back beyond that.

What worries me is that we were at the time escalating, we were involving ourselves more and more in the difficulty in South Vietnam. We know from the record what the thinking was in the Administration, having in their pocket a resolution ready to spring on us.

We had some evidence that the resolution, or a draft of a resolution was prepared before the Tonkin Bay incident ever occurred. It was to give to the President the authority that the Congress gave. I am willing to let history be the judge, eventually it will be recorded that it was a completely unconstitutional move . . .

The basic question is why were we following this course of action at that time in the Gulf of Tonkin when the South Vietnamese boats were going up there to make an attack? I think all the explanation of the Secretary, all the explanation of the Administration just ducks that problem.[24]

At this point, Senator Morse was repeating a charge that he had expressed on a number of occasions. If the naval commanders did not know what was going on, surely the same thing could not be said for the president and the secretary of defense. What were we doing there in the first place? What was our intent?

It was on this issue that Secretary McNamara sought refuge in the opacity of the human consciousness. In accord with the oldest of American traditions, the secretary implied that aggressive intent could only be censured if it was conscious and deliberate. To demonstrate this deliberation, it was necessary to show that the provocation had been planned and expressed verbally in the form of an actual conspiracy. If there was no evidence of this type, there was no such intent. In fact, as he had previously indicated, the charge was "monstrous."

> As a final point, I must address the suggestion that, in some way, the government of the United States induced the incident on August 4 with the intent of providing an excuse to take the retaliatory action which we in fact took. I can only characterize such insinuations as monstrous . . . I find it inconceivable that anyone even remotely famil-iar with our society and system of government could suspect the exis-tence of a conspiracy which would include almost, if not all, the entire chain of military command in the Pacific, the Chairman of the Joint Chiefs of Staff, the Joint Chiefs, the Secretary of Defense, and his chief civilian assistants, the Secretary of State, and the President of the United States.[25]

Of course, such a conclusion does not necessarily follow from the senator's charge. It is sufficient for the president to give his military commanders only the slightest hint of his intention and the latter will improve on the instruction. Commodore Perry has already dem-onstrated how the enthusiasm of an activist can flower from the suggestion of a few words. It is impossible to escape the moral di-lemma by reducing everything to concrete plans and specific in-structions.

Nevertheless, as the hearings came to a close, various members of the senate complimented the secretary on his sincerity and his can-dor. If it is possible to be disingenuous and candid at the same time, then it is possible that the secretary achieved this remarkable feat. For he was quite correct when he said:

> For seven years I have tried not to hide the actions of the Department. We have disclosed more to our nation and to our enemies, for that matter, about the national security of this country and the factors that we take account of in protecting it than has ever been disclosed before. I believe in disclosure, and I believe that the truth will support it-self . . .[26]

If candor means the disclosure of information, the secretary had, indeed, been candid. However, we are dealing here with a kind of unreflective sincerity, a sincerity in regard to acts, which is com-pletely devoid of introspection. With his great regard for concrete data and specific facts, the secretary placed all his confidence in data and in the disclosure of information. A computer could be equally sincere with anyone who knew how to interrogate it properly.

The lack of candor in the secretary's testimony consists of his re-fusal to come to grips with the matter of intent. The administration is presented as though it were a giant logic machine, which receives an external stimulus, computes the most appropriate response, and acts on the basis of that computation. There are no hunches, intuitions, or moral reservations. Thoughts that are not represented by specific, identifiable factual statements, do not exist at all. At no time in his testimony did the secretary admit to the slightest possibility that the United States could be, in any way, responsible for the incident in the Gulf of Tonkin or that any of our actions could have been provocative or could be considered as provocative. Mr. McNamara's account of U.S. policy is like Sartre's description of a woman who flirts without admitting to herself that she is flirting. She manages this act of bad faith by concentrating on the facts. Her movements, her gestures are merely what they are. They are devoid of any meaning beyond the present moment. She has no intentions, but she can be aroused if her companion causes something to happen to her.[27]

VI

The *Pentagon Papers*, which were published in 1971, suggest that President Johnson and his advisors "lied" to Congress and to the American people.[28] Both the Pentagon historians' and the *New York Times* account of these events strongly support the conclusion that the president had secret plans for bombing North Vietnam, that he concealed these plans until after the elections of 1964 and until he could get congressional approval for his resolution. There is a further suggestion in this account—implied, if not directly stated—that Congress and "the people" would not have approved of the president's plans if they had only known the truth.

The hearing by the Senate Committee on Foreign Relations gives us a picture of a secretary of defense with his back to the wall, his earlier bad faith clearly exposed, and now forced into a deeper cynicism. The senators appear relentless in their search for the causes of the Tonkin Gulf incident. But we must remember that this hearing was conducted in 1968, almost four years after the event. Were Congress and the American people really as innocent as we are led to believe? Were they really tricked by a crafty president and his secretary of defense who sought power for themselves, contemptuous of the desire of the people for peace? Did we inadvertently elect a scoundrel as president of the United States or did we—Congress and the people, you and I—really know what we were doing all along?

Let us begin with Congress. In his first testimony on behalf of the Tonkin Gulf resolution on August 6, 1964, we do not find Secretary McNamara under any serious pressure. Several basic "disagreeable questions" had been identified for which the administration expected it would have to provide answers in order to assure public support. Almost none of these questions were asked by Congress at that time.[29] As to the incident itself there was a certain vagueness on both sides. The secretary was able to speak in generalities. The navy "was not aware of any South Vietnamese actions." The *Maddox* was carrying out a "routine patrol." There was no connection between the patrol and "any action by South Vietnam."[30] Was the secretary consciously lying? Probably not. He was deliberately vague and somewhat abstract in his discussion of the "navy," having reference to two things at the same time. But he found justification for his vagueness on the ground that he was dealing with classified information.

In allowing him to gloss over the details, Congress accepted a euphemism in place of an outright lie. The euphemism serves a double purpose. It not only substitutes a nice inoffensive phrase for one that might be more detailed and direct; it also helps the individual hide exactly what he is saying from himself. At that time, of course, many of the specific messages from the *Maddox* were not available. Congressional leaders did not know of the American role in Operation 34A, and, what is more important, they probably did not want to know. The only exceptions were Senators Wayne Morse and Ernest Gruening, who voted against the resolution. (Both of whom faced a lack of support by their own constituents when they came up for reelection.) But several other details were available. Senator Morse had learned that boats manned by South Vietnamese crews had attacked two North Vietnamese islands on July 30, less than a week before the incident and that we had supplied the boats for the raid. At the same hearing Senator Frank Church asked Secretary of State Dean Rusk, "I take it that our government which supplied these boats . . . did know that the boats would be used for attacks on North Vietnamese targets, and that we acquiesced in that policy, is that correct?" Rusk replied, "In the larger sense, that is so, but as far as any particular detail is concerned we don't from Washington follow that in great detail."[31] This is another way of saying, "We let them have the boats, but we don't ask them what they are doing with them. We don't want to know."

When Senator George McGovern later mentioned the July 30 attacks during the debate on the Tonkin Gulf resolution, Senator Fulbright replied that he had been assured by the administration that "our boats did not convoy or support or back up any South Vietnamese naval vessels."[32] Although several liberal senators made critical remarks at the time the resolution was offered, it was clearly the support of Senator Fulbright that carried the day for the administration. Fulbright was a well-known opponent of escalation. But he was also, at that time, a close personal friend of President Johnson. Many congressmen allowed themselves to believe that if Fulbright supported the resolution it must be all right.[33]

But the passage of the resolution cannot be so easily explained. If one finds a group of liberal senators voting for a resolution to give the president authority to widen the war, one must ask why. Most of them recognized later that they had made a "mistake" in not opposing the resolution. How was such a mistake made? Clearly, Fulbright was influential, but he did not have to twist any arms. What was in it for the senators themselves? I believe there are three reasons (which I will mention in order of their importance) why the Tonkin Gulf Resolution found so much support in Congress. (1) The senators did not believe their constituents would support a direct opposition to the president on this matter. The war protest movement was in its infancy, and there was still strong opposition to a complete withdrawal from Vietnam. If the senators opposed the resolution their constituents might later accuse them of tying the hands of the commander-in-chief of our armed forces. Thus, although they felt uncomfortable about the war, they were also doubtful about the popularity of complete unqualified opposition. (2) The president offered to relieve their own responsibility by a resolution that would grant him a wider authority—and also a larger share of the blame for failure. These two factors were augmented by (3) the fact that most of the liberals were Democrats as was the president. They did not want the Republicans supporting an important aspect of administration policy while they opposed it. Thus came the great capitulation of liberals in the U.S. Senate. The resolution passed 88 to 2 in the Senate and 416 to 0 in the House. To say that all these senators and representatives were "tricked" by misinformation is to give the administration a much higher mark for credibility than it had at the time. If the congressmen were deceived, it was because they lacked a sense of the outrageous absurdity of the Vietnam War. Although they were later to argue with one another about who had spoken against the war first, it was clear that, in 1964 at least, congressional leaders believed there was a strong support for our continued presence in Vietnam.

Why, then, was Barry Goldwater not elected president? Certainly he was much more honest in regard to what he intended to do about the war. However, he also left no room for the people to deceive themselves about what he was doing. Goldwater made a fundamental mistake in his assessment of the American people. He knew there was strong support for the war in Vietnam, but he assumed that this support was based on a hard-headed acceptance of the position that we were advancing our own interest. He recognized our desire for success but not our need to have this success clothed in virtue. The American people like to be told that they are not really interested in personal gain, but that they are protecting mankind. Under this subterfuge we could lay waste a continent. But to justify all the killing on the grounds that we were out to improve our influence in the world—this sounded crass and rather inhumane. Furthermore, to say that we were going to bomb North Vietnam sounded provocative. It is American policy to provoke without intending to provoke, to wait for a response to this provocation, and then to attack in massive force. Johnson had it right all along. He promised us "no wider war" but he understood—and we understood, of course—that one cannot tolerate insults, deliberate attacks against a patrol ship "on the high seas."

VII

But now we come to the more serious charge of the *Pentagon Papers*, namely, that President Johnson had secret plans for bombing North Vietnam even while he was campaigning against Senator Goldwater and promising not to widen the war. Furthermore, it is asserted that there was a "general consensus" among Johnson's advisors to bomb North Vietnam at a White House strategy meeting on September 7, 1964.[34] President Johnson's account of the events of 1964–1965 varies, but in general he contends that he made no final decision to bomb North Vietnam until February 7, 1965, despite strong military pressure to do so.[35] In this statement he does not deny the extensive contingency plans for bombing and the selection of specific targets. He probably has reference to the fact that he had not yet given the final "go" signal and so, technically, he could still change his mind. In a similar manner President Kennedy allowed planning to continue for the invasion of Cuba, always in the belief that, since he had not yet given the order to launch the invasion, he could stop the operation at any moment. This attitude is characteristic of the Western compartmentalization of actions. To make contingency plans and to encourage others to believe that these plans will be carried out is to initiate a whole series of unseen acts and preparations for action. These actions were all part of the total movement toward expansion of the war.

The statement that the president "lied" about his war plans, as well as Johnson's later accusation that Fulbright really knew what the administration was planning all along,[36] are both misleading. Statements of this kind do not face up to the great cooperative project in bad faith that was a product of the efforts of both Congress and the administration at the time. There is no doubt that the administration misled Congress, both in regard to the full extent of our provocation in the Tonkin Gulf incident and in regard to administration plans for escalation of the war. But the misleading statements were made in the context of a general agreement that the Tonkin Gulf Resolution was necessary. There was a tacit assumption on the part of the administration that Congress wanted a convincing story that would justify their release of power to President Johnson. Therefore, the strongest possible case was prepared, including the use of certain ambiguous statements, which made it seem that we were attacked without provocation. When Congress failed to press hard for a complete revelation of our involvement, the administration assumed they had full support. On the other hand, no one *really knew* what Lyndon Johnson was going to do until he did it. Even on February 7, 1965, the date when Johnson admitted that he had decided to bomb North Vietnam and a full-scale attack was launched against Vietcong barracks in the North, the raid was announced as another reprisal for Vietcong raids and terrorist attacks in the South. Mr. Johnson ordered American families home from Vietnam at the same time, but he "made it clear, however, that the air strike was a limited response rather than a signal for a general expansion of the guerrilla warfare."[37] Like the 64 sortie "reprisals" that followed the incident in the Gulf of Tonkin, this air attack was described as a retaliation for something that had been done to us, a response rather than an expression of general policy.

VIII

The public justification for our involvement in Vietnam was that we were helping a "free people" fight communism. At the same time it was explained that we were not giving anything away. We had commercial interests in Vietnam as well. After 1964 the administration began to speak with increasing frequency, in its own private circle, of our need to remain in Vietnam to avoid a humiliating American defeat. Under such circumstances one might assume that we would avoid similar temptations to intervene in the affairs of another nation. However, on April 24, 1965, just nine months after Tonkin, a group of rebels in the Dominican Republic captured the major radio station in Santo Domingo and announced the overthrow of the government. Was this too a threat to the status of the United States as a world power?

NOTES

1. U.S., Congress, Senate, *Senate Executive Document 34*, 33rd Cong., 2d sess., p. 58; message of the President of the United States transmitting a Report of the Secretary of the Navy, in compliance with a resolution of the Senate of December 6, 1954, calling for correspondence, etc., relative to the naval expedition to Japan.

2. Ibid., p. 57.

3. Ibid., p. 8.

4. F. Dostoyevsky, *The Brothers Karamazov* (New York: Random House, 1950), pp. 264–332, 734–771.

5. D. D. Eisenhower, *Vital Speeches of the Day* (New York: City News Publishing, 1953), pp. 696–698.

6. On November 6, 1964, in a memo on U.S. aims, Assistant Secretary of Defense John T. McNaughton, placed "the protection of United States reputation" first on the list. By March 1965 he had quantified these aims, possibly at the request of Secretary McNamara. Protection of U.S. reputation was listed as 70 percent of our reason for continuing the war in Vietnam. See N. Sheehan, et al., *The Pentagon Papers* (New York: Bantam, 1971), pp. 365, 432.

7. Sheehan, *The Pentagon Papers*, pp. 234–241.

8. "Red PT Boats Fire on U.S. Destroyer on Vietnam Duty," *New York Times*, August 3, 1964, p. 1.

9. *New York Times*, August 6, 1964, p. 8.

10. Ibid.

11. *New York Times*, August 6, 1964, p. 8.

12. U.S., Congress, Senate, Committee on Foreign Relations, *The Gulf of Tonkin, The 1964 Incidents: Hearing*, 20 February 1968, p. 95.

13. Ibid., p. 26.

14. Ibid., pp. 44–45.

15. Ibid., pp. 49–50.

16. Ibid., p. 33.

17. Ibid., pp. 42–43.

18. Ibid., pp. 29–30.

19. Ibid., p. 31.

20. Ibid., p. 33.

21. Ibid., pp. 33–34.

22. Ibid., p. 97.

23. Ibid., p. 101.

24. Ibid., pp. 83–84.

25. Ibid., p. 19.

26. Ibid., p. 87.

27. J.-P. Sartre, *Existential Psychoanalysis*, trans. Hazel E. Barnes (Chicago: Henry Regnery, 1966), pp. 172–175.

28. Sheehan, *The Pentagon Papers*, pp. 307–330.

29. Ibid., pp. 257, 269.

30. Ibid., p. 265.

31. Ibid., pp. 265–266.

32. Ibid., p. 267.

33. In fairness to Senator Fulbright it should be mentioned that he was later to make several public apologies for his failure to inquire into the details of the Tonkin Gulf incident. His persistence in leading the later investigation of the incident was due, in part, to the feeling that he should make some attempt to counter the effect of his earlier support for the resolution. At the 1968 hearing he remarked:

> I went on the floor to urge passage of the resolution. You [McNamara] quoted me as saying these things on the floor. Of course, all my statements were based upon your testimony. I had no independent evidence, and now I think I did a great disservice to the Senate. I feel very guilty for not having enough sense at that time to have raised these questions and asked for evidence. I regret it. I have publicly apologized to my constituents and the country for the unwise action I took, without at least inquiring into the basis . . . I feel a very deep responsibility, and I regret it more than anything I have ever done in my life, that I was the vehicle which took that resolution to the floor and defended it . . . [*Washington Post*, February 25, 1968, section D, pp. 5–8, section E, pp. 1–2.]

Although Fulbright says he was misinformed, he does not offer this misinformation as a justification for his own behavior. He accepts the responsibility and does not attempt to deny the powerful role he played in influencing others to support the resolution. Senator Gore seems to have taken a position similar to that of Fulbright. He accused Secretary McNamara of having misled Congress and the people, but added, "I know I have been misled. It may be partly my fault. I am not excusing myself."

34. Sheehan, *The Pentagon Papers*, p. 307.

35. "As Lyndon Johnson Sees It," *Newsweek*, June 28, 1971, pp. 22–23.

36. Ibid.

37. T. Wicker, "Capital Is Tense," *New York Times*, February 8, 1965, p. 1

8

The
Intervention
in
Santo Domingo

I

As the previous chapter has indicated, there is sometimes a fine line between the process of self-deception (which is a socially acceptable form of behavior for American leaders) and the deliberate lie (which violates one of the important taboos of our culture). The American intervention in the crisis in Santo Domingo offers an opportunity to study the process of self-deception in more detail. It illustrates a point that has already begun to emerge from our previous investigations: that self-deception is, like the lie, a deliberate act, in which the decision to fool one's self must take place with the active will and cooperation of the self.

Sometimes the aides of an administrator may deceive him, but here, too, there must be a tacit aquiescence on the part of the leader, a refusal to question information critically because of a personal desire to see things in a certain way. Thus, although it is possible to be deceived by others or to be the "victim" of one's unconscious needs, the "victim" appears less innocent as we penetrate deeper into his dynamics. At some point, it appears, he asks to be deceived. He refuses to look at the information that might warn him, or he deliberately contrives a situation that will give him false information. He suggests, perhaps inadvertently, perhaps not so inadvertently, the kind of information he requires for the action he plans to take. If his aides and advisers know his proclivities, they will be able to "think for him" when they make inquiries. It is not necessary for the leader to find the false information and, being aware of its false nature, tell himself a lie. It is only necessary that he create the appropriate atmosphere and not make a critical examination of his sources.

Our policy in Santo Domingo was born in a moment of fear of communists. We implemented it with support for the military junta, which had toppled the elected government of Juan Bosch from power. To stabilize the situation, we found a General Imbert, whom we believed to be a national hero, and helped him form a government. By the time we recognized that he was not a popular figure among the Dominican people, he had achieved so much power that he was difficult to dislodge. During the process of his removal, the United States proposed a dizzying round of successors from Joaquin Belaguer, a chief figure in the Trujillo government, who had served the dictator for 30 years, to the more moderate Héctor Garcia Godoy. In a chapter of such limited scope we cannot hope to trace all of the factors behind this confusing series of actions. The most critical decision was that involving the American military intervention in the Dominican Republic and the suppression of the democratic revolution. It is this step that we will attempt to follow in the present analysis.

II

On May 31, 1961, General Rafael Trujillo, one of the most brutal dictators in South America, was assassinated on George Washington Avenue in Santo Domingo. Following his death many of the leaders of exiled democratic forces began to return to the Dominican Republic. In December 1962 Juan Bosch became the first president of the Dominican Republic to be placed in office through free elections. He was the candidate of the Dominican Revolutionary Party (PRD), a party respected throughout Latin America as the embodiment of the democratic left. Bosch had returned from 26 years of exile after spending a number of years in various South American countries. He had fled Cuba when Batista had ordered him deported to the

Dominican Republic. He returned to Cuba in 1959, but left again in 1960 when he became convinced that Castro had betrayed the Cuban revolution to communism. The election of Juan Bosch by a 2 to 1 majority was hailed by President Kennedy as a clear victory for the democratic forces in the Dominican Republic. In 1963 Kennedy sent Vice-President Johnson and Senator Hubert Humphrey to attend the inauguration of President Bosch.

On the morning of September 25, 1963, the short-lived democracy of President Bosch came to an end when he was overthrown by a military coup. The United States immediately withdrew all economic and military aid to the Dominican Republic, and the PRD began the struggle to return Bosch to power. On April 24, 1965, a group of military and civilian rebels captured the major radio station in Santo Domingo, announced the overthrow of the government and demanded the return of their exiled leader, Juan Bosch. Within hours, crowds of people filled the streets with their celebration, and the Dominican revolution was underway.

But somehow the attitude in the United States toward Juan Bosch had changed since the day of his inauguration. Diplomatic memories are short. There was a new administration in the United States and a new American ambassador to the Dominican Republic. The new American president had recognized the junta government on the grounds that it was anticommunist, and the government had provided evidence of its sentiment by initiating a military expedition against what was described as "communist guerrillas" in the Cibao region. This was followed by the killing of sixteen rebels including their leader, Manual Tavarez Justo.[1] So brutal was the killing that the junta-backed president, Emilio de los Santos, a Dominican elder statesman, had resigned in protest. Nevertheless, the junta government was on good terms with the United States, and its position strengthened against the return to power of Juan Bosch.

Thus, when the revolution began, the American embassy was less than enthusiastic about this new turn of events, which threatened to upset an anticommunist government, even if it meant the restoration of the Dominican constitution. Within a few days after the revolution began, messages were arriving in Washington from our embassy in Santo Domingo, suggesting a serious threat of communism in the revolutionary movement. However, the unpopularity of the government of the new Dominican leader, Donald Reid Corbal, had been evident ever since the resignation of the highly respected de los Santos.[2] When Reid asked for U.S. aid for his forces on April 25, he was given no encouragement.[3] It is reported that Juan Bosch asked for a "United States presence" to ensure an orderly transfer of power on the same date. He was also denied this assistance.[4]

But the rebels within the military had begun to arm civilians. They hauled several thousand guns into downtown Santo Domingo and began passing them out to crowds in the streets. They were evidently acting on the assumption that the people, if armed, would fight beside them. It was at this point that the CIA reported an eyewitness who "saw Castro/Communist leaders joining them [the rebels] in their work."[5] The arming of civilians continued through Tuesday, April 27. In the meantime Reid resigned and Colonel Pedro Bartolome Benoit was appointed head of the junta. On April 27 the rebel leaders presented themselves at the U.S. embassy, seeking the aid of the United States as a mediator in the crisis in order to avoid further bloodshed. There are contradictory stories concerning why the United States failed to mediate at this point, but it is clear that the rebel leaders returned from their interview with the American ambassador, William Tapley Bennett, convinced that the United States was not an uninvolved neutral, but a supporter of the loyalist forces, and that the refusal to mediate was based on a conviction that the rebel forces were losing the conflict.[6]

Actually the rebels themselves considered their situation desperate at the time of their appeal to Bennett. On the afternoon of April 27 General Wessin y Wessin's tanks were on the verge of entering the city of Santo Domingo. But for some reason the Wessin forces failed to press their attack, and the rebel forces gained further support. By the morning of April 28 an American military assistance officer, sent by Ambassador Bennett to San Isidro Air Base to gain some information, reported the loyalist commanders discouraged and disorganized. The advance on the city was halted.[7] Now it was the turn of the junta forces to ask for help from the United States. Ambassador Bennett responded with a request to Washington for communication equipment for the junta air force general. His request was denied, but after he had repeated it with the warning that the issue was between Castroism and its opponents, Washington finally complied.[8] However, it soon became clear that communication equipment would not do the job. The rebel forces had wide popular support. Armed civilians roamed the streets, and rebel machine guns were being installed on the roof tops. The morale of the junta forces was dangerously low. It was at this point that the decision was made to send in the U.S. Marines to crush the rebels. In order to avoid the accusation that the United States was engaged in a military intervention in the internal affairs of Santo Domingo, it was necessary to find some justification for this intervention.

Ambassador Bennett had already learned from his previous call for communication equipment, that if he did not use the right words in his requests, they would be denied.[9] The same thing happened in the first call for U.S. military support. In midafternoon on April 28 Colonel Bartolome Benoit, head of the junta asked a second time for U.S. troops to prevent a "communist takeover." His message was in writing, but it made no mention of the danger to American lives. The request was passed to Washington, and it was denied.[10] It is Senator Clark who tells us what happened next.

> Ambassador Bennett sent word back [to the junta], "I can't get away with bringing Americans in on that ground [Communist takeover] because the evidence is not clear. If you will change your request and make it in writing, and ask American forces to intervene in order to protect American lives, then I believe that we can persuade Washington to do it.[11]

It was in this manner that the understanding of how to phrase the request was communicated to the junta general in the field. Both parties knew the real purpose for the American troops, but the administration required a justification that did not violate the OAS charter and that would be acceptable to Congress and the American people. Senators and other opinion leaders who opposed the U.S. intervention in Santo Domingo were later to accuse Ambassador Bennett of deceiving the administration. If this were the case, he surely had extensive aid from within the highest quarters of the government. What probably happened is that the ambassador first deceived himself in regard to the extent of communist infiltration within the rebel movement.[12] Once he was convinced of the danger of a communist takeover, a certain poetic exaggeration of the situation seemed more justifiable.

The full extent to which the danger was exaggerated, and by whom, is still not clear. We do not know, for example, whether it was Ambassador Bennett or the president's own interpretation of Bennett's remarks that was responsible for the now famous "under-the-table" story. In any event, this tale arrived at the opportune moment, when President Johnson was briefing selected congressional leaders on the action it would be necessary for him to take to "protect American lives." Senator Smathers recalls that the president's remarks were interrupted by a telephone call from Ambassador Bennett who "said that he was at that moment under the table and the bullets were coming through the window and surging all around him."[13] The embassy later denied this story, and Tad Szulc, on the scene in Santo Domingo, reported there were no bullet marks on the walls of the American embassy.[14]

The president concluded his briefing for the congressmen and then made his official statement regarding U.S. intervention in the Dominican crisis on April 28. It was a brief report, announcing that

the threat to American lives was the basis for the action and appeal-
ing for a cease-fire.[15] A few days later he provided a longer account,
still maintaining the position that the U.S. armed forces had become
involved only to protect American lives and insisting that American
forces had "attacked no one." However, the second speech had a
more ominous note. It was clear by this time that the rebel forces
were moving rapidly toward victory. If the United States could not
oppose them with an effective military resistance, they would soon
control the country. It was at this point that President Johnson described the "communist takeover" of the revolutionary movement.

> The revolutionary movement took a tragic turn. Communist leaders,
> many of them trained in Cuba, seeing a chance to increase disorder, to
> gain a foothold, joined the revolution. They took increasing control.
> And what began as a popular democratic revolution, committed to
> democracy and social justice, very shortly moved and was taken over
> and really seized and placed in the hands of a band of Communist
> conspirators.[16]

Like the previous "under-the-table" story, this tale was not a deliberate fabrication. What had happened was that the United States had
opposed the pro-Bosch forces from the beginning and had actively
supported the formation of a strong military junta to crush them. In
the first few days of the revolution American officials anticipated a
communist threat long before it materialized. On Monday afternoon,
April 26, William Connett, the chargé d'affairs at the embassy
warned the U.S. State Department that, while Bosch's popularity
precluded direct U.S. intervention against his party, the pro-Bosch
movement must be stopped or there would be "extremism in six
months" in the Dominican Republic.[17]

From the time the U.S. Marines first landed in Santo Domingo,
American correspondents reported the evidence that U.S. forces
were opposing the rebel movement and giving logistic support to
their opponents.[18] Of course, it was impossible to conceal the true
purpose of American intervention from the U.S. military leaders.
Military commanders could not wait for each order from Washington before taking action. They must know the general approach, or
they might fail to do their job. The orders were intended for the top-
ranking officers and were not to be revealed to newsmen. But on the
day the American troops landed, one of the chief U.S. naval commanders made the statement that we were going in to crush the
communists.[19]

When Ambassador Bennett made it clear that he expected the
rebel forces to surrender, Molina Ureña and other democratic leaders
became disillusioned about the role of the United States in the re-

volution. Many of them left the pro-Bosch forces at this point. If the communists gained strength within the rebel movement, it was not due to their cleverness at infiltration, but the fact that the Americans had abandoned the rebel cause.[20]

III

If the first evidence of U.S. opposition to the pro-Bosch PRD party in Santo Domingo came from the American embassy, there was clearly a strong predisposition in Congress to believe that the PRD was "communist-dominated," even before the president included such remarks in his public speeches. The day after President Johnson's speech about intervention to "save American lives" and while he was still protesting U.S. neutrality, Representative Mendel Rivers asserted, as fact, that

> those now in charge [of the rebel forces] have been oriented, trained, and directly identified with Castro's Cuba and that they are Communists. There is no question about this. It has been established . . . Had he (President Johnson) not acted, Castro—and it was his intention to do so—could well have taken charge in the Dominican Republic. We cannot and must not permit such a thing to happen as happened in Cuba.[21]

His remarks were echoed by a number of other members of the House of Representatives. On that same day, on the other side of Capitol Hill, Senator Smathers also warned that the Bosch forces were infiltrated with communists and that the United States could not let the Dominican Republic become "another Cuba."[22]

Although Rivers and Smathers implied that the democratic forces within the Bosch movement had been replaced by communists, it was Senator Eastland of Mississippi who came out in opposition to Bosch himself. Speaking on behalf of Senators Dirksen and Hruska, as well as himself, he called for "a firm stand by the United States against the return to power in the Dominican Republic of Juan Bosch." While he had to admit that "Juan Bosch himself is probably not a Communist Party member," he insisted that Bosch would prove to be a "second Fidel Castro" and that he was already an "ideological Communist." Eastland concluded that the United States must, therefore, "take whatever action is required to prevent the establishment in Santo Domingo of another Communist bastion in the Western Hemisphere."[23] Toward the close of the Senator's remarks, Senator Hruska arose and the two of them sang an anticommunist duet together, ending with a chorus of the domino theory. After they described the inevitable fall of Haiti, which would

be a natural consequence of the communist takeover of the Dominican Republic, Senator Hruska remarked, "Once the dominoes started
to fall in that area further exploitation and further occupation would
surely follow."[24]

The Eastland speech was a clear manifestation of the opposition to
Juan Bosch among the conservatives in the United States. But it
revealed more than that. In the "evidence" that Eastland presented
there were comments by right-wing writers, newspaper columnists,
and excerpts from a memorandum prepared by the research staff of
the Internal Security Subcommittee that indicated a strong opposition to Bosch among the conservative forces in the United States
when he was first being hailed by the Kennedy Administration as
one of the enlightened reformers of South America. At that time it
was difficult to oppose him, since he had just been chosen as president in a free election in which he had received 58 percent of the
votes. However, once he attempted a return to power there was no
question that he was regarded as a dangerous man by those who
wished to prevent reform movements from spreading in South
America.

Thus, there were many influences in the United States (in addition to the information from the embassy) that formed the
background for the president's decision to send U.S. forces to Santo
Domingo. Although it is not clear to what extent the president was
willing to admit to himself what he was doing, it is evident that the
story he told the American people differed markedly from what was
happening. On Sunday, May 2, the day of President Johnson's
speech announcing that U.S. soldiers had "attacked no one,"[25]
paratroopers from the 82nd Airborne Division had already landed at
the junta-held air base at San Isidro and moved out against the rebel
forces on the Duarte bridge. They had captured the bridge under
heavy fighting, using bazookas, 106mm recoilless rifles and machine
guns, and penetrated into the city of Santo Domingo against rebel
counterfire. In the action on the bridge, Tad Szulc reports, four
American paratroopers were wounded in the fighting and "the extent of the casualties among the rebels and the civilian population of
the densely inhabited downtown section of Santo Domingo is not
known. But American troops had superior and devastating fire
power."[26]

Although American troops had set up an International Safety
Zone near the Hotel Embajador, the action on the Duarte bridge was
clearly not related to the protection of American lives. Again it was
Tad Szulc who clarified the situation.

> Since there were no American or other foreigners to be evacuated from
> the rural and urban areas lying between San Isidro and the Ozama

River [spanned by the Duarte bridge], the move by the Airborne Division obviously was a military operation designed to serve a political
purpose.

That political purpose was unquestionably to prevent the collapse
of the Benoit junta. . . . This was the first instance in which United
States troops had entered into direct combat with the organized forces
of Colonel Camaño [the rebel leader]. By any reasonable standard—or
so it seemed to many of the American newsmen on the scene—this
was also a direct intervention in the Dominican civil war, despite the
continuing claims in Washington that the U.S. still remained neutral
in the conflict.[27]

So much for the remark that American troops had attacked no one. In
the same Sunday speech the president also said that the form of the
Dominican government was "a matter for the Dominican people."[28]
At that moment, our former ambassador, John Bartlow Martin, was
negotiating with General Imbert, one of the conspirators responsible
for the ouster of President Bosch, to ask him to assume the leadership of a new Dominican government. At this point, a total of 14,000
American troops had landed in the Dominican Republic, a number
far beyond that necessary for the protection of American lives.

As Dean Rusk was later to remark, the negotiations between Martin and Imbert were "unofficial."[29] That is, Martin was not acting as
a salaried member of the State Department at the time. Nevertheless,
he had been called in as a consultant by the administration and there
was no doubt that he was representing the United States. Mr. Rusk
appeared rather embarrassed about this in his press conference. Both
Rusk and Martin tried to deny that there was any deliberate attempt
to set up a government. Such things happen, according to the American style, inadvertently and not because we intended it that way. If
a government is formed, everyone is surprised. Theodore Draper
described this inadvertent formation of a government as follows.

On May 26, Secretary of State Rusk blandly told a news conference:
"As far as the civilian–military group under General Imbert's leadership is concerned, we did encourage them to form a group that could
try to assure the normal process of the countryside which was not
involved in downtown Santo Domingo. From these words one might
infer that Imbert was "encouraged" to form a "group" to "help"
[whom?] to deal with [what?] problems outside the capitol. In fact,
Imbert set up what he called a "Government of National Reconstruction," which Mr. Martin says "began to behave surprisingly like a
government." Since by the time Mr. Rusk spoke, it had already appointed a foreign minister and representatives to the United Nations
and the O.A.S., and demanded all the rights and privileges accorded to
legitimate governments, it is difficult to understand the Secretary's
language. One can hardly recall a Secretary of State afflicted with such
squeamishness . . . We are asked to believe, then, that two "private
citizens," John Bartlow Martin and Antonio Imbert Barreras, had a

private little conversation out of which came a "group" which surprisingly behaved like a government.[30]

Because the human consciousness is opaque, it is not possible to determine exactly when an administration official is lying and when he is deceiving himself about what really happened. Of course, it is less dangerous if he is lying, for at least he knows what he is trying to do and his discussions with other officials involve deliberate moves to promote the ends he desires. However, there are aspects of our culture that work against this kind of lucidity. The need to be good as well as powerful is an American dilemma, and one need is often fused with the other in the execution of policy.

The imposition of a military junta on a people struggling for their freedom is not consistent with American values, even if it tends to promote American interest. As in the Gulf of Tonkin incident, the significance of such an action must be veiled by blinding one's self to the information available at the moment. If a decision is made swiftly, for immediate objectives such as keeping the peace, it is possible to isolate one's self from an awareness of its consequences. Both the rushing in of American troops and the selection of Imbert had immediate objectives that could be defended in terms of American interest. They were rationalized as temporary measures to keep the peace. The implication was that we wanted to stop the fighting and that we could give the people an opportunity to choose their government at some later date. But despite the size of the American forces, we could not restore order without making use of the only organized military force indigenous to Santo Domingo. Thus, our troops fought side by side with the junta forces in the name of expediency, a temporary measure to restore order. In doing so, we made it unmistakably clear which side we favored. One does not help the military kill rebel soldiers and then remain neutral in an election.

IV

One of the problems in examining any decision after the fact is that the decision maker has a strong tendency to explain his behavior in a cause-and-effect context. He is inclined to ignore such matters as his own preparatory set (his expectations of what is about to happen) and describe his behavior as though he made a series of logical decisions, based on the changes in the situation and the "evidence" he received. This tendency is, in part, a reflection of our cultural bias in the direction of explanation by evidence. It is also a means of concealing one's intentions. If every decision is merely a matter of the person making a logical deduction from present facts in the light of his memory of past events, like the operations of a computer, it is devoid of moral implications. If everything is a matter of logic, one can avoid altogether the problem of good and evil. Wrong decisions are merely "mistakes" based on an imcomplete knowledge of the facts or information that is later proved to be false. With this conception of human behavior, the question of an awareness of one's intention is irrelevant. One does not have to deny the existence of intent. One simply ignores it. It is there, but it does not play a part in the decision.

However, the attempt to conceal one's intent by a logical explanation of what happened often proves to be a cumbersome process. The more logical the reasons for behavior in a diplomatic crisis, the more people are inclined to feel there is something left unsaid. Sometimes the very profusion of facts and evidence that are marshalled to explain one's behavior gives people the feeling that one is protesting too much. For the first intimation that another person is being false comes, not from the facts, but from a sense of one's own feelings. It is an awareness that is based on our capacity for empathy with others. It is this hunch that induces us to push hard on the facts to see if they will give way.

It may have been the assertion of American "neutrality," as our warships steamed into the Caribbean, that first alerted newsmen to the fact that we had reached a crisis of intent, an intent that could not be openly avowed because it would not hold up in the eyes of the world. The claim of American neutrality toward the Dominican revolution was an exaggeration that passed even beyond the official U.S. attitude during the Cuban crisis—in which our sympathy with the Cuban exiles was admitted and we denied only military involvement.

As Senator Fulbright was later to remark, U.S. policy during the Dominican crisis was characterized by a lack of candor throughout the whole affair.[31] The sad story of a communist takeover prior to American intervention has never been confirmed. The implication that the administration was initially sympathetic to the pro-Bosch forces and changed its policy because of the evidence of communist infiltration is clearly false. These were the "facts" that were brought in after the intervention to support the American action in helping to crush the rebel forces. Theodore Draper has presented a brief, but convincing refutation of the administration position.

> President Johnson and other U.S. spokesmen have sought to concentrate public attention on the events of April 27 and 28, when U.S. lives were allegedly in immediate danger, the Boschist movement had allegedly collapsed, and the Communists had allegedly taken over, to

justify U.S. military intervention. They have been notably reticent about the actual policy in the first two to four days, except to imply that they were initially sympathetic to a popular democratic revolution that went out of control. This claim of initial sympathy has never been very persuasive because it was not matched by any actions that might have been expected to flow from it. The least that might have been expected was some slight effort to make contact with Juan Bosch, the avowed and acknowledged leader of the "popular democratic revolution" . . . The failure to show the slightest interest in Bosch was, however, only a negative reason for suspecting that official U.S. sympathy with the Boschist revolution might have been a literary afterthought to make the actual intervention somewhat more palatable. But now we have more positive reasons for this suspicion—the repeated Washington instructions in favor of a military junta, the increasingly anti-Bosch tenor of the embassy's messages, and above all, the evidence pointing to the military attaché's pressures before April 27 and possibly as early as April 24 for Dominican air and naval attacks on the pro-Bosch forces. The difference between what President Johnson said about the "popular democratic revolution that was committed to democracy and social justice" and what was done about it has become almost incredibly grotesque.[32]

V

Although Senator Fulbright had expressed criticism of both Democratic and Republican administrations and had warned against the American-backed invasion of Cuba, it had not been his style in the past to play the maverick and openly oppose an administration controlled by his own party. Somehow the Dominican crisis served as a turning point in his attitude. Following the suppression of the Dominican revolution by a United States-supported military junta he prepared a major foreign policy address in which he said, in effect, that our policy in the Dominican Republic had been a mistake and that this error was merely a reflection of the generally wrong direction in which U.S. policy had been moving in recent years.[33] It was a painful step for Fulbright. He had long been a personal friend of President Johnson, and he attempted to take the sting out of his words by saying that the president had been given poor advice. "On the basis of the information and counsel he received," said Fulbright, "the President could hardly have acted other than he did."[34] Senator Clark, who supported Fulbright, also insisted that his criticism of U.S. policy was not a criticism of the president. In response to a defense of the president by a Democratic colleague, he asserted:

I pointed out then, and I point out again, that nobody is attacking the President of the United States—neither the Senator from Arkansas [Fulbright] nor I . . . I think the Senator from Florida [Smathers] and the Senator from Louisiana [Long] really do a disservice and an injustice to the Senator from Arkansas by trying to say that he or I or anybody else is attacking the President of the United States . . . That is not the issue. The issue is: Was the advice that came to the President of the United States accurate?"[35]

Of course this was not the real issue. Both Fulbright and Clark were aware of this, but their own position as fellow Democrats and the tradition in the Senate against open criticism of the president of the United States had influenced them to mute their remarks to one of "faulty information." But there was never any question of the president's final responsibility for American actions nor his responsibility to question his sources of information. The president of the United States is not a machine that receives data, adds up the score, and produces an automatic response. The responsibility that the president bears is indeed a great one, but there has never been any doubt that it is *his* burden. In electing a human for president of the United States, we assume the existence of something beyond the ability to make logical deductions from information that has already been placed in neat categories like the bits in a computer. The human consciousness is not a black box that is independent of the data it receives. It becomes part of the data, merges with it, and extends into the world beyond it. Although it is possible to deal with the world in terms of categories and numbers, this is essentially a denial of one's full awareness, a denial of nuance and shades of meaning, a denial of the shifting transcendental nature of reality. This has never been as evident as it is today when machines can sense, categorize information, perform logical operations, and do almost everything except be aware of themselves and their relationship to the world.

There are many factors, often the very personal ones that make us human, that may interfere with judgement and cause us to deny certain things that are difficult to face. It may be that there is a limit to the capacity of anyone to face reality all the time. We cannot continue with our faculties extended at every moment. This is a problem faced by national leaders as well as other mortals, and it may have been a recognition of this fact that enabled Senators Fulbright and Clark to understand the president's reluctance to question the information he received from his own embassy—information that was so congruent with his expectations.

But what happens if we accept this "information failure" as an explanation of the problem? If we excuse the president for believing the ambassador, must we not also excuse the ambassador for believing his sources? Men who have faced the responsibility of high office and have had to make decisions under stress are all too familiar with the vulnerability of the human consciousness under such circumstances. Sometimes all decisions seem wrong. It is not surprising, therefore, that ambassadors, like presidents, have colleagues or former colleagues who will say, "It wasn't his fault; he received bad information." In commenting on the behavior of William Tapely Bennett, John Bartlow Martin, the former U.S. ambassador to the Dominican Republic remarks, "It is extremely disagreeable to second-guess any Ambassador. Moreover, no Ambassador can know everything; to a considerable extent he must rely on what he is told."[36]

If we agree with Senator Clark that the important question is whether the president had accurate information, we will become lost in the labyrinth of information know-how, where Americans are already second to none. If we see the problem as a technical one, involving a search for some "technique" to improve our information processing, we will attempt to solve this problem in the approved style of our culture. We will add another sprocket to the old machine and assume that this time it will work. However, it should be clear by now that if the problem of American policy were technical, we Americans would have solved it long ago. The problem that we faced—or failed to face—in the Dominican crisis, was one of character. To solve it, we will have to examine some of the basic assumptions of our society, our mores, and our "American way of life."

The statements of Senators Fulbright and Clark about the failure of information were, of course, social niceties. Everyone who reads the *Congressional Record* has noticed how polite the senators are to each other when they are on the attack. It is one of the gladiatorial conventions of the Senate floor that one's opponent is assumed to have made an honest mistake. But the senators' hesitation in criticizing President Johnson for the failure of our policy in the Dominican Republic also may have been due, in part, to a feeling that the intervention in the Dominican civil war was a part of the larger problem of American interventionism throughout the world, that criticizing a president—or even changing presidents—would not heal the basic flaw in American policy. Senator Fulbright described some of the attitudes that he felt were behind this policy failure in his speech on the Dominican crisis. It was a courageous speech for a man whose position depends on the votes of his fellow Americans, for it faced squarely some of the realities of present day American culture:

> It is not surprising that we Americans are not drawn toward the uncouth revolutionaries of the noncommunist left. We are not, as we like

to claim in Fourth of July speeches, the most truly revolutionary nation on earth; we are, on the contrary, much closer to being the most
unrevolutionary nation on earth. We are sober and satisfied and comfortable and rich; our institutions are stable and old and even venera-
ble; and our Revolution of 1776, for that matter, was not much of an
upheaval compared to the French and Russian Revolutions and to current and impending revolutions in Latin America and Asia and Africa.

Our heritage of stability and conservatism is a blessing but it also
has the effect of limiting our understanding of the character of social
revolution and sometimes as well of the injustices which spawn them.
Our understanding of revolutions and their causes is imperfect not
because of any failures of mind or character but because of our good
fortune since the Civil War in never having experienced sustained social injustice without hope of legal or more or less peaceful remedy.
We are called upon, therefore, to give our understanding and our sympathy and support to movements which are alien to our experience
and jarring to our preferences and prejudices.

We must understand social revolution and the injustices that give it
rise because they are the heart and core of the experience of the great
majority of people now living in the world.[37]

The senator was saying, in effect, that we Americans, as a nation,
are lacking in an awareness of how others feel and think. In this
sense our president represents us very well, for his failure in the
Dominican crisis was our failure. His inability to understand what
was really happening in the world is characteristic of the lack of
contact on the part of most middle-class Americans with hunger,
privation, and social unrest. In an affluent world such experiences
might well be a source of pride. But in the real world in which injustice is as common as Coca Cola, the American experience is unique.
It has set us apart from the majority of mankind. For a long time we
have denied the reality of this separation. Our desire to sustain the
image of our national virtue is the primary motive for this denial.
Our feeling of being in the right derives from the conviction that
American values are universal values, that Americans do not have a
national interest, but a world interest.

But the level of awareness is rising throughout the world to the
extent that it is becoming increasingly difficult to maintain this private fiction. The democratic revolutionary in South America is
angered when he finds a liberal democracy supporting a military
dictatorship in order to maintain law and order. The black man in
the American ghetto is outraged that a white liberal can participate
in a society that crushes him. The two situations are analogous. They
both reflect the fact that others are no longer willing to accept our
interpretation of reality in terms of our own needs.

NOTES

1. Although government reports called him a "communist," Juan Bosch describes Tavarez Justo as "an impassioned, honest leader, driven to constant activity in order to keep his party to a political line far enough to the left to prevent it from falling into the Communist camp." The youth in his movement openly admired Fidel Castro, making them vulnerable to communist penetration. But "Tavarez Justo had never allowed the Communists to gain control of his party." J. Bosch, *The Unfinished Experiment: Democracy in the Dominican Republic* (New York: Praeger, 1965), p. 223.

2. J.B. Martin, *Overtaken by Events* (Garden City, N.Y.: Doubleday, 1966), p. 638.

3. Statement by Senator J. W. Fulbright for P.M. release on September 15, 1965, p. 4.

4. This account is by Senator Fulbright (Ibid., p. 4). However, the situation as described by John Bartlow Martin, the former U.S. ambassador, was not as clear as Fulbright's account would indicate. Martin claims it was a minor functionary of the PRD (the party supporting Bosch) who called the American embassy and said Reid was willing to turn the government over to the PRD in the presence of a U.S. representative. Prior contact with Reid had provided no hint of such an offer, and Reid later denied it (see Martin, *Overtaken by Events*, pp. 646–647).

5. Martin, *Overtaken by Events*, p. 647.

6. Fulbright reports that the rebels were refused U.S. mediation because we believed they were dominated by communists (Fulbright, statement, p. 5). Martin says that the United States embassy did offer its help but that mediation efforts broke down because the loyalist air force officers left the meeting with the U.S. naval attaché to begin a combined air and naval bombardment of rebel positions (Martin, *Overtaken by Events*, p. 652.)

   Actually, however, as both Martin and Szulc indicate, the mediation request by the rebels finally turned into a suggestion, on the part of U.S. Ambassador Bennett, that the rebels surrender (see Martin, pp. 654–655). Bennett told Molina Ureña, the provisional president of the PRD, that his movement had been infiltrated by communists. Colonel Camaño, the leader of the rebel military forces, reports that Bennett told them "this is not the time to negotiate, this is the time to surrender [T. Szulc, *Dominican Diary* (New York: Delacorte, 1965), p. 36–38.] Although Molina Ureña abandoned the rebel cause after this interview and went into asylum, Camaño became firmly resolved to fight on, regardless of the consequences.

7. Martin, *Overtaken by Events*, p. 655.

8. Fulbright, statement, p. 6.

9. The messages sent by Bennett to Washington during this period have not been released for publication. But they were the subject of extensive discussion during a hearing by the Senate Committee on Foreign Relations. The committee was in executive session at the time, and the testimony is not open to the public. However, through the speeches of Senators Fulbright and Clark and others who sat in on the hearings, it has become possible to piece together the content of most of them.

10. Fulbright, statement, p. 6.

11. U.S., Congress, Senate, *Congressional Record*, 17 September 1965, p. 23366. Senator Fulbright has given a similar account: "This request [for American troops] was denied in Washington, and Benoit was thereupon told that the United

States would not intervene unless he said he could not protect American citizens
. . ." Fulbright, statement, p. 6.

12. The CIA was able to produce the names of only three communists who were said
to be connected with the revolutionary movement (see Senator Clark, speech, p.
23366). The American embassy in Santo Domingo had earlier reported a list of
"53" communists. This list was given wide publicity, but it turned out to be a
mere listing of names of communists and suspected procommunists in Santo
Domingo with no documentation in regard to the relationship of these men to the
rebel forces (Szulc, *Dominican Diary*, pp. 69–72).

13. U.S., Congress, Senate, *Congressional Record*, 15 September 1965, p. 23007.

14. Szulc, *Dominican Diary*, p. 45.

15. U.S., Congress, Senate, Committee on Foreign Relations, *Background Information
Relating to the Dominican Republic*, p. 51.

16. Ibid., pp. 55–60.

17. Szulc, *Dominican Diary*, p. 25.

18. Ibid., pp. 55–89. The reporters found they could monitor communications in the
American fleet by a transistor radio. Said Szulc, "What we heard was most revealing as to the part the United States was already playing in the Dominican civil
war." [p. 56]

19. Speech by Senator Clark, *Congressional Record*, Senate, p. 23007.

20. Theodore Draper ("The Dominican Crisis," *Commentary*, December, 1965, pp.
42–43) quotes a *Daily News* report in which Ambassador Bennett allegedly told a
group of reporters that Bosch's party (the PRD) had been collaborating with the
communists. In a later Associated Press dispatch a "U.S. government official"
describes a meeting between Colonel Camaño and members of three communist
organizations in which the communists are promised Camaño's support. Camaño
denied that such a meeting took place. Draper also points out that on the "Open
End" television program Tad Szulc described the ending to this story.

    Several days later we went back to Ambassador Bennett, I think quite a few of us
    did, and said, could we have a few more details because we cannot check it out.
    And we were told at the Embassy rather sheepishly well, it seems that we were
    misinformed about the alleged meeting between Colonel Camaño and the five
    top communists. This was never mentioned again. [p. 43]

21. Senate, *Congressional Record*, p. 8549.

22. Senate, *Congressional Record*, p. 8677.

23. Senate, *Congressional Record*, p. 8695.

24. Senate, *Congressional Record*, p. 8697.

25. Senate, Committee on Foreign Relations, *Background Information*, p. 57.

26. Szulc, *Dominican Diary*, p. 79.

27. Ibid., pp. 78–79.

28. Senate, Committee on Foreign Relations, *Background Information*, p. 59.

29. Ibid., p. 84.

30. Draper, "The Dominican Crisis," p. 52.

31. Fulbright, statement, p. 1.

32. Theodore Draper reports the president as saying in his speech on May 2, "we have
also maintained communications with President Bosch, who has chosen to remain in Puerto Rico . . ." I cannot find this remark in the official version of the
President's speech. Actually there was no communication with Bosch until he
called Abe Fortas, a confidant of President Johnson, and asked for U.S. transporta-

tion to the Dominican Republic. He was refused (see Draper, "The Dominican Crisis," p. 41).

33. Fulbright, statement.
34. Ibid., p. 1.
35. Senate, *Congressional Record*, p. 23367.
36. Martin, *Overtaken by Events*, p. 705.
37. Fulbright, statement, p. 3.

Spend
a
Billion

I

In his book, *The Strategy of Persuasion*, Arthur Meyerhoff suggested that America had failed to "sell itself" to the world. The reason for this, he said, was that the job had never been given to the people who know how to do it: the same people who popularized cornflakes and automobiles.[1] Complaining that the U.S. Information Agency is staffed primarily with newsmen and is lacking in representation from the advertising profession, he pointed to the defects of mere news in promoting American policies. The news story usually gives the facts and does not tell the person what to do. A good advertising campaign, on the other hand, moves people to action.[2] Ideas, if they are to be retained, must be defined in simple terms and repeated over and over again.[3] The USIA, he said, should "concentrate on delivering messages that are carefully calculated to promote our aims."[4] Emphasizing that "our very survival may depend on our ability to overcome an unscrupulous competitor," he was critical of the Kennedy program for sending Americans abroad to perform as

152

artists or musicians and lecture on history, philosophy, and literature. This approach, he argued, was not sufficiently persuasive.[5] He
spoke of the need to "condition people to understand our aims."[6] We
must not merely tell the other peoples of the world who we are, but
we must explain what we can do for them. At no point did Mr.
Meyerhoff suggest that we lie to anyone. We must simply help them
to understand the truth.

In this emphasis upon simplification and explanation, there is an
implicit assumption that American truth is universal. If we can only
succeed in making our aims clear to others, they will support us in
our objectives. However, there is a problem in telling people what
you are going to do for them when you are really not going to do
anything for them. This is not really such a terrible thing if we know
it and admit it to ourselves. But if we strive to tell the "real truth"
without understanding it ourselves, we will damage our own credibility without convincing others. The presentation of our offer to
spend a billion in Southeast Asia as a humanitarian gesture is
characteristic of this approach. It was made during a crucial turning
point in public opinion in regard to the war in Vietnam. It was an
attempt to use the techniques of public relations to bring the American public and world opinion in line with the policy of an American
president. And it failed. It was the last major effort of the Johnson
Administration to sell aggression—American style, that is, to strive
publicly for peace while stumbling inadvertently into a larger war.

II

In February 1965, after his successful campaign against Senator
Goldwater, President Johnson had begun a series of intensive air
attacks against North Vietnam. The result was an increasing hostility
on the part of the neutral nations and of France, a former belligerent
in Vietnam. On March 16 the University of Michigan announced a
one-day suspension of classes to protest the administration's policy
in Vietnam and a "teach-in" to examine the issues in the Vietnam
War. At that time, the president had the full support of the governor
and state senate of Michigan. The Michigan Senate adopted a resolution condemning the plan and requesting disciplinary action from
the university. Concerning the teach-in, Governor Romney of Michigan remarked, "That's about the worst type of example that profes-
sors could give to their students."[7] The athletes and several frater-
nities of the university protested and picketed the meetings that

were broken up several times by bomb scares, but the teach-in continued. At the conclusion of the meetings, both Columbia University and the University of Wisconsin announced that they, too,
would hold teach-ins.

At that date, opposite to the war and the fight for civil rights
were separate issues. Although the University of Michigan teach-in
was mentioned by the New York Times on page eight, the civil rights
marchers in Selma, Alabama, were in the headlines on the same day
when they were attacked and beaten by mounted police. The president gained the support of most liberals when he insisted on protection for the marchers and, when Governor Walace refused, called up
the National Guard and brought in 4000 troops to watch over the
marchers from Selma to Montgomery. It appeared that liberals were
still in the Johnson camp.

As the Easter season approached, there were many, both inside
and outside government circles, who were urging the president to
provide a dramatic bid for peace and reverse the course of world
opinion on the Vietnam War. On April 7, 1965, during a speech at
Johns Hopkins University, President Johnson finally made his move.
He announced that he would ask Congress to join in a billion dollar
American investment to improve the life of man in Southeast Asia
when peace was achieved. He coupled this statement with an offer to
begin unconditional negotiations to end the war. Just to make sure
the offer was communicated to the interested parties, copies of the
speech were dropped on North Vietnam by American planes on
April 17. We now know that it was during this same period that
President Johnson made his final plans for the extensive use of
ground troops for offensive action in South Vietnam. A Pentagon
analyst was later to describe this step as a pivotal change in the
enlargement of the war.[8]

From the beginning, the Johnson billion dollar speech was viewed
as a move to enhance his image as a peacemaker. The New York
Times carried the headline: PRESIDENT MAKES OFFER TO START VIET-
NAM TALKS UNCONDITIONALLY; PROPOSES $1 BILLION AID FOR ASIA.
Max Frankel reported that the offer was part of a "personal desire to
yield and to appeal to opinion at home." It was also, he said, a bid for
world opinion.[9] By the following week it appeared to the leadership
of the New York Times that the president had succeeded. In an unsigned editorial, the Times reported that the Johnson peace plan had
brought about a change in world opinion from opposition to support.[10] Many columnists seemed to agree. David Lawrence said the
speech was one of the best expositions of American foreign policy
that had been presented since the cold war.[11] Evans and Novak re-

garded it as a major coup in the field of public relations that enabled the president to pursue his war objectives while disarming his critics.

> In a deft display of the famous Johnson technique, the President disarmed his anti-war critics without really changing his hard line or alienating the hard-liners. In fact, he disarmed the peace wing of his Democratic party so thoroughly that a spate of anti-Vietnamese war speeches by Democratic Senators were postponed.[12]

In the criticism that was leveled at college teach-ins and at the young men and women who used their bodies to stop the movement of military vehicles and obstruct draft boards during this period, the resounding theme seemed to be that they had no need to use "violence" to attain their objectives. They were reminded that they lived in a democracy and should write their congressmen if they did not like what was going on. Although congressmen, no doubt, read their mail, it is evident that the media leave a much more forceful impression on them. President Johnson was an expert at capturing the attention of the media. From his "We Shall Overcome" speech on civil rights to his billion dollar offer to Southeast Asia, he managed to stifle the liberal opposition. The capitulation of the liberals (with two exceptions) following the incident in the Gulf of Tonkin was only the beginning. The postponement of the anti-Vietnamese War speeches reported by Evans and Novak was another example of the Johnson expertise in silencing his critics.

It is difficult to determine to what extent anyone really believed in the sincerity of the billion dollar offer. Many, no doubt, praised it because they believed they should stand behind the president in any peace move. Some opinion leaders professed that they regarded the offer as a great humanitarian gesture, and the fact that it came after two months of intensified bombing of the North was merely attributed to the realistic aspect in Mr. Johnson's policy. In this respect, the Johnson offer seemed to confirm Margaret Mead's image of the American struggle for success: the need to be virtuous but tough and practical at the same time. However, there was something about the way the speech was handled, coming at the Easter season, in time to catch the peace sentiment without interrupting the war policy, that made the combination of toughness, practicality, and humanity a bit too thick. Perhaps it was so American in its style that it represented not an ideal but a caricature. Joseph Alsop called it "A Great Speech," but in describing the president's proposal, a certain incongruity crept into his writing. He stretched common sense almost to the breaking point in his effort to link the president's craftiness and ruthlessness with his feelings of human warmth.[13]

Many of the initial statements of world leaders were favorable toward the Johnson offer, but sober reflection may have convinced them that a billion dollars was very little to pay for peace, considering the price the war was already extracting from the American taxpayer. Furthermore, it was an obvious, though unstated, condition of the Johnson offer that if the president did not like the peace terms, he was not obliged to spend any money at all.

Soviet and Chinese sources immediately described the offer as a hoax, an attempt at bribery. The Chinese press agency distributed a dispatch that said the president's proposal was "pursuance of the stick and carrot tactics."[14] "Observer," writing in the official newspaper of Peking, said the offer was an attempt to "buy over the Vietnamese people."[15] Republican Senator Dirksen was also critical. "Do you buy freedom for a humble people," he asked, "with a billion dollar package?"[16] Somehow the senator managed to escape the accusation that he was following the communist line. President Sukarno of Indonesia simply called the offer a bribe.[17]

But the notion that the billion dollar offer could be construed as a bribe was repugnant to many in the United States and the West generally. The *New York Herald Tribune* editorialized as follows: "The assertion by some Americans in and out of Congress that the President was trying to buy peace with his advocacy of a vast development plan for Southeast Asia is very wide of the mark."[18] Why, then, was the offer made? Was it simply a generous impulse, devoid of any connection with the war in Vietnam? Was it, as Mr. Johnson said, the product of a desire not to allow people to go hungry and naked while our own warehouses overflow? If this were the case, we might well begin in the ghetto and in those regions of the United States where people go hungry and naked. Was it mere hypocrisy? At first thought, this would seem to be the case. But hypocrisy implies a certain deliberation and an absence of the kind of noble intent with which the president was credited for his proposal. The answer, I believe, lies in the realm of self-deception. It is represented by a split between intent and deed that manages to preserve the virtue of the former without interfering with the latter.

The manner in which the average American manages to avoid looking at his own intentions varies from one region to another. In his brilliant work, *The Mind of the South*, W. J. Cash has examined the Southern style in detail: the protestation of one's high religious motives, the fondness for rhetoric, the resort to fantasy, and the building of noble legends. But Cash also places a strong emphasis on the unconscious nature of this deception. It is, he said, first of all a deception of the self.

> Hypocrisy? Far from it. There was much of Tartarin in the Southerner, but nothing of Tartuffe. His Puritanism was no mere mask put on from cold calculation, but as essential a part of him as his hedonism. And this combination of the two was without conscious imposture. One might say with much truth that it proceeded from a fundamental split in his psyche, from a sort of social schizophrenia. One may say more simply and more safely that it was all part and parcel of that naive capacity for unreality which was characteristic of him.[19]

There are various ways of hiding from one's self. One is to indulge in fantasy. Another is to conquer the world. The advertising culture of the northern big cities has provided this second approach as the national style. In the mobility of the last half-century in the United States, these two philosophies have merged in the idea of selling an illusion. One cannot listen to a group of admen arguing over the ideas for a sales campaign without gaining the distinct impression that these men know they are distorting the truth. One cannot hear some of the in jokes in the profession without a feeling that such distortion is considered quite acceptable, even humorous by those in the field. On closer inspection, however, the extent to which advertising people are unaware of what they are really doing is quite remarkable. In a standard textbook on the subject, *Modern Advertising* by H. W. Hepner, one searches in vain for any indication of reservation, doubt, or even a mention of the distortion and exaggeration that is such an integral part of the field. The introductory chapter is itself an advertisement for advertising. A few examples follow:

> Every alert person must recognize that advertising has been a stimulating influence in our modern civilization. It often has stimulated people to want the new and desirable. As such, advertising may be considered an "accelerator of civilization" . . . The claim that advertising increases costs is made by certain small businessmen wishing to counteract the popularity of competitors who do advertise . . . Any advertisement no matter how much hard-sell it contains, must inform the reader and seek to help him raise the standard of his living. As such, it is just as important to our American way of life as production.[20]

It requires an unusual naïveté to make such remarks in a textbook for students, where one might expect to find a greater attempt at veracity. Does the author realize he is exaggerating? I think not. Samm Baker, a veteran of 30 years in advertising, has remarked:

> During my years in advertising I fooled myself. I was aware of fakery, of course. *But I didn't realize consciously* the vast amount of "fraud" perpetrated in ads, including many of my own efforts. The adman becomes so accustomed to using the permissible lie that it becomes his natural approach in creating an ad and selling a product.[21]

Baker is not talking about an activity that is "unconscious" in the Freudian sense; that is, it is not so deeply repressed that it is unavailable for conscious recall. He is describing a form of self-deception.[22] It is a lack of awareness that involves, at some point, the decision to remain unaware. But it also depends on a cooperative milieu for its perpetuation. In order to remain unaware, one must live and circulate among people who have a similar attitude. It is an acquiesence in a shared illusion, an unspoken agreement that one will not struggle to wake up nor attempt to awaken others.

The advertiser has convinced himself that people will get along much better if he makes the decisions for them by manipulating their perceptions. They need to be encouraged to buy for their own good and the good of the nation. When the advertising philosophy is applied to American foreign policy, it amounts to a belief that American policy is good for the people of the world. It is only a matter of finding the right sales gimmick to sell them a program that is in their own best interest. The problem with such a philosophy is that although the salesman does not recognize his own deception, others see through him. Phillipe Ben, writing in the French newspaper, *Le Monde*, described the swift change in American policy that resulted in the offer to negotiate and to spend a billion:

> For a long time on the defensive the Americans now wish to profit from the occasion and "launch" in the marketplace of world politics a product which, from all appearances "sells good" and which has for its name, "unconditional negotiation and economic aid."
>
> This comparison of the foreign policy of a great power with public relations techniques might shock some people. It is necessary, therefore, not to forget that for the average American commercial publicity which "produces good sales" represents the most natural means and that all political propaganda should strive for nothing other than to do a good job of "selling" the United States abroad with the same methods and the same success that they sell toothpaste and vitamin pills in the United States. It is for this reason that in the coming weeks one will hear the Americans speak constantly of negotiations, of economic aid. One must expect numerous initiatives of this type in the United Nations. Thus, at least an illusion will be created: the war in Vietnam is not the only reality in Southeast Asia.[23]

III

It is difficult to determine to what extent President Johnson's success in coopting the liberals in his own party helped to discredit the older liberalism as a force in American politics, but it is clear that the opposition to liberalism became a moving, articulate force within the antiwar movement in the summer of 1965. It was this same summer of 1965 that saw the beginning of a unity between the antiwar and civil rights movements with the McComb, Mississippi, Freedom Democratic Party's antiwar statement in July and the antiwar statement by Julian Bond (of SNCC), who was denied his seat in the Georgia legislature for his stand. The change was not a sudden one. Criticism of liberals had been an aspect of the New Left as early as the Free Speech Movement at the University of California and was implicit in the Port Huron Statement of SDS in 1962. But it was Carl Oglesby, President of SDS, who crystallized this position and brought it to public attention in his speech at the November 27 march on Washington. On many occasions, protest groups had been careful not to offend liberals in the administration who represented their only hope of working within the existing political system. Now the lid was off, and liberalism itself was on trial. Said Oglesby:

> The original commitment in Vietnam was made by President Truman, a mainstream liberal. It was seconded by President Eisenhower, a moderate liberal. It was intensified by the late President Kennedy, a flaming liberal. Think of the men who now engineer that war—those who study the maps, give the commands, push the buttons, and tally the dead: Bundy, McNamara, Rusk, Lodge, Goldberg, the President himself.
> They are not moral monsters.
> They are all honorable men.
> They are all liberals.[24]

Oglesby's speech was also a recognition that American society could not be changed by throwing the "bad" men out of office and placing "good" men in power. The difficulty was deeper and more fundamental. There was a need for a complete change in American values. People had to want a more humane and just society to the extent that they would no longer accept the comfortable illusion peddled by public relations men.

The year 1965 was also a year of escalation, in both the war and the war protest movement. On January 5, the public first became aware of extended U.S. military operations when two American planes were shot down over Laos. On January 14, the press carried front page reports of U.S. fighter bombers knocking out a key Laotian bridge. On February 8 in a massive raid U.S. planes bombed Vietcong barracks in North Vietnam, and President Johnson ordered American families home from South Vietnam. On March 3, over 100 U.S. jets bombed South Vietnam. It was also in March that the teach-ins began and protests were mounted across the country from Oakland to New York and Washington. In April, Dean Rusk scolded the academic community and began to send representatives from the State Department to explain American policy. In October the attorney general began a probe of groups behind the antidraft movement. But the government was dealing with a new breed of rebels who would not be frightened away by the charge that they had communists among them or that they had been "duped" into opposing the war by a communist conspiracy.

Within the Democratic party, a growing body of dissidents, led by Senators Fulbright and Morse, was becoming increasingly concerned about the obvious escalation of the conflict, despite the president's repeated slogan that he wanted "no wider war" and his offer to spend a billion for peace. It was suggested in several quarters that despite the president's insistence that he would negotiate anywhere without any preconditions, the opportunities for peaceful settlement were not really being explored. Some with stubborn memories had recalled the earlier prediction by the Pentagon that major U.S. involvement in the Vietnam War would end by December 1965 and had publicly wondered if there had not been an unfortunate misunderstanding about the whole nature of the Vietnam problem. For over a year, the U.S. efforts to obtain military support from the nations of Europe and Asia had met with almost total failure. Even NATO countries were not willing to supply more than token support and President de Gaulle had publicly called the war "absurd." As the Christmas season approached, James Reston remarked in the *New York Times*, "the mood is solemn at the Christmas when the Pentagon led the American people to believe the boys would be coming back home."[25] In general, the American character is particularly responsive to thoughts of home and peace during the Christmas season. This attitude is inevitably heightened by special pleas and messages of hope from religious leaders at this time. It would have been an ideal time for some new move on the part of the administration to advertise its work toward world peace. However, it was at this very moment that news of the Hanoi peace feeler reached the American press.

On December 17 the highly reliable *St. Louis Post-Dispatch* published the news of a U.S. rejection of a peace offer from North Vietnam. The offer had come through Giorgia La Pira of Rome who had talked with Ho Chi Minh in Hanoi. Ho had allegedly offered to go anywhere and meet anyone, without conditions, to discuss peace. An attorney, Peter Weiss, who had heard the story in Rome, received only denials when he spoke to Ambassador Goldberg at the United Nations about the Hanoi offer. The implication of the story was that the administration was covering up the peace offer because it had been rejected and that President Johnson did not want peace.

Had this been the only instance of a rumored peace offer, the general public might have been less excited by the story, but it was only the *previous* August that the administration had rejected a proposed peace conference with North Vietnam, an offer that had been issued through U Thant, Secretary General of the United Nations. After months of denial that such a proposal had ever been made, it was reluctantly admitted in November. The apparent refusal of the Johnson Administration to consider the possibility of peace became a matter of national concern.

Clearly, there were many reasons why it would not be militarily advantageous for the United States to be negotiating for peace at this time. Most of these reasons had been advanced, naturally enough, by the military. In an article entitled "Vietnam Peace Prospects Feared," Rowland Evans and Robert Novak pointed out that "there is a high-level apprehension in Washington and in Saigon that a negotiated settlement today could be disastrous" and that "the U.S. generals think they can win the war militarily and destroy the Viet Cong." More specifically, they quoted "one high U.S. officer in Vietnam" who felt it would be "most embarrassing" if an offer to end the war without conditions were put forward by Ho Chi Minh. General Westmoreland was said to have remarked "privately" that the Saigon political structure would collapse if a settlement were made.[26]

This situation was well known by most American authorities on foreign affairs, and in some quarters it had increased the doubts that President Johnson was really interested in peace, as he had often maintained. Two days before the peace offer was disclosed, the *New York Times* carried an editorial describing the failure of Secretary Rusk to enlist the aid of Western European nations and attributing this failure to his "hard line" on Vietnam.[27] At this time, there was serious skepticism regarding the willingness of the administration to make peace under any terms.

After the disclosure of the Hanoi peace feeler by the *Post-Dispatch*, the pressure began to mount from all the news media for a complete disclosure of the details of both the offer and the assumed U.S. rejection. Finally, at 3 P.M. on Friday, December 17, the State Department released the full story of the "peace offer" including the complete text of a letter from Amatori Fanfani, President of the U.N. General Assembly, who had transmitted the substance of the proposal to Secretary Rusk. The proposal had not been rejected, said the State Department, it was being "studied."[28]

But now the press was really indignant. The State Department was deluged with a series of embarrassing questions that began in the briefing room that afternoon and lasted for several days. If the United

States had received word of a peace feeler almost a month ago, as the Fanfani letter indicated, why did the president say, on December 9, that North Vietnam had been "completely negative" on the question of negotiations?[29] Why had Secretary Rusk said there had been only a "discouraging response" to all efforts to bring about talks? Why did Rusk ponder over the letter for two weeks before making a formal reply? Why had the secretary taken such a hard line when he finally did reply, insisting that Hanoi clarify all the ambiguities of the offer? A New York Times editorial stressed the need for ambiguity in diplomacy.[30] If the administration was seriously considering peace, why had U.S. bombers made the first air strike on a major industrial target in North Vietnam just 11 days after Secretary Rusk's request for clarification of the offer? Arthur Krock, who called this a strange pursuit of "clarification," pointed out that 25 percent of the power and light facilities of Hanoi had been knocked out by the strike.[31]

But the most embarrassing question of all was the one that related to the State Department's disclosure. Why, if anyone was really taking the proposal seriously, did the State Department release the full text of the Fanfani letter? Hanoi must now surely repudiate the offer as it would embarrass Ho before the North Vietnamese people, the Viet Cong, and the Communist Chinese, who were supplying him with aid. The explanation is as obvious as it is tragic. The administration was seriously intimidated by the press and by a sense of moral failure in the eyes of the general public. The atmosphere of guilt and hasty decision making was evident in the process of the disclosure. The determination to release the story to the press came so fast that State Department personnel apparently did not have time to mimeograph the press release. Only the correspondents from the two main wire services were called in to receive it.[32] Once the government's resistance was broken down, there was an abrupt capitulation.

The gentlemen of the press were shocked not only by the extent of their own power, but by the insecurity of the administration. Said Max Frankel, "remarkably, the United States government decided that its word, against that of a single newspaper, would not suffice." He reported a frank admission by Ambassador Goldberg that "we have a great problem here maintaining our credibility" not only with foreigners, but with "our own people." There was, he said, widespread doubt not only whether the United States can be trusted to tell the truth about peace offers, but whether its leaders "really are pursuing what has been said is a path of peace."[33]

The disclosure of the Fanfani communication did not get the Johnson Administration out of difficulty. In fact, it seemed to intensify the problem of national confidence. The New York Times felt the disclosure was a serious mistake[34] and Drew Middleton reported that "diplomats from countries of all political coloration agreed that the publication of the letters between the United States and Mr. Fanfani was a 'calamity'."[35] Arthur Krock said it had "exploded any step toward peace."[36] Hanoi, of course, denied the offer and called it an American hoax.

There can be little doubt that President Johnson was seriously affected by the attitude he saw developing in regard to his own position on peace. A few weeks after the event, he was reported by "close associates" to be blaming himself for his "failure to conince Hanoi and Peking of American sincerity in seeking a settlement" and feeling that "the United States could do more to promote peace."[37] It is not clear how President Johnson's personal feelings came to the reporters. It is probable that the "close associates" presented the information in an informal session with reporters, asking not to be named directly. Even if the president deliberately planted the information, it is clear that he was making an effort to counter the picture of himself that had been appearing in the press for over a month. It was the picture of a man who, without a sense of conscience, concealed his intentions from his own people, who spoke of his desire for peace, but was secretly planning to expand the war. Although it had been developing for quite some time, this image had reached a certain crisis with the Hanoi peace feeler. The unfortunate disclosure of the full context of the Fanfani exchange and the administration's confession that it was fully aware that such disclosure killed any hopes for peace,[38] added the final touch to that negative image.

Mr. Johnson's concern about the picture of himself as opposed to peace was further demonstrated by the measures he took to erase this image. Up to this point, his major policy moves had been in the direction of further escalation of the war. It seems clear that the "peace offensive" that he initiated in the final days of December was a direct result of his attempt to prove his "sincerity" in the field of peace. If his peace moves had been planned before the fiasco over the Hanoi peace feeler, they would have been timed prior to the Christmas season so as to have the greatest effect on the American people. Instead, he was caught off balance by the Pope's Christmas message.

On December 19, Pope Paul VI called for a temporary halt in the fighting in a message that made oblique reference to a similar proposal by the Viet Cong:

> We know of some proposal for a truce; of a truce of arms at least for the blessed day of Christmas. And we know of many dedicated men of state who are seeking to resolve the difficult dispute.
> But we particularly know that millions of hearts are trembling,

suffering, waiting for peace to return. We applaud those who loyally
act to solve the menacing conflict.

We wish that at least—at least!—the proposal for a truce is accepted and put into effect! So that Christmas may be for all a day of
peace! We recommend this to the wisdom and the hearts of the leaders
responsible.[39]

On the same day that the New York Times carried the Pope's message, an editorial carried a report that President Johnson was planning to ask the Congress "for vastly expanded commitments in manpower and money in Vietnam." The peaceful hopes of the Pope and
the warlike attitude of the president were presented in striking contrast. Said the Times:

The best way to demonstrate the sincerity of American desires for unconditional discussions would be for President Johnson to respond to
the Pope's appeal by announcing a new pause in the bombing of North
Vietnam during which Secretary General Thant of the United Nations
or other intermediaries could explore the possibilities of a permanent
ceasefire.[40]

Soon Warren Rogers was reporting in the Los Angeles Herald-
Examiner that, acting on a plan prepared by the Joint Chiefs of Staff,
the president was about to "go all out" to end the war by escalating
the strikes against North Vietnam.[41]

In the face of the Pope's message, the Christmas season (in which
the boys were supposed to be home) and the growing doubts about
the sincerity of the administration's reaction to the various efforts to
promote peace, these rumors of the president's war plans sounded
very cold indeed. Pressure from the press, Congress, and the American people began to mount for some clear and decisive move toward
peace by the president. Senator McGovern allegedly called the White
House urging a 30-hour Christmas truce to which the president reluctantly agreed.[42] At first, the president denied all involvement in
the truce, claiming that all arrangements were being made in Saigon.
However, when the U.S. bombing raids against North Vietnam
ceased and were not resumed even after the failure of the Christmas
truce, it became apparent that an important policy move by the
United States was underway.

Officials at the White House and State Department refused to
comment on the bombing pause, despite persistent questioning by
reporters. But soon Vice-President Humphrey was off to Tokyo, Ambassador Harriman was on his way to Warsaw, major State Department figures seemed to be scurrying everywhere, and this time no
one would talk to the press. Having slowly and painfully extracted

its foot from its mouth, the administration was showing an exaggerated caution. It soon became known that Vice-President Humphrey had talked to Premier Eisaku Sato of Japan and had asked him to do anything he could to arrange a conference on Vietnam. Harriman, it developed, had talked to Polish Foreign Minister Adam Rapacki, and Poland was reported anxious to act as a mediator in Vietnam negotiations. News was coming in from all over the globe, but no one was saying anything in Washington and President Johnson left for Austin, Texas, for the holidays.

As McGeorge Bundy departed for Canada and airplanes began to roar down the runway bearing diplomats to various parts of the world, the silence of the administration began to seem as ostentatious as a 21-gun salute. Like a performer in a game of charades, President Johnson seemed to be waving his hands, rolling his eyes, wiggling his ears, in short, using everything but his voice to tell the world that he was making a mighty effort for world peace. Furthermore, his audience had already guessed what he was trying to tell them.

Finally, on the last day of the year, the president's press secretary was able to "confirm the obvious," according to John Pomfret, but he refused to go beyond the general statement that the various high ranking U.S. officials were part of an exhaustive U.S. probe to see if Hanoi was interested in peace.[43] The press secretary still refused to link the diplomatic missions with the cessation of bombing, nor would he say whether the president felt the climate for peace was better now than in the past few weeks. There was, however, a great emphasis on "sincerity" in the reports of all those who made contact with the administration. One of the subcolumn heads in the *New York Times* story by Tom Wicker, on page one, was SINCERITY EMPHASIZED. At the same time, within the article proper, an element of doubt was manifest: "One senior official here said in a private conversation that the effort was sincere and energetic. His attitude toward its prospects, however, was one of weary skepticism."[44]

IV

One might well stop at this point and ask the question: Just what is meant by the word *sincere* in this context? It is a word that was used with increasing frequency whenever President Johnson spoke of peace. Yet no one questioned the "sincerity" of his military objectives or described his "sincere" war policy. In general, the stories carried by the press indicate a long-range policy of gradual increase in the military effort by the administration. What, then, was the "peace offensive"? Was it a sop to public opinion? Was it an impulsive gesture, designed to take the edge off criticism, but devoid of any long-range intent? It would not be proper for anyone to suggest this directly, for President Johnson was doing exactly what his critics had asked him to do. Following the suggestion of the *New York Times* editorial and the urging of Senator McGovern, he had called a halt to the bombing and was sending intermediaries everywhere in search of peace.

However, there must have been something in the questions of reporters that suggested that the president was not really personally involved in his peace efforts, or perhaps the protestations of sincerity were a reaction against the doubts within the administration itself. In any event, on New Year's Day, Wicker was describing the president's attempt "to give added urgency and sincerity" to the call for negotiations. "High authorities" were also confirming the direct personal involvement of the president. The question of impulsiveness was more difficult to handle, but this was explained in terms of a "confluence of circumstances."

> The authorities emphasized, however, that Mr. Johnson's direction of the effort from Texas did not mean a division of opinion in the administration. Nor had it been a sudden impulse on his part, they insisted.
>
> Instead, Mr. Johnson was described today as having long sought the proper time and the method of making a concentrated drive for unconditional negotiations . . .
>
> Therefore, a knowledgeable source said today, a "confluence of circumstances" caused Mr. Johnson to launch the peace offensive at this time.[45]

There was, of course, little doubt that the decision was made in haste—that is, in a matter of a few days at a time when the president was under considerable pressure. The decision was made without consulting the South Vietnamese government and that government was informed only a few days before the mission began. Secrecy was a factor in the delayed notification, but if the plans had been made sufficiently far in advance, a briefing could have been prepared for Saigon.

The secrecy surrounding the mission was a product of the president's desire to prove his sincerity. The quiet channels of diplomacy were to offer a dignified contrast to the fanfare of publicity and the headline story. But the speed with which the mission was called and the rapid build-up of effort soon made secrecy impossible, and there were those unkind enough to believe that the president really wanted it that way. There was a suggestion in some of the commentary that the refusal to talk to reporters was merely a stimulus to the curiosity of the press.

On January 6, 1966, a column by Anthony Lewis reported that most Europeans backed the president's peace offer, but the body of the article contained, primarily, critical reports from Britain and France of President Johnson's inflexibility in refusing to negotiate with the Viet Cong and West German criticism of the "exaggerated publicity" of the peace campaign.[46] In his column James Reston remarked on the president's "airport diplomacy," his "spectacular diplomacy," his diplomacy that was "personalized and jet-propelled" and his "headline moves."[47] In an unsigned editorial, the New York Times also called attention to the means used by the president to convey his proposals and the doubts that these methods had aroused concerning his real intentions.[48] The strongest condemnation within the United States probably came from the Coordinating Committee to End the War in Vietnam. Here, the president's efforts were openly called a "hoax" and a "circus," a deliberate device to soften world opinion while he prepared for an intensification of the war in Vietnam.[49] Thus, despite the conclusion in Washington toward the end of January that "the world is now largely convinced that 'America wants peace',"[50] it would appear that President Johnson's peace mission was a failure.

In retrospect, it seems clear that the major peace offensive was not part of the president's long-range plans. Subsequent events have shown that he was, in fact, planning to escalate the war. With these plans in mind, it is obvious that the 37-day halt in the bombing, which he apparently felt compelled to initiate, was a serious setback to his own policy. As Joseph Alsop pointed out, the peace offensive threatened to topple the Ky regime at one point. It also allowed North Vietnam to repair most of the damage done by the previous eight-month effort to disrupt communications and destroy defenses in the North.[51] Had the peace policy been part of a plan for the total deescalation of the war, had it been made by a man who was determined to reduce the American commitment in Southeast Asia, it is possible that the results would have been more impressive. As a temporary interruption in an expanding war, it served only to increase the effort required for the following months in Vietnam.

Furthermore, the peace offensive mobilized resistance to the president's policy within his own party. When the time came to consider resumption of bombing in North Vietnam, several Democratic senators attempted to organize their colleagues in both houses to oppose renewed bombing. Meetings were held with Senator Ful-

bright to stiffen opposition to expansion of the war.[52] Many of these
senators later became a part of the permanent opposition to the president's policy in Vietnam. There seems little doubt that the president's "peace offensive" was incongruent with his own long-range
plans and that it only served to make the execution of these plans
more difficult.

The most impressive aspect of the peace campaign was the demonstration of the extent to which the president of the United States is
required to maintain an image of sincerity and goodness as well as
strength. He can afford a blemish on this image in a swift move in
which the military effort rises to a rapid peak and then declines. But
for the American people, a sustained conflict requires a sense of national virtue, and the only person who can represent this virtuous
intent is the president. The campaign also suggests that there are
limits to the extent to which advertising can be used in international
relations to create an illusion that something nice is about to happen.
Although the *Pentagon Papers* had yet to reveal the full extent of the
president's war plans during this period, it does not appear that the
press nor the protestors were being seriously misled. True, the vast
silent majority were still accepting the pronouncements from
Washington, but the antiwar movement had already begun to capture the media.

One can find a peculiar kind of indecision in the editorials of this
period. The inconsistencies in the president's policy are cited. His
false statements are held up to public view. His headline-grabbing
moves are ridiculed, but in the end, he is described as a warm and
sincere human being. Joseph Alsop's description of the president as
crafty but warmly human is only one example. After his critical remarks about the president's "spectacular diplomacy" and his "headline moves," James Reston warned his readers that President
Johnson was really sincere and that it would be "unfortunate and
perhaps even dangerous to interpret his unusual diplomatic moves
in any other way."[53] I do not know if Mr. Reston intended this remark as a sop to the president's wounded ego, after having
thoroughly mauled him in the earlier part of his article, but in any
event I believe Reston is striking at something very basic in the
American character when he closes with this happy ending to an
otherwise complete rejection of the president and his policies. It is as
if the sincerity of the president is so basic to our sense of national
morality that we must never really lose faith in it, or we will surely
be a lost people. Although it is always important for a man to have a
reputation for standing behind his word, Americans have conducted
a kind of romance with sincerity that is far afield from the specific

terms of any agreement. President Johnson's charade with the American people was an effort to reveal his heart as a good heart, not to fulfill an agreement.

V

The coalescence of dissident groups during the years after 1965 was a slow process. Despite the early antiwar stand by radical civil rights groups, such as CORE and SNCC, it was not until April 1967 that Martin Luther King and Benjamin Spock shared the same platform in a major peace demonstration in New York City. The following March, President Johnson announced the cessation of his bombing campaign and his decision not to run for another term in the White House. The Great Johnson Peace Campaign had failed, not only in its effort to achieve peace, but in its effort to convince the American people that the administration was really working for peace.

A factor in President Johnson's decision to halt the bombing of North Vietnam was an alleged understanding with the North Vietnamese that American reconnaisance planes would be permitted to fly over North Vietnam to the 20th parallel unmolested. As of this writing, it is not clear whether the "understanding" was offered to the North Vietnamese on a take-it-or-leave-it basis or whether there was actually some agreement between the two parties. The North Vietnamese have consistently denied any such agreement. In any event, the American insistence on the continuation of reconnaisance flights is congruent with our earlier attitude in the U-2 incident and the Open-Skies proposal that followed this incident.

In the U-2 incident President Eisenhower appeared ready to defend our right to look with the full force of American nuclear might on the grounds that our looking was devoid of "aggressive intent." At the last moment, he managed to climb down from this position and quietly drop the U-2 flights. In the following chapter, we will see how the issue of the American right to look was raised once again in connection with our surveillance of smaller nations and how we progressed from a position of outraged innocence to intensive and widespread bombing attacks in an alleged defense of our right to look.

However, it is important to remember that the earlier incidents of espionage (the Pueblo and the EC-121) occurred in Korea where we were attempting to maintain the status quo. In Vietnam the notion of ultimate victory (or Vietnamization, as it came to be called) was still the policy of the Nixon Administration. Thus, the new president was in the peculiar position of seeking some justification for the use of greater force while, at the same time, withdrawing troops and "reducing American involvement." It is for this reason that the attacks on the *Pueblo* and the EC-121 were suffered in a sense of moral outrage, but the attack on American reconnaisance planes over North Vietnam (like the incident in the Gulf of Tonkin) became the basis for "protective reaction strikes."

NOTES

1. A. Meyerhoff, *The Strategy of Persuasion* (New York: Coward-McCann, 1965), p. 17.

2. Ibid., p. 99.

3. Ibid., p. 100.

4. Ibid., p. 107.

5. Ibid., pp. 121–123.

6. Ibid., p. 108.

7. "Romney Criticizes Cancelling of Classes to Protest Vietnam." *New York Times*, March 17, 1965, p. 8.

8. N. Sheehan, et al., *The Pentagon Papers* (New York: Bantam, 1971), p. 382.

9. M. Frankel, "Johnson's Speech Viewed as a Bid to World Opinion," *The New York Times*, April 8, 1965, p. 1.

10. "Initiative for Peace," *New York Times*, April 11, 1965, p. E14.

11. D. Lawrence, "The President's Viet Speech," *New York Herald Tribune*, April 9, 1965, p. 21.

12. R. Evans, and R. Novak, "Inside Report: Quieting the Peace Bloc," *New York Herald Tribune*, April 14, 1965, p. 24.

13. J. Alsop, "A Great Speech," *New York Herald Tribune*, April 9, 1965, p. 20.

14. "China Cold to Johnson Bid on Talks as 'Full of Lies'." *New York Times*, April 9, 1965, p. 1.

15. "Peking Condemns Johnson Proposal on Talks as 'Hoax'," *New York Times*, April 11, 1965, p. 6.

16. "New Phase in Vietnam Conflict," *New York Times*, April 11, 1965, p. E1.

17. "Sukarno Bids U.S. Quit Vietnam," *New York Times*, April 18, 1965, p. 6.

18. Editorial, *New York Herald Tribune*, April 11, 1965, p. 22.

19. W. J. Cash, *The Mind of the South* (New York: Vintage, 1941), p. 60.

20. H. W. Hepner, *Modern Advertising, Practices, and Principles* (New York: McGraw-Hill, 1956), pp. 5–20.

21. S. S. Baker, *The Permissible Lie* (Cleveland: World Publishing, 1968), p. 15.

22. Ibid.

23. P. Ben, "Aux Nations Unies et dans le Monde," *Le Monde*, April 12, 1965, p. 2.

24. C. Oglesby, "Liberalism and the Corporate State," in *The New Radicals*, eds. Paul Jacobs and Saul Landau (New York: Vintage, 1966), pp. 257–266.

25. J. Reston, "Saigon: A Christmas Paradox," *New York Times*, December 17, 1965, p. 38.

26. R. Evans and R. Novak, "Vietnam Peace Prospects Feared," *Los Angeles Times,* December 23, 1965, part II, p. 6.

27. "NATO and Vietnam," *New York Times,* December 15, 1965, p. 46.

28. T. Wicker, "U.S. is Studying a Hanoi Feeler for Peace Talk," *New York Times,* December 18, 1965, p. 1.

29. "Peace Feeler or Not?" *New York Times,* December 19, 1965, p. E1.

30. "The Bombing Pause," *New York Times,* December 30, 1965, p. C22.

31. A. Krock, "Hanoi Peace Feeler. Chronology of Events," *Los Angeles Herald-Examiner,* December 24, 1965, p. C3.

32. "Peace Feeler or Not?"

33. M. Frankel, "A Crisis of Confidence Confronts the U.S.," *New York Times,* December 26, 1965, section E, p. 3.

34. "Crushed Hope in Vietnam," *New York Times,* December 19, 1965, section E, p. 8.

35. D. Middleton, "Some in UN Score US for Hanoi Step," *New York Times,* December 19, 1965, p. 1.

36. Krock, "Hanoi Peace Feeler."

37. "Peace, LBJ's Top Objective," *Los Angeles Herald-Examiner,* January 3, 1966, p. A5. See also J. D. Pomfret, "Vietnam 'Failure' Saddens Johnson," *New York Times,* January 1, 1966, p. 1.

38. "Vietnam: A Glorious Quiet for Christmas," *New York Times,* December 26, 1965, section G, p. 4. See also Frankel, "A Crisis of Confidence."

39. "Pope Appeals for Truce in Vietnam for Christmas," *New York Times,* December 20, 1965, p. 4.

40. "The Pope on Vietnam," *New York Times,* December 20, 1965, p. 34. (The full text of this editorial can be found in the Appendix.)

41. W. Rogers, "LBJ Talk May Order Big War," *Los Angeles Herald-Examiner,* December 29, 1965, p. 1.

42. D. Pearson, "Johnson Convinced Reds Don't Want Peace, Growing Irritable," *Los Angeles Times,* December 29, 1965, part II, p. 6.

43. J. D. Pomfret, "White House Says Aim Is Parley," *New York Times,* December 31, 1965, p. 1.

44. T. Wicker, "U.S. Peace Drive Said to Produce Offers to Assist," *New York Times,* December 31, 1965, p. 1.

45. T. Wicker, "President Gives Urgency to Drive," *New York Times,* January 1, 1966, p. 2C.

46. A. Lewis, "Europeans Back Peace Bid Widely," *New York Times,* January 6, 1966, p. 2C.

47. J. Reston, "Washington: Johnson's Jet-Propelled Diplomacy," *New York Times,* January 2, 1966, p. 12E.

48. "The Reply to Hanoi," *New York Times,* January 9, 1966, p. 12E.

49. D. Janson, "Vietnam War Opponents View Johnson's Peace Bid as 'Hoax'," *New York Times,* January 9, 1966, p. 5.

50. "Barriers to Talks," *New York Times,* January 23, 1966, p. 1E.

51. J. Alsop, "Harmful Effects of the Strange Interlude," *Los Angeles Times,* January 28, 1966, Part II, p. 6.

52. E. W. Kenworthy, "Six Democrats Try to Rally Senate Against Bombing," *New York Times,* January 27, 1966, p. 1.

53. J. Reston, "Johnson's Jet-Propelled Diplomacy."

10

On Looking and Being Looked At

I

Looking at people and things is one of the first steps to mastery of the environment. It is a means of knowing at a distance, a warning of impending contact, a way of experiencing the environment before we have to deal with it. The look and its interpretation are means for assessing the intentions of an adversary. Freud established the connection between the act of looking and the sense of shame, but in his emphasis on the sensual aspect of looking as "scoptophilia," he all but ignored the role of looking as an ego function and a means of mastery.[1] Both looking and its counterpart, being looked at, are related to sexual impulses, but they are also manifestations of the urge for power over others. Even the sense of shame, which we experience when we are observed in the act of looking at others, derives in part, from this function of looking in relation to mastery. In the adolescent who lowers his gaze when he is caught looking at a pretty girl, the look appears to have a purely sexual significance. But what happens in the look exchanged between two men?

I am sitting in the compartment of a train watching the man across from me who is facing toward the window. Suddenly his head turns and he looks directly into my eyes. I turn away at once with a feeling of embarrassment. But as my gaze wanders back in his direction, I can see, out of the corner of my eye, that he is now looking at me. Gradually the feeling of embarrassment changes to anger. I look at him directly and our eyes meet. Neither of us smiles. We continue to look at each other without a change of expression. The tension mounts. Thoughts race through my mind. "This is silly, childish. What does it prove?" But I continue to look and so does he. Neither will break the tension by turning away, although both of us wish for relief. The look has now been transformed into a contest for power. In this primitive impulse to look at the other, one can find all the psychological roots of warfare among mankind.

It is Sartre who has given us the most penetrating insight into the psychological significance of looking.[2] For Sartre shame is the result of this basic contact with the other. The look of the other makes me aware of myself. It is as though the other were present in my own consciousness, yet he cannot be there. His image of me is clearly different from my own, although I catch some intimation of it from his look. When we hear the distortions of a person afflicted with paranoia, the difference between these two images of the self becomes quite evident. But in the accusations of the paranoid there is a basic psychological truth. For, intentionally or inadvertently, the look is a form of attack. By looking at the other we make him aware of his quality as an object. We pull him back into himself and impair his ability to lose himself in the world in the sense of simply being there. To be looked at and to know one is being looked at is no longer to see the world and other people as objects but to become an object. It is also to become aware of the freedom of others to see us and use us as objects. Thus, although the sensation of looking and being looked at may flicker back and forth from one moment to the next, we cannot, while we are conscious of being looked at, see the other person as an object. We are imprisoned within ourselves by his look, forced to turn inward, distracted from our grasp of the world. We are, in short, vulnerable.[3] The look of the other constitutes a negation of the fluidity that we feel in our own being, the sense of a flickering and changing consciousness with evolving possibilities for action, as opposed to the more limited notion of a fixed object with "traits," as a "type" of person. Therefore, this look, while it violates our subjectivity, also attacks our freedom in a more fundamental and irrevocable sense than physical restraint. It may cling to us in memory long after the other has departed. It is a perpetual challenge to our very existence, as we know it and experience it.

II

When one nation spies on another the hostile and threatening aspect of looking is clearly paramount and the word, *espionage*, carries this same connotation. Committing an act of espionage against another nation suggests that the other has been *damaged* in some way or made vulnerable by our act of looking. But espionage has generally meant some illegal act inside the borders of another nation. There is another context in which looking can be construed as an innocent act or, at least, defensive rather than aggressive. This is looking as observation or reconnaissance.

The incident of the *Pueblo,* like the U-2, was one in which the United States took the position that it was not engaged in an aggressive act but simply collecting information that should be available to anyone. It was, in fact, not a simple situation in which one nation was right and the other wrong. There was a sharp difference in the perceptions of North Korean and U.S. leaders concerning the significance of the act itself.

When the American spy ship *Pueblo* was captured off the coast of North Korea on January 23, 1968, with the loss of one American life and the injury of several other crewmen, the chief question raised at the time of the incident was: "Why was this ship not provided adequate protection?" Despite the official answer that such ships had not been attacked in the past, there were, in fact, a series of precedents to suggest that spy vehicles were considered fair game by communist nations. The United States, on the other hand, has assumed the existence of an international "right to look" in addition to the informally recognized freedom of the seas. Our attitude stands in striking contrast to that of other nations in this regard.

The notion of "freedom of the seas" developed as a reaction to the act of piracy. Piracy, as it was originally practiced, meant the seizure of commercial vessels for plunder of economic goods. The pirate was either an independent entrepreneur or the agent of one naval power preying on the commercial shipping of another and using the black flag to disguise his nationality. The elimination of piracy was due to the more effective arming of merchant vessels, the provision of escorts, and to treaties between nations. Formal recognition has never been accorded to freedom of the seas (or the air) for spy craft of any kind, although the right to carry cargo or passengers in international waters is generally recognized. There was, at the time, no established international agreement that defined the limits of a nation's territorial waters or air space. Most communist nations claimed a 12-mile limit for territorial waters. The United States claimed three miles. The very notion of an act of piracy or aggression on the high seas has a rather different meaning when a ship is attacked far from shore carrying a commercial cargo and when it is attacked close to the shore of an enemy or potential enemy while in the act of gathering information on enemy defenses. Among their various missions, most of these spy vessels and aircraft require the collection of some data on radar frequencies in order to develop what is called an "electronic order of battle." Experienced reporters in the field of military affairs have suggested that this information is used to prepare penetration aids for strike aircraft so these aircraft can jam defensive radar, (or otherwise avoid defensive radar) and place their bombs on target. In other words, the information collected by spy ships such as the *Pueblo* and reconnaissance planes is directly related to military attack—not merely to defense purposes. They can be used not only to gather information, but to jam radar prior to an attack.[4] Therefore, it is not surprising—or at least it should not be surprising—that these reconnaissance activities are regarded as threatening to the security of the country being watched.

As a nation, the United States is particularly embarrassed by restrictions against looking, for our style has been to look openly, or to strive to look openly. All nations engage in some degree of undercover espionage and make secret penetrations into the territory of their neighbors for purposes of gathering information, but such acts are admittedly illegal and are not acknowledged. *It is the effort to change the world ethic in this regard that distinguishes the actions of the United States from those of other nations.* The effort to legitimize reconnaissance has been pushed almost exclusively by Americans, from the Eisenhower open-skies proposal to the Johnson attempt to base a cessation of bombing in North Vietnam on a North Vietnamese agreement to end shelling in the cities of the South and grant safe passage for U.S. reconnaissance planes. The acceptance of an international right to look might improve the prospects for peace. However, it is one thing to promote such a world ethic and quite another to act as though it already existed.

The American belief in a right to look is demonstrated by the risks taken by the United States in aerial reconnaissance. The RB-47, the U-2, the *Maddox* and *Turner Joy* in the Gulf of Tonkin, the *Pueblo*, and the EC-121, are only the more notable instances in which American aircraft or ships have been fired upon for actual or alleged penetration of the territory of another sovereign state. If we were able to back off from such ventures once they proved unprofitable, they would not be so dangerous. Our position that our looking is innocent and the enemy is the aggressor is what makes the situation so explosive.

Nevertheless, the notion that it is basically "unfair" to fire on an unarmed reconnaissance vehicle of any kind has persisted in the conduct of U.S. foreign policy. As a consequence of this tacit assumption, great pains are taken to avoid any show of armament in connection with such missions. According to Secretary McNamara, the *Pueblo* was not provided with air cover because it might have been "provocative."[5] Clearly, the Secretary was quite correct, as we shall see in the latter part of this chapter. Once a nation decides to provide armed support to an espionage vehicle, it must be prepared to go all the way into full-scale warfare. For the enemy may decide that the violation of its territory is insupportable, and it may be willing to expend any amount of armament and manpower to detain or destroy espionage vehicles (ships, planes, etc.) that it regards as having violated its territory. Presumably it was the issue of "provocation" that was behind the refusal to provide the *Pueblo* with any major defensive armament. Even the two .50-caliber machine guns on board were kept covered. Commander Bucher indicated during the naval court of inquiry on the incident: "Nor was I to provoke anyone by the use of these guns or by practicing with them or even having them in the presence of foreign shipping."[6] Extreme care was exercised to make sure that there would be no physical capability for armed aggression on or around the *Pueblo*, yet its mission was not considered provocative in itself.

The lack of protection afforded the *Pueblo* was not the only indication that the mission was regarded as innocent of all aggressive intent. It was the total lack of preparation for attack that was the most striking feature of the ship and its mission. Commander Bucher told the naval court of inquiry that his pleas for a destruct system to get rid of classified documents and equipment had been ignored. Even his last minute attempt to buy dynamite was rejected.[7] The apparent lack of concern for the *Pueblo* continued despite an obvious increase in belligerence on the part of the North Koreans. During the year prior to the capture of the *Pueblo*, the number of reported North Korean violations of the armistice agreements had increased tenfold, and 31 North Korean commandos had penetrated as far south as Seoul in an attempt on the life of President Chung Hee Park of South Korea just before the incident.[8] On January 20, just three days before the attack on the *Pueblo*, the North Koreans registered a strong protest against "the provocative act of dispatching spy boats and espionage bandits" to the coastal waters of North Korea, saying that if such acts continued, it could start another war. The statement concluded, "We have the due right to make a due response to your thoughtless play with fire. We will fully exercise our rights."[9] In a *New York Times* report of the investigation of the *Pueblo* affair by the Senate Committee on Foreign Relations it was noted that this statement was a clear indication of increasing belligerence by the North Koreans and that "prudence would have suggested that the *Pueblo* be ordered 25 to 30 miles at sea or else provided with protection." However, "those responsible for the overall management of American foreign policy were only dimly aware, if at all, of the *Pueblo's* mission and not at all aware of the timing."[10]

Here, again, is the issue of *awareness*, a matter that is crucial to an understanding of the entire *Pueblo* affair. Both Secretaries Rusk (State) and McNamara (Defense) took responsibility for approval of the *Pueblo* mission, but both men refused to identify the individuals within their departments responsible for the approval. The Committee on Foreign Relations concluded that the decision to go ahead with the *Pueblo* mission, despite the issue of timing, was made somewhere well down in the hierarchy of the departments. Somehow the administration as a whole, managed to go ahead with the *Pueblo* mission without really being aware of what it was doing and unaware of the dangers faced by Commander Bucher and his men.

In the testimony at the naval court of inquiry there are few clues as to why U.S. officials were unaware of the dangers faced by the *Pueblo*. The chief basis for the refusal of military support and the failure to provide a destruct system for classified data was apparently the belief that the North Koreans would not attack as long as the *Pueblo* remained outside their territorial waters. However, it is clear from the record that even in this area the *Pueblo* was pushing its limits. Concern was directed toward remaining outside North Korean territorial waters, *as viewed from the Pueblo*. There was no attempt to consider the effect of possible errors in navigation or errors in enemy monitoring devices, which may have made it appear that a violation of the territorial waters had occurred. In the court of inquiry, Lieutenant Murphy, the *Pueblo's* navigator, testified that the ship's Loran navigational system "could have been out of position by as much as five miles."[11] He further indicated that the *Pueblo's* steering was poor, that overcast weather severely limited celestial navigation, that the navigational charts had obvious errors, and that radar was only ordered five or six times in the ten-day voyage to check the *Pueblo's* position.[12] Yet Commander Bucher's orders permitted him to go within 13 miles of the shore, just one mile beyond the 12-mile limit claimed by the North Koreans as their territorial waters.

If one adds to this problem the possible errors in North Korean radar calibration, the size of the radar skin paint on the scope (which may easily have covered a two to three-mile area), and possible distortion in transmitting the radar report to a North Korean plotter (who was presumably maintaining a continuous record of the *Pueblo's* position), we have ample grounds for assuming that the North Koreans may have placed the *Pueblo* five or six miles closer to shore than its position as indicated on board ship. The failure to try to imagine what the North Koreans might be doing or thinking was certainly an important factor in placing the *Pueblo* in such an exposed position. The insistence that the record of the *Pueblo's* position, as maintained aboard the *Pueblo,* is the only acceptable evidence of this position, is another example of a peculiar narrowness in the American concept of what constitutes "international waters."

III

The *Pueblo* incident was good material for the presidential campaign of Richard M. Nixon. In several of his speeches before election, Mr. Nixon promised that there would be no repetition of an incident like the *Pueblo.* On January 24, 1969, after the crew of the *Pueblo* had been returned to the United States and the hearings begun, the *Los Angeles Times* urged President Nixon to place the problem posed by the *Pueblo* on his early agenda. Why, the *Times* asked, had the *Pueblo* been so inadequately armed and why was there such a lack of protection for similar missions? The issue was too important, said the *Times* editorial, to let the navy take a position of passing judgement on its own actions.[13] Apparently, however, the danger was construed as relating to ships such as the *Pueblo.* The alert capability was increased, and air cover was provided for certain missions. The problem was considered solved.

On April 14, 1969, an American naval electronic plane EC-121, was shot down off the coast of North Korea with 31 men aboard and the issue of the "right to look" was raised once again. As in the past, the United States made its point on the position of the plane when it was shot down. It was, the defense department reported, "90 to 100 nautical miles southeast of Chongjin, North Korea."[14] Nevertheless, the North Koreans claimed that the American plane had intruded into its "territorial air." Once again, we are in a situation that is a bit confusing as regards what is a nation's territorial air. Most nations permit free travel for passenger and cargo aircraft that have filed flight plans with the appropriate authorities. Russian passenger planes penetrate U.S. air space without objection and U.S. planes fly to Moscow. However, the United States does have what is known as an Air Defense Identification Zone (or ADIZ) that extends far out from our shores. Foreign aircraft that have not filed flight plans are subject to interception and, if they cannot be identified by the interceptor pilot, "forcible action in proportion to the threat posed would be taken."[15] Although this action is to be taken only if the aircraft "committed a hostile act or evidenced hostile intent," it is obvious that the definition of "hostile intent" must be made on the spot by the military authorities who are aware of the situation. If the U.S. pilot attempted to force the foreign aircraft to land and the unidentified plane attempted to escape, would he fire on the aircraft? It would appear that some kind of force would be required under these circumstances.

However, this would depend on the nation involved and our relationship with that nation at the time. If our Air Defense Command were on "red alert," we would probably attempt to destroy an unidentified aircraft or at least force it to land if it penetrated our ADIZ and came within 100 miles of our territory. On April 14, 1977, an unidentified Russian bomber penetrated to within 60 miles of the Florida coast without filing a flight plan. There was no alert condition, and our relations with Russia were peaceful. When the plane was still 200 miles from our shore, two of our jets were scrambled to intercept it, but the Russian aircraft moved below our radar coverage and the interceptors were not able to locate it. Whether they would have forced it to land or merely warned it away we do not know. Our policy is probably deliberately unclear on this point in order to discourage such penetrations.[16]

How far out to sea does the "territorial air" of the United States extend? The limits of our ADIZ can be found in the Federal Aviation Administration Regulations, a casual inspection of which indicates that ADIZ reaches 400 to 450 miles from our shores in some areas.[17] There are indications that the U.S. reconnaissance plane may have been a good deal closer than 100 miles when it was first sighted on North Korean radar. It may have been in flight to avoid capture when it was downed off North Korea. The statement released by the defense department indicates that the EC-121 was actually authorized to penetrate to 40 nautical miles by standing instructions and 50 nautical miles for the mission in question. Even this latter figure is well within what might be regarded as a Korean zone for air identification.

Yet President Nixon reported that the action by the North Koreans constituted a "completely surprise attack in every sense of the word and therefore did not give us the opportunity for protective actions."[18] Commenting on his statement the New York Times remarked: "it is incredible that the President should assert yesterday that the plane incident came as 'a completely surprise attack.' The fact that North Korean jets regularly rode shotgun on 190 earlier American intelligence flights this year should have been a warning, not a reassurance."[19]

Let us return, then, to the question that was asked at the beginning of this chapter. Knowing what we did about the belligerence of North Korea and the aggressive activities of our own spy vehicles, why did we not anticipate attack? After the *Pueblo* was captured, why was not further consideration given to the mission of the EC-121? Or perhaps a more pertinent question, why were these missions not more carefully reviewed to determine if the intelligence data collected was really worth the risk involved? The answer is that such high level reviews of policy are generally undertaken by men of cabinet rank or the president himself. The cancellation of a mission or a whole series of missions would mean a curtailment of activity and a budget cut for the service involved. The objective of the various service commands has always been to solve problems before they come to the attention of the president. This often comes to mean keeping the president unaware of potentially explosive situations. It was clear that President Eisenhower was not made aware of the timing of the U-2 flight as the summit conference approached, just as no one called President Nixon's attention to the exposed position of the EC-121, even after the loss of the *Pueblo*.

Congressional leaders are aware that many details of such missions are withheld from the president unless he learns what questions he must ask. After the first White House briefing on the EC-121 incident, both Senators Fulbright and Dirkson expressed some reservation about accepting the official report that "the plane did not get closer than 60 miles to North Korea at any time."[20] Senator Mike Mansfield stated publicly that the mission of the EC-121 "was carried on without the personal knowledge of President Nixon even as the incident of the U.S.S. *Pueblo* was carried on without the personal knowledge of President Johnson." Mansfield pointed out that the mission may have continued automatically "in the absence of an order to the contrary from the new Administration."[21] Mansfield suggested a new intelligence facility to let the president know what is going on in such missions.

However, the creation of such an intelligence capability is directly contrary to the American style in such matters. Our entire system of information transfer is designed to permit the president to maintain the national image of frankness and honesty, as befits the leader of an open society. In order to do this he must remain relatively free from awareness of our aggressive actions. This attitude is critical for the war-making potential of the United States. American effectiveness in a wartime situation comes from this sense of being in the right. The other nation must be seen as the aggressor. We must be the wronged party, if necessary, even the "patsy." Therefore, spy vehicles must be seen, not as aggressors, but as representatives of an open society, striving to achieve a maximum of world openness, keeping the world an honest place in which to live.

Although the highly advertised openness of American society has considerable substance, it has also a strong mythic content; that is, it serves as a justification for many of our beliefs and our actions regardless of its factual accuracy. Our openness serves as a basis for demanding that others be open with us. If they are not, there is an unspoken assumption that we have the right to "open them up." Since our openness makes us more vulnerable to the information-gathering techniques of potential enemies, we feel justified in forcing the lock on the more "closed" societies. In the process we are inclined to interpret our own behavior, not as a hostile intrusive act, but as a right to look, which is based on a universal application of our national ethic of openness. In this respect we are able to avoid facing the aggressive implications of our act.

IV

There was no retaliation for the loss of 31 lives aboard the EC-121 and the single death aboard the *Pueblo*. However, in Vietnam the situation was quite different. We have already noted that President Johnson retaliated against the attack on the *Maddox* and *Turner Joy* (in which neither ship was hit and no Americans killed or wounded) with a 64 sortie raid against North Vietnam. When President Johnson decided not to run for reelection and made his announcement of a bombing halt for North Vietnam, he was faced with a powerful military organization that was still urging further expansion of the military effort. There are indications that President Johnson could not obtain military endorsement for a bombing halt unless he was able to guarantee those forms of reconnaissance the military considered important.[22] In other words, it appears that the "understanding" that the U.S. reconnaissance planes would be permitted to fly over North Vietnam was the result of a bargain the president made with his top military officers in order to gain some measure of support for his policy—and not a bargain with the North Vietnamese.

When the Nixon Administration came into power, the escalation of the air war was justified, at first, on the basis of this alleged right to look—unrestricted right of observation of North Vietnamese territory. In the first few days after the bombing halt, the reconnaissance planes had flown unescorted. But when the aircraft were fired upon by the North Vietnamese, armed escorts were sent to provide "suppressive fire." The first intimation that we were moving into a new stage of the air war appeared on January 29, 1970, when an American fighter-bomber and a rescue helicopter were shot down in an air battle near a North Vietnam missile site. The American plane had attacked the missile site because the missile battery had fired on the American reconnaissance plane it was escorting. The State Department insisted at the time that the United States had not changed its policy and was not resuming the bombing of North Vietnam.[23] The North Vietnamese (Colonel Ha Van Lau) called the American action a brazen provocation and denied any agreement to permit reconnaissance of its territory by American aircraft.[24]

But it was not until the invasion of Cambodia that the Nixon Administration conducted the biggest air strike against North Vietnam since the formal bombing halt. On May 2, 1970, four days after the first American troops entered Cambodia, 120 American bombers attacked bases in North Vietnam "to protect reconnaissance planes." In contrast to the usual practice of ordering "suppressive fire" from escort aircraft this group of 120 planes was described as "augmented protective reaction" strikes. To the North Vietnamese charge that populated areas had been attacked by American planes, the Pentagon replied, "We conduct protective reaction when necessary to protect our unarmed reconnaissance planes against enemy attack."[25] Just as the Cambodian invasion was an effort to "protect American lives," the mission of 120 bombers was conceived of as an effort to "protect unarmed planes." But this was not to be construed as a change in policy or a resumption of the bombing of North Vietnam.

On December 26, 1971, a new series of heavy bombing raids began against North Vietnam. In one raid alone it was reported that 350 airplanes were involved, but the Pentagon refused to confirm or deny these figures. This time the raids were called "reinforced protective reaction strikes," and it was finally admitted that they amounted to a "limited selective resumption of the bombing."[26] This time, too, the justification had to be extended. They were, said Secretary of Defense Laird, necessary to protect our planes, but also to protect American service personnel still in Vietnam. When asked what was the difference between these new "reinforced protective reaction strikes" and the earlier bombing policies of Secretary McNamara, the new secretary replied that the current strikes were of "limited duration."[27]

By this time it was clear that more than the right to look was involved in American bombing operations. The contrast between our response to the *Pueblo* (and EC-121) near Korea and the increasing attacks to "defend" reconnaissance in Vietnam made it clear that our intent was quite different toward these two nations. The elusive notion of victory was still in the air.

V

Officially, our only intent was observation. We had no desire to widen the war or to be more aggressive. We were not to fire at enemy defensive installations in North Vietnam unless we were fired upon. Privately, however, field commanders were encouraged to be more aggressive. In fact, they were ordered to be more aggressive. On December 4 and 5, 1971, a conference was called in Honolulu by the Chairman of the Joint Chiefs of Staff. The Chairman told his field commanders they were not being aggressive enough.[28] But here again care was taken not to give them the *authority* to be more aggressive. This would have implied that the president himself had changed his policy in the air war. Instead, they were told to be more aggressive in using the authority available to them. For example, it was suggested that they could increase their reconnaissance activities and increase the number of armed escort aircraft to ensure effective damage to the enemy.[29] The atmosphere in Washington at this time was one that encouraged an expansion of the air war provided it could be managed without any change in public policy. This required an indirect pressure on the military from the Department of Defense on down to the wing commanders and the pilots who flew the missions. The result was a situation similar to that obtained between the secretary of the navy and Commodore Perry on his mission to Japan. The field commanders were urged to use their authority to the utmost and were assured that they would receive the full support of the Department of Defense. Said General Lavelle, Commander of the Seventh Air Force, in reviewing this situation:

> It was quite clear that we were first encouraged to be and then commended for being more aggressive: that we were told to be more flexible; that we were told to increase the frequency of reconaissance flights over NVN; that we were told to increase the number of fighter escorts with the reconnaissance aircraft to ensure effective results on protective reaction strikes; that Washington wouldn't question our aiming points and would back us up. It was also very clear that the JCS representative at the Honolulu conference, and higher authority, the JCS, CINCPAC and CINCPACAF, in messages, had made very liberal in-

terpretations of the rules of engagement (ROE) concerning protective
reaction strikes. . . . Higher authority had recommended, encouraged,
and then commended an extremely liberal target policy, well beyond the language of the ROE. This liberal interpretation by higher
authority of *what* could be struck, plus the encouragement to be more
aggressive and more flexible, influenced my determination to make a
similar, though I believe less liberal, interpretation of the conditions
under which we could strike.[30]

And so it goes on down the line. Our official policy was the same,
but the word was out that commanders would be rewarded for extra
initiative and aggressiveness in their conduct of the air war. What
aspiring commander could resist such a challenge? It is part of the
American way. You don't sit back and wait for people to tell you
what to do. You use your leadership and imagination to show the
Joint Chiefs of Staff and the Department of Defense that you are the
best in the business. It was in this spirit that General Lavelle began to
improve on the rules of engagement for the air war in Vietnam.

However, only a few months before General Lavelle took the initiative in the war away from the Joint Chiefs of Staff, he received in
his command a young sergeant named Lonnie Franks. Had he
known more about the character of Sergeant Franks, he would certainly have modified his urge for achievement. For it was the testimony of this obscure sergeant that finally led the general to the loss
of his command. We will examine how this came about in the next
chapter.

NOTES

1. S. Freud, *Basic Writings of Sigmund Freud*, ed. A. A. Brill (New York: Modern Library, 1965), pp. 546, 577, 593, 568–569.

2. J. -P. Sartre, *Being and Nothingness*, Trans. Hazel E. Barnes (New York: Philosophical Library, 1956), pp. 221–413.

3. Ibid., pp. 258–259.

4. R. Homan, "Lost Plane: a Pueblo-Type Spy," *Washington Post*, April 16, 1969, p. A6. "N. Korea Claims It Downed U.S. Plane," *Washington Post*, April 16, 1969, p. A6.

5. U.S., Congress, Senate, Committee on Foreign Relations, *The Gulf of Tonkin. The 1964 Incidents: Hearings*, 20 February, 1968, pp. 42–43.

6. B. Weinraub, "Admiral to Face Three Pueblo Queries," *New York Times*, January 29, 1969, p. 6.

7. B. Weinraub, "Bucher Pits Moral Judgment Against Naval Code." *New York Times*, January 27, 1969, p. 2.

8. E. W. Kenworthy, "Study on Pueblo Discerns Weakness in Control," *New York Times*, February 2, 1969, p. 47.

9. Ibid.

10. Ibid.

11. B. Weinraub, "Testimony of Pueblo Crewmen Raises Questions and Conflicts," *New York Times*, February 10, 1969, p. 6.

12. Ibid.

13. "Comdr. Bucher's Testimony," *Los Angeles Times*, January 24, 1969, part II, p. 8.

14. *New York Times*, April 17, 1969, p. 14.

15. Personal letter in response to my questions about air defense policy from Leigh Ratiner, Office of Assistant General Counsel, International Affairs, Department of Defense, dated 5 November 1969.

16. "Soviet Plane Flies Over U.S." *Los Angeles Times*, April 23, 1977, p. 1.

17. *Federal Aviation Administration Regulations*, Security Control of Air Traffic, 14 CFR pt. 99; referred to in letter from Mr. Ratiner.

18. Transcript of the president's news conference on foreign and domestic affairs, *New York Times*, April 19, 1969, p. 14.

19. "Intelligence for What?" *New York Times*, April 19, 1969, p. 32. (The complete editorial can be found in the Appendix.)

20. W. Chapman, "Hill Dubious About Initial U.S. Accounts," *Washington Post*, April 17, 1969, pp. A-1 and A-9.

21. Ibid.

22. W. Beecher, "The Risks of Those Reconnaissance Flights," *New York Times*, December 8, 1968, section E, p. 4.

23. T. Sell, "U.S. Planes Hit North Vietnam Missile Base after Attack by Red Jet," *Los Angeles Times*, January 30, 1970, p. 1.

24. "Hanoi Assails Air Attack as Provocation," *Los Angeles Times*, January 30, 1970, p. 10.

25. "120 U.S. Jets Hit Red Antiaircraft and Missile Sites," *Los Angeles Times*, May 3, 1970, p. 1.

26. W. Beecher, "Laird Warns Big U.S. Raids in North May Be Repeated to Protect G.I.'s in South," *New York Times*, December 28, 1971, p. 1.

27. Excerpts from Laird's news conference on the bombing of north and defense department activities in 1971, *New York Times*, December 28, 1971, p. 8.

28. U.S., Congress, Senate, Committee on Armed Services, Nomination of John D. Lavelle, General Creighton W. Abrams, and Admiral John S. McCain: Hearings, p. 103.

29. Ibid., p. 47.

30. Ibid., p. 51.

11

General
Lavelle's
Misunderstanding

I

In the American intervention in Santo Domingo, there were some strong indications that President Johnson and others in the administration had crossed that thin line between self-deception and the conscious lie to others. Nevertheless, the myth of inadvertence was maintained for the sake of public appearance. In the case of General Lavelle's unauthorized bombing strikes into North Vietnam, the appearance of inadvertence was more difficult to sustain. Over 20 bombing strikes were ordered in which the pilots were to bomb regardless of enemy reaction. Furthermore, the records of the strikes were falsified to make it appear that the North Vietnamese had fired first. The situation was complicated by the general's initial refusal to admit that he had made a mistake and his insistence that his superiors knew what he was doing. It was not until the Senate Armed Services Committee demanded a full hearing into his conduct that he discovered the importance of inadvertence in American political life.

On April 8, 1972, the air force announced the retirement of General John D. Lavelle, Commander of the Seventh Air Force in Vietnam, for "personal and health reasons" and his replacement by General Vogt. On May 8, General Lavelle was nominated for advancement on the retired list from major general to lieutenant general. In June, after considerable investigation by reporters and pressure from Congress, the full story of the general's unauthorized bombing raids over North Vietnam reached the public. The issue raised by these raids went considerably beyond the question of the general's insubordination. It was Senator Hughes of Iowa who raised the question:

> to what extent can the actions of a single combat commander, authorizing persistent violations of established orders over a period of four months, trigger a spiraling escalation of hostilities by both sides at a time when we are committed to winding down the intensity of the war and withdrawing?
>
> Now, an even graver question has arisen: To what extent were unauthorized air strikes ordered by General Lavelle responsible for the total collapse of the Paris peace talks last November? . . . Mr. President, it is imperative to note that, two weeks after the North Vietnamese agreed to meet and nine days before the meeting was cancelled, American war planes carried out "protective reaction strikes," as they were called by the American command in Saigon, against three North Vietnamese airfields. That was November 8, the same day fixed as the beginning of the Air Force investigation into the unauthorized air strikes. . . .
>
> These startling facts suggest parallels with the 1964 Gulf of Tonkin incident. Once again, we have been misled as to what actually occurred. We were told of the North Vietnamese retaliation but not about the allied attacks which preceded it.[1]

When called before the House Armed Services Committee on June 12 to explain why the details of General Lavelle's replacement had been kept from Congress and from the public, General Ryan, the air force chief of staff, replied, "I have avoided public discussion because I had no desire to add to General Lavelle's personal and health problems by publicizing other circumstances involved in this matter. He stated his reasons for requesting retirement and I considered them, then and now, highly personal and private business."[2] However, neither the House nor the Senate were very pleased with the general's explanation. It seemed that the effort to cover up the reasons for General Lavelle's dismissal was related to the concealment of a basic change in our goal in Vietnam. The Senate Armed Services Committee determined to conduct its own investigation of the unauthorized strikes and to examine, at the same time, the encouragement that the general may have had, from sources within the administration, to expand his authority and bomb North Vietnam.

The situation in Vietnam at the time General Lavelle assumed command was clearly moving toward a crucial decision point as a result of increasing hostilities by both sides that had been building for over three years. Before we go into the details of the Senate hearing, it would be best to review this background.

II

In April 1969 a few months after he assumed office, President Nixon announced that he had set in motion a plan to extricate the United States from Vietnam. In June he announced the first withdrawal of 25,000 American troops to be completed in August. In September, he announced the second round of withdrawal: 35,000 men. From 1969 through 1972, with the exception of the incursions into Cambodia, the Nixon policy was clearly aimed at reducing the involvement of American ground troops in Vietnam. Although he insisted he would take no notice of peace protesters, he was obviously moved by the strong disenchantment with the Vietnam War, which was widespread in the United States. However, the disenchantment was two-sided. Americans on the left wanted immediate withdrawal and those on the right were discouraged by the "no win" policy that they felt the Nixon Administration was continuing. They were angered to find a president, whom they had once considered to be one of their own kind, catering to liberals and "peaceniks."

The new president was faced with a difficult balancing act. If he would appease both sides, he must win the war while withdrawing troops at the same time. His solution was an attempt to speed up the process by which the South Vietnamese assumed greater responsibility for the war (the so-called "Vietnamization" program) along with a massive infusion of American air and naval power. Nevertheless, it was important that this additional military force should not appear as a change of policy or an attempt to escalate the war. For this reason, briefings to the press on the arrival of American air and naval forces stressed the "defensive" character of their mission. They were in Vietnam to "protect" the American program of withdrawal. The rules of engagement for air warfare remained the same as they were at the time of the 1968 bombing halt declared by President Johnson. A pair of escort craft would accompany our reconnaissance missions over North Vietnam, but they were not to bomb unless they were fired upon.

Soon the American military began to complain that the North Vietnamese were building up their defenses and suppressive fire was not really sufficient to halt this buildup, but President Nixon was not *willing* to put an end to the bombing restrictions imposed by President Johnson. One might well ask "why?" We maintained that the "understanding" between the previous administration and the North Vietnamese, who permitted U.S. reconnaissance over North Vietnamese territory, had been violated. If this were true, why did we still feel constrained to live up to our side of the agreement? The answer probably lies in the important role that public relations had come to play in the Vietnam War. The "understanding" was the only shred of legality that surrounded our reconnaissance mission, and we did not want to abandon it. We had never declared war against North Vietnam, and we were going to prove we were not at war by resolving it into a series of gun battles in which the other fellow had to go for his gun before we would return the fire. This would prove we were only fighting in self-defense.

Like the heroic gun slinger of the old West, we were expected to stand there, hands at our sides, until we saw him draw. In this case the restrictions were even more severe. We had to see the flash of his weapon before we could return his fire. At the same time, we ignored the aggressive nature of our presence in Vietnam and the violation of North Vietnamese territory by our reconnaissance.

However, there is something about the massive influx of air power into an area that changes the nature of our acts. If the power to bomb is present, there is a certain inevitability in regard to its use. Soon the reconnaissance aircraft, which were formerly accompanied by two escorts,were given four, eight, and even sixteen or more armed escort planes. The targets for the missions were preplanned. Earlier reconnaissance flights had already determined the location of enemy targets in the area. It was only necessary to assign these targets to the escort craft that accompanied the reconnaissance. In practice the whole character of the missions began to change from reconnaissance to bombing. Without any official change in policy, we had moved from the sending of unarmed reconnaissance aircraft over enemy territory to the position in which repeated, preplanned bombing of enemy targets was standard practice. The "looking" that was, at first, the real purpose of the mission was now used for cosmetic effect. As one informant described the situation,

> I am referring to the recent strikes in the north which are termed "protective reactions." To give you some background, last year reconnaissance flights were flown with our Crusaders into the north with some Skyhawks as protection. The photo planes were unarmed and the

briefing of the pilots consisted of emphasis on photo intelligence. Oc-
casionally, they were fired on which precipitated a protective reaction.
The picture is now changed considerably. The operation is called [de-
leted] and consists of ostensibly the same setup. However, the concentration in the briefing is on strikes—the reconnaissance pilot now sits
in the back of the room hardly noticed. The Skyhawks are armed with
our most sophisticated weapons and launched with the Crusader.
Now, however, the Crusader is giving the Skyhawk protection, not
from the SAM's but from the press.[3]

The implication of this letter, which was sent to Senator Case in
mid-1972, is that the reconnaissance aircraft (the Crusader) was used
to justify the nonaggressive character of the missions in case the
press began to ask questions. The following testimony from a wit-
ness before the Senate Armed Services Committee reveals a similar
change in the character of the North Vietnamese response.

The strikes ... were daily affairs ... At the beginning [November
1971] most of the strikes did not receive hostile reactions. In fact, it
was obvious to me or it seemed logical to me that their orders in North
Vietnam at least were not to shoot at our aircraft because even when
they were bombing they weren't receiving hostile reactions and it
seemed a flight would come back from North Vietnam and not get shot
at after they had bombed and I couldn't believe it because there was a
great deal of guns in North Vietnam. So it amazed me.
     After the middle of February [1972] they did really receive quite a
bit of ground fire and it seemed to me that the North Vietnamese were
finally reacting and finally allowed their gunners to shoot.[4]

It was obvious that the air war was escalating. Just who moved first
and by how much, we may never know. The North Vietnamese
claimed that they "had to" build up their defenses and increase the
flow of supplies because of our increased bombing. We maintained
that we "had to" bomb to prevent the buildup of their air defense
and impede the movement of their troops.

In June 1972 Seymour Hersh of the *New York Times* interviewed a
number of pilots and photo intelligence officers who reported that
preplanned bombing raids had been justified as protective reaction.
"Protective reaction," said one informant, "especially among the
pilots, was very much of a joke. It was very much a set up thing. It
was one of the outs that allowed us to go out and bomb North Vietnam all of the time."[5] Lengthy testimony before the Senate Armed
Services Committee makes it clear that bombing strikes were regularly planned over North Vietnam by both the navy and air force. The
fine point seemed to be, as far as navy testimony was concerned, that
even though the targets were planned in advance, they could always
call off the mission at the last minute if the enemy did not provide a
"hostile reaction." However, sometimes the idea of what constituted

a hostile reaction was rather vague in the mind of the pilots. In some cases, the mere presence of a Russian-built MIG aircraft on the ground was perceived as "hostile," even though the rules of engagement specified the contrary. At least one navy lieutenant showed considerable confusion on this point when questioned by the committee.

> LIEUTENANT MOORE: A MIG on the ground, if you want to talk rules of engagement, they may be one thing, but if you want to be logical about it, a MIG on the ground is a threat because a MIG can launch from a runway in 5 minutes.
>
> THE CHAIRMAN: Let's start over now. Under the rules of engagement as you understood them—
>
> LIEUTENANT MOORE: As I understood them—
>
> THE CHAIRMAN [continuing]: Was there any question about a MIG on the ground?
>
> LIEUTENANT MOORE: There was no question to me at the time. Right now I am trying to remember exactly what the rules are. And the rules are quite—there are quite a lot of them.
>
> THE CHAIRMAN: Yes, I am sure. I am not just trying to pick on them, I am sure you understand that, but as I have understood this testimony it was agreed that a MIG on the ground, inactive, was not hostile under the rules of engagement. . . . Was your mission to bomb the runway regardless of hostile action or no hostile action?
>
> LIEUTENANT MOORE: No, my mission was to bomb the runway in the event of hostile action.
>
> THE CHAIRMAN: Is a MIG, or was a MIG on the ground inactive considered hostile action toward you?
>
> LIEUTENANT MOORE: He is toward me, but he may not be in the rules of engagement, I am not sure on that.[6]

The rules of engagement were, for Lieutenant Moore, something rather theoretical, seemingly not very much related to the realities of air warfare. Commander Miller, the lieutenant's immediate superior and the man who would have been responsible for calling off the strike if he received no enemy reaction, considered the possibility of no enemy response hypothetical. The planes were always attacked, he asserted.[7] Technically speaking, he may have been correct for the time period he was describing, but the escalation to full air warfare was a gradual process. As we have already noted, the North Vietnamese did withhold their fire at certain times, particularly during 1971 and early 1972. For a military commander trying to conduct a war which was strictly "defensive" as far as the press and the public were concerned, but who was receiving private instructions to "be more aggressive," this unpredictability of the North Vietnamese was very frustrating. Suppose, for example, the weather was bright and clear, a perfect day for bombing, the targets had been carefully selected from previous reconnaissance missions, but the enemy failed to provide any hostile response. One might not find such a day again for some time, and the temptation to bomb was magnified by the fact that it was always easier and safer to land a plane from which the ordnance had been expended.

One possible solution to this problem for a commander was to transfer this anxiety and uncertainty down to the flight crews. One could let them know that it would not be a good idea to come back to the base with bombs in the plane's belly. This would leave the matter up to the pilot. He could decide that he had indeed received indications that he was acquired by enemy radar and that he had "observed" missiles in launch position. With a bit of imagination, he would see airborne MIGs or perhaps even a flash of antiaircraft fire. If he had scruples about reporting a reaction he did not see, he could fly low and roll in directly on the target in an attack position. This approach, called "trolling" in air force parlance, seldom failed to draw fire, even from the most reluctant enemy. Of course, it also exposed the pilot and his crew to great danger. For this reason, it was not considered proper for a commander to order trolling. However, if he did not specifically forbid it, the pilot's own need for advancement and his concern for the success of his mission would spur him on. In that case, he was on his own.

III

As men rise to positions of prominence in American military and government life, they develop a certain skill in the art of inadvertent aggression. It is always possible to communicate, in general terms, what must be done without becoming aware of the details. A hint, a nod, a casual remark, or a failure to inquire into certain practices are ways of letting a subordinate know that he will be rewarded for his achievement but that no one will ask embarrassing questions about his methods. As this attitude is passed down the chain of command, there is a certain loss of control over the specifics of an operation but the spirit of the executive's intent (if not his publicly proclaimed policy) is generally followed. This fuzziness about details is important for any nation that seeks both power and virtue at the same time. The American ethic is to be candid with the press and public, to be decent, civilized and humane, and despite all this goodness, to achieve success and power. The only way one can accomplish all of these things is to be unaware of what one is really doing.

On August 1, 1971, the Seventh Air Force in Vietnam received a new commander who was not given to self-deception. General John D. Lavelle was noted for his attention to detail and for his willingness to take full responsibility for his command. He had been conscientious in the execution of his past assignments—to the extent that he often exceeded the formal requirements of a given job. He had a tendency to ask himself not merely what were his orders, but what was his duty. In a previous assignment, he had been in charge of the development of a major defense communications program. At the end of one fiscal year, he had returned to the U.S. Treasury $700 million in unspent funds from his $2.3 billion budget. Such an act was most unusual among military managers who make a point of spending all their allocated funds in order to justify requests for more money. The returned balance aroused considerable controversy in military and government circles, but it received little public attention. A former Pentagon official, in describing the incident, remarked that "Lavelle was committed and didn't see spending the money just to spend it."[8] He was the sort of man who asked what was behind an order, what was really intended? In an environment where people learn to survive through hypocrisy, this is a dangerous question to ask.

General Lavelle had another characteristic that made it difficult for him to function in Vietnam. He had an almost obsessive sense of responsibility for the lives of the men in his command. He absolutely forbade trolling, which he considered an undue risk to the lives of his pilots. We do not know to what extent trolling was practiced before the general assumed command of the Seventh Air Force. Both the navy and the air force had accused each other of this practice, but no commander would admit to it himself. Said General Slay, the operations officer at Seventh Air Force Headquarters:

> A trolling strike, which General Lavelle absolutely forbade, was to attempt to stay within the rules of engagement by the letter by taking a recce [reconnaissance] aircraft or some aircraft, flying into the enemy defenses around and stooging around up in the vicinity of the enemy defenses until groundfire was actually observed and then having the strike aircraft lurking in the weeds—and the Navy liked to do it this way because they would get down right on the deck and as they saw the fire come up, pop up and roll in and do whatever strike they had to do—that is trolling.[9]

General Lavelle understood that he was charged with the responsibility for a more aggressive prosecution of the war, but he was not willing to pass on these vague instructions to his pilots and wink at their efforts to stretch the rules of engagement. He wanted to know exactly what was going on in his command. If anyone was to stretch the rules, it would be him and he would decide how far they were to be stretched. Again, in the frank and colorful testimony of his operations officer, we find an eloquent description of this tight control and the refusal to delegate important decisions.

> General Lavelle was the type of man who—he liked to keep a firm grip on his operation. As a matter of fact, on several occasions he would laughingly introduce me as his assistant ops officer and, in other words, "I am the ops officer; Slay is my assistant."
>
> I don't fault him for that. I probably would run 7th Air Force that way myself. He wanted to do it his way and I certainly would not blame him for that; but, as I said before, he would allow no one, not even his vice commander, I might add, to make the decisions to go into North Vietnam. When he was gone on a trip there were no incursions into North Vietnam even though he left his vice commander in charge. He had to make, personally make, those decisions.[10]

General Lavelle assumed command of the Seventh Air Force in August 1971, but it was not until November that he became so concerned about the build-up of defensive sites and troop movements in North Vietnam that he determined to strike at North Vietnamese installations whether or not he received enemy fire. In the meantime, he made several contacts with General Creighton Abrams, the theater commander, and with the Joint Chiefs of Staff, requesting authority to strike against the enemy build-up in North Vietnam. All requests were denied. There were occasional suspensions of the rules of engagement in which specific bombing raids were ordered by the Joint Chiefs of Staff, but no authority was given to the general to bomb at will.

Finally on December 2, 1971, American pilots reported the first attack on a B-52 bomber by a MIG fighter. It was as though a bomb had landed on the Pentagon. The enemy was fighting back in the air as well as on the ground, and the United States no longer had an assurance of air superiority. It is difficult for the layman to understand the tenderness that an air force general feels toward a B-52. The mere threat to such an expensive colossus was enough to set the Joint Chiefs on edge. It was at this point that the Chairman of the Joint Chiefs of Staff called the Honolulu conference in which he told commanders they were "not aggressive enough." General Lavelle described his response to this instruction: "So having been instructed we were not aggressive enough, we were not using the authorities we had, increase our reconnaissance flights, increase our escorts to be more effective, I assumed I should take the rules that I had and interpret them as fully as I could to operate under them and be more aggressive."[11]

In early December, Secretary of Defense Laird visited Saigon, and the general again asked for authority to strike into North Vietnam. However, at that time, the political climate was filled with news of the Democratic election campaign, and it seemed that every candidate was a peace candidate. President Nixon had announced the withdrawal of 45,000 more troops, but a Cornell University group studying the air war in Indochina had just concluded [November 7] that the Nixon Administration was curtailing ground combat by U.S. troops only to intensify the air war. The secretary told the general that he would support his actions, but that he could not give him any more authority. Said Lavelle, "Although I do not remember any of the Secretary's statements verbatim, the essence of his comments, as I understood them, was—don't come into Washington requesting new authorities, it was an inopportune time; make maximum use of the authorities we had and he would support us in Washington."[12]

Although the general had engaged in two questionable strikes prior to December, it would appear that it was after the meeting with the Joint Chiefs of Staff and the visit from Secretary Laird that he began to make regular strikes into North Vietnam regardless of enemy reaction. It was on January 23, 1972, that he insisted his pilots must report some enemy reaction on all strikes. His decision was prompted by the previous attack on the B-52, and his mission on January 23 was to strike the base at Dong Hoi where the MIGs were fueled. Although he may have been encouraged by Secretary Laird's suspension of the rules of engagement for five days in late December to allow for a series of raids into North Vietnam, raids that were hampered by bad weather, the rules of engagement were reimposed on December 31, and they were quite clear in their restrictions. Reaction was permitted when surface-to-air missiles or antiaircraft artillery fired on U.S. aircraft or were "activated against them".[13] The term *activated* was crucial in the developments that followed.

Two types of North Vietnamese radar could be detected by the American pilot on the radar indications equipment in the cockpit of his plane. One was Fire Can radar, associated with antiaircraft artillery; the other was Fan Song radar, associated with surface-to-air missiles (SAM II). Both were Soviet radars.[14] When the tracking Fan Song radar picked up a U.S. aircraft, the Radar Homing and Warning (RHAW) equipment in the cockpit alerted the pilot that he was being attacked by a missile unit.[15] However, in mid-December, the North Vietnamese were able to use their long-range Barlock or Whiff air defense radar to pass target information to the

Fan Song. The new tactic, the netting or interconnecting of radar communications, meant that the Fan Song could acquire information on the position of the U.S. aircraft before it could be detected by the RHAW. In short, there was no way to detect this passing of information and the U.S. aircraft was now deprived of advance warning. The rules of engagement forbade attacks on long-range radar or interceptor control (GCI) sites. Even after January 26 when the rules were relaxed to permit attacks on GCI sites, it was specified that hostile aircraft must be airborne at the time.[16]

Faced with this situation, General Lavelle made his own interpretation of the rules. In explanation to the Senate Committee, he said, "Being deprived of radar warning, perhaps one could make the judgment that you could no longer determine when the system was activated against U.S. aircraft. In the face of the new tactics, however, a more logical judgment appeared to be that, since U.S. aircraft were under constant surveillance by the air defense radars netted with the missile units, the system was constantly activated against us."[17] This assumption permitted the general to bomb at will. He conducted some 22 unauthorized bombing missions over North Vietnam from January 23 to March 9, 1972, and there is every evidence that his bombing policy would have continued had not the falsification of his records been exposed.

In his early testimony on the bombing incidents General Lavelle insisted that he knew what he was doing and that his actions had been known to those above him in the chain of command. His contention was not that he had made a mistake in his interpretation, but that he had tacit approval for what he was doing. "I had a lot of superiors and I'm not saying that they all knew—by any stretch of the imagination," said the general, but he added in response to questions, "I think General Abrams knew what I was doing."[18] The officers under him evidently made the same assumption. When asked whether he was concerned as to whether Lavelle really had the authority for the raids he was planning, General Slay remarked, "if you want to know the honest-to-God truth, I thought somebody was holding his hand."[19]

Sometime between June and September, it became evident that the general's superiors were not going to back him up. The heat was on in Congress; a new election campaign was underway. If someone had been holding the general's hand, he let go of it before the September hearings. By this time, it was evident that it would be safer to confess to an error of judgment and mismanagement of his command than to face a general court martial for insubordination. These were the only two alternatives that remained. It must have been a painful decision for a man who prided himself on his judgment and his detailed awareness of what he was doing. Nevertheless, General Lavelle confessed that "While I was of the opinion that my superiors were aware of the nature of our operations, it now appears that there was a different understanding than I thought existed."[20]

IV

It was, in fact, the general's determination to be in complete control of everything that happened in his command that made it so difficult for him to exert vague pressures and manage tacit understandings of who was to do what, without becoming fully aware of what he was doing. Had he not given specific orders against trolling or had he permitted "errors" in the reporting process, his responsibility might have been more easily spread through the lower echelons of his command. But in an organization run by General Lavelle, if anyone was going to make out a false report, he wanted another true report made out as well, to make sure that nothing slipped by him. This, it appears, was the mistake that cost him his command and not the unauthorized bombing per se.

If the pressure to expend ordnance induces a pilot to falsify a report on his own initiative, he is the only one who knows about it. If the commanding general orders the falsification of reports, the order must be passed down through the chain of command. In the Seventh Air Force, over 300 people finally became involved in the falsification process. This makes self-deception very difficult. It is particularly difficult at the end of the line where someone must knowingly lie about what happened. This is the position in which Sergeant Lonnie Franks found himself one day late in January 1972. He was assigned to the 432nd Tactical Reconnaissance Wing, Udorn, Thailand, in the Directorate of Operational Intelligence, where his duties involved the debriefing of pilots after missions and writing reports. Following are some excerpts from his testimony.

> SERGEANT FRANKS: This day . . . on the 25th of January, this was a reconnaissance crew and both the pilot and the navigator came in and gave me what would be considered an ordinary reconnaissance debrief. So when I asked them if they had received any ground fire or any hostile reactions they answered that they had not received any hostile reactions.
>
> THE CHAIRMAN: Had not?
>
> SERGEANT FRANKS: Had not received any hostile reactions, but

they had been told that they should report that they had received hostile reactions.

THE CHAIRMAN: How did you handle that?

SERGEANT FRANKS: I didn't really know how to handle it; I had been in Nakhon Phanom in Thailand as an intelligence specialist and was in my 6th month in Udorn and I had never heard of anyone doing this before, so I went to my NCOIC, my noncommissioned officer-in-charge, Technical Sergeant Voichita. He is a technical sergeant and asked him just what was happening, what I should be doing and why we were doing it, and basically he just told me to "make it look real; just make up some sort of hostile reaction."

I still was not convinced and he was relatively busy so I went to my OIC, my immediate officer-in-charge, Capt. Douglas Murray, and asked him what we were doing and why we were doing it and this whole time the pilot and navigator were waiting around; they really didn't understand why they were waiting around and so he told me that I should do as my NCOIC had instructed. . . .

So there is a separate form for debriefing if a flight does receive some antiaircraft artillery fire, some triple A fire; so I went through this form with them and I had a great deal of difficulty. It bothered me that I was doing it at the time; I didn't know why I was doing it, but I went ahead and did it and finally I came up with 10 to 15 rounds of 23 millimeter fire was fired at them and—

THE CHAIRMAN: Now to be sure that the record speaks clearly, you said you took it up with them—you mean the pilots, the navigators again?

SERGEANT FRANKS: Right; right.

THE CHAIRMAN: Yes; and came up with this 10 to 15 rounds?

SERGEANT FRANKS: They were trying to help me and I was trying to help them and we were trying to decide—you see it is a very detailed report as far as—because when a crew receives hostile reaction, especially in North Vietnam, it is very important that you pinpoint the exact location of the gun that is firing at them because it is very likely you are going to receive more from that same gun; so the report itself goes into such detail as the aircraft headings, the aircraft altitude, the exact type of maneuver the aircraft would be in at the time that it was receiving hostile reaction, the exact plot position that the aircraft had seen both a ground flash—there is a flash from the gun that goes off— and an airburst and exactly what distance the airburst missed the aircraft and what position the airburst was: an extremely detailed report, so that the gun can be pinpointed.

And to dream it up out of the clear blue sky takes—it had to be a reasonable report and it had to be perfectly reasonable, in fact, so you had to have a gunflash and a heading correct and an airburst correct and you had to have a correct number of rounds fired at correct interval. A 23 millimeter shoots at a certain rate of fire so you couldn't have an airburst every 3 seconds when it shoots a half-second interval; you should have an airburst every half a second.

So they were quite involved and it was quite difficult but I did finally get that and the crew did initial the sheet and I wrote up an OPREP-4 on this reconnaissance mission as I would write up any OPREP-4 except that it was falsified. . . .

THE CHAIRMAN: Before you leave the first one, what was the reason given you? What was the reason and cause assigned as to why you should do this?

SERGEANT FRANKS: Well—

THE CHAIRMAN: And who did it?

SERGEANT FRANKS: The pilots and my OIC told me that—you see, this mission was escorted from Danang so the pilots told me and my NCOIC told me the reason for reporting they were receiving a triple A reaction, a hostile reaction, was so that the strike escort, the strike aircraft, the escorts would be able to strike. On this mission we were escorted by Danang and Danang did not strike. The pilot and navigator of the reconnaissance groups, in fact, were upset by the fact that Danang had not struck.

THE CHAIRMAN: So as you understood it, it was necessary therefore to file a report as if Danang had struck; is that what you are saying?

SERGEANT FRANKS: Right. . . .[21]

At first, only the false information was recorded, but soon, an order came through to record both the true and the false information. The information was recorded side by side and passed on for the intelligence briefing. The commander had to know what was *really* happening.

SERGEANT FRANKS: Later it became much simpler because the correct information and the incorrect information would be put on debrief forms, on the debrief forms themselves side by side. Therefore, when you wrote the OPREP-4 you would know the incorrect information: struck antiaircraft artillery at such and such a site and results were not observed because of smoke and foliage. However, on just to the right or just to the left of the incorrect information would be the correct information, so it would be quite simple to tell which was correct and which was not correct. . . . I found out that Captain Murray was taking down the correct information and sending the information forward to 7th Air Force, the correct information forwarded to 7th Air Force.

THE CHAIRMAN: As well as the incorrect?

SERGEANT FRANKS: The incorrect information went out on an OPREP-4 which went to quite a few organizations.

THE CHAIRMAN: Yes.

SERGEANT FRANKS: I was told by Captain Murray that this information, the correct information, was only going to 7th Air Force.[22]

The extent of the falsification and the deliberate recording of both true and false information made it clear to Sergeant Franks that the orders had come from a high level within the command. But where? A few days later, he observed the wing commander and the vice-wing commander watching the falsification of a pilot report and discussing the correct and incorrect information. There was no longer any doubt that Colonel Gabriel, the wing commander, was fully aware of the falsification. Could the orders have come from Seventh Air Force Headquarters? If so, how could he report the falsification without reporting to the very person who had ordered it? He considered reporting to the Inspector General, but in the 432nd Wing, the vice-wing commander, Colonel O'Malley, was also the Inspector General—and O'Malley was part of the falsification procedure. "Unfortunately," said Franks:

> at my level I had no idea where the ultimate authority was coming from. It could have come from the—it could have come through the Chief of Staff and if I had written to the Inspector General of the Air Force (in Washington) and the Chief of Staff had been the person authorizing it and it was done against Presidential order, the Chief of Staff would have every reason to take action against me rather than against his own orders.

It took Sergeant Franks a month to decide what to do. Meanwhile, he tried to become occupied with other duties so he could avoid the falsification of reports as he found this procedure very uncomfortable. At last, he determined to write to Senator Hughes, the senator from his home state of Iowa. Hughes brought the matter before the air force Chief of Staff, General Ryan, who finally uncovered the falsified reports.

V

At first, General Lavelle denied that he had anything to do with the falsification. In the first hearing in June, he remarked that he didn't "think it was very smart" for his subordinates to fake combat reports, "but that's how it happened." "I believe somebody someplace got overeager," he said.[24] He admitted forbidding "no reaction" reports but denied ordering falsification. In the second hearing in September it was clear that each of his subordinates were to be called in and questioned. There was no longer any escape. At that time, he decided he must admit to an inadvertent order that resulted in the "accidental" falsification of reports. However, the general insisted that at no time had he "willfully" tried to conceal information from his superiors. "I fully understand and support the traditional U.S. principle with respect to civilian control of the military and I assure this committee that I have never knowingly violated these principles," he said.[25] General Lavelle, the man who was proud of his full awareness of what he was doing, had at last learned to strike the right note before Congress. He had done it all, he said, and he accepted full responsibility for his acts, but it was all the result of an inadvertent error.

> At no time did I intend to mislead my superiors concerning these missions. I did not lie about what I was doing nor did I order any of my subordinates to misrepresent the truth. It is true that some reports were falsified at a lower echelon of command, which probably resulted from my failure to make clear my objectives and my interpretation of the pertinent rule of judgment. When brought to my attention, the matter of false reporting was immediately stopped. In retrospect, it is clear that a misunderstanding did develop among my subordinates concerning the manner in which these air strikes should be reported. . . . I have never suggested that the responsibility was other than my own. In my earlier testimony before the House Armed Services Committee [the June hearing] I accepted full responsibility for these reports and I still do.[26]

It was the General's desire to accept full responsibility without admitting intent. He was responsible, in the technical sense that he was in charge, but he did not really intend to do what he did. The first mission in which the false reporting occurred was on January 23, 1972, following a strike on Dong Hoi airfield. The attack had been prompted by the widely reported B-52 incident, in which a MIG attacked a flight of three B-52's and fired heat-seeking missiles at them. The B-52's had not been struck, but the incident had upset the entire air force. The general explained it this way:

> I ordered the Quick Check Recce flight to launch with the objective of cutting the Dong Hoi runway [deleted]. The strike was successful [deleted]. The strike was so successful that the strike aircraft pulled off the target and out of the threat area without receiving enemy fire. The lead pilot reported [deleted] that he had struck Dong Hoi airfield, expended all ordnance, the mission was successful and no enemy reaction.
> I told my Director of Operations that we could not report "no enemy reaction." "Hostile radar" would have been a proper and, in my opinion, an accurate report. Unfortunately, as my instructions were passed from my Director of Operations probably to the wing commander, to the wing deputy for operations, to the squadron commander, to the intelligence officer on duty and, finally, to the sergeant technician who prepared the follow-up reports, the word apparently got distorted. Although I feel they should have reported "hostile reaction, enemy radar," the detailed follow-up report form was filled out indicating heavy AAA fire. . . . The inaccurate reports were OPREP-4 reports

which are formated, extremely detailed reports; readable only by a
technician or with a key to the format. These reports were routed to the
report section of my staff; I never saw them.[27]

There are several revelations in the general's statement. He said a
correct report would have been "hostile reaction, enemy radar," but
he did not say this to General Slay, Director of Operations. He merely
told him the pilots could not report "no reaction." A convenient
oversight for a man given to precise orders and one who followed up
an order to make sure it was carried out. Did he know what he was
doing? General Slay thought so. In describing the situation to the
committee, he said:

> I happened to be out at the—I guess I was at the tanker desk . . . but
> General Lavelle did tell me what had occurred and he said, "You see,
> those letters up there?" and the plotters would always have, you
> know, each day would have a code, like "no reaction" might be today
> [deleted] and it was [deleted] up there. He said, "God damn it; we can't
> have that. It's got to be 'reaction.' You have got to show 'hostile reac-
> tion'."[28]

Later, of course, General Slay was required to reinforce General
Lavelle's order.

> I said the rule still stands that the report comes in that you did have a
> reaction because this is General Lavelle's policy and his desire. My
> belief at that time was that General Lavelle was perfectly—in fact, my
> absolute conviction was that General Lavelle was completely cogni-
> zant of what he was doing. . . .[29]

In response to the question as to whether or not General Lavelle
knew the reports were being falsified, General Slay replied:

> Lavelle knew, sir, that regardless of whether there was reaction or not,
> it would be reported that there would be reaction. He knew that be-
> cause he directed it.
>
> THE CHAIRMAN: That came from him; correct?
>
> GENERAL SLAY: That came from him.[30]

Not only did the general know of the falsification, he followed up on
his initial order, chiding Colonel Gabriel, the wing commander, for
the incident on January 23 in which he reported "no reaction." Colonel Gabriel reports that at a commanders' conference in early February,

> The one comment that was made to me from General Lavelle at that
> meeting—he chided me personally about the call that was made
> January 23, about "no reaction; fighters expended."
>
> THE CHAIRMAN: You say he chided you?

COLONEL GABRIEL: Yes, sir, just as we were going into the meeting room. That was the only thing that he discussed with me directly. . . .

THE CHAIRMAN: Chiding is in fun in a way but I think it is important if you could remember; if it is possible, anyway, tell us what he said.

COLONEL GABRIEL: Sir, I don't remember precisely but the gist of it was that it is inconsistent, of course, to say there was no reaction but the fighters expended.[31]

It was General Lavelle's position that his pilots were always fired upon and, since one could not guarantee that he was not being fired upon, it was better to assume the enemy was firing. Said General Slay:

It was General Lavelle's comment at the time that "No one can fly over North Vietnam without being fired at, so why should I risk my pilots' lives by going up and waiting until I see a burst" and I remember on one occasion he said, "Slay, you have seen .51-caliber fire; you have seen 23-millimeter fire; you have seen 37 and 57." He said, "What can you—can you assure me when you fly somewhere that you are or are not getting .51 caliber fire?" and, of course, you cannot. I mean unless they are using tracers you can't. So it was his contention at the time that if you are in the vicinity of where the enemy has supplies, or where the enemy has a SAM site, they know that you are there to do them some dirt and you will get fired upon. . . .

I was in the command post [deleted] and General Lavelle passed the word back down to the wing that they could not report "no reaction", that they must report that the enemy has reacted. He got me right after that, as well as my chief in the command post [deleted] and explained the facts of life to us, that "Anytime you are over North Vietnam you have, just by definition, people who are going to shoot at you so you must report that you have been reacted upon."[32]

In General Lavelle's memory of the incident, the whole matter was more inadvertent. He had not intended to make a false report. There was a "misunderstanding" of his orders. He was "shocked" when he discovered that pilots had been ordered to report that they had been fired upon. When Sergeant Franks' account of the false reporting was read to him, he indicated he "did not know it was going on".[33] His one off-hand remark on January 23, he said, had resulted in the whole elaborate system of false reporting involving over 300 people in the command—and he knew nothing about it. "I didn't pay any attention to the reporting system," he said, "didn't see them, sir, never entered my mind to question them."[34] His defense was simple. He had told his director of operations he could not report "no reaction," but he had not said in so many words, "You must falsify the reports." Therefore, he had not really ordered the falsification of reports. His statements raised some doubts on the committee.

> SENATOR DOMINICK: You did not intend your instructions to the Director of Operations—"that we could not report 'no enemy reaction,'" as a general instruction?
>
> GENERAL LAVELLE: No sir.
>
> SENATOR DOMINICK: It was designed only for that particular raid?
>
> GENERAL LAVELLE: Yes, sir; that was the only raid; I mentioned this was the only raid that came to my attention. . . .
>
> SENATOR HUGHES: And you believe that all of the false reporting initiated from that one statement you made in the command and control tower when the strike was made on Dong Hoi airbase then; that is the only thing you can attribute it to?
>
> GENERAL LAVELLE: Yes, sir. . . .
>
> SENATOR HUGHES (after some questions about who was present at the time):   I would like to determine how this order originated, because it is obvious that it did originate somewhere; instructions were given and they were carried out. I don't think all of this could have been hypothetical; I think someone had to say, "Falsify reports." That is what I am saying.[35]

The Chairman (Senator Stennis) also wondered how the false reports could have been prepared without the general's knowledge.

> I just do not see how all that reporting happened right there under you, even though you did not see the reports, were not supposed to, and for all that period of time on these important matters that were marginal at best, according to your own interpretation, it is hard to see how all of that happened without your knowledge before this inspector came. Could you elaborate on that now? I may be totally mistaken but is hard to see. Do you not have a fuller or better or stronger explanation of that than you have given?
>
> GENERAL LAVELLE: No, sir, I do not have. Have you ever seen an OPREP-4 report, sir?
>
> THE CHAIRMAN: I have seen one and I could not tell much about it. . . .
>
> GENERAL LAVELLE: Sir, the OPREP-4 report, as I stated, is a very detailed formated report. It is automatically routed directly to the reports section. . . . To be honest with you, Senator, I had never seen an OPREP-4 report until General Wilson showed me the report.
>
> THE CHAIRMAN: Who got up the idea of a false report there, who did it? You said it was done under you. That is the first thing you told me in my office, and you were there, fully responsible. Who did it?
>
> GENERAL LAVELLE: I do not know, sir.

THE CHAIRMAN: If it caused you all this trouble, it would seem to me like you would have dug it up, frankly.

GENERAL LAVELLE: No, sir, I was not aware of it until it happened.

THE CHAIRMAN: I mean, since then.

GENERAL LAVELLE: The OPREP-4 report is made by the pilots after the mission.

THE CHAIRMAN: That is one of them, is it not? Let us pass it around to the membership so they can have a look at it. . . .

GENERAL LAVELLE: The pilots do this in a debriefing. . . .

THE CHAIRMAN: But the practice of it—it is inconceivable to me that all this could be borne there, and go on, and successfully keep it from the officer that they would do it in the first place.

GENERAL LAVELLE: It shocked me, sir, when I found out about it. . . .

THE CHAIRMAN: If you are blameless in it, has the Air Force investigated anyone else or taken any action against anyone else for doing it?

GENERAL LAVELLE: No, sir. It would be my responsibility to do this and under the circumstances since it probably stemmed from my remark I have accepted the responsibility for it as the commander, and since probably it did come from my remark. I did not feel that I could go down to these pilots who flew these missions over North Vietnam and take any action.

THE CHAIRMAN: You did not have much chance to do it. You were relieved of command. But anyway, skipping over that, what did you hear about it? Did you not go and accost some of these men when General Wilson [the inspector general] told you that these things were true, did you not at least talk to them? A man does not just take responsibility and turn around and walk off, does he?

GENERAL LAVELLE: No, sir, I did not go to the men, I did not talk to them about it.

THE CHAIRMAN: You felt like you should not under the circumstances?

GENERAL LAVELLE: I felt that it was a misunderstanding of something that I had said and, as I mentioned before—

THE CHAIRMAN: For the record at this point what was that that you had said, repeat that again, you said a remark you made.

GENERAL LAVELLE: I made the remark that they could not report no reaction.

THE CHAIRMAN: And from that you think all this springs—about 43 days of false reporting originated?

GENERAL LAVELLE: I think so.

THE CHAIRMAN: All right.[36]

The general's position, then, is that he made a remark about not reporting "no reaction" which he inadvertently failed to qualify. This remark was misunderstood by his Director of Operations and passed on down the line. But the Director of Operations, General Slay, recalls it somewhat differently. It was General Lavelle himself, he said, who passed the word on down the line that day.

> SENATOR DOMINICK [speaking of the first prohibition against re-porting "no reaction"]:   Was that the first time you passed the word down the line?
>
> GENERAL SLAY: Sir, I think General Lavelle personally passed the word down the line that day.
>
> SENATOR DOMINICK: Yes, but I mean to Udorn or to the wing commanders?
>
> GENERAL SLAY: That is what I mean; yes sir. I think he personally did it that day.
>
> SENATOR DOMINICK: You did not do it yourself?
>
> GENERAL SLAY: No sir, not that day.[37]

General Lavelle evidently failed to make inquiries as to how his order had been misunderstood and by whom, because he knew it had not really been misunderstood at all. If we are to believe General Slay, Lavelle not only personally called the wing, he called in General Slay to make sure he, too, understood that the command could not report "no reaction." Then, he followed up a few weeks later at the commanders' conference, twitting Colonel Gabriel, the wing commander, about reporting "no reaction." It was not, then, a casual off-hand remark, blurted out in a moment of stress, which he inadvertently failed to qualify with specific instructions. It was a deliberate policy of falsification. There is no other explanation for the fact that his order was "misunderstood" at least twice by two different people, and the intent of his chiding was also "misconstrued." The chiding was a "joke," but like many a joke, it had a very specific purpose.

VI

It should be noted at this point that the rules of engagement and the procedures for reporting on missions were known to all line officers in the command. Although they had all received their orders from General Lavelle, they knew these orders were improper. How did it happen that no one offered a protest until a lowly sergeant walked into the intelligence shop and discovered what was going on? General Slay maintained that the breach of orders was a relatively minor one—Lavelle was asking him to bomb military targets, not villages—and he believed the general had some tacit support for his behavior ("somebody was holding his hand"). However, there was no way he could check on this. General Lavelle closely guarded his prerogatives and would not have permitted General Slay to talk to General Abrams (Lavelle's immediate superior). When questioned on this point, Slay was quite emphatic. Speaking of the falsified reports, Senator Dominick asked Slay, "But you never took these and discussed these with General Abrams?" "No, sir; never," replied Slay. "General Lavelle would have chopped my head off."[38] As to the rules of engagement, Senator Hughes asked a similar question.

> SENATOR HUGHES: Did you discuss with any of Abrams' staff around him the rules of engagement you were operating under?
>
> GENERAL SLAY: No, sir.
>
> SENATOR HUGHES: Would this have been a breach of protocol for you to do that?
>
> GENERAL SLAY: Yes, sir.
>
> SENATOR HUGHES: Or you would have considered it that?
>
> GENERAL SLAY: I would have considered that.
>
> SENATOR HUGHES: So would General Lavelle, I suppose?
>
> GENERAL SLAY: Oh, boy; yes, sir.
>
> SENATOR HUGHES: Under the circumstances?
>
> GENERAL SLAY: The air war was run by General Lavelle and in the conduct, the detailed conduct of the air war it would have been the height of presumptuousness for me to go over and discuss a decision that he made with a ground officer over at MACV, with the MACV staff.[39]

The distinction is an important one in the military. Slay and Lavelle were air force generals; Abrams was an army general. For Slay, it was not only a question of breaking the chain of command, but of talking to someone from a rival service who outranked his boss and who, as a "ground officer," had no real understanding of the "air war." When Senator Hughes asked him, "precisely why you didn't question more than you did the orders that you had been given," Slay replied, "Sir, I spent all my life since 17 in the military service and that is all I know."[40]

Slay did not deceive himself. He knew the rules of engagement were being bypassed and the reports were being falsified, but he also had some familiarity with the interaction between generals and politicians. He assumed that Lavelle was being protected by forces behind the scenes that he did not fully understand and that it would not be proper for him to ask questions. Perhaps there were political reasons why our public policy proclaimed one thing and our military practice demonstrated another.

At the lower echelons of command, however, the detailed orders had to be more specific and a procedure had to be outlined for the falsification. For the men deeply absorbed in these details, once they had accepted the order to change the reports, there was apparently a need to cover their behavior with some form of rationalization. What they were doing was not *really* wrong, it was not really lying, but only writing an "incomplete" report. Captain Douglas Murray, the chief of the intelligence branch where the false reports were uncovered, found the questions of the committee most disconcerting. He would not use the term *falsification* in any of his replies.

> THE CHAIRMAN: . . . Did anything happen to these young fellows, these men under you? Did they respond in any way, talk to you about it, these false reports, the false part of it?
>
> CAPTAIN MURRAY: There definitely was some comment, but to my knowledge there was no strong opinion expressed by anyone that what was being carried on was, in fact, a falsification of the reports because, again, most of the information was available and was being sent forth in the other reports. . . .
>
> SENATOR HUGHES: When did you begin falsifying reports?
>
> CAPTAIN MURRAY: The procedure that I outlined, sir, we began in the early February time frame; I can't recall the exact time. . . .
>
> SENATOR HUGHES: When information came back that trucks and POL and so, the soft targets, had been hit; what did you do?
>
> CAPTAIN MURRAY: We didn't do any more than we would normally do with any other report of the same stature, the same nature.
>
> SENATOR HUGHES: What was that?
>
> CAPTAIN MURRAY: In this particular case, for instance, in the North Vietnam instance?
>
> SENATOR HUGHES: Yes.
>
> CAPTAIN MURRAY: The OPREP-4 went out with the results of the mission.
>
> SENATOR HUGHES: Saying you hit trucks and POL?
>
> CAPTAIN MURRAY: No, sir; as I said before—
>
> SENATOR HUGHES: Saying you did not hit them?

CAPTAIN MURRAY [continuing]: That the target listed on the OPREP-4 was normally defensive weapon systems.

SENATOR HUGHES: Triple A or SAM defenses?

CAPTAIN MURRAY: Yes sir. . . .[41]

What the captain is saying is that soft targets, illegal targets, such as trucks and POL, were reported as triple A or SAM missiles. But it was difficult for the senator to pull it out of him, so insistent was he that the procedures were "normal" and "the same as any other mission of the same stature." It is difficult to tell if the captain is trying to lie to the senator, to himself, or to both at the same time. When asked about Sergeant Franks, he found it difficult, at first, to recall Sergeant Franks raising the question of falsification.

SENATOR HUGHES: Do you remember Sergeant Franks coming to you and asking why he was issuing a different report?

CAPTAIN MURRAY: I don't remember a specific occasion but he very well could have asked me, I am sure.

SENATOR HUGHES: First, let me ask you, do you know Sergeant Franks?

CAPTAIN MURRAY: Yes.

SENATOR HUGHES: He did work in your shop?

CAPTAIN MURRAY: Yes. . . .

SENATOR HUGHES: But his coming to you and asking a question did not strike you as being—it probably didn't make any impression on you at all—you can't hardly remember it or do you remember it?

CAPTAIN MURRAY: No; I remember him asking—a discussion in the office.

SENATOR HUGHES: Do you remember what you said to him?

CAPTAIN MURRAY: . . . I said, in short, something to the effect that these were the procedures that we had been following and had been handed down to us to be followed in handling these cases.

SENATOR HUGHES: And to go ahead and report them that way?

CAPTAIN MURRAY: Yes, sir.

SENATOR HUGHES: Did that raise any questions in your mind?

CAPTAIN MURRAY: No, sir.

SENATOR HUGHES: Why not? Do you have any idea why you were not alerted—some alarm didn't go off when someone questioned filing false reports?

CAPTAIN MURRAY: Sir, let me describe it this way: I think you have to look at the framework of thought here. . . . Yes, the reporting procedure was different; we have had different procedures before . . . taking all of this into consideration, you operate under a concept or an assumption of legitimacy and that is not to question orders unless you feel there is some illegality in the orders and in the system of trust. And the last factor I think to consider was the fact this was not done in secrecy; no one was called in separately; the procedure was outlined to the entire office and there was never any attempt by anyone to conceal the procedure. . . .

SENATOR HUGHES: Since it wasn't secret and since everyone around knew about it, are you surprised to hear that General Abrams didn't know about it, the commanding general of the theater of operations?

CAPTAIN MURRAY: Yes. . . .

SENATOR SYMINGTON: Do you feel that you were doing anything wrong under instructions from superior officers in this connection with respect to what the actual facts were?

CAPTAIN MURRAY: At the time, no, sir.

SENATOR SYMINGTON: You did not? You had no suspicions in your mind then of anything that was incorrect?

CAPTAIN MURRAY: No, sir; I didn't.

SENATOR SYMINGTON: If you were actually told to report things that didn't happen, why wouldn't that be considered wrong in your mind?

CAPTAIN MURRAY: Sir . . . I think you have to look at a couple of things and a couple of factors. First of all, at the level we were at, we were not involved in the determination of policy and likewise with the definition and interpretation of the rules of engagement.

SENATOR SYMINGTON: Would this be a determination of policy or a determination of fact?

CAPTAIN MURRAY: What I am saying is that at the level that we were at we didn't have access to the reasoning and the thoughts that went into the orders that came down to us. . . .[42]

There are two important aspects of Captain Murray's response. The first, and I believe the less important, is the fact that he was operating under a direct order and was subject to punishment if he refused to obey that order. The second, more important consideration is the style of thinking involved. Although he was acting under orders, his cooperation was voluntary. He believed in what he was doing—not in the specific sense, but he accepted his role as a function in a larger system of experiencing and thinking about the world. I have called this the "systematization of thought."

In this process, certain ideas or considerations are excluded from consciousness because they are assumed to have taken place at another level. It is a product of the functional approach to decision making that is characteristic of modern American bureaucracy—not merely the military system. It differs from the totalitarian model in that the individual surrenders his own will voluntarily. He never makes the assumption that he has no right to question orders. He assumes, instead, that he simply does not have the *necessary information* and that those who do have the information are performing their function properly. His cooperation is further ensured by the fact that he is kept very busy attending to the details at his own level. "It is not my job," he says. There is, therefore, a restriction of thought and perception into a series of functions, and thinking takes place in stages by different people in the manner of an assembly line, with minimum communication between one stage and the next.

VII

In the September hearing by the Senate Armed Services Committee, General Lavelle firmly defended his right to make a "liberal" interpretation of the rules of engagement. He did not feel he was guilty of insubordination or of acting without authorization. He believed, in fact, that he had been treated unjustly by the order that relieved him of his command.[43] General Slay, his subordinate, and the officers above him in the chain of command were unanimous in their belief that he *had* violated the rules of engagement. General Creighton Abrams, Commander, U.S. Forces, Vietnam, General Lavelle's immediate superior, insisted there was no ambiguity in the rules of engagement that would have permitted General Lavelle to conclude he could attack whenever an enemy radar was activated. Lavelle, he said, had never discussed with him the possibility of making this interpretation of the rules of engagement.[44] Admiral Thomas H. Moorer, Chairman of the Joint Chiefs of Staff, also indicated that Lavelle's interpretation of the rules of engagement was not justified.

> ADMIRAL MOORER: . . . I do not think that the authority could be expanded to that degree. I just do not think that is a correct interpretation. In the first place, you should not interpret authorities. But on that basis, he would have carte blanche to bomb anything, because once you get up there [deleted]. I know he said he interpreted it that way, but that was certainly not spelled out.
>
> SENATOR CANNON: That was in your opinion an erroneous interpretation?

ADMIRAL MOORER: That was an erroneous interpretation in my opinion and has never been discussed in my presence as being a possible interpretation of the Rules of Engagement. . . .[45]

The rules still required that the aircraft be fired upon first. That is really the key to the rule. And the pilots had to be instructed that they should be fired upon first and not told at the outset that they were to attack regardless of whether they were fired on or not. I think that is the crux of this thing. . . . So, General Lavelle, I do not think, has been called to task for the targets he struck but for planning in advance to strike targets regardless of whether he got fired upon. I do not think the targets are really the issue.

THE CHAIRMAN: I will read here for the record his [General Lavelle's] last comment. It says:

This liberal interpretation (by JCS) of what could be struck, plus the encouragement to be more aggressive and flexible, vitally influenced my determination to make a similar, though I believe less liberal and very reasonable, interpretation of the conditions under which we could strike.

ADMIRAL MOORER: . . . If General Lavelle was concerned about this, he did not see fit to discuss it with me when I was there, Or neither have I seen a message from him expressing his concern or describing his interpretations of this message.[46]

It seemed clear that the general had no specific orders to do what he did, but a certain uneasy doubt remained with the committee. Had he received encouragement or pressure to go beyond the rules of engagement? Was there a tacit assumption that he could expand his authority as long as he managed to conceal what he was doing? Even with over 300 people involved in the falsification process, there is every indication that no one in the military chain of command above General Lavelle would have discovered the falsification of reports or the unauthorized strikes had not Sergeant Lonnie Franks written to Senator Hughes. The general's work was examined by his superiors. Photographs of his strikes were looked over in detail, and he was criticized at least once for inaccurate bombing. *But the other possibility—that he might be bombing beyond his authority—was never questioned because no one wanted to know.* No one questioned his increased expenditure of ordnance. Although it is true that he was reprimanded on the one occasion that he did report bombing without enemy reaction (the attack on Moc Chau), he quickly learned how to correct this problem by simply reporting enemy reaction on future bombing runs. How can we explain the failure of those above General Lavelle to detect his unauthorized strikes? Was their "not knowing" a form of looking the other way while the General did what they had covertly encouraged him to do?

Senator Stennis, the senate committee chairman, asked the question of General Ryan, the air force Chief of Staff.

> THE CHAIRMAN: Here is the matter—I am getting right down to the heart of this thing—here is the matter with a man with a good record, and fine enough as a lieutenant general for you to ask that he be retired at that rate, and in this highly responsible position. . . . It is tied in with the proposition that before this venture as to a strike was ever made, there was preparation of it, it was planned that they would use their ordnance whether they were fired on or not.
>   The charge has been made repeatedly that there was bound to be, or it seems there was, some kind of an encouragement or some kind of implication or implied authority for this general to go and follow a course of conduct like that.[47]

General Lavelle raised the same question of intent in a somewhat different way when he concluded his own argument.

> It was brought out during the testimony that had I elected to "troll", i.e., send an aircraft and crew into the area as bait to draw fire, the strikes would then have been considered authorized under the pertinent rule of engagement. Mr. Chairman, I just couldn't do this in the environment in which my crews were flying. Even if a tactic of trolling would have made these strikes legal with respect to the enemy, it would not have been morally right in that hazardous area, with respect to my crews. Quite apart from that, it should be remembered that in the final analysis the practice of provoking enemy fire through trolling was done in order to execute air strikes involving precisely the same degree of preplanning as those which I directed. Consequently, as regards the preplanned aspects of the strikes, I respectfully submit that this tactic cannot be fairly differentiated.[48]

What the general is saying is that he could have exerted the same kind of pressure on his pilots that his superiors exerted on him—and he could have avoided the responsibility for the consequences. He could have castigated his pilots for returning to base with unexpended ordnance. He could have accused them of cowardice if they were not fired at (without necessarily ordering them to troll). In short, he could have made it hot for them if they failed to get the results he wanted, without allowing himself to "know" about the risks they were taking to get these results.

Of course, he could have complied with his orders by simply increasing the number of reconnaissance flights and letting it go at that. However, the general's previous history, what little we know of it, indicates that he was never satisfied with minimum compliance with an order. He wanted to understand the job to be done and exceed the expectations of his superiors. He had the kind of drive for personal achievement that makes for success in public administration and military command. However, he lacked the capacity for self-deception that is the second essential requirement. He could not conceal from himself the full consequences of an order he gave to his men. Because he refused to play the bureaucratic game of passing on the pressure, he placed his own career on the line rather than risk the lives of his pilots.

The fall of General Lavelle was the result of placing a man with a reputation for honesty and conscientiousness in an environment where bad faith was necessary for survival. In Vietnam during 1970–1972, there was a requirement to win the war without being aggressive—that is, without taking the initiative in battle. Every good soldier knows this is impossible, but there was no other way to prove to ourselves that we were both good (i.e., nonaggressive) and great (i.e., powerful) at the same time.

In retrospect, it would appear that General Lavelle did know what he was doing in both the unauthorized strikes and in the falsification of reports, although he may not have understood the complexity and the amount of time consumed in the falsification. If he presented the senate committee with a "misunderstanding," it was because he knew this was the only explanation that would preserve the system of military command and the logic of the government organization that directed it. Instead of saying, "I did it knowingly and deliberately because I was fed up with a public relations war in which my pilots were asked to risk their lives to make Washington look good," he acknowledged the error of his ways and, in return, he was treated lightly. He was relieved of command, but he received the retirement pay of a four-star general (because of a disability at that level). No one wanted to punish him more than necessary. In contrasting the general's situation with that of the man who resists killing, James Reston remarked:

> It [the U.S. government] is telling its soldiers on the battlefield to obey orders or go to the brig, and threatening its deserters who jump the country that they will be incarcerated if they come home. There is no freedom here for men who refuse to engage in killing when so ordered, but General Lavelle, who admits to bombing and killing on his own authority, is quietly retired on a four star general's salary of $2,250 a month.[49]

Perhaps a partial explanation for this difference lies in the fact that the general, by his admission of inadvertence, avoided raising moral issues. He preserved the illusion that his mission was to gather information and that our government had no hostile intent in North Vietnam. Another reason may lie in the nature of the act of killing itself. One can kill inadvertently, but it is difficult to refuse to kill inadvertently.

VIII

It is necessary to remember that the extensive program of pre-planned strikes conducted by the Seventh Air Force from early 1970 to March 1972 was designed, at least officially, for the defense of our right to look. The American position that there is or should be an internationally recognized right to look is actually part of a larger issue. It relates to the general question of how we come to know things in this world. Is it possible to look at something and know about it without having an influence on the thing we are observing? Is it possible to separate looking and acting in such a way that the look is innocent and there is no involvement prior to action, or is looking itself a form of involvement?

NOTES

1. H. E. Hughes, statement, *Congressional Record,* June 14, 1972, pp. S9311–9312.

2. J. D. Ryan, statement, *Congressional Record,* June 14, 1972, p. S9313.

3. U.S., Congress, Senate, Committee on Armed Services, Nomination of John D. Lavelle, General Creighton W. Abrams, and Admiral John S. McCain: Hearings. Washington, D.C.: U.S. Government Printing Office, 1972, p. 436.

4. Ibid., pp. 166–167.

5. S. M. Hersh, " 'Reaction' Strikes Called Cover-Up," *New York Times,* June 15, 1972, p. 1.

6. Senate, Committee on Armed Services, Nomination of Lavelle, Abrams, and McCain, p. 404.

7. Ibid., p. 430.

8. "A Businesslike General," *New York Times,* June 14, 1972, p. 20.

9. Senate, Committee on Armed Services, Nomination of Lavelle, Abrams, and McCain, p. 302.

10. Ibid., p. 291.

11. Ibid., p. 48.

12. Ibid., p. 50.

13. Ibid., p. 5.

14. Ibid., p. 377.

15. Ibid., p. 5.

16. Ibid., p. 103.

17. Ibid., p. 6.

18. S. M. Hersh, "General Testifies He Made 20 Raids Without Orders," *New York Times,* June 13, 1972, p. 1.

19. Senate, Committee on Armed Services, Nomination of Lavelle, Abrams, and McCain, p. 302.

20. Ibid., p. 99.

21. Ibid., pp. 159–162.

22. Ibid., pp. 165–166.

23. Ibid., p. 167.

24. U.S., Congress, House of Representatives, Armed Services Committee, *Unauthorized Bombing of Military Targets in North Vietnam: Hearing,* Washington D.C.: U.S. Government Printing Office, 1972, p. 30.

25. *Senate Hearings,* Op. Cit., p. 3.

26. Ibid., p. 4.

27. Ibid., p. 7.

28. Ibid., p. 299.

29. Ibid., p. 291.

30. Ibid., p. 317.

31. Ibid., pp. 203, 223–224.

32. Ibid., p. 290.

33. Ibid., p. 15.

34. Ibid., p. 13.

35. Ibid., pp. 26, 36.

36. Ibid., pp. 88–90.

37. Ibid., p. 299.

38. Ibid., p. 301.

39. Ibid., p. 308.

40. Ibid., p. 310.

41. Ibid., pp. 226–228.

42. Ibid., pp. 231–238.

43. Ibid., pp. 36, 84.

44. Ibid., pp. 142–143.

45. Ibid., p. 451.

46. Ibid., p. 473.

47. Ibid., p. 247.

48. Ibid., p. 99.

49. J. Reston, "The Double Standard," *New York Times,* June 14, 1972, p. 47.

12

Watergate:
Inadvertent Aggression in Politics

I

On June 17, 1972, during the campaign for president of the United States, five men were arrested inside the Watergate offices of the Democratic National Committee. They were wearing surgical gloves and carrying electronic bugging equipment and burglary tools. One of the men, James W. McCord, Jr., was identified as the security chief for the Committee for the Reelection of the President. On August 29 President Nixon announced that, based on a complete investigation by White House counsel John Dean, he could say categorically that no one on the White House staff and no one in his administration was involved in the break-in and bugging of the Watergate complex. However, it was subsequently discovered that two of the chief planners of Watergate, G. Gordon Liddy and E. Howard Hunt, were not only members of the White House staff but part of a special investigations unit within the White House designed to gain information on security leaks and other matters for the Nixon Administration.

As General Lavelle's "misunderstanding" provides a demonstration of the extent to which our assumed right to look may be carried in the international arena, the Watergate scandal reveals some of the domestic implications of such an attitude. It contrasts, on the one hand, the technician's view that information is necessary and neutral no matter how it is acquired, and the more human view that some forms of looking constitute acts of aggression by one party against another. It also raises, once again, the role of inadvertence in acts of aggression by the American government.

It should be noted that most of the major countries of the world, with the exception of Great Britain and the United States, have no laws against government wiretapping of private citizens. These restrictions then, which do exist in the United States, constitute an unusual and important protection for a political party that opposes the administration in power—that is, they constitute such a protection if the government is willing to abide by them.

However, we have already observed that in U.S. international relations we have developed an assumed right to "open up" those "closed" societies that conceal information from us. This was a central aspect of our violation of Soviet air space in the U-2 incident. It was the basis for our protective reaction strikes in Vietnam. Some form of espionage or reconnaissance is carried on by all of the major world powers. It is not in the act of reconnaissance that we are different from other nations. It is the attempt to legitimize this behavior that is characteristically American. It was not the U-2 flights themselves but our insistence that they had "no aggressive intent," that they were therefore justified and that they would continue, that opened an irreparable breach with the Soviets and ended the summit conference. It was not our reconnaissance activity in North Vietnam, but our insistence that this activity was legal (based on an "understanding" with the North Vietnamese that had been repudiated by the North Vietnamese) that led to the protective reaction strikes.

If we take a close look at this assumed right to open up other societies, the reasoning goes something like this: "We Americans are more open than the other nations of the world. We are more open because we are honest and have nothing to hide. Our openness is, therefore, an indication of our honesty and our virtue. Only dishonest people have a need to conceal what they are doing." One finds this attitude in various aspects of American life, from the encounter group to the public hearing. Such reasoning would not stand close examination if it were used as an explicit aspect of our policy. Instead, it is implicit in much of our behavior and our beliefs. Therefore, there is no attempt to reconcile it with government and business secrecy.

When the attempt to "open up" a secretive opponent is applied to domestic politics the reasoning clearly does not hold. The opposition party is not a "closed" society and there is no Democratic Party Iron Curtain behind which an opponent can hide, secure from American laws. It would appear, however, that this pervasive attitude of a legitimate "right to look" on the part of the government was extended in a rather unthinking manner to domestic as well as foreign policy. In fact, the use of the CIA (an organization specifically designed for intelligence gathering in the international arena) for assistance in implementing domestic espionage suggests that in the minds of some officials in the Nixon Administration the distinction between spying on an enemy nation and spying on a rival political party had begun to break down.

A special senate committee was appointed to investigate Watergate and, as key Nixon Administration officials were implicated one after another, the defense of simple denial had to be dropped (as it was finally dropped in the U-2 incident). There was a brief attempt by the Republican high command to maintain that they had to get information on possible "radical" activity sponsored or supported by the Democrats that might threaten the life of the president, but it was soon clear that this defense could not be used to legitimate espionage in domestic politics. The last line of defense proved to be the same one that had been used so often in American foreign policy—the inadvertence of the president.

On Monday evening April 30, 1973, almost a year after the burglary of the offices of the Democratic National Committee by his own reelection committee, President Nixon provided the following explanation in a televised speech. He announced that he wanted to speak to the American people "from my heart." He indicated that he knew nothing of the burglary during its planning and implementation stages and was completely unaware of any attempt to cover up the connection between the burglary crew and the White House staff. He announced the resignation of several White House aides, some of whom, he claimed, had misled him about the affair. He disapproved of the burglary and the attempted electronic espionage of the Democratic National Committee, he said, and would certainly have stopped it had he known of it in advance. However, like General Lavelle, President Nixon was not usually the type of man to leave the details to others. In the past he had insisted on taking personal charge of his election campaign. Therefore, a more detailed explana-

tion was required as to how he happened to be unaware of what was
going on. He said:

> Political commentators have correctly observed that during my 27
> years in politics I have always previously insisted on running my own
> campaigns for office. But 1972 presented a very different situation. In
> both domestic and foreign policy 1972 was a year of crucially impor-
> tant decisions, of intense negotiations, of vital new directions, particu-
> larly of working toward the goal which has been my overriding con-
> cern throughout my political career—the goal of bringing peace to
> America and peace to the world. That is why I decided, as the 1972
> campaign approached, that the Presidency should come first and poli-
> tics second. To the maximum extent possible, therefore, I sought to
> delegate campaign operations . . .
>
> For the fact that alleged improper actions took place within the
> White House or within my campaign organization, the easiest course
> would be for me to blame those to whom I delegated the responsibility
> to run the campaign. But that would be a cowardly thing to do. I will
> not place the blame on subordinates—on people whose zeal exceeded
> their judgement, and who may have done wrong in a cause they
> deeply believed to be right. In any organization, the man at the top
> must bear the responsibility. That responsibility, therefore, belongs
> here, in this office. I accept it.[1]

Like General Lavelle, President Nixon accepted the blame for
Watergate, but not the guilt, for he followed his remark with the
statement, "and I pledge to you tonight, from this office, that I will
do everything in my power to ensure that the guilty are brought to
justice . . ."[2] He continued, at a later point, with a general statement
about the virtue of government employees, including, presumably,
himself. "I have been in public life for more than a quarter of a century. Like any other calling politics has good people and bad people.
And let me tell you, the great majority in politics in the Congress, in
the federal government, in the state government, are good people."[3]
He concluded with further implicit denials that he would or could
do anything that was contrary to the welfare of the American people:

> I want these to be the best days in America's history, because I love
> America. I deeply believe that America is the hope of the world, and I
> know that in the quality and wisdom of the leadership America gives
> lies the only hope for millions of people all over the world that they
> can live their lives in peace and freedom. We must be worthy of that
> hope, in every sense of the word. Tonight I ask for your prayers to help
> me in everything that I do throughout the days of my Presidency to be
> worthy of their hopes and of yours. God bless America and God bless
> each and every one of you.[4]

There was, in this speech, no suggestion that he had done anything
to encourage the Watergate break-in, either directly or indirectly.

F. L. Zimmerman writing in the *Wall Street Journal,* a newspaper generally friendly to the Nixon Administration, referred to the president's speech as a "sentimental plea." He had claimed that he was misled by his aides about the extent of White House involvement, but, said Zimmerman, he "can't command the messy affair to go away."[5] In the same article several senators were quoted who insisted the president must still show he was totally isolated from the Watergate affair. As the offers of executive clemency for McCord, one of the burglars in the break-in, began to emerge from the senate Watergate hearings the implications of presidential involvement in the coverup became more explicit. No one could offer executive clemency except the president. Had the offer been made with his approval? A host of other questions were raised by the hearings and by other investigations. Perhaps the most damaging revelation was the secret espionage plan exposed by White House counsel, John Dean. It indicated that the president had authorized a nationwide system of burglary and espionage against private citizens involving a cooperative effort by the CIA, the FBI, the National Security Agency, and the Defense Intelligence Agency and that the only thing that prevented this plan from being implemented was the strong objection of J. Edgar Hoover, Head of the FBI. As *Newsweek* suggested, the plan may well have helped to spawn the Watergate break-in, the break-in at the office of Dr. Ellsberg's psychiatrist in the Pentagon Papers case and a series of other burglaries perpetrated by the government.[6] Clearly, the president was involved indirectly if not directly in the general expansion of espionage activities and in the approval of burglary and espionage as a way of life in Washington. A further explanation appeared necessary.

On May 22 the White House released two statements for the press covering more details of both Watergate and espionage generally. In the first statement was the declaration that other national security activities were "totally unrelated to Watergate" and, at a later point, the statement that the president "neither authorized nor encouraged subordinates to engage in illegal or improper campaign tactics."[7] In the full statement Mr. Nixon gave more details. He admitted approving the nationwide spy system, which he described as "a directive to strengthen our intelligence operations."[8] He also admitted that he had authorized the development of a special investigations unit within the White House, which came to be known as the "plumbers." This organization was designed to stop security leaks from the White House and, according to Mr. Nixon "to investigate other sensitive security matters." He acknowledged having impressed on Mr. Egil Krogh the extreme gravity of the Ellsberg case and the "vital

importance to national security" of Krogh's efforts to secure information on Ellsberg and his associates. As the president had already approved a system for clandestine burglaries for the FBI, CIA, and other
agencies, it is not surprising that Mr. Krogh felt he was authorized to
conduct his investigation in a similar manner. The president even
included in his statement the remark that:

> because of the emphasis I put on the crucial importance of protecting
> the national security, I can understand how highly motivated individ-
> uals could have felt justified in engaging in specific activities that I
> would have disapproved had they been brought to my attention. Con-
> sequently, as President, I must and do assume responsibility for such
> actions despite the fact that I, at no time approved or had knowledge of
> them.[9]

But he adds that the special investigations unit also had other duties
and that "their intelligence activities had no connection with the
break-in of the Democratic Headquarters or the aftermath."[10]

Although there was widespread approval for espionage and
burglary against private citizens authorized by the president within
the Nixon Administration, he maintained this activity had no connection with the Watergate break-in. Obviously Mr. Nixon was referring to the fact that the reason for each break-in was different. In this
way they were not connected. But in the larger sense, in the sense
that they were part of an attitude of "anything goes as long as you get
the information," they were clearly connected. In fact, several members of the "plumber's squad," E. Howard Hunt and G. Gordon Liddy
in particular, were directly involved in planning the Watergate
break-in. There was a connection not only in the general White
House climate at the time, but in the specific people involved in both
White House and Watergate operations. Hunt and Liddy, no doubt,
received their training and inspiration for Watergate from their work
on the plumbers squad within the White House itself.

As to Mr. Nixon's involvement in the attempts to cover up Watergate and its connection with the White House, his second statement
did admit a deeper involvement. But again it was in the form of responsibility without guilt. "I wanted justice done with regard to
Watergate," he said:

> but in the scale of national priorities with which I had to deal—and
> not at the time having any idea of the extent of political abuse which
> Watergate reflected—I also had to be deeply concerned with ensuring
> that neither the covert operations of the CIA nor the operations of the
> Special Investigations Unit should be compromised. Therefore I in-
> structed Mr. Haldeman and Mr. Ehrlichman to ensure that the investi-
> gation of the break-in not expose either an unrelated covert operation
> of the CIA or the activities of the White House investigations unit—and

> to see that this was personally coordinated between General Walters, the Deputy Director of the cia, and Mr. Gray of the fbi. It was certainly not my intent, nor my wish, that the investigation of the Watergate break-in or of related acts be impeded in any way.[11]

At this point Mr. Nixon seems to be saying that he did order the concealment of the connection between the Watergate personnel and the White House investigations unit but that he did not intend to obscure the connection between these people and the White House. A very fine point. It is difficult to conceal one aspect without the other, since Hunt and Liddy were involved in both operations. However, it was in his concluding statement that the president made his defense of inadvertence more specific:

> It is clear that unethical, as well as illegal activities took place in the course of that [1972] campaign. None of these took place with my specific approval or knowledge. To the extent that I may in any way have contributed to the climate in which they took place, I did not intend to [italics mine]. To the extent that I failed to prevent them I should have been more vigilant.[12]

This time there was no "God bless America" or "pray for me." It was a straight statement of fact with the assertion that, if he had said anything that fostered or encouraged the actions of Watergate it was completely inadvertent and without aggressive intent.

II

The evidence strongly suggests that the president was not a member of the small group that made the decision to go ahead with the Watergate operation. This group, according to one of the key witnesses, Jeb Stuart Magruder, consisted of the White House Counsel, Mr. Dean; an advisor, Mr. Larue; an assistant to Mr. Haldeman, Mr. Strachan; the head of the committee and former U.S. Attorney General, Mr. Mitchell (who made the final decision to go ahead with the project); Magruder himself, who was Mitchell's assistant; and finally Mr. Liddy who proposed the plan.

It is in this decision process that we must raise, once again, the question of inadvertence that has been a central issue in this study. Can the chief legal officer and law enforcement authority in the United States really make a decision committing his government to burglary and illegal espionage inadvertently? Around this question and its many ramifications revolves the central thesis of this book. Also central to this question is the state of mind of the decision

maker. I think an administrator can make such a decision inadvertently or without thinking about what he is really doing—if he prepares his mind for such an act. This is what Sartre has called "bad
faith."[13] However, bad faith is not something that infects the mind
from outside. At some point, the person must make a project to be in
bad faith. Although certain systems for decision making seem designed to enhance our capacity for bad faith, they do not preclude
individual reflection. It is the willingness to acquiesce, to give one's
self over to such a system that is the initial act of bad faith.

Under questioning by the Senate Committee on Watergate, Mr.
Magruder described the Watergate decision in detail. The picture
that emerges is one of a determined Mr. Liddy who began his espionage proposal with an elaborate design and an estimated budget
much larger than he could hope to have approved. But through his
own persistence and his aggressive, rather flamboyant personality,
he finally overcame the objections of the other members of the decision group. He allowed them to negotiate him down to a smaller
proposal, which looked modest only because it was compared with a
budget four times its size, and, although it was clearly illegal, it did
not seem nearly as illegal as his original proposal. Having cut the ex-
penses, it seemed to the decision group that moderation had prevailed. Besides, the decision came at the end of a long hard meeting
and everyone was tired.

There were three meetings in all, during which Liddy's original
proposal for a million dollar budget, the use of prostitutes to lure
Democratic candidates into compromising situations, and the kid-
napping of potential radical demonstrators at the Republican convention, was reduced to a budget of $250,000 and the proposal for
burglary and espionage of the Democratic National Committee. It
was Senator Baker who questioned Magruder in detail about the decision, in this last meeting, to go ahead with the project. (Mr. Dean
was not present at this last meeting.)

> Q. (Baker) . . . It is important for me to know exactly how the assent
> was given.
>
> A. (Magruder) . . . We discussed the pros and cons, Mr. LaRue and
> Mr. Mitchell and I, not any great feeling of acceptance to this plan,
> with the exception that supposedly these individuals were profes-
> sional, the information could be valuable. Mr. Mitchell simply signed
> off on it in the sense of saying, "Okay, let's give him a quarter of a
> million dollars and let's see what he can come up with. . . ."
>
> Q. Was there any question in your mind that the plan was agreed to
> by Mr. Mitchell?

A.   No, sir, there was no doubt. But it was a reluctant decision. I think that is important to note. It was not one that anyone was overwhelmed with at all. But it was made and he did make it.

Q.   Tell me more about why it was a reluctant decision.

A.   We knew it was illegal, probably inappropriate. We didn't think that much would come of it. We had at least thirty decisions we made that day about even greater sums of money than that $250,000.

Q.   Did you have any decisions to make that day that involved any illegal action?

A.   No, sir.

Q.   Or any clandestine activity.

A.   No, sir.

Q.   Did that stand out in your mind, why you made that decision reluctantly?

A.   Yes, sir. I think so.

Q.   Did you ever express any reservations about it?

A.   Yes, sir.

Q.   What did you say?

A.   Well, that it was illegal and that it was inappropriate and that it may not work.

Q.   To whom did you say that?

A.   To Mr. Mitchell, Mr LaRue, Mr. Strachan.

Q.   What was Mr. Mitchell's reply?

A.   I think he had similar reservations, sir.

Q.   What did he say?

A.   Well, by this time, we had some indications of lack of compatibility with Mr. Liddy's behavior and we knew that this was possibly an inappropriate program.

Q.   What was Mr. LaRue's reaction?

A.   Similar. He was not overwhelmed with the program.

Q.   What was your reaction?

A.   I was not overwhelmed with the program, but you must, I think, understand that I had personal feelings relating to Mr. Liddy and I was concerned about letting those personal feelings overcome a possible decision that might be made. [Liddy had argued with Magruder and threatened to kill him. Liddy was known to carry a gun.]

Q.   What was Mr. Strachan's reaction?

A. I think he felt uncomfortable with Mr. Liddy. But again, I think we have to, in all honesty, say that we thought there may be some information that could be very helpful to us and because of a certain atmosphere that had developed in my working at the White House, I was not as concerned about its illegality as I should have been at that time . . . I fully accept the responsibility of having made an absolutely disastrous decision, or at least having participated. I didn't make the decision, but certainly participated in it.

Q. A decision really that is going to affect history that was made in almost a casual way.

A. Yes, sir.

Q. When did you first begin planning the coverup?

A. I think there was no question that the coverup began that Saturday when we realized there was a break-in. I do not think there was ever any discussion that there would not be a coverup.

Q. An historic decision to go forward with this plan was followed with another historic decision to cover it up without any great debate or discussion of the matter.

A. That is correct, sir . . .[14]

Gordon Liddy was the man in charge of developing the Watergate "option," and he pushed his point hard. Had we not already observed the decision process in the Cuban invasion, it would be tempting to conclude that it was merely Mr. Liddy's aggressive personality and his persistence that eroded the opposition of the other members of the decision group. However, there was already an attitude and a series of precedents in White House policy that gave an implicit acceptance to wiretapping. After each meeting Liddy was told that his plans were not satisfactory, but no one told him to discontinue working on the project. The longer he continued, the more pressure mounted to make some use of his time and the money that was already allocated. The pressure in this direction was further increased by a call from Charles Colson to Jeb Magruder before the third meeting with Mitchell. Colson warned Magruder that the election committee would have to fish or cut bait, that it was absurd to have Liddy and Hunt working for the committee if they were not going to be used. If the committee could not use them, said Colson, he could make use of them himself.[15]

Mitchell did not want to make trouble. Referring back to this incident John Dean later remarked of Mitchell, "He is a nice person and doesn't like to have to say no when he is talking with people he is going to have to work with."[16] About the same time Magruder also received a call from Robert Haldeman's office, asking about the progress of intelligence-gathering efforts against the Democrats and wondering why no information was forthcoming. Whether or not the specific bugging plan was mentioned by Strachan (Haldeman's assistant) is not clear, but he showed his impatience and, by implication, the impatience of the president for immediate intelligence on the activity of the opposition. This may well have served as the final push to "try harder."[17]

It was not, then, Liddy's personality that dominated the decision group. In all probability they knew that they were going to accept some variation of the bugging proposal when they appointed Liddy to develop the plan; that is, they knew it without admitting it to themselves. The decision process was a means of making it appear to the participants that they had considered all the alternatives, that they were dealing with objective facts, and that they were not influenced by personal feelings. For example, Magruder failed to voice his reservations about Liddy *because* of his personal feelings toward the man. He regarded these feelings as not relevant to the decision at hand. They may have been the most relevant data in the decision situation. The decision makers did not deceive themselves about *what* they were doing, but they did deceive themselves about *the significance* of what they were doing. They placed the decision at the end of the meeting agenda and managed to convince themselves that it was relatively routine and unimportant.

III

It seems clear that President Nixon did not give a direct order for the Watergate operation. But surely the sense of fatalism that surrounded the decision process, the feeling that the committee members knew they were going to have to approve the plan, even though no one seemed to like it, the general acceptance of wiretapping and political espionage as a way of life, resulted directly from the personality and the attitude of Richard Nixon. There was a heavy-handed pressure from the White House to get information. The pressure came directly from Nixon to Haldeman to Colson and Strachan, and from both of these men to Mitchell. John Dean tells how these pressures worked on Mitchell.

> "Well, I have a lot of theories," I [Dean] began. "My strongest one is that Colson was all over you on the Liddy plan and Haldeman was sending down pressure through Strachan. I know you weren't too excited about it, but I figure you finally said what the hell and approved

it to get them off your back. My theory is that you just threw the dice
on it."

Mitchell turned to look at me for the first time. He was holding his
pipe in his hand, leaning slightly forward in his chair. "Your theory
is right," he said quietly, "except we thought it would be one or two
times removed from the Committee."[18]

Gordon Strachan, assistant to Haldeman, attended the meeting in
which the decision was made. Strachan must certainly have conveyed the plan of the Watergate operation to Haldeman. If Haldeman
did not describe the specific details to Mr. Nixon before the break-in,
it was only because he knew the president should be protected from
this kind of knowledge. The president, as John Dean remarked, must
have "deniability."[19] He must be at least one step away from all
questionable orders so that his name cannot be connected with anything illegal or unethical. This preservation of deniability was already a common practice in the Nixon White House at the time John
Dean first accepted his position.

We began this study with a series of incidents in which the
phenomenon of inadvertence appeared rather subtle, a product of
the situation and the general characteristics of the American temperament. But in this instance it seems clear that the inadvertence was
more a façade than a reality. The president *deliberately* designed a
system of decision making in which his wishes could be carried out
without his being "aware" of the details. We are no longer dealing
with the kind of inadvertence that characterized the U-2 incident
and the Cuban invasion.

The preservation of one's innocence through inadvertence is a
dangerous game. If one is to remain truly innocent of all aggressive
intent, one cannot take part in the act of concealing one's intentions
from one's self. John Dean has described the elaborate tickler system
that operated in the White House.[20] It was a system through which
the president could conceal the source of an order, but it was a relentless system that ensured the implementation of his intent. One
cannot maintain a high level of innocence and a high level of efficiency at the same time. In the Nixon White House inadvertence
had degenerated into fraud.

IV

It would be comforting if we could lay out the details of the
Watergate case to show that it was a conscious act of conspiracy by a
group of evil men who are now, thank God, forever removed from

power. However, the sad truth about Watergate is that it is perfectly congruent with a set of American values that has been developing in government circles in recent years. Like many previous acts of aggression against other countries, this act against another political party was, in part, inadvertent. It was inadvertent in the sense that most of the people involved did not realize the essential wrongness of their acts until they were brought under public scrutiny. To say that they were evil men, we would first have to believe that we were morally superior to them. In many cases, at the lower echelons of power, they came forward to reveal all the details of the case, without requesting immunity from prosecution, once they were aware of the magnitude of the crime itself. Like the hundreds of captains and sergeants who participated in the falsification of reports of General Lavelle's "protective reaction strikes," they were part of a plan that they believed to be technically illegal but justified in some larger sense because the enemy would not play fair.

But these were not the men who were to be protected by the myth of inadvertence. It was the inadvertence of President Nixon that was crucial to the final explanation for Watergate. The edited transcripts of the president's conversations leave no doubt that he was involved in the cover-up, once the arrests were made. Mr. Nixon knew that he knew the details of Watergate, but he wanted to pretend (to himself and to others) that he did not know. Here the transcripts are most revealing. It is clear from Mr. Nixon's conversations with Dean, Haldeman, and Ehrlichman that he *did not want to know* if illegal acts had taken place with the involvement of White House staff, that he *wanted to be told* that White House staff were *not* involved. At all times he was careful not to ask Mitchell directly what happened in those meetings on the Liddy plan, nor did he push Magruder for the details. He asked others to conduct "investigations" for him, but he made it clear to those others (Dean, Haldeman, Ehrlichman) that he did *not want* to know the details, only the general statement. Without saying it in so many words, he invited others to tell him that he and his staff were not involved with the dirty details of Watergate. His concern, as revealed by the transcripts, is with what witnesses can be expected to hold up in court. Who will crack under questioning? Who will reveal what?

However, John Dean, the president's counsel grew increasingly uneasy. Mr. Nixon was expressing his concern about keeping the investigation away from the White House without really knowing the full extent of White House involvement. On March 20, 1973, in the evening, Dean called the president to arrange a meeting in which Mr. Nixon would be told all the details of Watergate and be able to make his own judgment on what to do. During the telephone call the president again asked Dean to reassure some of his cabinet that the White House was in the clear. Dean again urged the president to wait until he knew all the facts before he offered any further reassurance. The president said he really did want to know, but he persisted with his concern for some public statement. He did not want to appear to be holding back information from the public. On the other hand, he did not really want to reveal anything. If Dean pretended to investigate, but revealed nothing, this might keep people satisfied. The conversation continues.

> THE PRESIDENT: You've got to have something where it doesn't appear that I am doing this in, you know, just in a—saying to hell with the Congress and to hell with the people. We are not going to tell you anything because of Executive Privilege. That, they don't understand. But if you say, "No, we are willing to cooperate," and you've made a complete statement, but make it very incomplete. See, that is what I mean, I don't want a, too much in chapter and verse as you did in your letter, I just want just a general—
>
> DEAN: An all around statement.
>
> PRESIDENT: That's right. Try just something general. Like, "I have checked into this matter; I can [sic] categorically, based on my investigation, the following: Haldeman is not involved in this, that and the other thing. Mr. Colson did not do this; Mr. so and so did not do this. Mr. Blank did not do this. Right down the line, taking the most glaring things. If there are any questions let me know. See?
>
> DEAN: Uh, huh. I think we can do that.[21]

Of course Dean did not do that. By this time he had begun to worry about the responsibility he was carrying. For he knew that when the facts were finally revealed, Mr. Nixon would be able to claim that he did not know anything about the coverup, that he was relying on John Dean, his "investigator," to get all the facts and John Dean had failed him. Dean insisted on giving the president all the information, all the messy details, and leaving him with the decision of what he would tell the public. This violated all the rules for a good team player. The responsibility should be properly spread around so that no one is really responsible. Dean would not have it that way.

The next morning the president and Dean met at the White House. Haldeman entered the room later. This was the famous meeting in which Dean warned that there was a cancer growing around the presidency. He layed out all the facts: Magruder's involvement, the decision to go ahead with Watergate, made by Mitchell, his own involvement (his presence at the first two Watergate meetings.) He warned that Gordon Strachan, Haldeman's aide, had been in on

Watergate from the beginning and that he had been reporting to Haldeman. Hunt, one of the Watergate defendants, had been given money, and Ehrlichman, Haldeman, Dean, and Mitchell were all involved in that. He warned that there would be continued blackmail of the White House by Hunt and other defendants, and he used the word *blackmail* several times. The president was distressed by the blackmail, but he seemed unable to act at once. "It seems to me we have to keep the cap on the bottle that much, or we don't have any options." he said. Finally Dean told him, "If this thing ever blows, then we are in a coverup situation. I think it would be extremely damaging to you." The president cut in with a firm agreement, but he wondered why Dean had lost his confidence that they could all ride through the mess. Dean said everyone was getting scared and someone would surely break soon. Too many people knew about it. Dean urged the president to tell the attorney general the facts. After all, this was really the first time he really knew the full extent of White House involvement. Dean said he might have to go to jail for obstruction of justice, but he was prepared to go. The president could not believe it; this was not really obstruction of justice. Dean urged that we "cut our losses," and "minimize the further growth of this thing, rather than further compound it."

But the president again urged that Dean brief the cabinet and tell them that neither Ehrlichman nor Haldeman was involved: "Answer questions basically on the basis of what they told you, not what you know." They decided on another meeting that afternoon, and the president reassured Dean that "the way you put it out there, letting it all hang out, it may never get there." Haldeman entered the room, and there was more talk about the pressure from Hunt for more money. The president told Dean he had no choice but to come up with the money for Hunt. There was more talk about the danger of further embarrassing information coming out and Haldeman showed increasing concern about the extent of the problem. At this point, Mr. Nixon remarked, "Bob, it's not so bad. It's bad, but it's not the worst place."

"I was going the other way there," said Haldeman, "I was going to say that it might be to our interests to get it out."

Mr. Nixon responded to this in terms of controlled leaks, leaking bits of information, but keeping most of it under control.

This was the critical meeting for the president. There is much more information than I have been able to record here, and the reader should certainly cover the entire transcript of this meeting and the one that followed. To me it appears that, at this meeting, Dean presented Mr. Nixon with his last opportunity to pretend that he now understood, for the first time, the real details of Watergate. He clearly advised the president to get all the facts out, to turn everything over to the Attorney General. Robert Haldeman, too, seemed to be leaning in the same direction. But even after he knew all the facts, the president minimized the severity of the situation. Without ever saying "let's cover this thing up," he implied that full disclosure was not necessary, and he delayed any decisive action. Once they saw the way he was moving, Dean and Haldeman fell into line and supported his position. Neither man opposed him directly or told him he was making a mistake. In fairness to both men, however, it must be said that the president's decision to continue the coverup was never really made. He let it hang, and they may well have thought that he would decide that afternoon.

By delaying a decision to reveal the information, he, in effect, made it necessary to continue the coverup until such time as he was ready to tell all. However, he must have known what he was doing, as we see him pressing, all the more firmly, for a Dean report that same afternoon. It was clear that if the information were not revealed at once, the president would need some justification for his failure to act. He would need a report from John Dean full of reassurances that the White House was not involved.

In the meeting that same afternoon, with the president, Haldeman, Ehrlichman, and Dean, Mr. Nixon urged Dean to write his report. Haldeman and Ehrlichman, sensing the president's nondecision, also pressed Dean in the same direction:

> THE PRESIDENT: . . . John, I asked for a written report which I do not have, which is very general, understand . . .

> EHRLICHMAN: I think the President is in a stronger position later. The President is in a stronger position later, if he can be shown to have justifiably relied on you at this point in time.

> DEAN: Well, there is the argument now that Dean's credibility is in question. Maybe I shouldn't do it. Maybe someone else—

> THE PRESIDENT: As a matter of fact, John, I don't think your credibility has been much injured . . . you are going to make a hell of a good impression . . .

> THE PRESIDENT [in another conversation]:   . . . I think this should be a letter to me. You could say that, "Now, now that hearings are going on, I can now give a report that we can put out."

> HALDEMAN: That is what you can say. In other words, he gives you a report because you asked him for it, regardless of the timeliness . . .

> DEAN [following further conversation]:   Well, I see in this conversation what I have talked about before. They do not ultimately solve

what I see as a grave problem of a cancer growing around the Presidency. This creates another problem. It does not clean the problem out.

THE PRESIDENT: Well . . .

EHRLICHMAN: But doesn't it permit the President to clear it out at such time as it does come up? By saying, "Indeed, I relied on it. And now this later thing turns up and I don't condone that. And if I had known that before, obviously I would have run it down."[22]

Dean resisted, never refusing outright, but always raising objections and reminding the others that there were too many people involved, that it would all come out sooner or later. There was a feeling implied in what was being said but never expressed openly by anyone, a growing feeling on the part of Dean that the other members of the group would like to make him a fall guy, that they were all turning to him and expecting him to write a report that would cover them all. Again, on the afternoon of March 22, with Nixon, Haldeman, Mitchell, and Ehrlichman present, the president again urged Dean to make his report, and he was supported by the others.

DEAN: . . . I haven't gone through the exercise yet in a real effort to write such a report, and I really can't say until I do it where we are and I certainly think it is something that should be done though.

THE PRESIDENT: What do you say on the Watergate [inaudible]

DEAN: We can't be complete if we don't know, all we know is what, is what—

THE PRESIDENT: It is a negative in setting forth general information involving questions. Your consideration—your analysis, et cetera. You have found this, that. Rather than going into every news story and every charge, et cetera, et cetera. This, this, this—put it down—I don't know but—

DEAN: I don't think I can do it until I sit down this evening and start drafting.

HALDEMAN: I think you ought to hold up for the weekend and do that and get it done.

THE PRESIDENT: Sure.

HALDEMAN: Give it your full attention and get it done.

THE PRESIDENT: I think you need—why don't you do this? Why don't you go up to Camp David?

DEAN: I might do it, I might do it . . .

EHRLICHMAN [after further conversation]:   and I am looking to the future, assuming that some corner of this thing comes unstuck, you [the President] are then in a position to say, "Look, that document I published is the document I relied on, that is, the report I relied on."

THE PRESIDENT: That is all we know.

HALDEMAN: That is all the stuff we could find out—

EHRLICHMAN: And now this new development is a surprise to me—I am going to fire A, B, C and D, now.

DEAN: John, let me just raise this. If you make the document public, the first thing that happens is the press starts asking Ziegler about it . . . Keep in mind every item, there will be a full day of quizzing. It will keep up day after day after day.[23]

It is clear that the president and John Dean began to move further apart from this date. Dean felt he had told Nixon everything, and Nixon was still trying to keep it quiet. An increasing caution and a note of hypocrisy creeps into their conversations with each other from this point onward.

The purpose of the proposed report was very clear. It was to be used to coverup the details of Watergate as long as possible, to deny White House involvement and presidential knowledge. Dean never prepared it. Later, on May 22, 1973, after Ehrlichman, Haldeman, and Dean resigned, President Nixon tried to make use of the Dean "investigation" anyway. In a statement on that date he denied any attempt to obstruct the investigation of Watergate and maintained that he had relied on John Dean, that Dean had given him all the information he had at the time.

It now seems that later, through whatever complex of individual motives and possible misunderstandings, there were apparently wide-ranging efforts to limit the investigation or to conceal the possible involvement of members of the Administration and the campaign committee.

I was not aware of any such efforts at the time . . . In the weeks and months that followed Watergate, I asked for, and received, repeated assurances that Mr. Dean's own investigation (which included reviewing files and sitting in on FBI interviews with White House personnel) had cleared everyone then employed by the White House of involvement . . .

With hindsight, it is apparent that I should have given more heed to the warning signals I received along the way about a Watergate coverup and less to reassurances.[24]

Mr. Nixon was telling the truth, in a very literal sense, when he said, "I asked for, and received, repeated assurances . . . ." That was the real problem. Instead of asking for an investigation he asked for assurances that there was no problem. Later when the involvement of White House staff in Watergate was revealed, he tried to use the Dean "report" even though it had never been written. He referred to the report on August 15, 1973. But at that time the proposed Dean report had undergone a marvelous transformation in the mind of Mr. Nixon.

> From the time when the break-in occurred, I pressed repeatedly to know the facts and particularly whether there was any involvement of anyone in the White House. I considered two things essential: First, that the investigation should be thorough and above-board; and second, that if there were any higher involvement, we should get the facts out first . . . I knew that the Justice Department and the FBI were conducting intensive investigations—as I had insisted that they should. The White House counsel, John Dean, was assigned to monitor those investigations, and particularly to check into any possible White House involvement . . .
>
> It was not until March 21 of this year that I received new information from the White House counsel that led me to conclude that the reports I had been getting for over nine months were not true. On that day I launched an intensive effort of my own to get the facts out. Whatever the facts might be, I wanted the White House to be the first to make them public.
>
> At first I entrusted the task of getting me the facts to Mr. Dean. When, after spending a week at Camp David, he failed to produce the written report I had asked for, I turned to John Ehrlichman and to the Attorney General—while also making independent inquiries of my own. By mid-April I had received Mr. Ehrlichman's report, and also one from the Attorney General based on new information uncovered by the Justice Department.
>
> These reports made it clear to me that the situation was far more serious than I had imagined . . . I ordered all members of the Administration to testify fully before the grand jury.[25]

In retrospect it is now clear that Mr. Nixon was aware of the serious nature of the situation on March 21, not mid-April. But even in August, when the above statement was made, he was still refusing to turn over his recorded conversations to the Watergate Committee. He still believed he could hold out against demands for full disclosure of all matters related to Watergate. It was only after the release of the president's taped conversations that the sham of the proposed Dean report was revealed—and the later Ehrlichman report as well. After Dean had refused to write his report clearing those close to the president, the job was passed to Ehrlichman.

Inadvertence has come a long way from the early days of the Truman Administration. It seems to have moved from a certain general lack of awareness to a conscious and cynical belief that one must appear to be inadvertent because that is the only thing the American people will accept. We must pretend that we didn't know what we were doing.

Is this really true in the United States today? If it is, our great technological development and our enormous systems for gathering and processing information are useless. We can do a better job of pretending that we don't know what we are doing if we do not have all this equipment and personal investigators feeding us detailed information. We have created a great fiction that our decisions are made in a logical, rational manner, and we have created an enormous system to support this fiction. But in the last stages it always appears that some mistake is made. Is it possible that the systematization of thought is itself responsible for some of these mistakes? If we had not placed so much emphasis on gathering, processing, and analyzing information, if we did not believe that decisions are based on objective "reports," filled with facts, we might be more willing to look at the personal factors in the decision process. We will examine this question in more detail in the next chapter.

NOTES

1. Presidential Documents. Administration of Richard Nixon. Volume 9, No. 18, May 5, 1973, pp. 433–38, Washington D.C.: National Archives and Records Service, 1973.

2. Ibid.

3. Ibid.

4. Ibid.

5. F.L. Zimmerman, "Resignations of Aides Ease Some Nixon Woes But Create New Ones," Wall Street Journal, May 1, 1973, p. 1.

6. "Blueprint for a Super Secret Police," Newsweek June 4, 1973, p. 19.

7. R. M. Nixon, press release accompanying a statement by the president, May 22, 1973.

8. R.M. Nixon, statement, May 22, 1973.

9. Ibid.

10. Ibid.

11. Ibid.

12. Ibid.

13. J. -P. Sartre, Being and Nothingness, trans. Hazel Barnes (New York: Washington Square Press, 1972), pp. 89–90.

14. Hearings Before the Select Committee on Presidential Campaign Activities of the United States Senate 93rd Congress. Watergate and Related Activities. Washington D.C.: U.S. Government Printing Office, 1973, Book 2, pp. 812–816.

15. Submission of Recorded Presidential Conversations to the Committee on the Judiciary of the House of Representatives by Richard Nixon Wash. D.C.: U.S. Government Printing Office, April 30, 1974, pp. 177–178.

16. Ibid., p. 176.

17. Ibid., pp.178–179.

18. J. Dean, Blind Ambition (New York: Simon & Schuster, 1976), p. 224.

19. Ibid., p. 33.

20. Ibid., pp. 32–88.

21. *Submission of Recorded Presidential Conversations* Op. Cit., p. 168.

22. Ibid., pp. 257–262.

23. Ibid., pp. 283–285.

24. *Presidential Documents. Administration of Richard M. Nixon,* Volume 9, No. 21, May 28, 1973, pp. 693–698.

25. *Presidential Documents. Administration of Richard M. Nixon.* Volume 9, No. 33, Aug. 20, 1973, pp. 984–991.

13

The Systematization of Thought

I

We have examined a series of incidents in which there is evidence of a conflict between the desire for power and the desire for virtue. I have taken the position that Americans desire power, but we have a kind of prudery about admitting our aggressive impulses. The modern American reacts to aggression the way his Puritan ancestor reacted to sex. He likes to engage in it without admitting to the world what he is doing. Sometimes he does not even admit it to himself. There are at least two major consequences of this situation:

1. Our desire for innocence could make us vulnerable. The need to appear good and peace-loving may cause us to delay preparations for war until some other nation has the force to overpower us. In the nuclear age this could mean our destruction.

2. Our desire for innocence could make us dangerous. There is a danger we will provoke others or try to destroy them without recognizing what we are doing. This could also lead to our own destruction in a mutual exchange of nuclear attacks.

Both conclusions are reasonable if we accept the original premise.

However, as I have already indicated, I feel the current danger for the world and for ourselves is the second possibility, namely, that our destructive impulses will get out of hand. In fact, the more we become aware of the first possibility *only* (without recognizing or attempting to correct for the second), the more dangerous we are likely to become. There is already a substantial movement in this country to make us aware of our innocence in regard to our vulnerability, but the people involved in this effort (most of whom have considerable influence in the government) have carefully avoided the suggestion that we may also be dangerous.

Herman Kahn has taken a position not unlike my own in regard to American prudery about aggression. He even compares this attitude to our earlier prudery about sex. But in the morality tales of Herman Kahn, innocence leads to vulnerability. He begins his book on *Thinking about the Unthinkable* with the story of English girls who were forced into white slavery in the Victorian period. Kahn says:

> One reason why this lasted as long as it did, was that it could not be talked about openly in Victorian England; moral standards as to subjects of discussion made it difficult to arouse the community to necessary action. Moreover, the extreme innocence considered appropriate for English girls made them easy victims, helpless to cope with the situations in which they were trapped. Victorian standards, besides perpetuating the white slave trade, intensified the damage to those involved.[1]

He follows this tale with the story of American vulnerability to nuclear attack because of our unwillingness to talk openly about our aggressive needs, to assess the risks of war and to decide how many people we would be willing to sacrifice in order to save those that remain. To talk openly about these problems would not only help us to understand them, it would put our enemy on notice that we will no longer be innocent victims. He warns us that we must do some hard, realistic thinking about aggression if we are to survive in the real world.

I support Herman Kahn's position that we need realistic thinking, but we differ markedly in what we might call "realistic." I do not think our situation is comparable to the English girls forced into prostitution. It is more comparable to that of the young man who has been making use of a "white slave" and who has been enjoying her dependency while telling himself that she is in love with him. One day she flies into a rage at him and he cannot understand her anger. He had imagined that she regarded him as her protector. He, too, is innocent, but it is an innocence in regard to his destructive potential and his capacity for evil.

Both kinds of innocence are possible, of course. It is the second kind of innocence about which I am most concerned in this study, because this is the kind that is more difficult to discover. It is less flattering to one's self-concept as a virtuous person. In fact, I would contend that it is, in part, our effort to correct the first kind of innocence by the development of a cold and calculated realism that has led us into the innocence of the second type. There are many reasons why this has occurred. One is the change in the nature of warfare itself. This change has worked to separate the intellect from emotion and to enhance the possibility for innocence in regard to our intent.

With the advance of civilization and the expansion of technology, human aggression has moved from the body to the mind. With the decrease in body contact and the diminished reliance on a sensory perception of danger, man's awareness of his fear and his anger has decreased accordingly. Man no longer feels his aggressive impulses with the same intensity. Aggression is viewed more and more with the intellect. It is seen as a problem to be solved in a cool, detached manner. In an earlier period sensation, emotion, thought, and action were more closely connected. Primitive man sensed danger from a crackling in the underbrush. He changed his posture and his body tension, he listened more intently, he readied himself for action or he acted and observed the results of his action. He thought about what he should do next, but his thoughts were informed by an immediate sensory contact with the environment.

The warrior king had to make more extensive preparations for action, but he often went into battle at the head of his troops and his anger found an outlet in the immediacy of conflict. As warfare became more technical a certain distance developed between the leader and his men. At the head of the army was a general who often removed himself to a distant hill where he could get an unobstructed view of the battlefield and where couriers could ride to inform him of the details that he could not determine from his greater distance.

At this point there was already a certain coolness on the part of the professional soldier. He wanted to win, but more as a matter of professional pride than because of any great commitment to the aims of his nation's leader. The immediacy of death being somewhat removed he could develop a certain detachment from his work. Information came to him not by direct sensory contact but indirectly through his courier. However, he had an overview of the battle, and he could conceive of the details and fit them into the total picture when they were explained to him. He continued to deal in concrete realities of the moment.

With the advent of more advanced weapons it became necessary for the general to remove himself even further from the scene of combat. He worked more with maps and charts, using vectors to represent opposing forces. He attempted to achieve the objectives of the national leader by formulating certain symbols and thinking in terms of these symbols. Increasing technological sophistication has continued this use of symbols, but the speed of information transfer is more rapid. The map of the general has become automated. With the development of radar, it became possible to observe an air battle by watching electrical impulses projected on a picture tube. The information was almost immediate, although the aircraft themselves were represented by small blips of light on the scope. Major disturbances in the environment were still visible, however. A nuclear burst became apparent by the existence of a rapidly spreading cloud on the surface of the radar scope. It could be confirmed by turning a height-finder scope on the object in question. Here, the familiar mushroom-shaped cloud was clearly visible.

With the development of the digital computer we have reached a higher level of abstraction. Information from many radar receivers is sent to a central computer where it is analyzed and displayed on a master scope for a battle district. One no longer sees the blip, which is an analog picture of an aircraft in space. Instead the computer generates an electronic symbol that *represents* the position of an aircraft. Furthermore, if a return from the radar is missing, the computer (having stored the position, speed, and velocity of the aircraft) calculates the point where it should be and generates a symbol for that new position. However, with several radar sites sending information to a master scope, it is no longer feasible to display the clouds, strobes, and other sources of electronic "noise" in the environment. Such additional data would overload the information capacity of the system. Therefore, the electronic picture is wiped free of interference, presenting only "clean" data. Such changes also eliminate the analog picture of a nuclear explosion. Nuclear bursts must be detected through another system, an extremely accurate sensing device that takes the thermal signature of an explosion and cannot be triggered by conventional weapons. The signal from this device is digital; that is, it provides a yes or no type answer. On the display at military headquarters a nuclear burst over New York City is indicated merely by a single light. However, this digitalization of the data further removes the sensory contiguity between the observer and the event. If the observer is at a point outside the city, he can feel the shock wave and see the burst through dark glasses or by means of a height-finder radar scope. He experiences the full complexity of the event itself. There is no doubt in his mind that he is observing a nuclear explosion. If he merely notes the change in color of a light, the credibility of the event is not quite the same. By presenting the individual with a set of symbols, certain important cues are lost, as is the feeling of really *knowing* that something has happened (in the sensory meaning of this term). By teaching the individual to rely on the *symbolic representation* of events rather than his own awareness, which springs from the sensory complexity of his environment, we have made his perception of danger into a strictly intellectual–logical experience rather than something that involves his whole body.

II

The requirement for planning, an inescapable attribute of technological development, tends to further remove the military commander from the sensory experience of combat. The weapons of tomorrow must be designed today, and their design and development require specialized knowledge. It is not enough to view the battlefield from a distance, the modern military leader must look into the future and foresee the consequences of his actions years before they will occur. Under such circumstances danger is further removed from the intuitive fear that "something doesn't feel right" and one prepares for aggressive acts without a feeling of anger— without, in fact, any real intent that one's planned moves will occur. They are merely contingency plans, and their execution depends on circumstances as yet unknown.

For a culture such as that of the United States, whose people are already predisposed to deny the reality of their aggressive ambitions, the modern technological society serves as the perfect vehicle. All of our tendencies are accentuated by the necessity that presses upon us. We are removed in both space and time from the physical sensations and from the emotions that generally accompany aggression. If it were only the military commanders who were forced into this detached mode of thought by the pressure of technology, national policy might find a source of correction from the leaders in industry and government. But our technological development has dictated a similar type of thinking in terms of symbols and advanced planning in both industry and government. The task is too big for one individual, and the steps from thought to action must be separated. A new technological system is created by a series of steps. The following represents a general outline of these steps.

1. Outline system objectives (in military terms the "mission" of the system).
2. Determine the system requirements.
3. Plan the general system design.
4. Analyze the tasks required.
5. Divide the tasks and assign teams to work on them.
6. Perform tasks.
7. Assemble final product.
8. Test product.
9. Prepare product for industrial use (in military terms, "implement" the new system).

These steps bear a close relationship to the type of thinking associated with the formal description of scientific method as described by the early philosophers of science. Experiments were to be planned in advance. They were expected to follow a sequential pattern:

1. Outline scientific objectives.
2. Plan method.
3. Make observations.
4. Perform analysis.
5. Derive results.
6. Draw conclusions.

The practice of science at its best was often quite different from its verbal representation. However, the myth of science has become the reality of technology. The linear method of thought has become the scientific ideal of our century, as embodied in the technique of systems analysis. With the increasing reliance of government leaders on technological sophistication, this "scientific" ideal has also become the model for the decision process in the higher echelons of government, including the formulation of national policy. This development is more evident in the United States. John Seeley has said that everything in America becomes an industry. "By industry I mean nothing more than some enormous organization in which some input is put in, brought under a process characterized by a maximum of 'rationality' (minute subdivision of labor, immense organization, and exact application of calculated means to ends), and thereby some output is put out."[2]

Real-life decisions in both science and policy formulation are, of course, much more erratic, disorganized, and creative than the process suggested by this linear model. The influence of this "ideal" systematic mode of thought on the real thinking process varies from one organization to another and from one level of command to another. In Chapter 2 I presented the comments of a number of foreign observers who have noted the American susceptibility to this kind of thinking, due to a predisposition for rationalization and for an emphasis on the external, the visible, the concrete, and the measurable. But it would be difficult to maintain that this tendency is exclusively American. American "technique" and know-how are rapidly being exported and imitated. Furthermore, it is not the mere availability of techniques of linear problem solving that makes them dangerous, but an undue reliance on all technical and external sources of evidence to the exclusion of internal, emotional factors in the problem situation.

Some of the most complicated policy problems have been subjected to this type of intellectual assembly line in the form of a "study" of alternative courses of action. It is assumed, of course, that the purpose of such studies is merely to clarify the possibilities available to an executive, not to make his decisions for him, but the enormous expenditure of capital, time, and the supposed expertise of the participants often produces strong pressures on the executive. He is embedded in a technological system that includes not just his military policy but his total environment. A certain rigidity is imposed upon his thought by the nature of the society in which he lives. Galbraith has described the constraints of the technological society and their consequences in terms of a generally limited flexibility for the decision maker.[3]

The digital computer has proved effective in coordinating the mass of interlocking processes involved in technological development. It is not surprising that it should also be used in the complicated interplay between technology and policy. The result is a certain rigidity in policy, the conviction that a given process must continue because there are so many other developments that "feed into" it and are dependent on it. The role of the digitalization of data is by no means evident to those who criticize our present system of technological planning.

In his celebrated attack on the National Security Industrial Association, Paul Goodman charged that systems analysis had been used to perfect the methods of warfare and that on the domestic scene it had resulted in "standardization, centralization, and bureaucratic control." But there was a reservation in his attack. These evils, he remarked, resulted from the character of the individuals and were "not necessary in the method." He chided the scientists and their military colleagues for their failure to "feed your computers indefinite factors and unknown parameters where spirit, spite, enthusiasm, revenge, invention, etc., will make the difference."[4]

Unfortunately the nature of the digital computer is such that one cannot feed it such "indefinite factors." In our present binary system of machine logic, the digital computer is designed to process data that has already been categorized on a two-choice, yes–no basis. In order to fit data into this digital framework, it is necessary to remove the ambiguity from each piece of information before it is processed. The old analog type of data perception, which recognized shades of difference and nuance, must be discarded during this procedure. This means that a certain *artificial cleanliness* is imposed on the data from the beginning.

However, if the result of a careful sequence of steps seems to clash with one's intuitive feeling for the situation, it would seem possible to stop the process and go back over the work. C. West Churchman has pointed out that the systems analyst may find it necessary to reexamine the thinking in earlier steps based on information developed later in the process.[5] In practice, however, Churchman's caveat is all too often forgotten. There is something about laying out a sequence of steps that sets a certain atmosphere for the study. Most studies are placed under a time constraint. Ideally there should be several iterations of the thinking process. In practice there is often a requirement for preliminary recommendations after the study has been under way for only a brief period. This leads to a division of labor in order to provide some results as rapidly as possible. The division of labor often takes place by assigning each step in the thinking process to a different team of intellectual workers. This means that one team may examine the objectives, another may prepare a diagram of the information flow through the system, another may develop a list of system components, another may attempt to represent these components in a mathematical model, etc. Each individual may do extensive work on his own portion of the study before the group gets together to consider the various steps in relation to each other. By this time there has developed a certain personal investment in the work. Each step, in other words, has an ego attached to it—the ego of the assigned worker or the collective identity of the work team. The rethinking that could be done by an individual in evaluating the steps in his own work is not so easy in such a team.

Some experienced systems scientists and planners are aware of these problems. Churchman emphasizes the importance of the first phase in the system's approach, the determination of objectives. He points out that the customer—that is, the person who has requested the services of a systems analyst—may not be able to specify accurately the objectives of the system because of his need to present these objectives in a positive light. This may be because he wants to create a favorable public image, but it also may be because he does not want to admit, not even to himself, all the *real* objectives of his system. On the other hand, the responsible system scientist must be concerned, not only with the objectives of his customer, but—if he is dealing with a public system—the objectives of the general public. Thus, he must not only be concerned with the measure of throughput on a freeway system, but problems of preservation of land contours and highway beautification. In short, we have come back once again to the question of intent. If the system scientist follows his own advice, if he always looks for the larger system in which his system is embedded, he discovers that the objectives he is attempting to describe are matters of morality as well as information.[6]

The system scientist will tell us that he recognizes this fact, and he does not pretend that systems analysis can answer these ultimate questions. Even the modest issue of national security is beyond his reach. Speaking in September 1967, after more than 20 years of the evolution and development of systems analysis, G. H. Fisher, of the Rand Corporation remarked:

> My own feeling is that in some areas a good deal of progress has been made in the way of clarification of issues and providing a basis for sharpening the intuition and judgment of the decision-makers. Examples of a few of the more important of these are the following:
>
> (1) The mix of airlift, sealift and prepositioning.
> (2) The force mix of land-based and sea-based tactical airpower.
> (3) The mix of manned aircraft and missile forces in the strategic offensive missile area.
> (4) The balance among different damage-limiting measures (both offensive and defensive) in nuclear war preparedness.
>
> Of course, the ultimate question is whether systems analysis as practiced today is helping to promote better national security decisions than would be the case without this specific type of analytical input to the process. I do not know whether such a question can be answered definitely by anyone.[7]

Such modesty is commendable, but it brings us face to face with the fundamental conflict of the systems analyst. Although he may be acutely conscious of his own limitations, it is not good business to state these limitations clearly at the time he is applying for a contract. Furthermore, if he wishes to stretch the imagination and expand the vision of the policy maker, he finds that he must formulate system objectives in such a way as to cover the full range of problems facing the decision maker. These two considerations tend to pull the analysis in two directions at the same time. The result is a brainstorming phase in which the global view is encouraged, and the objectives are stated with the widest possible ramifications, followed by a series of more detailed steps in which an attempt is made to measure system performance in relation to objectives. Ideally the first phase of the study never ends. The responsible systems analyst will probe every statement made about the system objectives by comparing it with the way the system operates. He will restate and reformulate the objectives in these operational terms and return to the administrator to ask, "Is this what you really mean?"

In practice, however, certain objectives lend themselves to the development of criteria that can be measured. Although they may be more important, others are more difficult to measure. The same considerations apply in the selection of variables. Goodman's *spirit* and *enthusiasm* are not operational terms. They are the kind of noisy, messy human variable that the scientist would prefer to ignore. This does not mean that they are never mentioned. It does mean, however, that they cannot be processed by the total system of methodologies employed. Therefore, they are likely to be set aside without being specifically excluded. In this regard the systems approach is more insidious in its disregard for human considerations than the older methods of the efficiency expert. The efficiency expert admitted, quite frankly, that he wanted to improve the efficiency of a factory. He had a single measure for success, and he was willing to use humane methods or inhumane methods, whichever proved to be more successful in turning out the greatest number of pieces of his product at a given time. He was not concerned with the long-range effect of his methods on the human resources involved or the extent to which his goals were congruent with national planning objectives. He had a problem to solve, and he felt he could identify it.

On the other hand, the systems analyst begins his approach without any preconceived notion of the problem to be solved. He is prepared to study a general area of endeavor, such as transportation or defense policy, and to try to clarify the choices available to the administrator or assist in the planning process. But in practice the approach is basically tied to technological or operational factors that can be more readily defined and measured. In this way human considerations are squeezed out of the study, *not because anyone has made a decision that they are unimportant, but because the energy of the intellectual effort has been diverted elsewhere.*

III

The shift from human to technological considerations is a subtle means of avoiding the problem of intent altogether. This shift is not due to any conscious conspiracy on the part of administrators, planners, and scientists. It is inherent in the method of thought employed. We will not find the source of our difficulty in the increasing popularity of the digital computer. This is but a symptom of the more general belief that policy decisions are essentially problems in data collection and that the operations of the human mind can be duplicated by the operations of a machine.

Jacques Ellul has described this process in the increasing emphasis on "technique" in modern society. By this he means, not only the increase in technological development and machine replacement of humans, but the extent to which man, himself, has begun to search for more systematic, step-by-step, machinelike procedures for making decisions. By means of technique, man changes not only the method by which he thinks *but the content of what he thinks about.* The process of reaching a decision is simplified, but it is also more simple-minded. Decisions are no longer made by any one individual but by a group of men, each of whom supplies a step in the total system of thought.

> Human beings are, indeed, always necessary. But literally anyone can do the job, provided he is trained to it. Henceforth, men will be able to act only in virtue of their commonest and lowest nature, and not in virtue of what they possess of superiority and individuality. . . . In this decisive evolution, the human being does not play a part. Technical elements combine among themselves and they do so more and more spontaneously. . . . In this sense it is possible to speak of the "reality" of technique—with its own substance, its own particular mode of being and a life independent of our power of decision . . . Technique is organized as a closed world. It utilizes what the mass of men do not understand . . . The individual, in order to make use of technical instruments, no longer needs to know about his civilization. And no single technician dominates the whole complex any longer. The bond that unites the fragmentary actions and disjointedness of individuals, coordinating and systematizing their work, is no longer a human one, but the internal laws of technique. The human hand no longer spans the complex of means, nor does the human brain synthesize man's acts. Only the intrinsic monism of technique assures cohesion between human means and acts. Technique reigns alone, a blind force and more clear-sighted than the best human intelligence.[8]

Although Ellul's description may be overdrawn, it does convey an important psychological truth, namely, the sense of individual helplessness in the face of an advancing technology. Herbert York makes a similar point when he asks, "To what extent is the increasing complexity of modern weapon systems and the need for instant response causing strategic decision-making authority to pass from high political levels to low military-command levels and from human beings to machines?"[9]

It is true that man appears to be squeezed out of the decision process by forces beyond his control, but it may be that this sense of human helplessness is an illusion created by the very method of thought we have employed. In the previous chapters we have examined the tendency of Americans to avoid facing the reality of their intent. Can it be that the sense of human helplessness in the face of technology is not only a fear but a wish? Can it be that we have not only a fear of no longer being able to make our own decisions, but a strong *desire* to escape that terrifying responsibility? If this were true, it might help to explain why human thinking in regard to policy matters becomes increasingly machinelike, logic-oriented, and systematized, despite the many complaints that we are being dehumanized by this very process. When technological considerations, such as weapon capability and response time, take precedence over the will and intent of the individual, it becomes increasingly possible to avoid awareness of one's intent. The situation may be structured in such a way that a national leader seems to be *forced* into a particular decision by events that are beyond his control.

If a person can look to a machine or a set of procedures to guide his thinking, he is less responsible for the result. The machine or the method becomes a kind of god—even if it is a god that was created by man only a short time ago, the limitations of which he is well aware. It is something he can turn to in an emergency if he becomes frightened by a sudden consciousness of his freedom. Like the religious man who runs over the beads of his rosary, the modern scientific man, who has rejected the notion of a god as "unreasonable," will run over his thinking procedures or feed data into his computer. Instead of calling a priest to advise him, he will call his expert, his interpreter of the "method." He will try any technique to avoid facing the terrors of uncertainty, the knowledge that he alone decides what he will do and that he is responsible for what happens. Thus, the technique, which was originally designed as an "aid" to decision, becomes a way of avoiding contact with one's own will, one's intent, one's very self.

One might say that, once we have placed ourselves in a position where we are surrounded by complex weapons, our statesmen have already abandoned a great deal of their decision-making authority.

We will not find that point at which the human decision is made and at which intent is manifest unless we retrace our steps to a point before the funds were allocated for weapons development.

But this decision, too, can be seen as one that is *forced* on the individual through the pressure of lead time in technological development or operational planning. It is tied to the notion that one must "keep one's options open," one of the favorite axioms in national security management. The discovery of the options available for action and their clear delineation is, of course, an essential feature in all planning. But keeping one's options open is a different matter. It represents a form of commitment without facing the fact that one is committed. If an executive is unable to decide on a particular course of action, he may isolate one or more options and carry them further by assigning study teams to develop implementation plans, provide feasibility studies, or begin the initial research and development on the equipment that may be required. In this way he tells himself that he has not really made a decision, but merely wants to have a better look at the problem. In some instances he feels *compelled* to keep his options open because technology is moving ahead all over the world and he may be left behind. In this way he avoids examining his intent.

The influence of the technological factor is even more significant if one option requires significantly more technological effort than another. In such cases, the need to keep an option open may be the critical factor in the initial commitment of funds. This is particularly true in the case of military hardware where the systems analyst and the intelligence expert, through their supposed access to complex and esoteric sources of information, have an inordinate influence on the decision maker. Both tend to support the notion that the decision maker should keep his options open, in order to maintain the widest possible range of decision latitude. This approach assumes that the creation of options is a strictly technical act and that the options themselves are merely "there" to be used by the decision maker whenever he feels the need for them. But options are attached to planning staffs, and individuals and organizations develop a vested interest in seeing their plans brought to fruition. This is particularly true when funds are granted to a research corporation such as Rand, SDC, SRI, MITRE, etc. The firm is given a small contract to study the feasibility of a particular idea. There was at one time a myth, which has been largely discredited, that these firms, since they are "not-for-profit," could take an objective view of a proposal. But it is well known by the individuals participating in the study that the adoption of a particular project can mean significant professional advancement. In some instances a new corporation is created to manage the implementation of a recommended program, with the former project leader as president of the corporation. Thus, the objective of the "study" centers around making the strongest possible case for its continuation or for the further allocation of funds for research and development.

However, it would be a mistake to picture the crafty scientist conspiring with his colleagues to bilk the government of millions of dollars. The reasoning is deceptive, but not knowingly conspiratory. This is what makes it so dangerous. Conspiracies can be exposed once a member of the group decides to tell all. But a clever rationalization goes unnoticed by the government, the public and even the scientists themselves. Herman Kahn has provided a classic example of this type of thinking. The act of pressing for commitment of government funds becomes a public duty since, if the "cheap" (i.e., $2,000 to $200,000) decisions are made early, it will shorten the lead time required for research and development. Furthermore, one needs money to gather information in order to "formulate specific recommendations and make the kind of case that could persuade all the echelons of decision makers and thereby get the rest of the programming underway."[10] In short, it is necessary to persuade the decision makers to allocate funds in order to gather information that will be used to persuade them to make further commitments of funds—all in the name of scientific objectivity and cost reduction.

It is Herman Kahn who compared the systematic study of warfare with the activity of a surgeon. It takes an iron will and an unpleasant degree of detachment to go about the study of war, he said. "In fact, the mind recoils from simultaneously probing deeply and creatively into these problems and being conscious at all times of the human tragedy involved. This is not new. We do not continually remind the surgeon while he is operating of the humanity of his patient."[11] It is significant, I think, that Kahn begins his analogy at that point where the surgeon has already convinced the patient than an operation is necessary. The time when the surgeon should be aware of the humanity of the patient is during that period when he is considering the advisability of an operation. If we are his patient, we would like to feel that the chief motive of the surgeon is our welfare and happiness and not his own interest in exploring a "curious" case, his desire to get us on the operating table in order to exercise his skill, or his desire to earn a large fee. The same considerations apply in systems analysis. One would like to believe that the systems analyst has allowed himself to become fully aware of what he is doing, in the human rather than the mechanical sense, *before* he strives to convince a government official that more money is needed to study a particular war option or to develop a particular weapon system.

We have come face to face with a fundamental human conflict. In order to find "truth," the analyst believes that he must be objective, detached, disinterested in the results. In order to make money and enhance his prestige, he must be sure of himself. He must establish a reputation for knowing where he is going. It is to his personal advantage if his early hunches are supported by his later detailed investigations. In order to get money for further research, he must push his ideas. He must be aggressive and persuasive. But the more he concentrates on being persuasive with others, the more he is likely to deceive himself. The more he tries to get others to take his mathematical model seriously, the more he is likely to become too serious about it himself. Leading scientists in the field have recognized this problem for some time. Herman Kahn and Irwin Mann have warned of the dangers of taking the model for the reality, the confusion of various types of uncertainty and many other common pitfalls in systems analysis.[12] C. West Churchman points out that the management scientist frequently deceives himself with his idealized model in which he has supposedly considered all the objectives and worked out a proper compromise. In the straight-faced seriousness with which he develops his model, he omits certain important human values. Ideally, says Churchman, the systems approach should involve the creation of a "theory of deception" in which the individual tries to understand the ways in which he is deceived about the world and learns to look at things from different points of view. In this deception–perception approach to systems there would be no experts.[13]

But as systems analysis is practiced today, there is an army of experts, each one having his favorite techniques of estimation, mathematical analysis, model building, criterion development and his own, often unspoken, notion of what constitutes "legitimate" data for study. Although the analyst may read the caveats of Kahn, Churchman, and others, he is under no obligation to consider them. Furthermore, it is not advantageous for him, at least in the short run, to present his report in such a way that he reminds the decision maker of the limited applicability of the results. Thus, while he may often warn that judgment is necessary in the interpretation of results, he seldom highlights some of the more questionable assumptions behind his procedures or suggests limits on the generalizations that one can make, based on his conclusions. Speaking of this problem,

Kahn and Mann remark, "It is very much as if the analyst thought that judgment was like salt or pepper, something to be added at the very end to bring out the flavor when all the other work is finished."[14]

Of course, one can argue that someone with technical knowledge must point out the options available and that sometimes it is not really possible to understand the significance of a particular option without further study. But perhaps it is necessary to allocate some resources to the study of the decision system itself, involving, as it does, the process by which a staff of analysts, planners, and other associated personnel persuade the influential department heads and advisors, one after another, until the proposal, or the "option," becomes a *fait accompli*.

This process of persuasion through expertise is characteristic not only of systems analysis per se but decision making in general in our rationalistic culture. It would appear that this was true, to a large extent, in the decision to go ahead with the CIA-sponsored invasion of Cuba. Planning for what appeared to be an option had passed the paper-and-pencil stage without anyone really recognizing what had happened and, by acquiring a large military force, the planners were able to face the president and his staff with a "disposal problem." He must either proceed with the invasion or accept the disillusionment and the bad publicity generated by the disbanded Cuban refugee army. The seemingly passive and inert "option" had suddenly become the motivating force in the decision process. The individual decision maker was in the grip of his own decision system. The same thing happened to Richard Nixon when John Dean faced him with the facts on Watergate and he decided to "keep his options open" by holding back the information a bit longer.

IV

In the discussion of planning staffs and implementation agencies we have already passed beyond systems analysis. The CIA planners were not systems analysts. They were part of a large organization of government agencies responsible for the planning and implementation of policy. Just as the digital computer represents only one of many tools used in systems analysis, the full range of techniques in systems analysis represent only a part of the larger structure in the total systematization of thought. In the larger sense the systematization of thought is manifest in any linear method in which thinking is ordered in sequence (objectives, observations, analysis, conclusions) and the tasks given to several different individuals. This requires the symbolic representation of information that was at one time sensory in character and the development of a consensus through the manipulation of symbols. This process does two important things: (1) it reduces complex and ambiguous phenomena to simple forms of representation through the mediation of an expert with the requisite technical skills and, (2) it removes the experience of "knowing" or awareness from the private to the public (or external) domain, from the individual to the group. Through this process the individual learns to accept group perception of reality over his own private sensory awareness.

To some extent, of course, learning to see the world as other people see it is part of the process of acculturation in all societies. However, in most instances the individual retains a certain elemental trust in the responses of his own body. In the systematization of thought the private sensory experience of individuals is abstracted into a model. As the process of thought continues, it is the model of reality, rather than reality itself, that serves as a basis for discussion. In many instances the nominal decision maker or group leader has not made sensory contact with the physical phenomena with which the decision is concerned. Although the selection of the particular method for the manipulation of data is an intuitive matter, this, too, is the work of an expert, someone skilled in the various rational methodologies available and one who is presumably capable of sensing the most effective and meaningful technique.

There is little doubt concerning the efficiency of this rational consensus approach for the accomplishment of technical objectives, such as the building of an improved automobile or the development of a program for increasing sales. If one were to measure the system of thought by its results, its power in controlling man and nature, it is clearly successful. The practical man will tell us with a certain smugness that if the method does not cover all aspects of the human situation, it *does* get the job done. Don't knock it; it works. In this view, such products as industrial pollution, the arms race, and the proliferation of ghettos and slum areas are not regarded as consequences of the method, but unfortunate side-effects that can be corrected by a more intensive application of the method itself. One need only state the goals clearly before the analysis begins. The problem in the past is seen as a too narrow specification of system goals, not a failure of the method itself.

In his book, *International Conflict,* Roger Fisher makes this point; he deplores the fact that we have become so sophisticated about making threats and that we do not have a comparable sophistication in making peace offers.[15] He cites the instance of President Johnson's offer to spend a billion in Vietnam as an example of this lack of sophistication. The offer, he points out, was not credible, whereas our threats are generally quite credible. Fisher proposes certain methods for the analysis of peace initiatives that are similar to the analytic techniques presently employed for the improvement of our war strategy. There is an assumption, inherent in Fisher's approach, that logical manipulation of information is a tool for enlightenment and that it can be used as readily in one direction as another. It further assumes that President Johnson's peace offer was not credible simply because he lacked sophistication in the area of peace. If his information had been better organized and if the logic of the possible Vietnamese response had been carefully examined, the president would have devised a more credible offer.

Logically speaking, Fisher is quite correct. But the problem of world peace is as much a question of intent as it is one of logic. Very often the reason we fail to examine a certain alternative lies in the fact that we don't want to use it. Furthermore, the very system of data gathering and analysis that we have already constructed makes it possible to avoid facing the influence of our methods upon the decision process itself.[16] The system has a built-in bias of which we are unaware.[17] Basic to this approach is the assumption of some kind of separation between an individual and his world. There is a conviction that one can observe, measure and even predict the outcome of events without affecting these events or changing the outcome. The physical scientist learned some time ago that there was a limit to his ability to remain outside the situation he was observing. The physicist, Heisenberg, discovered that it was not possible to determine both the position and velocity of subatomic particles because of the influence of his measuring instrument. In short, he found that by observing an event he had an effect on one of the two aspects he wanted to measure (i.e., position or velocity). Concerning the results of his experiments and the later "Copenhagen interpretation" of quantum theory that followed, Heisenberg remarked:

> To what extent, then, have we finally come to an objective description of the world? In classical physics science started from the belief—or should one say from the illusion?—that we could describe the world or at least parts of the world without any reference to ourselves. . . quantum theory reminds us, as Bohr has put it, of the old wisdom that when searching for harmony in life one must never forget that in the drama of existence we are ourselves both players and spectators.[18]

Matson has followed the implications of what Heisenberg called his Principle of Uncertainty for the social and political sciences.[19] Both physical and social scientists have begun to warn us that we cannot observe the course of events in the world without affecting these events. There is no such thing as an innocent bystander or an innocent observer.

When one is dealing with human beings instead of subatomic particles, the influence of the observer is generally more obvious. It is more difficult to imagine that we are neutral or objective observers of another person if he looks back at us and we become conscious of ourselves. "I see myself," says Sartre, "because somebody sees me."[20] The observer is transformed into an object. He is conscious of his vulnerability. He develops a moral sensitivity, a consciousness of his potential for evil. An individual cannot conceive of himself as evil in relationship to himself, but the presence of the other (or the possibility of this presence) leads him to reflect on his actions in relationship to the other. "Here I am bent over the keyhole; suddenly I hear a footstep. I shudder as a wave of shame sweeps over me. Somebody has seen me. I straighten up."[21] It is this sense of shame in relationship to the other that represents the moral aspect of looking.

But what happens if the observer is part of a study team? He has been sent into the field to gather certain "data." He is "under orders." He does not represent himself; he is a pair of eyes for a powerful government. His experiences in the field may arouse in him certain moral reservations about what he is doing, but he is not instructed to convey these feelings to his government. If he volunteered such information, his conduct would be considered unprofessional. At the same time, the person who has generated the requirements for certain information makes no sensory contact with the event being observed. He receives data in the form of numbers or categories of behavior. His actions are deprived of the sensory contact that arouses emotion and informs our moral sensibility. As a result, he is not fully aware of what he is doing when he asks for certain information.

Suppose, for example, a statistician in Washington would like to aid his chief by obtaining information on the progress of the war in Vietnam. He decides that a count of the number of enemy killed would make an excellent measure. He informs his chief, who sends word to the field commanders that they must make a count of enemy dead after each engagement. This sounds simple enough. It is assumed that each side is striving to kill the enemy anyway. What possible effect can a body count have on the course of the engagement? However, a field commander does not merely carry out an order. He wonders about its possible significance. If the number of enemy dead constitutes some kind of measure of effectiveness, surely he should keep his count up as high as possible in order to obtain a high efficiency rating. In like manner, his decision on promotions for his men in the field will be influenced by the body count per engagement achieved by those commanders under him — and so on down the line to the squad leader who operates a machine gun. If the objective is to search out and kill the Vietcong in a given peasant village, the emphasis on body count encourages an indiscriminate slaughter of all the people in the village. "Body count" does not specify whether the enemy is a man, woman, child, or an old person. One body is as good as another. Once they are dead they can all be counted as Vietcong. Here is one account of an army court martial in which the policy was revealed in some detail.

> Long Binh, Vietnam (UPI) — Two young American infantry officers told an Army court today they were under pressure from their commanders to report killing as many communist soldiers as possible. A civilian defense attorney called the officers to the stand in an effort to prove Army "body count" policies forced Lt. James B. Duffy, 22, of Claremont, California, to order the execution of a Vietnamese man seized by his platoon in September 40 miles southwest of Saigon.
> Attorney Henry Rothblatt of New York called Lt. John D. Kruger . . . and Lt. Ralph C. Krueger . . . Both testified "body counts" were a gauge for advancement in the Army. "Your OER (Officer Efficiency Report) is based on how many enemy killed," Lt. Kreuger told the court. "It's that simple."[22]

The medium of statistics becomes a device for separating the decision maker from the realities of warfare. No one planned it that way. It is inherent in the method employed. My Lai and Hamburger Hill are further consequences of this abstraction of the act of killing. There is a break in sensory continuity between the data analyst who tabulates the body count and the man in the field who experiences the physical reality of lifting the body out of the swamp and dragging it to a clearing where it is laid in a row with many others. While he is working, the man in the field smells the odor of rotting human flesh. He sees all the dirty details and the ambiguity inherent in each decision. Is the corpse a friendly peasant or a Vietcong? Should we go through the agony of touching the dead bodies or fly over them and make an estimate? As long as the field man and the data analyst do not talk to each other, it is possible for the analyst to maintain his aseptic notion of logical categories and measures of efficiency. But if he splashes down in the jungle, the stench in his nostrils gives him a different message. He learns that it is possible to "know" things in a more global way, that there is a certain aspect of human awareness that is distinctly physical and sensory in character and that this physical aspect of reality contains information that cannot be apprehended if reality has been cleaned up and presented to the cerebral cortex rather than the whole body.

V

In the United States the problem of war atrocities is still seen in terms of throwing the "bad" people out of office and replacing them with "good" people. Then we can use the same methods to produce a more humane society. Next time, the analysts will not forget to "input" human needs to the total decision system. Somehow these human needs will be abstracted and represented by mathematical models. The data on human responses will be categorized and thus better understood and used. The extent to which this process of abstraction and analysis dehumanizes thought is not yet fully recognized. Furthermore, the chance of it being recognized by people in a position of power is diminishing rather than increasing. We are moving toward a society in which influence is increasingly related to technical competence and technical competence is beginning to mean the categorization, quantification, and other forms of abstract representation of information.

However, control of the decision process is far from certain. If influence is proportional to technical competence it may mean that the man with greater technical competence will dominate the man with less technical competence regardless of the organizational chart. On the surface this sounds very democratic. There is more open communication. A man rises to power on the basis of his "worth" rather than his official position. If the task is a technical one, technical influence makes sense. But in matters of national defense and national policy, morality and technology are interwoven to the extent that they are inseparable. Suppose the "official" leader has been elected by the people to be president of the United States. Is it really democratic to have such a man unduly influenced by people who happen to have a high degree of technical competence? One can answer that it is no worse than having the president in the pay of a man who happens to have a great deal of money, but this is to miss the point entirely. A bribe is explicit. It can be discovered and exposed. The influence of the technician invades the very psyche of a national leader. An honorable man will say no to a financial favor, but if a technical expert from the CIA tells him the "evidence" points to an impending military attack by the Soviet Union, how is he to examine the details?

Although he may question the expert and ask him the basis for his statement, the time for decision is short. In a world where technical considerations have gathered such impressive strength, they may succeed in obliterating other factors. President Kennedy remarked after the fiasco of the Cuban invasion, "If someone comes in to tell me this or that about the minimum wage bill, I have no hesitation in overruling them. But you always assume that the military and intelligence people have some secret skill not available to ordinary mortals."[23] The problem with technical influence is that it does not stop with technical matters, and the intent of the technician may not be the same as the intent of the president. Thus, the real meaning of a statement of fact or probability may be veiled. The rational meaning is obvious, but it may be critical for the president to evaluate the *intent* of his expert as well. This may have been what Kennedy had in mind when he examined his own interaction with the chief of the CIA in the light of the Cuban invasion: "It's not that [Alan] Dulles is not a man of great ability. He is. But I have never worked with him, and therefore I can't estimate his meaning when he tells me things."[24]

VI

We have reached a peculiar paradox in the relationship between the national leader and his expert. The expert sells himself on the basis of his neutrality, his objectivity, and his lack of commitment to specific policies. He presents himself as a tool to be used by the administrator in any way the latter desires. With such immense analytic power available to him, the administrator feels rather foolish if he places much weight on a vague personal hunch, a casual observation of his own, a physical sensation of fear, anger, or revulsion. Because of the supposed power of this analytic tool, the administrator feels he must use it and, in the process, we often find that the tool uses the man. On other occasions the administrator may use his tool to provide himself with the information he wants, in order to make a decision that he would like to make for more personal reasons. In this way it becomes possible for him to disguise his intentions from himself through the charade of "information transfer." This was evident in some of the communications sent to the White House during the crisis in Santo Domingo. In both cases there is an unwillingness to trust the inner perceptions and emotions of the individual but to find some external and seemingly "objective" justification for action. In our society there is an inclination to believe that such objective and logical justification makes human action more responsible than would be the case if it were subject to influence by the highly individualistic and personal sensory and emotional environment of the body.

In reality all decisions made by human beings are part logical and part personal. All acts are related to the self whether or not one is aware of one's personal reactions and whether or not one attempts to exclude one's personal reactions. The use of logical procedures, if one attempts to use them exclusively, can become a device for concealing part of the data of the decision process. Harold Lasswell has remarked "logical procedures exclude from the mind the most important data about the self. Directed thinking, whether about the self or something else as an object, is impatient of the seemingly trivial, and this impatience with the seemingly trivial is the rationally acceptable guise in which the impulse to avoid rigorous self-scrutiny gets itself accepted."[25] It is this self-scrutiny that forms the basis for all moral judgment.

Contrast this self-scrutiny with the typical decision process in a government planning staff. Work starts immediately in a flurry of efficiency: schedules, milestones, flow charts, courses, routes, targets. The work is carefully compartmentalized. There is a division of labor in a manner that assures the most rapid "output" of the product. There is often an unspoken competition between study teams to see which team can make the best case for its particular alternative. Thus, the men who are in the best position to see the defects of a particular alternative are least inclined to do so. In this manner project members remain unaware of the issue of *intent* through their absorption in the details. The decision maker remains unaware of his intent through the belief that he cannot really evaluate the project until the details are worked out. In this way it becomes possible to delay decision and mitigate one's responsibility and, at the same time, to maintain the personal conviction that one has spared no expense or effort in order to discover the "right" answer to a particular problem. Directed thinking by study teams, when applied to the process of planning and decision making, greatly reduces the responsibility of any one individual while increasing the number of people involved in a mechanical or peripheral fashion. The man who collects the data has many choices, but no responsibility. The decision maker has the responsibility, but after he has been briefed on the data, he may feel that he no longer has any choice.

The problem is further complicated by what Irving Janis has called "groupthink" in the senior staff.[26] The pressures for conformity on the group members and their sense of loyalty to the group prevent them from questioning the basic assumptions of the group or presenting a radical new alternative not previously considered.[27] As a result, even the man who collects important data and is responsible for presenting these data to the decision staff, may slant his information or change it if he feels it is contrary to the group norms. In the Cuban invasion Allen Dulles was not a mere outside expert who presented intelligence results to the White House Staff, he was an ongoing member of that staff. In his own account of the events leading up to the Cuban invasion, Dulles makes it clear that there was no assumption on the part of the CIA that the landing by Cuban refugees would touch off widespread popular revolt. Nevertheless, this was one of the basic assumptions of the staff, of which Dulles was a member. Schlesinger remarked:

> We all in the White House considered uprisings behind the lines essential to the success of the operation, so too did the Joint Chiefs of Staff, and so, we thought did the CIA. It was only later that I learned about the Anzio concept; it certainly did not come across clearly in the White House meetings. . . . Dulles and Bissell themselves reinforced this impression (of an uprising). When questioned early in April about the prospects of internal resistance, instead of discounting it, which seems to have been their view, they claimed that over 2500 persons presently belonged to resistance organizations, that 20,000 more were sympathizers.[28]

In fact, it turned out that the Intelligence Branch of the CIA, which would have been involved in making such estimates, was never directed to the question of whether an invasion would produce an uprising of the Cuban people. They did not know that such an operation was being contemplated as they had no "need to know."[29] It appears that the root of the problem was that Dulles and Bissell did not want to violate the group norm. They sensed the way the decision was going and provided briefings that supported the group's decision—not out of a malicious desire to sabotage the president but because they were good team players and were deeply identified with the mission as it had been outlined by the previous administration.

Dulles and Bissell were more deeply involved in the details of the plan than other members of the staff. For such men, the problem of remaining unaware of what was happening must have been difficult. There is something about the experience of facing the details of an impending operation day after day that induces a process of reflection. For a thoughtful person, generalities have a way of leaping out of the details. Reflection upon one's personal role in the decision is almost inescapable—even for a man who is determined not to become involved in moral issues. However, if one does not have responsibility for the final "go" decision, it is possible to take the stand that one's personal opinions must be kept out of things. It is more professional to be discrete, impersonal, and to stick to the facts.

Thus, the systematization of thought, which was developed to provide a larger more comprehensive view of the possibilities for action, can become a means of avoiding the ambiguity inherent in problems of morality. If everyone takes a step in the decision process, the consciousness of the decision maker is protected, not only from a sense of his personal involvement, but from the knowledge of his own freedom and from the essential loneliness of his act.

NOTES

1. H. Kahn, *Thinking about the Unthinkable* (New York: Horizon Press, 1962), p. 17.

2. J. R. Seeley, *The Americanization of the Unconscious* (New York: International Science Press, 1967), p. 6.

3. J. K. Galbraith, *The New Industrial State* (New York: New American Library, Signet, 1967), pp. 25–29.

4. P. Goodman, "A Causerie at the Military Industrial," *The Age of Protest*, ed. Walt Anderson (Pacific Palisades, Calif.: Goodyear, 1969), pp. 9–19.

5. C. W. Churchman, *The Systems Approach* (New York: Delacorte Press, 1968), pp. 12–13.

6. Ibid., pp. 30–33.

7. G. H. Fisher, "Some Comments on Systems Analysis" (Santa Monica, Calif.: Rand Corporation, p-3637, September, 1967), pp. 5–6.

8. J. Ellul, *The Technological Society* (New York: Vintage, 1964), pp. 92–94.

9. H. York, "Military Technology and National Security," *Scientific American*, vol. 221, no. 2 (1969), p. 12.

10. H. Kahn, *On Thermonuclear War* (Princeton, N.J.: Princeton University Press, 1960), p. 318.

11. Kahn, *Thinking about the Unthinkable*, p. 24.

12. H. Kahn and I. Mann, "Ten Common Pitfalls" (Santa Monica, Calif.: Rand, Astia 133035, July, 1957).

13. Churchman, *The Systems Approach*, pp. 228–231.

14. Kahn and Mann, "Ten Common Pitfalls," pp. 1–2.

15. R. Fisher, *International Conflict* (New York: Harper & Row, 1969), pp. 113–127.

16. C. Hampden-Turner, *Radical Man* (Cambridge, Mass.: Schenkman, 1970), p. 13.

17. Ibid., p. 13.

18. W. Heisenberg, *Physics and Philosophy* (New York: Harper & Row, 1962), pp. 55–58.

19. F. Matson, *The Broken Image* (New York: Braziller, 1964), pp. 129–262.

20. J. -P. Sartre, *Being and Nothingness*, trans. Hazel E. Barnes (New York: Citadel, 1964), p. 236.

21. Ibid., p. 253.

22. *I. F. Stone's Bi-Weekly*, April 6, 1970, p. 1.

23. A. M. Schlesinger, Jr., *A Thousand Days* (Greenwich, Conn.: Fawcett, 1967), p. 242.

24. Ibid., p. 258.

25. H. E. Lasswell, *Psychopathology and Politics* (New York: Viking, 1968), p. 33.

26. I. L. Janis, *Victims of Groupthink* (Boston: Houghton Mifflin, 1972).

27. Ibid., p. 5.

28. Schlesinger, *A Thousand Days*, p. 232.

29. Ibid., p. 233.

14

The
Changing Nature
of
Aggression

I

In the previous chapters I have emphasized that the chief danger of American aggression is the extent to which it is rationalized and represented as a decision based on the logic of the situation and the "available" data. But this statement is not adequate to convey the content of the American consciousness. All nations rationalize their policy in an attempt to provide legitimacy. If no body of law exists, soldiers in the field will make their own rationale. No man fights for the spoils alone. Each prefers to convince himself that there is some moral basis for his actions. Even in the time of Caesar, it was rare for a warrior nation to go into battle without some explanation. In his description of the German attack on Gaul, Caesar gives us a clear account of his own justification and that of Ariovistus, the German leader.

> He [Ariovistus] insisted that he had crossed the Rhine not on his own initiative, but at the urgent request of the Gauls. He had committed no aggression—just the opposite: the Gallic states had combined to attack him, and in a single battle he had inflicted a crushing defeat upon their armies. ... Turning to the introduction of the German hordes, he

urged that this was a defensive, not an offensive, measure, and based his assurance on the fact that he came only because he was invited, and had acted thereafter not as an aggressor, but merely in self-defense. . . . He finished by offering me a substantial bribe to withdraw . . . I spoke at considerable length in an endeavor to explain why we could not abandon our present course of action. It was incompatible with my own principles and Roman practice to desert our faithful allies. . . . If priority of time was to be the criterion, Roman sovereignty in Gaul was well established. . . . At that point it was reported that Ariovistus' cavalry were moving closer to the knoll, riding up to hurl stones and javelins at our men.[1]

The rationalizations of Caesar and Ariovistus were consciously used as delaying actions. The rationale of the modern American culture is both more subtle and more pervasive. It is part of the fabric of society. It is not designed to support an immediate tactic. Its aim is more ambitious—to change the nature of reality. The similarities between ourselves and the ancient negotiators are both obvious and superficial. The differences are more profound. In Caesar's time, negotiations were generally conducted when warfare was imminent. The negotiators were men of stature who would command the armies or order them into battle. The justifications advanced by each side were tentative maneuvers, likely to be interrupted at any moment by an outbreak of fighting that would make all talk superfluous.

Today, the use of verbal persuasion has gained considerable prominence. It is no longer necessary for the military commander or the national leader to be present at negotiating sessions in order to postpone actual conflict. Justification is now directed not only at one's armies and one's enemies, but at world opinion. The concept of aggression itself has changed. Today, it is perceived in terms of the planning and testing of weapons as well as in the use of weapons against another nation. Negotiation is no longer confined to the exchange of diplomats, but it involves the world media. The frequently quoted remark by Clausewitz[2] that war is a continuation of politics by other means, might well be extended to say that all international exchange is part of a psychopolitical struggle to define world reality. The forum of the United Nations, the world press, television, the sheer size of a nation's population, the evidence provided by scientific studies and the size of the gross national product are all used to convince others of our view of reality. If the nonmilitary pressures are strong enough, an opponent will yield without the use of physical force. The modern world is one in which the effectiveness of these other forms of pressure is rapidly increasing. Unless we understand the continuous nature of this struggle and the subtle forms it can take, we are likely to become caught up in specific instances of the use of physical force and the effort to decide what is or is not a case of "aggression." I have said that the U.N. definition of aggression is satisfactory for legal purposes, but if we are to allow ourselves to become too deeply anchored in such a concrete definition, we will fail to recognize how the use of force is changing from the physical to the psychological realm. Stanley Hoffmann describes the process as follows:

> When the physics of power declines, the psychology of power rises. Also, reality was usually defined in terms of who controlled what and who possessed what. The same new factors have led states to transfer their greed and expectations from physical mastery to the shaping of the international milieu—from tangibles to intangibles. What constitutes success and failure in such a quest, what is "real" gain, or merely "symbolic" or "illusionary" achievement is hard to say. Again much depends on perceptions. Perhaps international politics today should be defined less as a struggle for power than as a contest for the shaping of perceptions. When force loses some of its prominence, power—my exercise of control over you—becomes the art of making you see the world the way I see it, and of making you behave in accordance with that vision. International politics in the past was often an arena of coercion without persuasion; it is tending to become an arena of persuasion, more or less coercive.[3]

The nature of aggression is changing, in part, because of the sense of transience that pervades the modern world.[4] Everything is temporary, including the shape and size of one's territory, and the total pressure that the people of the world exert on each other is constantly increasing. This is due to an increase in world population, but it is also due to increased communication, increased mobility, and increased technological capacity (including the capacity to develop weapons that act at a greater distance from their point of origin). The United States is on the leading edge of this transformation in the nature of aggression, not only because we are a highly developed nation in the technological sense, but because in our international style we have exhibited a growing tendency to use persuasion (admittedly, at times, a highly coercive persuasion) in place of the conquest of territory. If a nation maintains a myth that it has no national interest, it is driven toward the effort to shape the international milieu in accord with its own unspecified needs.

This change in the nature of aggression means two things. Aggression is becoming less totally physical, but it is also becoming more global, more ambitious, more grandiose, more "American." On the surface, it would seem that if the physical component of aggression is decreasing, aggression should become less dangerous to human life in the long run. But it is apparent that this is not the case. If a nation can no longer hold territory with any sense of permanence, it can no longer dig in and relax after a conquest. It must continue to build its image, its connections, its economic and political sources of influence, or it will begin to decline as a world power. If it is tempted into the use of physical force to preserve its image, the very psychological nature of the conflict means that the dangers of defeat are greater. It stands to lose not mere territory, but perhaps the whole world. One can determine where soldiers stand, and it is possible to measure their gain and loss of territory on a daily basis. But one's image is intangible. It can sweep across the world overnight.

The famous "domino theory" in regard to the American presence in Southeast Asia was *not* based on a belief that Asian governments would decline due to a progressive increase in the *physical power* of the communist governments in that region, but a fear that the loss of Vietnam would threaten our "image" in all of Asia, Latin America, and Africa without any change in our physical strike capability. This is evident from some of the documents prepared by the Joint Chiefs of Staff to justify a continuation of the American effort in Vietnam when the threat of defeat first became manifest in 1964.

> the Joint Chiefs of Staff are of the opinion that the United States must be prepared to put aside many of the self-imposed restrictions which now limit our efforts, and to undertake bolder actions which may embody greater risks. . . . In a broader sense, the failure of our programs in South Vietnam would have heavy influence on the judgments of Burma, India, Indonesia, Malaysia, Japan, Taiwan, the Republic of Korea, and the Republic of the Philippines with respect to U.S. durability, resolution and trustworthiness. Finally, this being the first real test of our determination to defeat the communist wars of national liberation formula, it is not unreasonable to conclude that there would be a *corresponding unfavorable effect upon our image in Africa and in Latin America.* [Italics mine][5]

As the conflict intensified, this threat to our "image" became the central focus of our effort. On March 24, 1965, John T. McNaughton prepared an advisory memo for Secretary McNamara which begins as follows:

> *U.S. Aims*
> 70%—to avoid a humiliating U.S. defeat (to our reputation as guarantor).
> 20%—to keep SVN (and the adjacent) territory from Chinese hands.
> 10%—to permit the people of SVN to enjoy a better freer way of life . . .[6]

We are not, then, moving *away* from physical conflict and *toward* more refined and less dangerous forms of aggression. Instead, the increased psychological component in aggression appears to contribute to a more intensified, more protracted, and more desperate physical conflict.

II

The changing nature of aggression on the international scene is reflected in a similar change *within* nations. Repression, the national counterpart of international aggression, has also become more psychological. But here again, as in the international model, the change is manifested not only in the type of aggression but in the will, the intent of the aggressor. And here, too, it is the United States that serves as a prototype for a change in style that is rapidly becoming worldwide.

George Orwell has given us a grim account of the older totalitarian model of psychological repression in his *1984*. But in the Orwellian state, the manipulation of the people was a conscious act on the part of those who were doing the manipulating. Lies were deliberate. Old newspapers and magazines were actually altered and republished to change past events in order to conform with the new reality ordained by the state. I do not believe that this form of deliberate and conscious repression can survive the communication environment of the modern world. It is no longer possible—or it will not be possible much longer—to create one reality for the *subjects* of a nation and a different reality for the *elite*. People and messages are crossing international boundaries at an ever increasing rate. As the people of the world are bombarded with communication, they have become more eager for variety and less tolerant of deliberate efforts by government to omit any messages. It is becoming apparent that the experts in the social sciences and in communications must work with uncontaminated sources of information if they are to do an effective job of supporting the position of their own nation. In short, they must have access to world reality if they are to support the national reality. As the number of these experts (and their assistants and secretaries) increases, the difficulty of keeping forbidden information from the people increases also. In a world where people are becoming more sophisticated about the uses of propaganda, the clumsy creation of a nonevent and the heavy-handed exercise of censorship are self-revealing.

The opposition to censorship in all international negotiation and the insistence that all nations share in deliberations that will influence the welfare of mankind is a popular position. Although private diplomacy has certain advantages, the pressure for open discussion is increased by the presence of the uncommitted nations. Even the Soviet Union, with its controlled press, has become the champion of the free flow of information on the international level and the great opponent of secrecy. The Soviet delegate to the U.N.

disarmament meeting in London was merely continuing the Soviet effort to gain the support of the uncommitted nations when he said, on August 27, 1957:

> in the United Nations Sub-Committee, they [Western powers] refuse to hear the views of states standing outside the military blocs and showing a sincere concern to preserve peace, as for instance India, which requested the Sub-Committee to give it a hearing. This attitude of the Western Powers betrays their fear of a broad discussion of this important problem with states which are not members of their exclusive military groups.
>
> In addition, the Western Powers have compelled the Sub-Committee to work secretly, in private, with the result that public opinion has been kept in ignorance, and has on many occasions been completely misinformed about the true state of affairs in the Sub-Committee. This situation apparently suits the ruling groups of the Western Powers. It enables them to use the secrecy of the Sub-Committee's work as a pretext for evading direct answers to questions about the progress of the talks raised in parliaments and by the Press. . . . The time when professional politicians and diplomats could decide questions affecting the basic and vital interests of people secretly and behind their backs has gone forever. . . . In all countries the people are day by day playing a more active part in political life . . .[7]

When a nation's representatives take such a position in order to influence world opinion, they cannot avoid having an influence on their own people. Despite travel restrictions, Soviet citizens are subject to a constantly increasing exposure to world media. Statements of this kind, if they are not reported in the Soviet press, are reported throughout the world.[8] They are reported with increasing frequency by the press of Soviet bloc countries for their own purposes.

Protests within the Soviet Union against the suppression of information and criticism have mounted rapidly in recent years. In February 1966 the trial of Sinyavsky and Daniel in the Soviet Union aroused protests in the communist presses of France, Italy, England, Sweden, Denmark, and Austria.[9] Louis Aragon, noted French poet and member of the Central Committee of the French Communist Party, attacked the action of the Soviet Union as more damaging to socialism than anything the two men could write.[10] Even in Russia itself, where the press was controlled, intellectuals were critical of communist authorities and Aleksander Yesenin-Volpin, son of a Russian revolutionary poet, was the leader of a public demonstration in Moscow to demand an open trial for the two authors, thus calling attention to the fact that the Soviet people were denied free access to information of the proceedings.[11] Although it did not force a completely open trial, the demonstration was probably responsible for the Soviet government's decision to allow selected Soviet observers, but no Western journalists. It was from the notes of one of these observers that the record of the trial was finally reconstructed and leaked to the Western world.

The following year, the Peoples' Court in Moscow began to hear the case against five Soviet intellectuals who were critical of the government, some of whom had sent manuscripts to the West. Outside the court, there occurred one of the most vigorous protests seen by Western observers in many years. When policemen came to break up the disturbance, demonstrators demanded that the court try the policemen for brutality. When one of the protestors, a former army general, complained to the local police against the harassment of his group by party activists, his arguments were politely heard, a contrast to previous police tactics. Even Western correspondents were admitted to the trial on this occasion. But perhaps the change of major significance in Soviet policy was the Russian attempt at news management, American style. Instead of pressuring Western newsmen to stay away from the trials, the Soviets treated them politely and assigned a press officer to "brief" them on the proceedings.[12]

The more obvious forms of repression are decreasing in the Soviet Union because of the need for more open access to information and because of the inefficiency of rigid controls. This has induced Bennis and Slater to issue the rather optimistic prediction that "democracy is inevitable."[13] Clearly, we are witnessing a trend toward the open society, but openness of information and democracy are not the same thing. We may be in the initial stages of the development of more subtle, less obvious forms of repression. If the open society is the society of the future, the government that learns to dominate the media of the open society will have the major long-range influence on the world information system.

III

The American example illustrates that it is not necessary to censor the news media if the people will accept the intent of the administration. The average American is quite willing to admit that terrible things have happened in his country, and he will even concede that those in authority have been responsible. But his answer is that someone has made a mistake, an inadvertent error that derives from insufficient knowledge. It is therefore a matter of technical competence. We need more information so the mistakes will not happen again. With this attitude, there is no need for a conscious conspiracy to suppress minorities or a secret coalition to advance American imperialism. Conspiracies can be found out. But the subtle kind of agreement I am describing can operate within an open society. It cannot be detected because it is not explicit. It is possible for the chief executive to maintain a policy of telling the truth if others learn when to lie for him and when to conceal information from him. In this way, deception can take place without becoming a part of national policy. The intent of the national leader is concealed not only from the people but from himself as well.

A similar process obtains in all the echelons of command. Junior military officers, junior State Department executives, and rookie policemen soon learn that there are certain practices the "old man" would rather not hear about. Thus, it becomes possible for the "old man" to be "honest" and open in his dealings with the press and the public. If illegal and repressive acts occur, they occur without his knowledge and, by implication, without his intent. In a society in which there are laws designed to provide freedom of information, it is impossible to conceal acts of injustice—and it is not really necessary. If such acts can be isolated from the intent of the administrator, they become "mistakes" or "failures in communication." If one cannot find a repressive intent in the written directives of the police department or in the words of a briefing officer, the acts themselves become the product of individual idiosyncrasy, nothing more. In a similar manner, acts of international aggression are explained in terms of a failure in communication or a failure to get all the facts. This is particularly true for acts of aggression that turn out badly for one reason or another.

Censorship occurs, but it is a self-censorship that operates within the mind of the reporter when he withholds certain facts because he feels he is being a "responsible journalist." One does not create false information, but information can be shaped and transposed if the perceptual process of the media experts has been taken captive so that they no longer recognize that they are distorting. It was Tocqueville,[14] long before Orwell,[15] who saw this change coming about. In the second chapter, we noted his remark that monarchs institute material repression, but that democratic republics had made repression entirely an affair of the mind. This form of repression is most effective if the elite are not themselves aware of the repressive nature of their acts. Policy arises from a particular acceptable way of thinking about the world. The control of others becomes a form of "good management" in which the repressive nature of the control is never obvious. The success of this American approach has made it increasingly popular throughout the world. Jean-Jacques Servan-Schreiber recommends the use of American methods in Europe. He reports that European life is changing toward the American model through a rigidity in European leadership that cannot adapt to the modern view and is still hobbled by "old methods of exerting pressure."[16] The new "tools of action" such as the mass media, says Servan-Schreiber, have not been used by those in power, who nevertheless complain that the masses are being Americanized.[17]

Servan-Schreiber does not want Europe to become Americanized, and to prevent this he prescribes a stronger dose of American methods. Like other aspirants, who condemn American culture but who admire American achievement, he fails to recognize that the road to the second objective inevitably leads to the first. The novice, be he student or businessman, is determined to learn the "method," gaining wealth and power for his people while preserving the cherished traditions of his own culture. If he learns well, he discovers that he must fill his mind with his objective and that no detail is too small for his attention. He learns that it is not only the acts themselves, but the team spirit and the success ethic that are critical. The adaptation to the affluent society begins as though it were a convenience, an easier and more effective way of getting things done. It ends by making over the individual.

Without telling anyone what he *must* think, certain ways of thinking are rewarded with financial success and increased status. In this way, the "common" people are left free to think as they like, but if they wish to obtain status and power, they must learn to think in the approved manner. This kind of coercion is only effective if the individual can tell himself that he is not being coerced. The *result* of his thinking is never specified in advance. It is up to him to determine the conclusion. Only the means for reaching the conclusion are specified, and this is accomplished by the subtle process of emphasis; never by fiat.

In the examination of the psychological pressures in the United States, we are talking about something quite different from political freedom. All the outward signs of freedom are on the increase in the United States. Since the end of World War II, civil rights—in the formal and legalistic sense—have improved. The American black man, who was formerly considered an inferior soldier, is now welcomed by the armed forces. In fact, if he is not careful, he may find himself part of a large mercenary force designed to advance the cause of white imperialism. To recognize how far we have exceeded even the predictions of Tocqueville in this direction, it is necessary to look at the early American attitude toward military conscription. Observing the United States in 1835, Tocqueville remarked, "The notions and habits of the people of the United States are so opposed to compulsory recruitment that I do not think it can ever be sanctioned by the laws."[18] Many foreigners came to our shores to escape this form of servitude. But only recently, and perhaps temporarily, we have abandoned a selective service system that was part of a vast network designed not merely to increase the direct military power of the United States, but to exert a psychological pressure on the youth of the nation toward certain forms of work and education that we regard as productive. The many ways of avoiding military service make this subtlety possible.

The process of coercing people into certain types of activity is deliberate in the sense that it is planned and specified, but it is inadvertent in the sense that it is not consciously repressive. Generally, neutral words are used to describe this pressure when it is enunciated as a part of national policy—words like *channeling*. *Channeling* is the title of one of ten documents in an orientation kit published by the selective service. It was issued in July 1965, but it was later withdrawn, altered, and reissued when excerpts were published in *Ramparts*. However, the very fact that a document like *Channeling* can be published by a government agency and released for open distribution suggests that the repressive nature of the policy was not apparent at the time it was developed and described. Only later did it become embarrassing. If repression in the United States can be described in great detail, including such phrases as "pressurized guidance" and "forced choice" without anyone becoming aware of what we are really doing, then it is not surprising that we can commit acts of aggression against other nations without recognizing the significance of our acts. I have quoted a few exerpts from *Channeling* for illustration.

> One of the major products of the Selective Service classification process is the channeling of manpower into many endeavors, occupations and activities that are in the national interest . . . The club of induction has been used to drive out of areas considered to be less important to areas of greater importance in which deferments were given. . . . It is in this atmosphere that the young man registers at age 18 and pressure begins to force his choice. . . . The psychological effect of this circumstantial climate depends upon the individual, his sense of good citizenship, his love of country and its way of life. He can obtain a sense of well-being and satisfaction that he is doing as a civilian what will help his country most. . . . In the less patriotic and more selfish individual it engenders a sense of fear, uncertainty and dissatisfaction which motivates him, nevertheless, in the same direction. He complains of the uncertainty which he must endure; he would like to be able to do as he pleases; he would appreciate a certain future with no prospect of military service or civilian contribution, but he complies . . .

> The psychology of granting wide choice under pressure to take action *is the American or indirect way of achieving what is done by*

> *direction in foreign countries where choice is not permitted* [Italics
> mine] ... The device of pressurized guidance, or channeling, is em-
> ployed on Standby Reservists of which more than 2½ million have
> been referred by all services for availability determinations. ... From
> the individual's viewpoint, he is standing in a room which has been
> made uncomfortably warm. Several doors are open, but they all lead
> to various forms of recognized patriotic service to the nation. Some
> accept the alternatives gladly—some with reluctance. The conse-
> quence is approximately the same.[19]

This strange Kafkaesque sense of indefinable pressure is characteristic of modern democratic imperialism. As the United States
strives to become a world power, it must use increased psychological
pressures to control and direct the lives of its citizens. It is not feasible, in a democratic state, to arrest citizens for political dissent. Such
acts break the illusion of civil rights and political freedom. Hazel
Barnes has provided an eloquent description of the more indirect
pressures required:

> Our legal recognition of such obvious rights as freedom of religious
> belief, freedom of speech, equality of race and sex have progressed
> beyond the first intent of the constitution. The more subtle pressures
> for conformity have increased and are perhaps more deadly because
> they are more insidious and offer less opportunity for clear-cut mo-
> tives for revolt. It takes courage to fight for civil rights in Alabama, but
> at least it is clear that there is injustice to be opposed, that there is a
> principle worth defending. The half-secret attack on spontaneity and
> personal preference for one's own style of life is experienced without
> ever being fully grasped. It is like those thermal blankets in which the
> threads are so loosely woven that they seem to hold more empty
> spaces than substance, yet the result is an artfully contrived insulation
> against the outer environment more complete than any tight-woven
> textiles can provide. Against such suffocating pressures, one must
> fight one thread at a time, and each in itself seems too insignificant to
> justify a violent revolt.[20]

IV

It is not strictly accurate to say that repression is never conscious
or that American society is completely open in regard to the flow of
information. It is not unusual for an administration to conceal embarrassing information, to exert pressure on individual reporters or
to provide special rewards in the form of an exclusive news release
for favored columnists. However, these are the more obvious and
less dangerous forms of repression. Repression is always more effective when the individual is not aware that he is being coerced in any

way, when his very will is taken captive. In the absolute sense, of course, this is not really possible. No one surrenders his will to another without receiving something in return. No one gives up his power over his own destiny without some desire to become powerless. Yet we have watched the Congress of the United States turn over enormous powers to the president on the condition that the president accept full responsibility for American foreign policy. This is not the intent of our Constitution, but it has happened. Marcus Raskin has described this erosion of power in some detail.[21] He observes that it has not occurred without the complicity of Congress. But Congress has an ally in this abdication of responsibility. It is the American people. In exchange for freedom of responsibility, individual congressmen vote away some of their power. Then they complain that they are powerless to change things. Although they retain the power of the purse, they maintain that it would not be "responsible" to deprive the president of the funds he needs to carry out American policy. In regard to national and international affairs, a similar relationship exists between the American middle class and their elected representatives. Those who are genuinely repressed are the various minorities: cultural, intellectual, and racial, along with the youth and the poor. The power that the government has taken from the middle class is the result of a massive abdication.

All of this puts a rather different light on an old-fashioned word like *repression*. The term is actually a hangover from the period when the living standard of a monarch was widely divergent from that of his people. He could live in luxury and spend much of his time hunting and enjoying himself. Today, the American president lives well, but not luxuriously and he works harder than most of his countrymen. The interest of the monarch was different from that of his people, and he understood that he must control them by force. The American president justifies his quest for power on the grounds that it is a burden that he did not seek but that is necessary if he is to provide the good things in life for his people and preserve them from the threat to their security. Thus, the "need" of the president for ever greater power is justified on the basis of the people's "need" for more and more material things and a higher standard of living than any nation in the world. We do not willingly submit to domination, except through our desire to dominate others.

Is this a trick, a deliberate act of deception? Certainly, deception is often involved in the elaboration of American foreign policy. But the major deception is the contention that we can provide peace and freedom for the world while constantly increasing the economic distance between ourselves and the underdeveloped nations. Do the American people really "know" better than this? Here again we come to that critical question of knowledge. We have accepted the superiority of a way of knowing that is abstract, "objective," and divorced from human feelings. Clearly, all Americans do not think in this way, but we have faced the "reality" that government decisions must be arrived at through this kind of knowledge. Otherwise, we believe, we will not be safe or the machinery of government will break down.

In an earlier chapter I suggested that there might be a motive for looking at things in this way. This kind of thinking, when it is used exclusively, makes it possible for the individual to avoid that painful confrontation with himself that is the basis for another kind of knowing. If the citizen has turned his government over to experts (and those who control the experts), if he has been convinced that he does not know enough to participate in the major policy decisions,[22] his lack of knowledge is not merely due to a clever trick that has been played upon him by those in power. The experience of "not knowing," then, is only partly due to the deception, the distortion, and the psychological repression of the administration. It is based, in large measure, on a will to be deceived.

The way of thinking maintains the status quo. If a serious rent is made in this system of thought, it might tear apart. Thus, the middle class supports not only the system of thought itself, but the deliberate deceptions that serve to protect this system. As the administration protects the consciousness of the people by subtle forms of coercion and deception, the people protect the administration. When a cover story is exposed (as in the U-2 incident)[23] or a blatant act of aggression is unmasked (such as the attempted invasion of Cuba), the people rally to the side of their president with an incredible show of public support. They understand that the president was really acting in their interest—that American interest that is forbidden open expression—and they do not want him to experience the full pain and the reality of what he has done. This might bring about a change in policy that no one really wants.

In an open society—and we still have an open society in this country—no real deception is possible without some cooperation on the part of those being deceived. Through this mutual cooperation, there is no single person or agency that deprives the people of their freedom. If the people are coerced and managed and if they are unaware of the extent to which they are coerced and managed, it is because they have made the effort to shield themselves from this awareness at some point. They do not really want to accept the responsibility for what they are doing (or what their government is doing in their name). In this sense, the phrase "psychological repression" is both an accurate and a misleading way to describe the American experience. It is accurate in the sense that many of us are engaged in a vast conspiracy to repress our own awareness and that of our national leaders. It is misleading because the term *repression* implies the existence of a clever tyrant who manipulates us and bends us to his will—a will that is *his* and not *ours*. If we are repressed, there is an implication that someone else is restraining or coercing us. In reality, we are coerced because we have refused to accept our own power to change things and the responsibility that is an inherent aspect of that power.

"To be too aware of the inner workings of the political process," say Dvorin and Simmons, "might make government intolerable."[24] There is, then, a motive for this lack of awareness and the perpetuation of the myth of majority rule. It is that awareness generally brings an element of severe discomfort and the great bulk of the people would prefer to have the government rule in their name, even if it rules unjustly and causes them occasional personal unhappiness, if they can be spared the greater pain of self-confrontation and the responsibility for directing their own lives.

This is not just an American phenomenon. There is a tendency toward this kind of abdication of responsibility in all democratic states. Bertrand Russell described his anger at the British government for having lied to the people and tricked them into involvement in World War I, but as he began to talk to the people and observe their enthusiasm for the war he discovered he had been wrong."I naively imagined that when the public discovered how he [Sir Edward Grey] had lied to them, they would be annoyed; instead of which they were grateful to him for having spared them the moral responsibility."[25] The tradition of British foreign policy training and the style of a former monarchy may influence the degree to which the diplomats and the national leaders *knowingly* lie to the people, but in their willingness to accept the lie, the British people resemble the Americans.

Can we really say that the people are controlled and deceived if they participate in the deception and are grateful for being deceived? I believe we can, for once a people submits to deception, it is difficult for individuals to struggle against a pervasive attitude of their own culture. Furthermore, once the mechanisms of deception and control are in place, they can operate with or without the will of the people.

It is as though a peasant were being forced into heavy labor by a powerful knight who rides behind him on horseback. The knight wears a helmet with the visor closed and the peasant cannot see his face. The knight carries a weapon, but he does not use it. He neither raises his weapon nor threatens violence. Yet the peasant knows what he must do. He has forgotten the purpose of his task and does not know why he is afraid of the knight. He only knows that the knight is more important and powerful than he, and he must obey. At last, after the peasant has labored for many years, the horse stumbles. The knight falls to the ground, lying motionless. The peasant finally summons his courage to open the visor on the knight's helmet and finds, to his terror, that he is looking into his own face.

V

Would it be possible for the government to control the behavior of the people in the United States if this control were exercised deliberately and consciously by government officials? There have already been a few moves toward a deliberate effort to condition and control the behavior of all Americans. The *Channeling* article suggests this kind of open acknowledgement of a nationwide effort at behavior control. But once published, it was withdrawn and republished to eliminate revealing phrases such as "pressurized guidance" and the analogy of the overheated room. It is as though someone made a mistake by openly admitting what we were doing, and the activity had to be reinterpreted in more neutral terms. However, at least one prominent social scientist in the United States appears to believe that such concealment is not necessary. B. F. Skinner, an American psychologist, has suggested that our entire culture can be managed by a technology of behavior;[26] that is, approved actions can be rewarded in such a way that we can control the behavior of our people and design the kind of culture we desire. In this way we will have less need for laws to restrain people. This is the point where psychology and politics become one. The professional psychologist and the professional policy planner are both designing an environment that will control human behavior. The psychologist applies his knowledge of how to condition human beings in the development of a more efficient system of control in much the same manner that the physicist applied his knowledge of the atom to the development of an atomic bomb for the use of the government.

In Skinner's view, it is not the urge to dominate and control others that provides our greatest danger, but "the literature of freedom and dignity." This notion of free will and moral responsibility for one's acts are, for Skinner, the chief causes of our present difficulties. They perpetuate the use of punishment and stimulate the individual to act against society. What we need, says Skinner, is more control, not less, "and this is an important engineering problem."[27] He would have us apply some of the same technological principles that have worked so well in the design of automobiles to the design of human behavior.[28] The literature of freedom and dignity, he says, tends to undermine this worthy development and interfere with the psychological adjustment of those who come under its influence. "A literature of freedom may inspire a sufficiently fanatical opposition to controlling practices to generate a neurotic if not psychotic response. There are signs of emotional instability in those who have been deeply affected by the literature."[29]

The crux of Skinner's argument is that everyone exerts some control over the behavior of others, even those who speak of freedom and dignity. So why limit ourselves? Why not study the problem and design a culture in which we have an "effective" control, a control that works to ensure the survival of the culture?

Skinner believes that war, crime, overpopulation, and many other ills of our society can be resolved if we perfect a technology of behavior.[30] The fact that such measures have not yet solved our problems means only that the technology we have applied is not sufficiently effective. The literature of freedom and dignity and the archaic belief in an autonomous man have held us back, he says. By complaining about control, those who believe in a free and autonomous man have forced us to disguise our control and limited us to "weak measures."[31] Skinner argues that a technology of behavior is ethically neutral. It can be used by a villain or a saint.[32] The protest that such measures sometimes arouse is due to the fact that the control is not effective. It has adverse consequences that are evident to the person being controlled. Presumably if we could develop a truly effective technology of behavior, it would have few adverse consequences, and hence, protest would be minimized or eliminated altogether.

In many respects, Skinner seems to be advocating a more deliberate effort to do what we are already doing in the United States, namely, developing methods for the efficient management of human behavior without the use of the more obvious and coercive forms of control. However, there is an important difference. Skinner has proposed that we make the control of others an open and explicit part of our policy. It is this aspect of his work that has aroused the wrath of the professional politician. With the classic intellectual courage of the man in pursuit of truth, Skinner has been willing to face the full implications of what he is proposing. He admits that the application of his ideas would mean the end of such "obsolete" ideas as the freedom and dignity of man. The professional politician, on the other hand, understands that if he is to be successful in the art of management, he must operate under the myth that he is only carrying out the will of the people. Furthermore, if he is to be truly effective within the American system, he must believe this myth himself. In this regard our former vice-president, Spiro Agnew, was quite "sincere", in the unreflective sense, when he attacked Skinner's book, *Beyond Freedom and Dignity*. Warning that behavioral psychologists are proposing a "new kind of despotism," a "radical surgery on the national psyche," Agnew maintained that Skinner's "thinking must be taken seriously and countered with logic and reason. It is potentially very dangerous, and is completely at odds with our basic belief in the dignity and worth of the individual."[33] Agnew was seeking to maintain the right of the administration to do what it was doing inadvertently, without acknowledging to itself or to the people the growing effort toward the centralization of power.

Thus, we come back, once again, to the problem of innocence with which this book began. Just as Richard Nixon would prefer to believe that the United States became a major world power "without asking for it," so the growing centralization of power in the office of the president is supposed to take place without any intent toward total control on the part of the administration. In like manner, the power elite, which C. Wright Mills observed in 1956, continues to grow in wealth and power despite apparent changes in political administrations.[34] This elite is supported by a middle class that is oppressed by a sense of its own powerlessness and by a willingness to accept certain material rewards in lieu of power. We have indeed moved a long way in the direction of the kind of manipulated society Skinner envisions without the help of the professional psychologist. It is not surprising, therefore, that Skinner's proposal should be greeted by a sense of outrage from the administration in power. He seeks to make explicit a process that has been implicit in American society for almost half a century. To do deliberately and consciously what we have been doing "inadvertently" would require that we write and talk about what we are doing and make this information available to others. This, in turn, might awaken that sleeping giant, the American electorate, into a concerted opposition to all forms of government surveillance and control.

Of course, Skinner does not believe this would occur. His view of man does not include the concept of an inner autonomous self that can act independently of the stimuli from the environment. For

Skinner, the self is "a repertoire of behavior appropriate to a given set of contingencies."[35] Therefore, if the external stimuli are pleasurable, the person will seek to perpetuate the circumstances that gave rise to these pleasurable stimuli.

Clearly, this is the kind of thinking that has come to dominate our foreign policy. It was the reasoning behind President Johnson's offer to spend a billion in Southeast Asia. It is congruent with the general belief that we can control the behavior of other less powerful nations if we can receive advance information on the development of revolutionary forces and change the environment in such a way that these incipient revolutions subside. The same approach is applied to the domestic scene. At the same time there is a persistent denial of the desire to become powerful or to centralize and extend government control. Why is this denial necessary? Skinner would contend there is no need for it, that if the government means well and produces a minimum of adverse consequences for the individual, he will not resist the extension of this control. To a remarkable extent Skinner has been right, for this is what has been happening in the United States. A minority continues to protest, but the threads of constraint are so loosely woven, as Hazel Barnes has described it, that rebellion seems foolish and out of place in such a comfortable environment. Watergate aroused a protest because it was an act by one political party against another. Similar bugging or spying against private citizens has continued for years. Only recently have we seen evidence of a real concern for privacy by the individual and an attempt to prosecute agents of government who spy on the citizen. Until recent years it has been possible to reserve overt violent repression for the nations of the Third World and keep our own people in line by an unacknowledged system of information collection and behavioral control, to gentle them into submission like an unruly horse.

But perhaps there is an aspect of man that Skinner has not recognized, an inner self that strives to create a goal of its own, that resists all forms of external control, no matter how benign. To make such a statement implies that man has the capacity to become aware of himself as a free being and will seek to throw off external control and determine his own destiny. I think we recognize this inner self in our policy formulation. The very fact that government officials have rejected Skinner's proposals for a technology of behavior, while acting on them "inadvertently," suggests that there is an unspoken fear of this phenomenon of awareness.

This does not mean that Skinner is completely wrong. Man is both controlled by his environment, and, at the same time, he resists this control. His freedom varies depending on the circumstances. He is more responsive to the control of another single individual if he feels that such a person (parent, educator, psychotherapist) is merely attempting to help him realize his own full potential. There is a certain eye-to-eye contact involved in such relationships that makes it possible for the controllee to assess the motives of the controller on a moment-to-moment basis. He is also more responsive to external control when he is less aware of himself, when he is hungry, tired, or greedy for possessions. Under such circumstances, he is more easily manipulated by a simple system of subtle punishments and rewards. He is more responsive to external control when he is less aware of the intent and the private interest of the controller, that is, if he believes the control emerges from the "conditions of the world" and is therefore inescapable. If a government controls the "conditions of the world" by long-range planning, the individual is more resistant than if he feels the government is a victim of current circumstances. However, if the need for planning can be seen as forced upon the government by the hectic pace of our present society, he becomes more accepting. For this reason, it has become fashionable for U.S. government officials to criticize a planned economy as an example of "creeping socialism" while nevertheless extending specific areas of government planning on the grounds that it is "necessary" to protect us from the plans of others. Galbraith remarks,

> What is not supposed to exist is often imagined not to exist. In consequence the role of planning in the modern industrial society remains only slightly appreciated. Additionally, it is the sound instinct of conservatives that economic planning involves, inevitably, the control of individual behavior. The denial that we do any planning has helped to conceal the fact of such control even from those who are controlled.[36]

It is evident, then, that the American denial of the intent to become powerful, which we examined in the first chapter, extends to all efforts at global or long-range control of others. We deny the intent to control while at the same increasing our control as unobtrusively as possible. The government will acknowledge a casual effort at news management, but the kind of massive behavioral conditioning that was implied in the *Channeling* article must be concealed. At the same time, since we cannot allow ourselves to become aware of what we are doing, documents like *Channeling* are published from time to time because some government official has failed to sense that one does not speak of such things openly. The need to repress public awareness of our efforts at behavioral control must be sensed. It cannot be ordered for this would require a conscious conspiracy to deceive the general public. A conscious conspiracy would violate the basic belief in human freedom on which this country was founded. It has become a requirement for survival of the American government official that he continue to believe in freedom and dignity while at the same time he helps to extend government control over the lives of his fellow citizens.

Thus, under the guise of a humanist view of man, a belief that man is free and should be encouraged to shape his own destiny, we are moving rapidly toward a planned, regulated, and controlled society, a society that controls its own middle class by a subtle system of punishments and rewards and uses a not-so-subtle system of control upon the minorities within the United States and the Third World nations. The most dangerous thing about this control (and here I think Skinner and I would agree) is that it is unacknowledged. We have denied what we are doing in both our foreign and our domestic policy. We have denied it not only in order to fool others, but we have deceived ourselves as well.

The continuation of the "American way of life" as we know it today depends on the perpetuation of this state of unawareness in the great majority of our people. Our style of control and our style of warfare have become a product of our way of knowing and understanding the world. This situation is extremely unstable. It depends on the systematic exclusion from consciousness of a whole realm of human experience. Of course, it is not simply an American phenomenon. Some elements of this way of thinking are characteristic of all modern highly industrialized nations. However, in the United States this situation has been accentuated by a strong desire for personal innocence and a concentration of power unprecedented in the history of the world.

VI

This state of unawareness cannot continue indefinitely. Just as foreign nations come to recognize that they are being exploited by a total system of international control directed by a few major powers, individuals come to recognize when their own efforts toward self-fulfillment have been thwarted by a total system of national control. Furthermore, they come to recognize that the two systems are interrelated, that one is a direct consequence of the other, and that both are a consequence of a system of thought that attempts to treat nations and people as though they were responsive to the laws of New-

tonian physics. Richard Barnet has characterized this way of thinking as it applies to the national security manager:

> From his vantage point in the national security bureaucracy, the Na-
> tional Security Manager sees revolution in the underdeveloped world
> as a problem in the management of violence. . . . The primary problem
> is aggression. The principal cause of aggression is weakness and in-
> stability. Unless aggressors are systematically opposed by "situa-
> tions of strength" they will strike at their weaker neighbors. Nations
> act in accordance with Newtonian laws, rushing to fill up "power vac-
> uums" wherever they find them.[37]

To recognize that this system is based on a value judgment and
not an "objective" or a "scientific" view of reality would involve the
rediscovery of personal intent for the American citizen. It would
mean that the citizen, and hence Congress, would change from a
passive supporter of presidential policies to an active participant in
the formulation of policy. If this is to happen, there must be a change
in our level of awareness and in our way of knowing and understanding the world. With the emergence of the United States as a
world power, we can no longer take refuge in the innocence of our
intentions, in the belief that our power was thrust upon us by the
circumstances of the modern world. If the president is indeed responsive to the will of the people, as we so often maintain, we must
curb his ambition or admit that his moves toward an American Empire *are a reflection of our desires.*

VI

Up to this point I have outlined what I believe to be a problem in
the way American policy is developed and perceived by the people.
The problem arises from our unwillingness to come to grips with our
intent. In the final chapter I have suggested some changes in our
approach that might bring the individual citizen into a more direct
contact with the consequences of American foreign and domestic
policy. Some of these changes are already underway. However, I
recognize that the proposed changes do not follow as a logical consequence of the problem itself. There are several means of bringing
the citizen into closer sensory and emotional contact with his intent.
I am aware that my personal bias against some of them may be unjus-
tified. However, I have tried to indicate that bias toward those
methods I regard as gimmicky or theatrical.

NOTES

1. J. Caesar, *Caesar's War Commentaries*, ed. John Warrington (New York: Dutton, 1958), pp. 24–25.

2. C. von Clausewitz, *On War*, vol. III (New York: Barnes & Noble, 1956), p. 121.

3. S. Hoffman, "Perceptions, Reality and and Franco-American Conflict," *Journal of International Affairs*, vol. 21, no. 1 (1967): 57–71.

4. A. Toffler, *Future Shock* (New York: Random House, 1970).

5. N. Sheehan et al., *The Pentagon Papers* (New York: Bantam, 1971), pp. 274–275.

6. Ibid., p. 432.

7. "Soviet Statement on the Disarmament Talks, August 27, 1957," *Documents on Disarmament, 1945–1959. Volume II* (Washington, D.C.: U.S. Government Printing Office, 1960), pp. 865–866.

8. Ibid., p. 867.

9. "Russia: Setback for Free Speech," *New York Times*, February 20, 1966, section 4, p. 1.

10. "French Red Poet Angry," *New York Times*, February 17, 1966, p. C13.

11. P. Grose, "2 Writers' Trial Scored in Soviet," *New York Times*, Feburary 21, 1966, p. 3.

12. "Tidy Tyranny," *Newsweek*, October 21, 1968, p. 18.

13. W. G. Bennis and P. E. Slater, *The Temporary Society* (New York: Harper & Row, 1968), pp. 1–19.

14. A. de Tocqueville, *Democracy in America*, vol. I (New York: Vintage, 1955), pp. 274–275.

15. G. Orwell, *1984* (New York: Harcourt, Brace and Jovanovich, 1971).

16. J.-J. Servan-Schreiber, *The American Challenge* (New York: Atheneum, 1968), p. 183.

17. Ibid., pp. 185–186.

18. Tocqueville, *Democracy in America*, p. 236.

19. "Channeling," a reprint from *Ramparts*, December 1967. This was the 1965 version of *Channeling*; I have tried to obtain a copy of this 1965 version from Selective Service, but received instead the 1967 version in which phrases such as "forced choice," the analogy of the hot room, and other more overt indications of government pressure on the individual were removed.

20. H. Barnes, *An Existential Ethics* (New York: Knopf, 1967), pp. 284–285.

21. M. G. Raskin, "The Erosion of Congressional Power," *Washington Plans an Aggressive War*, ed. R. Stannis, R. J. Barnet, and M. G. Raskin (New York: Vintage, 1971).

22. R. E. Lapp, *The New Priesthood* (New York: Harper & Row, 1965), p. 2.

23. W. H. Blanchard, "National Myth, National Character and National Policy: A Psychological Study of the U-2 Incident," *Journal of Conflict Resolution*, vol. 6, no. 2, (1962): 143–148.

24. E. P. Dvorin and R. H. Simmons, *From Amoral to Humane Bureaucracy* (San Francisco: Canfield, 1972), p. 28.

25. B. Russell, *The Autobiography of Bertrand Russell*, vol. II (New York: Bantam, 1969), p. 4.

26. B. F. Skinner, *Beyond Freedom and Dignity* (New York: Knopf, 1971).

27. Ibid., p. 177.

28. Ibid.

29. Ibid., p. 165.

30. Ibid., p. 138.

31. Ibid., pp. 83–100.

32. Ibid., p. 150.

33. S. Agnew, Address to the Farm Bureau, Chicago, November 1971.

34. C. W. Mills, *The Power Elite* (New York: Oxford University Press, 1959).

35. Skinner, *Beyond Freedom and Dignity*, p. 199.

36. J. K. Galbraith, *The New Industrial State* (New York: New American Library, Signet, 1967), p. 34.

37. R. J. Barnet, *Intervention and Revolution* (New York: World, 1968), p. 25.

15

The
Will
to
Know

I

Throughout this book, I have made the point that aggression per se is neither morally wrong nor unhealthy for a society, particularly if it is kept within manageable limits. The real danger, in the world of the superweapon, is that we may become so fearful of aggression that we will restrict its expression and conceal it with euphemism and rationalization. This sets the stage for an accident or an inadvertent outbreak of violence that may reach thermonuclear proportions before it can be controlled. Such incidents are called "mistakes," but the word *mistake* is really a general term to conceal our ignorance. It means that the individual was not aware of any intention to act the way he did, that he misperceived reality and acted in accord with this misperception. To the extent that we cover the expression of aggression in our society by the polite phrase of the public relations expert, we are creating the conditions for this misperception of reality. The use of a phrase like "sunshine units" to describe poisonous nuclear radiation, the creation of the term "clean bomb" and the

announcement that the government's effort to search out and destroy
Vietcong is a "pacification program" are all a part of this process of
obfuscation. In some cases, it is a half-conscious adoption of the
ethics of the advertising industry. In other instances, it is a deliberate
policy of pretense and concealment. Such was the case in a directive
issued to military officers who brief the press in South Vietnam. The
directive, entitled "Let's Say It Right," banned the use of certain
terms and substituted others. Vietcong deserters were to be referred
to as "ralliers" or "returnees." Mercenaries were part of the "civilian
irregular defense group." A search and destroy mission was called
"search and clear."[1] In the advertising culture, no one lie is very
important. In one sense, we are not really lying since all the statements have been discounted in advance. In another sense, however,
we are creating an atmosphere that makes self-deception easier.
Politicians flatter us by telling us we are a generous and compassionate people with no desire to advance our own interest and we
elect them because we want to believe them. We know what we are
doing, but we prefer the illusion that we are doing something else.

I am reluctant to use the term *unconscious* to describe this American self-deception. If we were unconscious of our conflicting desires
for power and for virtue, it would mean that the information was not
available for recall, that we could not make use of it without professional help even if we wanted to. I would maintain, instead, that
wanting to face our conflicting desires—*the will to know*—is our
real difficulty. In this regard the press, the government, business,
advertising, and the American people have been, at times, partners
in the same act of obfuscation. It is the corruption of our language
that forms the basis for this kind of distortion of reality. There are
some who would maintain that language is "only words" and one
cannot really change things with words. This is certainly true for the
soldier who has direct contact with "pacification." He knows what
he is doing. But most of us are protected from a sense of direct responsibility. More importantly, the great majority of government bu-
reaucrats and decision makers deal primarily with symbols and paper. Decisions are made, in part, because of the way data is colored
by words and because our perceptions are altered by words. In the
modern world we create a large part of our reality through the words
we use. And the initial impulse to use some of these words comes
from a willingness to participate in mutual deception—not always
deception about the same thing, but the act of deception itself.

However, the problem is not merely one of semantics. People become unaware of what they are doing not only because they use the
wrong words to describe their acts, but because they can arrange to
have others act for them. The police can be used to prevent obstruc-

tion of traffic in front of a business establishment or to quiet a celebration in the home of a neighbor. The armed forces can be used to keep the channels of commerce open overseas to ensure a regular supply of raw materials for industry and to prevent the rise of unfriendly governments. The professional military man and the policeman usually know what they are doing, but their code of ethics prevents them from speaking directly to the public. Only on rare occasions, such as in the remarks of General Smedley Butler quoted in the second chapter of this book, do we find a military man who will ignore the niceties of diplomatic language and reveal the character of his actions.

Even such a bold statement as General Butler's does not bring us to our senses because it is grossly oversimplified. In its very unreflective quality, it contains a certain lack of balance that makes us doubt its credibility. We may get into many of our wars for commercial reasons, but we do not stay in them for profit. The cost of the Vietnam War as of November 1972, according to economist Robert Lekachman, had already exceeded $400 billion.[2] This does not include the loss of American lives, the misapplied skills, wasted resources, lowered productivity, loss of social programs, and the inflation. The cost has far exceeded the meager supplies of tin and tungsten that President Eisenhower hoped to get from Southeast Asia. War grows and expands because we do not have a sensory connection with the conflict. We do not perceive our own loss of resources, and we have no real awareness of the acts being committed in our name. We do not feel anger toward the people we are fighting, and we cannot feel remorse. This same lack of sensory and emotional contact is at the root of domestic violence as well. When the police are used in a repressive manner against whole communities, we have already begun to deal with images or symbols of people rather than the real people themselves.

II

While this study was underway, I came across a book by Richard Sennett on the problems of the city entitled *The Uses of Disorder*. Sennett deals with the problem of aggression and conflict on a smaller scale, but there appear to be some clear parallels between his work and mine. The tendency of governments, whether they are city governments or national governments, to equate advance planning and control with peace and stability seems to increase as modern technology gives these governments the ability to exercise control. Sennett describes the city planner as one who imposes his concept of a city upon the real, disorderly, messy conglomeration of buildings and people. If the city does not develop according to the plan or if some parts of the plan conflict with others, there is said to be a "failure" of the plans. But in reality, some degree of conflict is part of the human experience. It is the effort to make everything orderly and "purified" that conflicts most of all with the way people work and live. The insistence that people function according to plans tends to increase the degree of conflict. The planners, instead of trying to understand why cities grow in unexpected ways, call for greater policing powers and new regulations to enforce their original plan. In this way, they try to avoid friction and disorderliness within the city. Sennett proposes, instead, an effort to develop cities that allow for intracommunity conflict. We could have communities in which it is not possible to call in the police to settle minor disputes. If people of different ethnic and socioeconomic backgrounds are in close proximity and if they discover they must solve their own problems without help from the outside, they will begin to know each other, to negotiate with each other and will develop a tolerance for individual differences.

> What researchers are beginning to glimpse about affluent working-class communities is that the cries for law and order are greatest when the communities are most isolated from other people in the city. In Boston, for example, the fear of deviance and conflict is much greater in an Irish area called South Boston, which is cut off geographically from contact with the city at large, than in another Irish area, North Cambridge, which is stuck in the midst of the city and is to some extent penetrated by blacks and college students.[3]

Sennett refers to his proposal as a form of limited anarchy. However, he does not advocate the abolition of city government, only the tolerance for greater community conflict and an insistence that this conflict be resolved by forces within the community and not by a total plan for control.

There is a striking similarity between Sennett's view of the city planners and Richard Barnet's description of the national security manager who would balance the forces of the world to avoid "power vacuums" that might, in turn, produce revolutions or other forms of disorder in international relations. In fact, some of the more ambitious city planners speak of a world plan for the balancing of urban and rural areas, which would be brought into harmony with economic and political values throughout the world. In the end, they call for a complete integration of social and physical structures. Speaking of one such planner, Sennett remarks, "These are not the words of a mad superman. They are rather a clear statement of the goals of a large and influential segment of the profession that plans modern cities."[4]

This type of thinking equates regularity and order with reason and reason with virtue. The "bad" people are those who upset the system and who prevent the orderly implementation of plans. In this new puritanism, there is an effort to develop areas of uniformity, to minimize friction within communities and within nations, in the belief that this will also prevent conflict between communities and between nations. The prevention of minor conflict and minor forms of violence becomes the first step in the prevention of major violence. The result is a growing belief that all aggression is wrong. The vision of "peace" that emerges from such an attitude is one of total passivity and an absence of all strife. In such an environment, it is not surprising to hear people say that the behavior of peace protesters proves that they could not possibly be for peace. After all, they are producing disorder and instability. They are angry, and anger may lead to violence. The entire structure of our attitudinal systems, our beliefs, and even our definitions of words tends to conform to this idea. Webster defines the word *peace* in several ways, most of which support the idea of order and calm.[5] Peace is "a state of security or order within a community provided by law and custom." It is "freedom from disquieting or oppressive thoughts or emotions." It is "harmony in personal relations." And finally, it is "a pact or agreement to end hostilities between those who have been at war." Now it seems to me that in order to achieve the condition described by the last of these definitions, we must be willing to forego the earlier ones. The peace that comes about through the termination of the international system of warfare will be characterized by a lack of tranquility, an increase in civil disturbance and in disquieting thoughts, disharmony in personal relationships and, most of all, a breach in the customs and laws of a community that provide for a state of order and security. It is well known that in order to prosecute a war efficiently, one must have domestic order, relatively strict adherence to the laws, and particularly the customs of a society, and minimal civil unrest. Therefore, in a civilization that has become habituated to warfare as a way of life, peace (in the sense of a cessation of war) can only be maintained by an alert citizenry that is in a constant state of disquiet: restive, suspicious of every government pronouncement, and ready to erupt into disorder at the slightest awareness that it is being prepared for mass mobilization. There is, here, I believe, a parallel between the uses of disorder within a city and within a nation.

A peace-oriented society would require the complete restructuring of our present system of national and international controls. It would require a change in the idea of what constitutes manhood and courage. It would mean a breach of customs, an invocation of the absurd in order to heighten our awareness of the absurdity of our present way of life. This awareness that changes the shape of a human life is, in part, an intellectual experience, a matter of understanding. But it also has elements of another kind of experience, a physical contact with the unknown, a willingness to experience the kind of change that has not been anticipated in one's plans.

It should be evident by now that the world cannot be sweet-talked or reasoned into peace. This does not mean we must discard all our intellectual resources. It does mean, however, that the intellectual explanation that peace makes good sense is not sufficient to evoke the necessary action to preserve it. In the context of really bringing about a reduction of major international conflict, peace means that we must accept the reality of minor conflicts, a certain limited disorder within the international community. In the previous chapters, we have noted that Americans, who live in an affluent society, are more isolated from the conditions of human deprivation that form the basis for revolutionary movements. Senator Fulbright has described our condition as "sober, satisfied and comfortable. Our understanding of revolutions and their causes is imperfect not because of any failures of mind or character but because of our good fortune. . . . We must understand social revolution and the injustices that give it rise because they are the heart and core of the experience of the great majority of people now living in the world."[6]

When the Senator speaks of understanding in this context, he is talking about something different from the kind of knowledge that one can provide in classrooms for young people. Abraham Maslow spoke of two kinds of knowing. The knowing that comes from learning facts and abstract principles and the other more emotional and physical contact with experience—an "affective" (emotional and sensory) education.

III

Having admitted the importance of the emotions, should we, then, call in an "expert in emotions" to solve our problem? The notion of an encounter group to handle the decision process in the White House sounds absurd and rightly so. To call in such an outside expert, a "group facilitator" would be to make the same mistake we have made in turning to our technical experts for the solution of our problems. The only one who can integrate the intellectual and emotional aspects of a problem is the individual or individuals who have the personal knowledge, the intellect, and the responsibility to deal with it. He must acquire the ability, the emotional balance, to handle this problem before he encounters it. Certainly there are changes in our educational system that can improve the process of decision making. I recently had the privilege of serving as a consultant in the final stages of a unique book by Eugene Dvorin and Robert Simmons called *From Amoral to Humane Bureaucracy,* in which the authors outlined some of the principles for an "affective" approach to the education of future administrators.[7] They decided to avoid a lengthy description of techniques and special courses, and have provided the reader with a sound rationale for such a program. The decision to avoid specific techniques was a wise one. The need for an affective element in education has been known for several hundred years, since the time of Rousseau's *Emile.*[8] But the problem with this approach is that some emotional experience is required for the student to "know" something in the emotional sense. In order to provide this experience the educator resorts to a series of tricks and gimmicks to make us "feel." Yet all the situations seem artificial. Rousseau's own work is flawed by these clever tricks and we find them, in a somewhat altered form, in many of the techniques of modern affective education.[9] There are exceptions, such as the Tutorial Community Program of Gerald Newmark.[10] But this program is unique in that it is not merely affective education, but a total educational process in which an attempt is made to integrate both *intellectual* and *emotional* aspects of education. At the present time Newmark's program is designed primarily for elementary and secondary education. Much of adult affective education is still strongly oriented toward emotional awakening as though the intellect were not an important element in education.

There is, of course, a sound basis for this emphasis on emotional involvement in affective education with adults. For those who have already been indoctrinated into the methods of systematic and quantitative thinking, it may be that some *shock* is essential if they are to break free of this mechanical notion of thought. But this raises an important ethical question for the instructor, facilitator, or whatever he calls himself. A minor shock is usually ineffective. It may even do a disservice in that it pretends to be a deep and moving experience. If a shock is to provide some personal knowledge, it must involve some risk to the emotional stability of the individual, possibly also to his sense of identity, perhaps even to his life. Is it right for the educator to make this decision for someone else? Perhaps the best affective education for the individual can be provided by those who are not interested in his education and have no ethical responsibility for his personal survival: the student of sociology who travels in the South to join a Civil Rights movement, the future public official who spends several years living in an underdeveloped country, or the urban planner who lives in the ghetto is providing himself with an affective education in which the situations are real, not contrived. He is making the move on his own initiative and on his own responsibility. At his best, the specialist in affective education can probably do no more than demonstrate the need for such experience.

IV

The individual does not come to "know" something in an emotional-sensual-experiential way without some risk, some shock, and some disruption of his identity. A nation also requires some kind of profound shock if it is to be roused from national complacency to reexamine its way of life. These shocks are sometimes painful and disheartening, but, in a people with the resiliency to master them, they can stimulate the self-understanding necessary for survival and growth. In the United States we have had a number of these shocks in recent years. Each in its own way has produced a rent in some area of our national identity: Watergate, the Vietnam War, the Arab oil boycott, the campus revolts, Civil Rights marches, militant minorities, and new, more critically perceptive, communications media.

It is possible that the current style of American aggression is a transitory stage in our development that has been maintained because of our geographic distance from other world powers in our early history. Our development was so rapid that we were not obliged to see the world as others saw it. It was up to them to understand us and to try to reach our level of achievement. The mere opening of the doors of travel by means of the jet airplane would not be enough to change this narrow American provincialism, for in the early part of the jet era, we brought our American money with us and purchased our own standard of living everywhere in the world with our powerful dollar. People who share a common culture tend to reinforce each other's beliefs, and a few weeks of travel outside this closed system is not enough to dispel our illusions. In a fascinating little book, *Outgrowing Self-Deception,* Gardner Murphy describes the difficulty in teaching people to look objectively on their own culture. He was working with an anthropologist who was responsible for social-science education of American officers. After he familiarized these men with anthropological methods of observation, the scientist hoped that he might have also taught them to view their own culture as an outsider, but this did not seem to work. "They had learned to look upon the civilization of the United States as a sort of standard."[11]

But the anthropologist was using a strictly intellectual approach for overcoming self-deception. The Arab oil boycott and the decline of the American dollar have diminished our physical comfort, but they have expanded our perception of the world. They have made us aware that the resources of the earth are not limitless, and we have been disturbed to discover that there is nothing permanent about American economic superiority. The wage-earners in Sweden and Germany have already surpassed our average wage and the Japanese are gaining rapidly. The world is changing to the point that we will soon be forced to deal with the problem of an equitable distribution of world resources. The unreflective "Pageant-of Peace" speech of President Nixon, in which he took pride in the disproportionate wealth and the abundance of consumer goods in the United States, would sound strange today. In his State of the Union message in January 1975, President Ford said, " . . . the State of the Union is not good. . . ."

> Economic disruptions we and others are experiencing stem in part from the fact that the world price of petroleum has quadrupled in the last year. But, in all honesty, we cannot put all of the blame on the oil-exporting nations. We, the United States, are not blameless. Our growing dependence upon foreign sources has been adding to our vulnerability for years and years, and we did nothing to prepare ourselves for such an event as the embargo of 1973.[12]

This sense of growing awareness of the demands of other people and the limits of American power were reinforced by President Carter in his inaugural address January 20, 1977:

> We have learned that *more* is not necessarily *better,* that even our great Nation has its recognized limits, and that we can neither answer all questions nor solve all problems. We cannot afford to do everything, nor can we afford to lack boldness as we meet the future. So together, in a spirit of individual sacrifice for the common good, we must simply do our best. . . .
> The world itself is now dominated by a new spirit. Peoples more numerous and more politically aware are craving, and now demand-

ing, their place in the sun—not just for the benefit of their own physical condition, but for basic human rights. . . .

Within us, the people of the United States, there is evident a serious and purposeful rekindling of confidence. And I join in the hope that when my time as your President has ended, people might say about our Nation:

—that we had remembered the words of Micah and renewed our search for humility, mercy, and justice;

—that we had torn down the barriers that separated those of different race and region and religion and where there had been mistrust, built unity, with a respect for diversity;

—that we had found productive work for those able to perform it;

—that we had strengthened the American family, which is the basis of our society;

—that we had ensured respect for the law and equal treatment under the law, for the weak and the powerful, for the rich and the poor; and

—that we had enabled our people to be proud of their own government once again.

I would hope that the nations of the world might say that we had built a lasting peace, based not on weapons of war but on international policies which reflect our most precious values. . . .

We are not yet certain that this shock is sufficient to bring about change. It may be that we will require a series of electrical blackouts before the individual American experiences this problem in a direct way in his own home. But the leadership of our nation is aware of it. If they can muster the courage to make the necessary unpopular decisions, we may still escape some of the more serious consequences of our declining resources.

The war in Vietnam represented an even greater shock to American dreams of omnipotence and personal virtue. We owe much that we have learned from this experience to the courageous resistance of the young men who refused to fight in the war on the basis of conscience and refused all the legal means of avoiding military service. The pardon of President Carter may yet bring them back to our society. If they are once more willing to work with us, we could use their capacity for seeing through self-deception. Although the college campuses are quiet once again, some of the young people who were part of the revolt of the 1960s are now taking their place in the adult world. The campus revolt had its fringe elements who loved to trash a city block for the fun of trashing, but the leadership in this movement represented some of our brightest and most capable people, as a number of studies of this period have demonstrated.[14]

It was the perceptive Tocqueville who warned of a revolt of the minorities in the United States if our system of majority rule became too oppressive.

> If ever the free institutions of America are destroyed, that event may
> be attributed to the omnipotence of the majority, which may at some
> future time urge the minorities to desperation and oblige them to have
> recourse to physical force. Anarchy will then be the result, but it will
> have been brought about by despotism.[15]

Here, too, our American people have received a shock in the discovery that some people are so unhappy in our society that they would be willing to sacrifice their minimal security and even risk their lives to protest against it. All of these people—war resisters, campus rebels, and minorities—have now begun to take positions in Congress, as city mayors, councilmen, and in the business world. As individuals, they might easily be coopted, but in larger numbers they should reinforce each other. We will need their experience and their capacity to see through the myth of America's invincibility and her endless resources if we are to move from a society of innocent, wasteful consumption and inadvertent provocation toward the position of a responsible world power.

Perhaps the most encouraging sign of a movement away from American innocence is the development of a more critical press and television. In the chapter on the Cuban invasion, I described the surrender of the press to the administration. Clearly, President Kennedy exerted considerable pressure to bring about press compliance, and he was angered by the few reporters bold enough to print some information on the invasion plans. But after it was over, he remarked that, had the press insisted on printing everything about the invasion, the administration might have been saved from a colossal mistake. He also arranged for more private discussions with his staff, urging them to come forth with their unfettered opinions. In regard to the staff, Schlesinger remarked, "For our part we resolved to be less acquiescent the next time. The Bay of Pigs gave us a license for the impolite inquiry and the rude comment."[16] Thoughts similar to this may have crossed the minds of the reporters and editors who had accepted the notion that the "responsible" journalist was one who supported the administration. The gadfly is not a pleasant fellow. He is always facing us with an unpleasant side of reality. But we cannot grow and develop unless we learn to face and overcome our own self-deception.

Television and press reporting of the Vietnam War was relentless. If a person could hide from it during the day, it was there facing him with the morning paper and it greeted him in the evening from the television set. There was no escape from the details of burning peasant villages, the body count, the defoliation, and the slaughter of Hamburger Hill and My Lai. These constant visual and auditory re-

minders that ours was not a "compassionate army," as well as the
coverage given to antiwar demonstrators, were much cricitized by
the Johnson and Nixon Administrations. Nevertheless, the media
played a central role in influencing our decision to withdraw from
Vietnam. The media did not manufacture this information; it simply
refused to suppress dramatic and newsworthy stories that contained
direct or implied criticism of the administration.

V

Although the reporter hungers for the dramatic and significant
story, there may be important national issues that do not have a
readily apparent dramatic impact. There may be sources of conflict
within the system that cannot or will not be covered by the reporter
in search of a story for today. If internal conflict is good for an administrative system and if people are to be encouraged to express this
conflict, there must be some means provided to ensure that this expression reaches the level of decision for which it is intended. Obviously, it would be impossible for every government worker to talk to
the president every time he thinks he has something important to
say. On the other hand, an official paid to "listen to complaints"
would be equally ineffective. The name for a system of conflict expression and the official mechanism by which it works are less important than the spirit of such a program. The ombudsman idea is a
good one. It was adopted in Sweden, Finland, Denmark, Norway,
and New Zealand. But in the United States, of the 60 ombudsmen
bills proposed in 1967, only one was enacted—for Hawaii.

Perhaps American skepticism of the system was well founded.
Unless an ombudsman functioned at the national level and had a
staff of inspectors to carry out an investigation of complaints, the
state-elected representative would serve just as well. But when is an
ombudsman or a national inspector of government policy truly independent? The inspector general system in the U.S. Air Force
clearly places an insurmountable barrier between the enlisted man
and the higher levels of command. When Sergeant Lonnie Franks
sought to make his government aware of the unauthorized strikes
and falsified reports in the Seventh Air Force, under the command of
General Lavelle, he found he could not turn to the local inspector
general for his wing because this was General O'Malley, the vice-
wing commander, who was fully aware of the falsification of reports,
as was the wing commander, who had authorized the falsification.

Clearly, the ombudsman must not only be outside of government, but ideally he should not have to operate on government funds. His office should not be subject to budget cuts from Congress or the president.

The future of citizen control of government will reside in the effectiveness of citizen organizations such as John Gardner's Common Cause and Ralph Nader's Center for the Study of Responsive Law, which seek to maintain a nonpartisan stance and attack issues. Hopefully, such organizations will provide "affective" education for the bureaucrat, not because they have a desire to educate him, but because they must force the needs of their constituents upon him. If these efforts are effective, we could see a reversal of the concentration of power in the hands of the president of the United States, a process that has intensified in the last decade and one that has alarmed the U.S. Senate Committee on Foreign Relations as indicated in their report of April 16, 1968.

> Our country has come far toward the concentration in its national executive of unchecked power over foreign relations, particularly over the disposition and use of the Armed Forces. So far has this process advanced that, in the committee's view, it is no longer accurate to characterize our Government, in matters of foreign relations, as one of separate powers checked and balanced against each other.[17]

This centralization of power is reversible. Congress can assert its control of the budget and cut off expenditures for policies it does not approve. This negative control also implies a positive control. The president could be forced to bargain and to permit the passage of social legislation if he believed Congress would really make use of its power. On April 30, 1970, there was a move by senators from both parties to cut off funds for President Nixon's invasion of Cambodia. This may have influenced his early termination of American involvement in that adventure. On June 24 of the same year, the Senate voted a repeal of the Tonkin Gulf Resolution and adopted the Cooper-Church amendment to limit presidential action in Cambodia. In early 1973 there was a congressional effort to cut off funds for the war in Vietnam.

But Congress can go only so far without the support of the people. Congressmen will not really cut off all funds from a major war effort unless they believe that the American people are prepared to face the consequences of such a drastic step. In this chapter I have tried to suggest some ways in which this conflict might be resolved. Sennett's suggestions for increasing the degree of personal interaction between people, the initiation of affective education for public officials, the move on the part of Congress to regain some of the power it has abandoned, and the development of citizen action groups—all of these are steps in helping the people to gain greater responsibility for national policy.

However, the critical aspect in all of this movement toward social change is that the American people must learn to recognize when their desires are incompatible. This requires the kind of self-scrutiny that Lasswell recommended in his study of politics. In the end the deeper study of politics means a confrontation with one's self. Churchman arrived at a similar conclusion about the study of the universe, but he also added that a deep look into one's self is not without a certain danger, that it has been viewed with suspicion throughout history:

> The suspicion is a sound one, as all the wise men of history have told us. He who seeks to understand himself seeks the devil in himself as well as his God. The view that his understanding may open up may be too much for his contemplation, for it may display to him what he really is: perhaps the agent of all that is decadent in nature . . .[18] If men begin to understand what they are trying to do, they may understand the worse as well as the better about themselves. Can they stand to understand?[19]

It is at this point that we come face to face with the problem of "openness" as an American virtue. I do not believe that the openness of the well-meaning public official, the openness of the entertainer, or the openness of the encounter group will really bring us closer to the decadence and the evil in ourselves. In a society or a group where openness is expected, we tend to learn the lingo of openness quickly in order to get group approval. We learn to tell little stories about ourselves—an adultery, some little dishonesty, a malicious thought—because this is expected of an open person. It is all a part of what Ramparts has called "the rhetoric of openness."[20] It is designed to show others we are innocent because we believe we have nothing to hide.

It is a paradox that this superficial openness may actually serve to enhance the process of self-deception. If a public official feels compelled to be open, he may be inclined to avoid looking too deeply into his motives and into the conflict in some of our national aspirations. If the nation, the group, or a popularity poll is substituted for one's conscience, one's standing is enhanced by retaining an unreflective sincerity. We do not look too deeply into ourselves when we expect others to judge our motives for us.

What we really need, then, is not openness in the sense of open and public negotiations, but openness in our right of inquiry. We do not need "open covenants openly arrived at." We do need the right to inquire into what agreements our public officials have made. We cannot and should not try to compel a public official to reveal his heart, to be sincere and honest with us regarding his innermost thoughts. We do need laws that prevent him from concealing his actions and specific directives. In short, we should not be asked to trust our public officials because they are "good" people. We should be in a position to keep them honest. The openness we need in this country can be achieved by allowing maximum freedom for the media and the individual investigator, including the right of these investigators to protect their sources. Many leaks to reporters are self-serving, but there are other cases in which a scientist or public official will leak information because he believes the public has a right to know. Current events suggest a growing recognition of the need for the citizen or reporter to make his own inquiries—in short, to keep his officials honest, regardless of what they say about openness.

In recent years there have been a series of legal decisions that support the expression of dissent and the freedom of information. In 1971 the District of Columbia Appeals Court handed down a decision that broadcasters who sell time for commercials may not refuse to sell time for the broadcast of opinion on controversial issues. In 1973 Ralph Nader cited the 1966 Freedom of Information Act when his Tax Reform Research Group tried to get information from the Internal Revenue Service on investigations of radicals and militants. When he was denied the information he responded with a suit, and the IRS was forced to open its books. As a result of this pressure and that of other concerned citizens, the Freedom of Information Act was considerably expanded and liberalized in December of that year. The new changes require a government office to reply to any request within ten working days and limit duplicating charges to actual costs. If an individual sues for information and wins, the agency will now have to pay his attorney's fees.

VI

This long struggle for openness, with its victories and defeats, the urge for power and, at the same time, the growing recognition of the importance of human rights suggests to me that both aspects of this great American conflict between power and virtue are still very much with us. Can we develop an American policy that will harmonize and integrate these two aspects of our national character? If we are prepared to recognize both aspects of this dynamic—the desire for both power and goodness—we will be forced to admit that our own desire for power interferes with our capacity to develop a fine impartiality in world affairs. Because of our own involvement in the outcome of a decision in an international conflict, we cannot really decide which nation is "in the right" and commit our armed might to support our version of "justice." It is for this reason that a judge disqualifies himself from presiding in a case in which he has a personal interest. In doing so, he admits that he is human and subject to bias. In like manner, as a nation, we need to admit we are human beings, not gods.

Does this mean we should take no moral position at all? On the contrary, the United States can support certain moral principles, such as human rights, and use such a stand to become an effective force in world opinion. But moral leadership is a difficult and hazardous adventure. The bugaboo of national interest inevitably raises its head when moral questions arise. President Carter's willingness to talk with Soviet dissidents was commendable. It would be more convincing, however, if we welcomed a Marxist champion of human rights from among the dissidents in some authoritarian "capitalist" state, such as the dissidents in Chile, who oppose the current military dictatorship. There has long been, in this country, an implication that all capitalists represent the "free" world and that all atheists and Marxists deprive their citizens of human rights as a matter of doctrine. If we really believe this, we will perceive a deprivation of human rights in all states that are admittedly Marxist. In reality, there is no fundamental incompatibility between Marxism and human rights, although it is certainly true that Marxist regimes have deprived their citizens of human rights, as have monarchies and capitalist states. The history of the past 40 years might have been very different if we had been able to acknowledge this possibility. Our entire future could change if we cease becoming the enemy of all revolutions no matter where or why they begin.

Although a president can take the leadership in this kind of policy, he can make no significant progress without the American people. Unless there is a strong national commitment to human rights, regardless of ideology, which a later president dare not violate, we will find ourselves welcoming the champions of human rights during one administration and supporting foreign tyrannies in the next. If we are not convinced that the nonmilitary support for human rights throughout the world is in our long-range national interest, we probably cannot sustain such a policy. This means we must recognize such a policy for what it is. Not merely that it satisfies our need for a sense of national virtue, but that it can also be used, in a very practical way, to pressure other nations, to open them up to investigation, to encourage internal dissent, and to make them as vulnerable as we have made ourselves. If we are willing to back such a policy, to "mean it," and to make it convincing, it could become a new and more effective form of aggression—American style.

However, if it is only used when it has an obviously self-serving motive, we will not find it to be very effective. It will have a phoney and pretentious quality, as much of our talk about American goodness has today. Herman Kahn has taught us one thing: If a weapon is to be effective, the "enemy" must be convinced that we know how to use it and have the will to use it. A strong human rights policy is a weapon against authoritarian societies in the great psychological battle for the mind of man, a battle that is being waged every day by diverse means throughout the world. It may be the strongest weapon in our arsenal if we, ourselves, have the strength to use it. But it is not a weapon for the soft and self-indulgent. It is not for those who want to preserve their standard of living at the expense of others or who will support any foreign leader as long as he declares himself pro-American. Our powerful military weapons have required great financial sacrifice for their design and construction. We now have a president who has proposed a new weapon, one that will require great personal sacrifice. Only the future will decide whether we have the courage and the conviction to use it.

NOTES

1. "Let's Say It Right," *New York Times*, January 11, 1970, section IV, p. 5.

2. R. Lekachman, "$400,000,000,000 Plus," *Saturday Review*, December 1972, pp. 44–49.

3. R. Sennett, *The Uses of Disorder* (New York: Random House Vintage, 1970), p. 194.

4. Ibid., p. 94.

5. *Webster's New Collegiate Dictionary* (Springfield, Mass.: G. & C. Merriam, 1961), p. 618.

6. W. Fulbright, statement for P.M. release, September 15, 1965.

7. E. P. Dvorin and R. H. Simmons, *From Amoral to Human Bureaucracy* (New York: Canfield Press, 1972).

8. J. J. Rousseau, *Emile* (London: J. M. Dent, 1911).

9. See, for example, W. H. Blanchard, "The Encounter Group and Society," *New Perspectives on Encounter Groups*, eds. L. N. Solomon and Betty Berzon (San Francisco: Jossey-Bass, 1972); and W. H. Blanchard, "Ecstasy Without Agony is Baloney," *Psychology Today* (January 1970): 9–10.

10. G. Newmark, *This School Belongs to You and Me* (New York: Hart, 1976).

11. G. Murphy, *Outgrowing Self-Deception* (New York: Basic Books, 1975), p. 43.

12. *Weekly Compilation of Presidential Documents,* vol. 2, no. 3 (Washington, D.C.: National Archives and Records Service, 1975), pp. 45–53.

13. *Weekly Compilation of Presidential Documents,* vol. 13, no. 4, pp. 87–89.

14. K. Kenniston, *Young Radicals* (New York: Harcourt, Brace & World, 1968); and C. Hampden-Turner, *Radical Man* (Cambridge: Schenkman, 1970). See also the numerous studies cited in the bibliographies of these books.

15. A. de Tocqueville, *Democracy in America,* vol. I (New York: Vintage, 1955), p. 379.

16. A. M. Schlesinger, Jr., *A Thousand Days* (Greenwich, Conn.: Fawcett, 1965), p. 278.

17. *Report of the U.S. Senate Committee on Foreign Relations,* April 16, 1969.

18. C. W. Churchman, *Challenge to Reason* (New York: McGraw-Hill, 1968), p. 108.

19. Ibid., p. 116.

20. *Ramparts,* October, 1974, p. 78.

Appendix

Castro's Motives

The break in U.S.–Cuban relations raised two main questions about Castro's course. They are: Why has he deliberately sought to portray the U.S. as Cuba's enemy? And why push to the breaking point now?

As to Castro's general anti-Americanism course, the principal reason advanced is the unrest within Cuba. Taxes are high, shortages have been increasing, the future remains bleak. As things have worsened, the Castro Government has become increasingly shrill with its anti-American propaganda to busy minds that otherwise would be preoccupied with dissatisfactions at home.

Bound up with this, it has been suggested, is Dr. Castro's fierce desire to become a front-rank leader of Latin America and a world figure to be taken seriously; defiance of the mighty nation to the north seemed a likely road to that end, and Dr. Castro took it. His attacks on the U. S. have in fact found a response among some Latin Americans, and Cuban agents in other Latin republics have been working hard to exploit it.

As to why the breaking point should be reached now, observers point to the number of Cubans seeking visas to flee to the U.S. Most are middle-class and professional people—the same sort who provided the initial support for the revolution. The U.S. consulates have been processing 1,000 visa applications a week, representing an outflow of professional people, technicians and skilled workers the country can ill afford to lose.

Thus by ordering the U.S. to reduce its staff to eleven officials, the Castro regime apparently figured they would be unable to cope with the flood of visas and the emigration would be stopped, or at least reduced to a trickle.

Another reason advanced is that Dr. Castro wanted to cut down on the number of diplomatic reports to Washington—especially those on Communist arms shipments. The Castro Government has taken elaborate security measures to cloak their arrival, but leaks will occur.[1]

Intelligence for What?

President Nixon has given a reasonable and responsible answer to the shameful North Korean attack on a United States reconnaissance plane. Galling as it is to all Americans to accept the loss of the plane and its 31-man crew, the President showed good sense in eschewing futile saber-rattling.

His low-key but persuasive statement of the American case is welcome as evidence of a new sobriety in the management of American power in world affairs. It reflects a recognition that enormous military might can be a restraint as well as a shield, forcing the strong to swallow humiliations from puny malefactors.

The country has no option at this stage except to take on faith the Administration's decision that more intelligence flights in the vicinity of North Korea are vital to the national interest. If they are essential, unquestionably the men engaged in such missions must have the protection the President has now promised them—a promise that comes too late for the men of the downed EC-121.

It is evident from the EC-121 case, however, that intelligence-gathering alone cannot insure the security of United States forces. Last January, Times correspondent Peter Grose reported from Washington that "Government policy planners detect an ominous pattern emerging in the words and deeds of North Korea leading them to fear that the Nixon Administration may be confronted with a new challenge of the Vietnam type in the next four years."

Earlier, American military authorities in Seoul had linked Pyongyang's new aggressiveness with the capture of the American spy ship Pueblo, even though the facts in that case—as President Nixon acknowledged yesterday—were far less clear-cut than those in the EC-121 incident.

In view of these danger signals and many more recent indications of North Korea's belligerent disregard for the normal rules of international conduct, it is incredible that the President could assert yesterday that the plane incident came as "a completely surprise attack." The fact that North Korean jets regularly rode shotgun on 190 earlier American intelligence flights this year should have been a warning, not a reassurance.

Of what use are high-risk, sophisticated intelligence operations if the American defense establishment is incapable of responding with adequate precautions against dangers that any schoolboy could deduce from the public words and deeds of an avowed enemy?[2]

The Pope on Vietnam

The call issued yesterday by Pope Paul VI for a cease-fire, followed by negotiations to end the fighting in Vietnam, ought to provide the impetus for a fresh attempt to restore peace in Southeast Asia. The Pope's plea focuses on a Christmas lull, but—welcome as any suspension of the death toll would be—so short a halt would obviously be little more than symbolic.

The real need is for a United States initiative to rekindle the peace hopes stirred by the short-lived mediation efforts of Italian Foreign Minister Fanfani. The American reply to the supposed negotiation feeler from North Vietnam was essentially affirmative, but its effect was diluted by argumentation that would be better left for the conference table. Quite clearly, differences between Washington and Hanoi on the proper interpretation of the 1954 Geneva agreements will be pivotal issues in any negotiations; to debate them in advance simply blocks the road to peace talks. This is particularly true in the light of the tangled interrelations that affect the Communist side of the negotiating equation—Hanoi, Moscow and Peking.

The best way to demonstrate the sincerity of America's desires for unconditional discussions would be for President Johnson to respond to the Pope's appeal by announcing a new pause in the bombing of North Vietnam, during which Secretary General Thant of the United Nations or other intermediaries could explore the possibilities of a permanent cease-fire.

There would, of course, be risks in such a pause. Yet, as the Pope has noted, the risks are even greater if the conflict keeps growing. The President is reported planning to ask Congress for vastly expanded commitments in manpower and money for the Vietnamese war when the new term begins next month. Before such an expansion is undertaken, the American people and the world are entitled to a fuller demonstration that every resource of diplomatic ingenuity has been exhausted in pursuit of peace.

One footnote to the collapse of the Fanfani overtures appears in order. The conduct of international affairs often depends on the confidentiality of diplomatic exchanges. For newspapers this consideration raises, on many occasions, the question of whether a particular bit of information ought to be published or whether its publication will torpedo negotiations that could be of the utmost importance to world peace. The State Department felt obliged to release

the Rusk-Fanfani documents because of an erroneous press report
that it had rejected a new Hanoi peace bid. Whether, in the end, the
Fanfani efforts might have led to some useful conclusion can now
never be known.[3]

NOTES

1. *New York Times*, January 8, 1961, Section 4, p. E1.
2. *New York Times*, April 19, 1969, p. 32.
3. *New York Times*, December 20, 1965, p. 34.

Index